THE top10★
OF EVERYTHING
2001

THE top10★

OF EVERYTHING

2001

RUSSELL ASH

Reader's Digest

The Reader's Digest Association (Canada) Ltd.
MONTREAL

Contents

Dorling DK Kindersley

READER'S DIGEST CANADA

Project Editor Andrew Jones
Designer Cécile Germain
Art Director John McGuffie
Copy Editors Gilles Humbert, Judy Yelon
Production Manager Holger Lorenzen
Administration Elizabeth Eastman
Researchers Françoise Giovannangeli, Nanda Lwin
Inputter Eiko Takeda
Proofreader Judy Yelon

DORLING KINDERSLEY

Project Editor David Tombesi-Walton
Senior Designer Tracy Hambleton-Miles
Production Silvia La Greca, Elizabeth Cherry
Managing Editor Stephanie Jackson
Managing Art Editor Nigel Duffield

Produced for Dorling Kindersley by
Cooling Brown, 9–11 High Street,
Hampton, Middlesex TW12 2SA

Published in Canada in 2000 by
The Reader's Digest Association (Canada), Ltd.
1125 Stanley Street, Montreal, Quebec H3B 5H5

For information on this and other Reader's Digest products
or to request a catalogue, please call our 24-hour
Customer Service Hotline at 1-800-465-0780

You can also visit us on the web at
www.readersdigest.ca

Canadian Cataloguing-in-Publication Data

The top 10 of everything

Annual.
Includes index.
ISBN 1209-3882
ISBN 0-88850-697-X (2001 edition)

1. World records. 2. Curiosities and wonders.
I. Reader's Digest Association (Canada)
II. Title: the top ten of everything 2001.

AG243.A75   031.02'05   C97-301371-0

READER'S DIGEST and the Pegasus logo are registered
trademarks of The Reader's Digest Association, Inc.

00 01 02 03 / 5 4 3 2 1
Reproduction by Colourpath, London
Printed and bound by Printer Barcelona, Spain

top10★

Introduction

Looking Back

This is the sixth Canadian edition of *The Top 10 of Everything* and the first to be published in the new century and the new millennium. We start with a look back at the 20th century in A Century of Change before moving on to chart many of the developments of the 1990s.

Information Overload?

The Internet is a mixed blessing: on the one hand, it gives increased access to information, especially official figures; on the other, we are increasingly overwhelmed by the sheer volume of data. Perhaps today more than ever the value of *The Top 10 of Everything* is that it distills down all this available information to a manageable level, which is why, despite the Internet, books like this still have a place.

Listomania

During the past dozen years, the number of published lists has increased inexorably, and the 20th century ended with a tidal wave of lists of the best movies, books, and recordings of all time. Scarcely a day goes by when I am not inspired with an idea for a new list, such as the top advertising campaigns, leading fat consumers, latest assassinated monarchs, deadliest serial killers, fastest roller coasters, largest mollusks, and champion cowboys, as featured here.

Not Just the Best

The book focuses on superlatives in numerous categories and also contains a variety of "firsts" or "latests," which recognize the pioneers and the most recent achievers in various fields of endeavor. Lists of movies are based on worldwide box-office income, and those on recorded music, videos, and books are based on sales, unless otherwise stated.

History in the Making

The Top 10 of Everything now spans three decades and has become a historical resource. Schools use older editions when undertaking projects on social changes, while others buy *Top 10* to commemorate births and other family events, as a "time capsule" of the year.

A Neverending Task

While I endeavor to ensure that all the information is as up to date as possible, certain statistics are slow to be collated and published. At the same time, lists relating to bestsellers and sporting achievements can change almost daily. Even lists that one would not expect to alter do: a revised height for Everest was published while I was at work on this book.

The Research Network

Compiling *The Top 10 of Everything* has been a pleasure and a revelation to me: in the course of my work on it I have discovered numerous interesting facts, increased my library, and, in particular, met many people who have gone on to become consultants on the book. My thanks to all of them and to everyone who has contacted me with helpful information.

Keep in Touch

If you have a correction, comments, or an idea for a future Top 10 list, you can contact Reader's Digest on their World Wide Web site at www.readersdigest.ca (where you can play an interactive Top 10 quiz) or e-mail me directly at ash@pavilion.co.uk.

Special Features

- More than 1,000 lists make this the most wide-ranging
  Top 10 of Everything ever.

- Maple leafs highlight Canadian lists unique to this edition.

- A Century of Change surveys some of the fascinating
  Top 10s of the 20th century.

- Double the number of pages have been devoted to
  some of the most popular subjects.

- Illustrated SnapShots add extra information to many lists.

- "Did You Know?" entries offer unusual sidelights
  on the subjects explored.

- "Why Do We Say?" features explain the origins of
  popular words and phrases.

- Challenging Canadian quiz questions with multiple-choice
  answers appear throughout the book.

- Dramatic vertical spreads add to the visual appeal.

A CENTURY OF CANADIAN MILESTONES

YEAR	MILESTONE
1917	Canadian soldiers capture Vimy Ridge, winning the first unequivocal Allied victory on the Western Front in WWI. The resulting 10,000 casualties help precipitate the Conscription Crisis in Quebec.
1922	A research team at the University of Toronto demonstrates the value of insulin as a therapy for diabetes mellitus, leading to Canada's first Nobel Prize in 1923 for Frederick Banting.and John J. R. Macleod.
1944	Voters in Depression-battered Saskatchewan elect a Cooperative Commonwealth Federation government, ushering in a nationwide series of social reforms that would eventually become today's "social safety net."
1956	Canada condemns the British and French invasion of Egypt and creates the framework for U.N. peacekeeping interventions. Lester B. Pearson is awarded the Nobel Peace prize in 1957.
1967	Florence Bird takes the chair of the Royal Commission on the Status of Women. The Commission's 1970 report gave Canadian women equal status in virtually every walk of life.
1967	Expo '67 in Montreal gives Canadians and Quebecers an exhilarating sense of national and cultural achievement.
1969	Native people angrily reject federal proposals to offer them full equality as Canadian citizens and demand special rights due to their Aboriginal status.
1982	Pierre Trudeau signs the Constitution Act, giving Canada the right to amend its own basic law. Quebec refuses to ratify the new constitution.
1988	Canada re-elects a Conservative government which passes the Free Trade Agreement with the U.S.
1995	Quebec narrowly rejects a second referendum on sovereignty.

Source: *Professor Desmond Morton, McGill Institute for the Study of Canada and author of* Canada: A Millennium Portrait

TEEMING MILLIONS

China began the 20th century with some 400 million inhabitants and ended it with 1.2 billion.

MOST HIGHLY POPULATED COUNTRIES, 1900–2000

	1900	1950	2000
1	China	China	China
2	India	India	India
3	Russia	USSR	US
4	US	US	Indonesia
5	Germany	Japan	Brazil
6	Austria	Indonesia	Russia
7	Japan	Germany	Pakistan
8	UK	UK	Bangladesh
9	Turkey	Brazil	Japan
10	France	Italy	Nigeria

TOP 10 MOST HIGHLY POPULATED CITIES, 1900

(City/population*)

1 London 6,581,000   **2** New York 3,437,000
3 Paris 2,714,000   **4** Berlin 1,889,000
5 Chicago 1,699,000   **6** Vienna 1,675,000
7 Wuhan, China 1,500,000   **8** Toyko 1,440,000
9 Philadephia 1,294,000   **10** St. Petersburg 1,265,000

* Including adjacent suburban areas

☘ A CENTURY OF CANADIAN POPULATION

(Year/population*)

1901 5,371,000 **1911** 7,207,000 **1921** 8,788,000
1931 10,377,000 **1941** 11,507,000 **1951** 13,648,000
1961 18,238,000 **1971** 21,568,000 **1981** 24,820,000
1991 28,031,000 **2001**# 31,050,000

* Includes Newfoundland since 1951
 # Figure represents growth projections based on 1999 population estimates

Source: *Statistics Canada*

Did You Know? United Nations estimates for world population in 2050 predict a 50 percent increase on today's 6 billion, bringing the total to about 9 billion.

TOP 10 ★

MOST EXPENSIVE MOVIES OF THE 20TH CENTURY

	DECADE	MOVIE/YEAR	COST (US$)
1	1900–09	*For the Term of His Natural Life* * (1908)	34,000
2	1910–19	*A Daughter of the Gods* (1916)	1,000,000
3	1920–29	*Ben-Hur* (1925)	3,900,000
4	1930–39	*Gone with the Wind* (1939)	4,250,000
5	1940–49	*Joan of Arc* (1948)	8,700,000
6	1950–59	*Ben-Hur* (1959)	15,000,000
7	1960–69	*Cleopatra* (1963)	44,000,000
8	1970–79	*Superman* (1978)	55,000,000
9	1980–89	*Who Framed Roger Rabbit* (1988)	70,000,000
10	1990–99	*Titanic* (1997)	200,000,000

* *Australian; all others US*

FRANKLY, MY DEAR...

Gone with the Wind, *starring Clark Gable and Vivien Leigh, was the most expensive movie ever made, allowing for inflation. It was also the most successful.*

TOP 10 ★

SUCCESSIVE HOLDERS OF THE TITLE "WORLD'S TALLEST HABITABLE BUILDING" IN THE 20TH CENTURY

	BUILDING/LOCATION	YEAR	STORIES	M	FT
1	**City Hall**, Philadelphia	1901	7	155	511
2	**Singer Building,** * New York	1908	34	200	656
3	**Metropolitan Life**, New York	1909	50	212	700
4	**Woolworth Building**, New York	1913	59	241	792
5	**40 Wall Street**, New York with spire	1929	71	260 282	854 927
6	**Chrysler Building**, New York with spire	1930	77	282 319	925 1,046
7	**Empire State Building**, New York with spire	1931	102	381 449	1,250 1,472
8	**World Trade Center**, New York with spire	1973	110	415 521	1,362 1,710
9	**Sears Tower**, Chicago with spires	1974	110	443 520	1,454 1,707
10	**Petronas Towers**, Kuala Lumpur, Malaysia	1996	96	452	1,482

* *Demolished 1970*

UNBEATEN CITY HALL

Once the world's tallest building, Philadelphia City Hall remains the largest and most expensive municipal building in the US.

The Universe & The Earth

Star Gazing

TOP 10 STARS NEAREST TO THE EARTH*

	STAR	LIGHT YEARS	KM (MILLIONS)	MILES (MILLIONS)
1	Proxima Centauri	4.22	39,923,310	24,792,500
2	Alpha Centauri	4.35	41,153,175	25,556,250
3	Barnard's Star	5.98	56,573,790	35,132,500
4	Wolf 359	7.75	73,318,875	45,531,250
5	Lalande 21185	8.22	77,765,310	48,292,500
6	Luyten 726-8	8.43	79,752,015	49,526,250
7	Sirius	8.65	81,833,325	50,818,750
8	Ross 154	9.45	89,401,725	55,518,750
9	Ross 248	10.40	98,389,200	61,100,000
10	Epsilon Eridani	10.80	102,173,400	63,450,000

* Excluding the Sun

A spaceship traveling at 40,237 km/h (25,000 mph) – which is faster than any human has yet reached in space – would take more than 113,200 years to reach the Earth's closest star, Proxima Centauri. While the nearest stars in this list lie just over four light years away from the Earth, others within the Milky Way lie at a distance of 2,500 light years.

CLOSE TO THE EARTH

The name of Proxima Centauri, a red dwarf star in the constellation of Centaurus, literally means "nearest of Centaurus," and it is indeed the Earth's closest star beyond the Sun.

TOP 10 ★
BODIES FARTHEST FROM THE SUN*

	BODY	AVERAGE DISTANCE FROM THE SUN KM	MILES
1	Pluto	5,914,000,000	3,675,000,000
2	Neptune	4,497,000,000	2,794,000,000
3	Uranus	2,871,000,000	1,784,000,000
4	Chiron	2,800,000,000	1,740,000,000
5	Saturn	1,427,000,000	887,000,000
6	Jupiter	778,300,000	483,600,000
7	Mars	227,900,000	141,600,000
8	Earth	149,600,000	92,900,000
9	Venus	108,200,000	67,200,000
10	Mercury	57,900,000	36,000,000

* In the Solar System, excluding satellites and asteroids

Chiron, a "mystery object" which may be either a comet or an asteroid, was discovered on November 1, 1977, by American astronomer Charles Kowal. It measures 200–300 km (124–186 miles) in diameter.

AMERICAN DISCOVERY

The Solar System's smallest planet, Pluto, found in 1930, is the only planet to have been discovered by an American – Clyde Tombaugh.

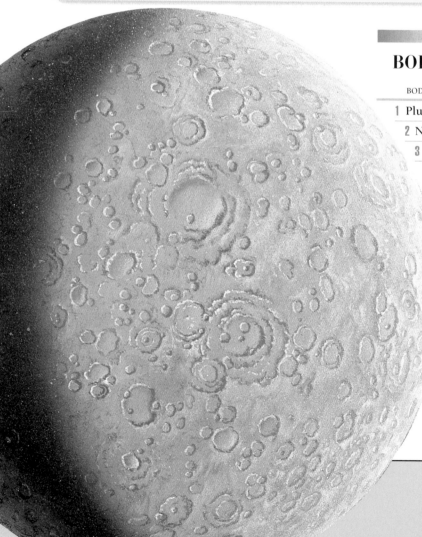

TOP 10 ★
BRIGHTEST STARS*

	STAR/CONSTELLATION	APPARENT MAGNITUDE#
1	**Sirius**, Canis Major	-1.46
2	**Canopus**, Carina	-0.73
3	**Alpha Centauri**, Centaurus	-0.27
4	**Arcturus**, Boötes	-0.04
5	**Vega**, Lyra	+0.03
6	**Capella**, Auriga	+0.08
7	**Rigel**, Orion	+0.12
8	**Procyon**, Canis Minor	+0.38
9	**Achernar**, Eridanus	+0.46
10	**Beta Centauri**, Centaurus	+0.61

* Excluding the Sun

 # Based on apparent visual magnitude as viewed from the Earth – the lower the number, the brighter the star

At its brightest, the star Betelgeuse is brighter than some of these, but its variability disqualifies it from the Top 10. More distant stars naturally appear fainter. To compensate for this effect, absolute magnitude estimates the brightness of a star at an imaginary fixed distance of 10 parsecs, or 32.6 light years, enabling comparison between the "true" brightness of different stars.

RINGS OF ICE

Saturn's ring system was not discovered until 1656. Composed of ice, the rings are up to 270,000 km (167,770 miles) in diameter.

TOP 10 ★
LARGEST BODIES IN THE SOLAR SYSTEM

	BODY	MAXIMUM DIAMETER KM	MILES
1	**Sun**	1,392,140	865,036
2	**Jupiter**	142,984	88,846
3	**Saturn**	120,536	74,898
4	**Uranus**	51,118	31,763
5	**Neptune**	49,532	30,778
6	**Earth**	12,756	7,926
7	**Venus**	12,103	7,520
8	**Mars**	6,794	4,222
9	**Ganymede**	5,269	3,274
10	**Titan**	5,150	3,200

Most of the planets are visible with the naked eye and have been observed since ancient times. The exceptions are Uranus, discovered on March 13, 1781 by British astronomer Sir William Herschel; Neptune, found by German astronomer Johann Galle on September 23, 1846; and, outside the Top 10, Pluto, located using photographic techniques by American astronomer Clyde Tombaugh. Its discovery was announced on March 13, 1930; its diameter is uncertain but is thought to be about 2,302 km (1,430 miles).

TOP 10 ★
LONGEST DAYS IN THE SOLAR SYSTEM

	BODY	LENGTH OF DAY* DAYS	HOURS	MINS
1	**Venus**	244	0	0
2	**Mercury**	58	14	0
3	**Sun**	25#	0	0
4	**Pluto**	6	9	0
5	**Mars**		24	37
6	**Earth**		23	56
7	**Uranus**		17	14
8	**Neptune**		16	7
9	**Saturn**		10	39
10	**Jupiter**		9	55

* Period of rotation, based on 23-hour, 56-minute sidereal day

 # Variable

TOP 10 ★
GALAXIES NEAREST TO THE EARTH

	GALAXY	DISTANCE LIGHT YEARS
1	**Large Cloud of Magellan**	169,000
2	**Small Cloud of Magellan**	190,000
3	**Ursa Minor dwarf**	250,000
4	**Draco dwarf**	260,000
5	**Sculptor dwarf**	280,000
6	**Fornax dwarf**	420,000
7 =	**Leo I dwarf**	750,000
7 =	**Leo II dwarf**	750,000
9	**Barnard's Galaxy**	1,700,000
10	**Andromeda Spiral**	2,200,000

These and other galaxies are members of the so-called "Local Group," although with vast distances such as these, "local" is a relative term.

TOP 10 ★
MOST MASSIVE BODIES IN THE SOLAR SYSTEM*

	BODY	MASS#
1	**Sun**	332,800.000
2	**Jupiter**	317.828
3	**Saturn**	95.161
4	**Neptune**	17.148
5	**Uranus**	14.536
6	**Earth**	1.000
7	**Venus**	0.815
8	**Mars**	0.10745
9	**Mercury**	0.05527
10	**Pluto**	0.0022

* Excluding satellites

 # Compared with the Earth = 1; the mass of the Earth is approximately 73,500,000,000,000 tonnes.

Who is Canada's longest-serving Parliamentarian?
see p.65 for the answer
A Mackenzie Boswell
B Azellus Denis
C Hippolyte Montplaisir

Asteroids, Meteorites & Comets

MOST RECENT OBSERVATIONS
OF HALLEY'S COMET

1 1986
The Japanese Suisei probe passed within 151,000 km (93,827 miles) of its 15-km (9-mile) nucleus on March 8, 1986, revealing a whirling nucleus within a hydrogen cloud emitting 18–45 tonnes of water per second. The Soviet probes Vega 1 and Vega 2 passed within 8,890 km (5,524 miles) and 8,030 km (4,990 miles) respectively. The European Space Agency's Giotto passed as close as 596 km (370 miles) on March 14 of the same year. All were heavily battered by dust particles, and it was concluded that Halley's comet is composed of dust bonded by water and carbon dioxide ice.

2 1910
Predictions of disaster were widely published, with many people convinced that the world would come to an end. Mark Twain, who had been born at the time of the 1835 appearance and who believed that his fate was linked to that of the comet, died when it reappeared in this year.

3 1835
Widely observed but noticeably dimmer than in 1759.

4 1759
The comet's first return, as predicted by Halley, thus proving his calculations correct.

5 1682
Observed in Africa and China and extensively in Europe, where it was observed on September 5–19 by Edmund Halley, who predicted its return.

6 1607
Seen extensively in China, Japan, Korea, and Europe, described by German astronomer Johannes Kepler and its position accurately measured by amateur Welsh astronomer Thomas Harriot.

7 1531
Observed in China, Japan, Korea, and in Europe on August 13–23 by Peter Appian, German geographer and astronomer, who noted that comets' tails point away from the Sun.

8 1456
Observed in China, Japan, Korea, and by the Turkish army, which was threatening to invade Europe. When the Turks were defeated by Papal forces, it was seen as a portent of the latter's victory.

9 1378
Observed in China, Japan, Korea, and Europe.

10 1301
Seen in Iceland, parts of Europe, China, Japan, and Korea.

Before Edmund Halley (1656–1742) studied and foretold the return of the famous comet that now bears his name, no one had succeeded in proving that comets travel in predictable orbits. The dramatic return in 1759 of the comet Halley had observed in 1682 established the science of cometary observation. There have been about 30 recorded appearances of Halley's comet. The most famous occurred in 1066, when William of Normandy (later known as William the Conqueror) regarded it as a sign of his imminent victory over King Harold at the Battle of Hastings; it is clearly shown in the Bayeux Tapestry.

TOP 10 MOST FREQUENTLY
SEEN COMETS
(Comet/years between appearances)

❶ Encke, 3.302 ❷ Grigg-Skjellerup, 4.908
❸ Honda-Mrkós-Pajdusáková, 5.210 ❹ Tempel 2, 5.259
❺ Neujmin 2, 5.437 ❻ Brorsen, 5.463
❼ Tuttle-Giacobini-Kresák, 5.489 ❽ Tempel-L. Swift, 5.681
❾ Tempel 1, 5.982 ❿ Pons-Winnecke, 6.125

COMETS COMING
CLOSEST TO THE EARTH

	COMET	DATE OF CLOSEST APPROACH	DISTANCE AU[#]
1	Lexell	Jul 1, 1770	0.0151
2	Tempel-Tuttle	Oct 26, 1366	0.0229
3	IRAS-Araki-Alcock	May 11, 1983	0.0312
4	Halley	Apr 10, 837	0.0334
5	Biela	Dec 9, 1805	0.0366
6	Grischow	Feb 8, 1743	0.0390
7	Pons-Winnecke	Jun 26, 1927	0.0394
8	La Hire	Apr 20, 1702	0.0437
9	Schwassmann-Wachmann 3	May 31, 1930	0.0617
10	Sugano-Saigusa-Fujikawa	Jun 12, 1983	0.0628

[#] *Astronomical Units: 1 AU = mean distance from the Earth to the Sun (149,597,870 km/92,955,810 miles)*

ROCK OF AGES

Visitors are encouraged to touch the 3.4-m (11-ft) Ahnighito, the largest meteorite on public display, and to appreciate that it is as old as the Solar System – some 4.5 billion years.

THE 10 ⭐
FIRST ASTEROIDS TO BE DISCOVERED

ASTEROID/DISCOVERER	DISCOVERED
1 **Ceres**, Giuseppe Piazzi	Jan 1, 1801
2 **Pallas**, Heinrich Olbers	Mar 28, 1802
3 **Juno**, Karl Ludwig Harding	Sep 1, 1804
4 **Vesta**, Heinrich Olbers	Mar 29, 1807
5 **Astraea**, Karl Ludwig Hencke	Dec 8, 1845
6 **Hebe**, Karl Ludwig Hencke	Jul 1, 1847
7 **Iris**, John Russell Hind	Aug 13, 1847
8 **Flora**, John Russell Hind	Oct 18, 1847
9 **Metis**, Andrew Graham	Apr 25, 1848
10 **Hygeia**, Annibale de Gasparis	Apr 12, 1849

Asteroids, sometimes known as "minor planets," are fragments of rock orbiting between Mars and Jupiter. There are perhaps 45,000 of them, but fewer than 10 percent have been named.

ASTEROIDS

Since the discovery of Ceres, the first and largest asteroid, over 6,000 have been found, 26 of them larger than 200 km (120 miles) in diameter. Gaspra, pictured here, measures only 20 x 12 km (12 x 7 miles), but was closely studied by the *Galileo* spacecraft in 1991. The total mass of all the asteroids is less than that of the Moon. It is believed that, on average, one asteroid larger than 0.4 km (¼ mile) strikes the Earth every 50,000 years. As recently as 1994, a small asteroid with the temporary designation 1994XM, measuring a modest 18 m (33 ft) in diameter, came within 112,600 km (69,594 miles) of the Earth – making it the closest recorded near-miss.

SNAP SHOTS

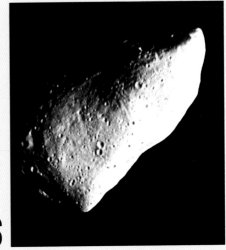

TOP 10 ⭐
LARGEST METEORITES EVER FOUND

SITE/LOCATION	ESTIMATED WEIGHT TONNES
1 **Hoba West**, Grootfontein, Namibia	54.4
2 **Ahnighito ("The Tent")**, Cape York, West Greenland	52.0
3 **Campo del Cielo**, Argentina	37.5
4 **Canyon Diablo***, Arizona	27.2
5 **Sikhote-Alin**, Russia	24.5
6 **Chupaderos**, Mexico	21.9
7 **Bacuberito**, Mexico	20.0
8 **Armanty**, Western Mongolia	18.1
9 **Mundrabilla#**, Western Australia	15.4
10 **Mbosi**, Tanzania	14.5

* *Formed meteor crater; fragmented – total in public collections is around 10.4 tonnes*

In two parts – 10.4 and 5.5 tonnes

The Hoba meteorite was found on a farm in 1920. A 2.73 x 2.43 m (9 x 8 ft) slab, it consists of 82 percent iron and 16 percent nickel. In 1989, 36 Malaysian soldiers with the UN Peacekeeping Force attempted to hack pieces off it as souvenirs, causing an outcry. "The Tent," known by its original Inuit name of Ahnighito, was discovered in 1894 by the American Arctic explorer Admiral Robert Peary. Now in the Hayden Planetarium at the New York Museum of Natural History, it is the largest meteorite in the world on exhibition.

TOP 10 🍁
LARGEST METEORITES FOUND IN CANADA

SITE/DATE	ESTIMATED WEIGHT KG
1 **Bruderheim**, Alberta, 1960	303.0
2 **Iron Creek**, Alberta, 1869*	175.0
3 **Madoc**, Ontario, 1854	167.5
4 **Abee**, Alberta, 1952	107.0
5 **Springwater**, Saskatchewan, 1931	67.6
6 **Dresden**, Ontario, 1939	47.7
7 **Osseo**, Ontario, 1931	46.3
8 **Peace River**, Alberta, 1963	45.8
9 **Manitouwabing**, Ontario, 1962#	39.0
10 **Saint-Robert**, Quebec, 1994	25.4

* *Reweighed in 1999 at 145.2 kg*

Date found. Year of impact estimated to be 1949

Source: *Geological Survey of Canada*

The Iron Creek meteorite had been greatly venerated by the native people of Alberta for generations. They saw the features of a face in the markings of its surface, and they made it offerings of beads and knives before setting out on hunts. The number of meteorites falling has been calculated to amount to some 500 a year across the whole globe, although many fall in the ocean and unpopulated areas, where their descent goes unnoticed. Fifty-three meteorites have been found and identified in Canada.

Did You Know? A car damaged by a 10-kg (22-lb) meteorite in Peekskill, New York, in 1992 was sold to the Montana Meteorite Lab for US$69,000 – complete with the meteorite.

Space Firsts

THE 10 ★ FIRST BODIES TO HAVE BEEN VISITED BY SPACECRAFT

	BODY	SPACECRAFT	COUNTRY	YEAR
1	Moon	Pioneer 4	US	1959
2	Venus	Mariner 2	US	1962
3	Mars	Mariner 4	US	1965
4	Sun	Pioneer 7	US	1966
5	Jupiter	Pioneer 10	US	1973
6	Mercury	Mariner 10	US	1974
7	Saturn	Pioneer 11	US	1979
8	Comet Giacobini-Zinner	International Sun–Earth Explorer 3 (International Cometary Explorer)	Europe/US	1985
9	Uranus	Voyager 2	US	1986
10	Halley's Comet	Giotto	Europe	1986

THE 10 ★ FIRST ANIMALS IN SPACE

	NAME/ANIMAL	COUNTRY	DATE
1	Laika, dog	USSR	Nov 3, 1957
2=	Laska and Benjy, mice	US	Dec 13, 1958
4=	Able and Baker, female rhesus monkey and female squirrel monkey	US	May 28, 1959
6=	Otvazhnaya, female Samoyed husky, and an unnamed rabbit	USSR	Jul 2, 1959
8	Sam, male rhesus monkey	US	Dec 4, 1959
9	Miss Sam, female rhesus monkey	US	Jan 21, 1960
10=	Belka and Strelka, female Samoyed huskies	USSR	Aug 19, 1960

THE 10 ★ FIRST WOMEN IN SPACE

	NAME/SPACECRAFT	DATE
1	Valentina V. Tereshkova, *Vostok VI*	Jun 16–19, 1963
2	Svetlana Savitskaya, *Soyuz T7*	Aug 19, 1982
3	Sally K. Ride, *Challenger STS-7*	Jun 18–24, 1983
4	Judith A. Resnik, *Discovery STS-41-D*	Aug 30–Sep 5, 1984
5	Kathryn D. Sullivan, *Discovery STS-51-G*	Oct 5–13, 1984
6	Anna L. Fisher, *Discovery STS-51-A*	Nov 8–16, 1984
7	Margaret R. Seddon, *Discovery STS-51-D*	Apr 12–19, 1985
8	Shannon W. Lucid, *Discovery STS-51-G*	Jun 17–24, 1985
9	Bonnie J. Dunbar, *Discovery STS-61-A*	Oct 30–Nov 6, 1985
10	Mary L. Cleave, *Discovery STS-61-B*	Nov 26–Dec 3, 1985

On January 22–30, 1992, Dr. Roberta Bondar became the first Canadian woman in space, accompanying 13 Canadian life science experiments aboard the US space shuttle *Discovery*.

THE 10 ★ FIRST MOONWALKERS

	ASTRONAUT/SPACECRAFT	TOTAL EVA* HR:MIN	MISSION DATES
1	Neil A. Armstrong, *Apollo 11*	2:32	Jul 16–24, 1969
2	Edwin E. ("Buzz") Aldrin, *Apollo 11*	2:15	Jul 16–24, 1969
3	Charles Conrad, Jr., *Apollo 12*	7:45	Nov 14–24, 1969
4	Alan L. Bean, *Apollo 12*	7:45	Nov 14–24, 1969
5	Alan B. Shepard, *Apollo 14*	9:23	Jan 31–Feb 9, 1971
6	Edgar D. Mitchell, *Apollo 14*	9:23	Jan 31–Feb 9, 1971
7	David R. Scott, *Apollo 15*	19:08	Jul 26–Aug 7, 1971
8	James B. Irwin, *Apollo 15*	18:35	Jul 26–Aug 7, 1971
9	John W. Young, *Apollo 16*	20:14	Apr 16–27, 1972
10	Charles M. Duke, *Apollo 16*	20:14	Apr 16–27, 1972

* Extravehicular Activity (i.e. time spent out of the lunar module on the Moon's surface)

MOON ROCKET
Apollo 11 blasts off from Cape Canaveral on July 16, 1969. Aboard are Americans Neil Armstrong and "Buzz" Aldrin, destined to be the first men to walk on the Moon.

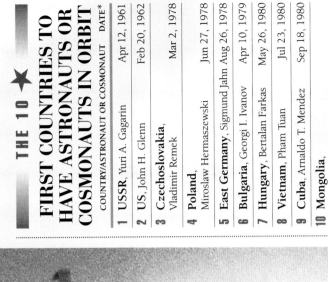

THE 10 ★ FIRST COUNTRIES TO HAVE ASTRONAUTS OR COSMONAUTS IN ORBIT

COUNTRY/ASTRONAUT OR COSMONAUT	DATE*
1 **USSR**, Yuri A. Gagarin	Apr 12, 1961
2 **US**, John H. Glenn	Feb 20, 1962
3 **Czechoslovakia**, Vladimir Remek	Mar 2, 1978
4 **Poland**, Miroslaw Hermaszewski	Jun 27, 1978
5 **East Germany**, Sigmund Jahn	Aug 26, 1978
6 **Bulgaria**, Georgi I. Ivanov	Apr 10, 1979
7 **Hungary**, Bertalan Farkas	May 26, 1980
8 **Vietnam**, Pham Tuan	Jul 23, 1980
9 **Cuba**, Arnaldo T. Mendez	Sep 18, 1980
10 **Mongolia**, Jugderdemidiyn Gurragcha	Mar 22, 1981

* Of first space entry of a national of that country

THE 10 ★ FIRST SPACEWALKERS

ASTRONAUT	SPACECRAFT	EVA* HR:MIN	EVA DATE
1 **Alexei Leonov**	Voskhod 2	0:23	Mar 18, 1965
2 **Edward H. White**	Gemini 4	0:36	Jun 3, 1965
3 **Eugene A. Cernan**	Gemini 9	2:07	Jun 3, 1966
4 **Michael Collins**	Gemini 10	0:50	Jul 19, 1966
5 **Richard F. Gordon**	Gemini 11	0:33	Sep 13, 1966
6 **Edwin E. ("Buzz") Aldrin**	Gemini 12	2:29	Nov 12, 1966
7 = **Alexei Yeleseyev**	Soyuz 5	0:37	Jan 16, 1969
7 = **Yevgeny Khrunov**	Soyuz 5	0:37	Jan 16, 1969
9 = **Russell L. Schweickart**	Apollo 9	0:46	Mar 6, 1969
9 = **David R. Scott**	Apollo 9	0:46	Mar 6, 1969

* Extravehicular Activity

Leonov's first spacewalk almost ended in disaster when his spacesuit "ballooned" and he was unable to return through the air-lock into the capsule until he had reduced the pressure in his suit to a dangerously low level. Edward H. White was killed in the Apollo spacecraft fire of January 27, 1967.

THE 10 ★ FIRST PEOPLE TO ORBIT THE EARTH

NAME/SPACECRAFT	COUNTRY OF ORIGIN	DATE
1 **Yuri A. Gagarin**, Vostok I	USSR	Apr 12, 1961
2 **Gherman S. Titov**, Vostok II	USSR	Aug 6–7, 1961
3 **John H. Glenn**, Friendship 7	US	Feb 20, 1962
4 **M. Scott Carpenter**, Aurora 7	US	May 24, 1962
5 **Andrian G. Nikolayev**, Vostok III	USSR	Aug 11–15, 1962
6 **Pavel R. Popovich**, Vostok IV	USSR	Aug 12–15, 1962
7 **Walter M. Schirra**, Sigma 7	US	Oct 3, 1962
8 **L. Gordon Cooper**, Faith 7	US	May 15–16, 1963
9 **Valeri F. Bykovsky**, Vostok V	USSR	Jun 14–19, 1963
10 **Valentina V. Tereshkova**, Vostok VI	USSR	Jun 16–19, 1963

Yuri Gagarin, at the age of 27, orbited the Earth once, taking 1 hour 48 minutes. Titov, the youngest-ever astronaut at 25 years 329 days, performed 17 orbits during 25 hours. The first American to orbit the Earth, John Glenn, is the oldest on this list at 40; he has since gone on to become the oldest astronaut of all time.

FIRST IN SPACE

In 1961, Soviet cosmonaut Yuri Gagarin became the first human to enter space and orbit the Earth. His flight aboard Vostok 1 lasted just 108 minutes. After receiving his country's highest honors, Gagarin was killed in a MiG-15 plane crash in 1968.

Space Explorers

SPACELINK

In 1995, the US's 100th crewed flight, Atlantis STS-71, linked up with Russian space station Mir for the first time, exchanging astronauts and cosmonauts between the two spacecraft.

TOP 10 ★
MOST EXPERIENCED SPACEMEN*

	SPACEMAN	MISSIONS	TOTAL DURATION OF MISSIONS			
			DAYS	HOURS	MINS	SECS
1	Sergei V. Avdeyev	3	747	14	22	47
2	Valeri V. Polyakov	2	678	16	33	18
3	Anatoli Y. Solovyov	5	651	0	11	25
4	Viktor M. Afanasyev	3	545	2	34	41
5	Musa K. Manarov	2	541	0	29	38
6	Alexander S. Viktorenko	4	489	1	35	17
7	Sergei K. Krikalyov	4#	483	9	37	26
8	Yuri V. Romanenko	3	430	18	21	30
9	Alexander A. Volkov	3	391	11	52	14
10	Vladimir G. Titov	5#	387	0	51	03

* To January 1, 2000

\# Including flights aboard US space shuttles

All the missions listed were undertaken by the USSR (and, latterly, Russia). In recent years, a number of US astronauts have added to their space logs by spending time on board the Russian *Mir* space station, but none has matched the records set by Russian cosmonauts. While Valeri Polyakov holds the record for the longest continuous space flight, Sergei Avdeyev exceeded Polyakov's cumulative record on June 20, 1999, by spending his 679th day in space.

TOP 10 ★
MOST EXPERIENCED SPACEWOMEN*

	SPACEWOMAN#	MISSIONS	TOTAL DURATION OF MISSIONS			
			DAYS	HOURS	MINS	SECS
1	Shannon W. Lucid	5	223	2	52	26
2	Yelena V. Kondakova	2	178	10	41	31
3	Tamara E. Jernigan	5	63	1	25	40
4	Bonnie J. Dunbar	5	50	8	24	44
5	Marsha S. Ivins	4	43	0	27	43
6	Kathryn C. Thornton	4	40	15	15	18
7	Janice E. Voss	4	37	21	10	18
8	Wendy B. Lawrence	3	37	5	23	20
9	Susan J. Helms	3	33	20	16	31
10	Nancy J. Currie	3	30	17	23	46

* To January 1, 2000

\# All US except two (Russian)

Shannon Lucid became both America's most experienced astronaut and the world's most experienced female astronaut in 1996. She took off in US space shuttle *Atlantis STS-76* on March 22, and transferred to the Russian *Mir* Space Station, returning on board *Atlantis STS-79* on September 26 after traveling 121 million km (75.2 million miles) in 188 days, 4 hours, 0 minutes, 14 seconds – also a record duration for a single mission by a US astronaut.

Did You Know? The greatest number of people in space at the same time was 13, when, on March 14, 1995, a space shuttle, a Russian spacecraft, and the *Mir* space station orbited simultaneously.

TOP 10 🍁

FIRST CANADIAN ASTRONAUTS*

ASTRONAUT/PROFESSION	FLIGHT DATES
1 **Marc Garneau**, Electrical engineer	1) October 1984 2) May 1996
2 **Roberta Bondar**, Neurologist	January 1992
3 **Steven MacLean**, Laser physicist	October 1992
4 **Robert Thirsk**, Medical doctor/mechanical engineer	June 1996
5 **Bjarni Tryggvason**, Engineering physicist, mathematician	August 1997
6 **Ken Money**, Physiologist	No space missions
7 **Col. Chris Hadfield**,# Mechanical engineer, test pilot	November 1995
8 **Captain Mike McKay**, Engineer	No space missions
9 **Dave Williams**, Emergency physician	April 1998
10 **Julie Payette**, Electrical/computer engineer	May 27, 1999

There are currently seven Canadian astronauts. Roberta Bondar resigned in September 1992, Ken Money in July 1992, and Mike McKay in early 1995

Chris Hadfield will become the first Canadian to perform a "space walk" on his second space flight, scheduled for April 2001

Source: *Canadian Space Agency*

Marc Garneau is scheduled for a third flight in November 2000.

TOP 10 ⭐

LONGEST SPACE MISSIONS*

NAME/MISSION DATES	DAYS
1 **Valeri V. Polyakov** Jan 8, 1994–Mar 22, 1995	437.7
2 **Sergei V. Avdeyev** Aug 13, 1998–Aug 28, 1999	379.6
3 = **Musa K. Manarov** Dec 21, 1987–Dec 21, 1988	365.9
3 = **Vladimir G. Titov** Dec 21, 1987–Dec 21, 1988	365.9
5 **Yuri V. Romanenko** Feb 5–Dec 5, 1987	326.5
6 **Sergei K. Krikalyov** May 18, 1991–Mar 25, 1992	311.8
7 **Valeri V. Polyakov** Aug 31, 1988–Apr 27, 1989	240.9
8 = **Oleg Y. Atkov** Feb 8–Oct 2, 1984	237.0
8 = **Leonid D. Kizim** Feb 8–Oct 2, 1984	237.0
8 = **Anatoli Y. Solovyov** Feb 8–Oct 2, 1984	237.0

**To January 1, 2000*

Space medicine specialist Valeri V. Polyakov (born April 27, 1942) spent his 52nd birthday in space during his record-breaking mission aboard the *Mir* space station.

"ASTRONAUT"

In a pioneering science-fiction novel, *Across the Zodiac*, published in 1880, British writer Percy Greg (1836–89) presented the first fictional account of interplanetary travel by space ship, calling his vessel *Astronaut* (from the Greek for "star sailor"). By the late 1920s, the word had become used to mean a space *traveler*, rather than his ship, and, once the space age began, it was this sense that became established in the West, with cosmonaut as the Russian equivalent.

WHY DO WE SAY?

SPACE-AGE WOMAN

With three further missions since her first flight aboard Space Shuttle Endeavor STS-57 in 1993, NASA astronaut Janice Voss has earned a place among the world's most experienced spacewomen.

Waterworld

DEEPEST OCEANS AND SEAS

OCEAN OR SEA	GREATEST DEPTH		AVERAGE DEPTH	
	M	FT	M	FT
1 Pacific Ocean	10,924	35,837	4,028	13,215
2 Indian Ocean	7,455	24,460	3,963	13,002
3 Atlantic Ocean	9,219	30,246	3,926	12,880
4 Caribbean Sea	6,946	22,788	2,647	8,685
5 South China Sea	5,016	16,456	1,652	5,419
6 Bering Sea	4,773	15,659	1,547	5,075
7 Gulf of Mexico	3,787	12,425	1,486	4,874
8 Mediterranean Sea	4,632	15,197	1,429	4,688
9 Japan Sea	3,742	12,276	1,350	4,429
10 Arctic Ocean	5,625	18,456	1,205	3,953

The deepest point in the deepest ocean is the Marianas Trench in the Pacific at a depth of 10,924 m (35,837 ft). The Pacific is so vast that it contains more water than all the world's other seas and oceans put together.

LONGEST RIVERS

RIVER	LOCATION	LENGTH	
		KM	MILES
1 Nile	Tanzania/Uganda/Sudan/Egypt	6,670	4,145
2 Amazon	Peru/Brazil	6,448	4,007
3 Yangtze–Kiang	China	6,300	3,915
4 Mississippi–Missouri–Red Rock	US	5,971	3,710
5 Yenisey–Angara–Selenga	Mongolia/Russia	5,540	3,442
6 Huang Ho (Yellow River)	China	5,464	3,395
7 Ob'-Irtysh	Mongolia/Kazakhstan/Russia	5,410	3,362
8 Congo	Angola/Dem. Rep. of Congo	4,700	2,920
9 Lena–Kirenga	Russia	4,400	2,734
10 Mekong	Tibet/China/Myanmar (Burma)/ Laos/Cambodia/Vietnam	4,350	2,703

LONGEST GLACIERS

GLACIER	LOCATION	LENGTH	
		KM	MILES
1 Lambert-Fisher	Antarctica	515	320
2 Novaya Zemlya	Russia	418	260
3 Arctic Institute	Antarctica	362	225
4 Nimrod-Lennox-King	Antarctica	290	180
5 Denman	Antarctica	241	150
6 =Beardmore	Antarctica	225	140
6 =Recovery	Antarctica	225	140
8 Petermanns	Greenland	200	124
9 Unnamed	Antarctica	193	120
10 Slessor	Antarctica	185	115

LONGEST RIVERS IN CANADA

RIVER	LENGTH (KM)
1 Mackenzie	4,241
2 St. Lawrence	3,058
3 Nelson	2,575
4 Churchill (Saskatchewan)	1,609
5 Peace	1,521
6 Fraser	1,370
7 North Saskatchewan	1,287
8 Ottawa	1,271
9 Athabasca	1,231
10 Yukon*	1,149

* Canadian portion only. If the total length of the Yukon (3,185 km) was considered, it would be No. 2 on this list.

TOP 10 DEEPEST DEEP-SEA TRENCHES

(Trench/ocean/deepest point in m/ft)

1 Marianas, Pacific, 10,924/35,837 **2** Tonga*, Pacific, 10,800/35,430 **3** Philippine, Pacific, 10,497/34,436 **4** Kermadec*, Pacific, 10,047/32,960 **5** Bonin, Pacific, 9,994/32,786 **6** New Britain, Pacific, 9,940/32,609 **7** Kuril, Pacific, 9,750/31,985 **8** Izu, Pacific, 9,695/31,805 **9** Puerto Rico, Atlantic, 8,605/28,229 **10** Yap, Pacific, 8,527/27,973

* Some authorities consider these parts of one feature

JUNGLE FEEDER

It was not until 1953 that the source of the Amazon was identifed as a stream called Huarco, flowing from the Misuie glacier in the Peruvian Andes mountains. It joins the Amazon's main tributary at Ucayali, Peru.

TOP 10 ★
COUNTRIES WITH THE GREATEST AREAS OF INLAND WATER

COUNTRY	PERCENTAGE OF TOTAL AREA	WATER AREA SQ KM	SQ MILES
1 Canada	7.60	755,170	291,573
2 India	9.56	314,400	121,391
3 China	2.82	270,550	104,460
4 US	2.20	206,010	79,541
5 Ethiopia	9.89	120,900	46,680
6 Colombia	8.80	100,210	38,691
7 Indonesia	4.88	93,000	35,908
8 Russia	0.47	79,400	30,657
9 Australia	0.90	68,920	26,610
10 Tanzania	6.25	59,050	22,799

Large areas of some countries are occupied by major rivers and lakes. Lake Victoria, for example, raises the water area of Uganda to 15.39 percent of its total. In Europe, three Scandinavian countries have considerable percentages of water: Sweden 8.68 percent, Finland 9.36 percent, and Norway 5.05 percent.

TOP 10 ★
HIGHEST WATERFALLS

WATERFALL	LOCATION	TOTAL DROP M	FT
1 Angel	Venezuela	979	3,212*
2 Tugela	South Africa	947	3,107
3 Utigård	Norway	800	2,625
4 Mongefossen	Norway	774	2,540
5 Yosemite	California	739	2,425
6 Østre Mardøla Foss	Norway	656	2,152
7 Tyssestrengane	Norway	646	2,120
8 Cuquenán	Venezuela	610	2,000
9 Sutherland	New Zealand	580	1,904
10 Kjellfossen	Norway	561	1,841

* Longest single drop 807 m (2,648 ft)

FALL AND ANGEL

Angel Falls in Venezuela were discovered in 1933 by American adventurer James Angel, after whom they are named. Their overall height is equivalent to two-and-a-half Empire State Buildings.

TOP 10 ★
DEEPEST FRESHWATER LAKES

LAKE	LOCATION	GREATEST DEPTH M	FT
1 Baikal	Russia	1,637	5,371
2 Tanganyika	Burundi/ Tanzania/Dem. Rep. of Congo/ Zambia	1,471	4,825
3 Malawi	Malawi/ Mozambique/Tanzania	706	2,316
4 Great Slave	Canada	614	2,015
5 Matana	Celebes, Indonesia	590	1,936
6 Crater	Oregon, US	589	1,932
7 Toba	Sumatra, Indonesia	529	1,736
8 Hornindals	Norway	514	1,686
9 Sarez	Tajikistan	505	1,657
10 Tahoe	California/ Nevada, US	501	1,645

TOP 10 ★
LARGEST LAKES

LAKE	LOCATION	APPROX. AREA SQ KM	SQ MILES
1 Caspian Sea	Azerbaijan/ Iran/Kazakhstan/ Russia/Turkmenistan	371,000	143,205
2 Superior	Canada/US	82,413	31,820
3 Victoria	Kenya/ Tanzania/Uganda	68,800	26,570
4 Huron	Canada/US	59,596	23,010
5 Michigan	US	58,016	22,400
6 Aral Sea	Kazakhstan/ Uzbekistan	40,000	15,444
7 Tanganyika	Burundi/ Tanzania/Dem. Rep. of Congo/Zambia	32,900	13,860
8 Great Bear	Canada	31,150	12,030
9 Baikal	Russia	30,500	11,775
10 Great Slave	Canada	28,570	11,030

TOP 10 ★
LARGEST LAKES IN NORTH AMERICA

LAKE	LOCATION	APPROX. AREA SQ KM	SQ MILES
1 Superior	Canada/US	82,413	31,820
2 Huron	Canada/US	59,596	23,010
3 Michigan	US	58,016	22,400
4 Great Bear	Canada	31,150	12,030
5 Great Slave	Canada	28,570	11,030
6 Erie	Canada/US	25,719	9,930
7 Winnipeg	Canada	24,553	9,094
8 Ontario	Canada/US	19,477	7,520
9 Athabasca	Canada	7,920	3,058
10 Reindeer	Canada	6,330	2,444

The Great Lakes together form the largest area of freshwater on the Earth. They comprise Superior, Huron, Michigan, Erie, and Ontario, which together have an area of 245,055 sq km (94,616 sq miles).

What is Canada's most popular alternative therapy?
see p.54 for the answer

A Acupuncture
B Chiropractic
C Homeopathy

Islands of the World

TOP 10 LARGEST VOLCANIC ISLANDS

	ISLAND/LOCATION	STATUS	APPROX. AREA SQ KM	APPROX. AREA SQ MILES
1	**Sumatra**, Indonesia	Active volcanic	443,065.8	171,068.7
2	**Honshu**, Japan	Volcanic	225,800.3	87.182.0
3	**Java**, Indonesia	Volcanic	138,793.6	53.588.5
4	**North Island**, New Zealand	Volcanic	111,582.8	43.082.4
5	**Luzon**, Philippines	Active volcanic	109,964.9	42.457.7
6	**Iceland**, Indonesia	Active volcanic	101,826.0	39,315.2
7	**Mindanao**, Philippines	Active volcanic	97,530.0	37,656.5
8	**Hokkaido**, Japan	Active volcanic	78,719.4	30,394.7
9	**New Britain**, Papua New Guinea	Volcanic	35,144.6	13,569.4
10	**Halmahera**, Indonesia	Active volcanic	18,039.6	6,965.1

Source: *United Nations*

TOP 10 ★ LARGEST ISLANDS

	ISLAND/LOCATION	APPROX. AREA* SQ KM	APPROX. AREA* SQ MILES
1	Greenland	2,175,600	840,070
2	New Guinea, Papua New Guinea/Indonesia	800,000	309,000
3	Borneo, Indonesia/ Malaysia/Brunei	744,100	287,300
4	Madagascar	587,041	226,657
5	Baffin Island, Canada	504,751	195,942
6	Sumatra, Indonesia	424,760	164,000
7	Honshu, Japan	230,966	89,176
8	Great Britain	229,957	88,787
9	Victoria Island, Canada	217,290	83,902
10	Ellesmere Island, Canada	196,236	75,772

* Mainlands, including areas of inland water, but excluding offshore islands

Australia is regarded as a continental land mass rather than an island: otherwise it would rank first at 7,618,493 sq km (2,941,517 sq miles), or 35 times the size of Great Britain. The largest US island is Hawaii, which measures 10,456 sq km (4,037 sq miles), and the largest off mainland US is Kodiak, Alaska, at 9,510 sq km (3,672 sq miles).

TOP 10 ★ LARGEST ISLANDS IN EUROPE

	ISLAND/LOCATION	AREA SQ KM	AREA SQ MILES
1	Great Britain, North Atlantic	229,957	88,787
2	Iceland, North Atlantic	103,000	39,769
3	Ireland, North Atlantic	83,766	32,342
4	West Spitsbergen, Arctic Ocean	39,368	15,200
5	Sicily, Mediterranean Sea	25,400	9,807
6	Sardinia, Mediterranean Sea	23,800	9,189
7	North East Land, Barents Sea	15,000	5,792
8	Cyprus, Mediterranean Sea	9,251	3,572
9	Corsica, Mediterranean Sea	8,720	3,367
10	Crete, Mediterranean Sea	8,260	3,189

Great Britain became an island only after the end of the last ice age, some 8,000 years ago, when the land bridge that had previously existed was inundated and the North Sea became connected with the English Channel. Until then the Dogger Bank, now a notable fishing ground, was land, and the Thames River was a tributary of the Rhine.

TOP 10 🍁 LARGEST CANADIAN ISLANDS

	ISLAND	APPROX. AREA SQ KM	APPROX. AREA SQ MILES
1	Baffin	507,451	195,942
2	Victoria	217,290	83,902
3	Ellesmere	196,236	75,772
4	Newfoundland	108,860	42,034
5	Banks	70,028	27,040
6	Devon	55,247	21,332
7	Axel Heiberg	43,178	16,672
8	Melville	42,149	16,275
9	Southampton	41,214	15,914
10	Prince of Wales	33,338	12,873

Covering 31,284 sq km (12,080 sq miles), Vancouver Island would be No. 11 on the list. Canada's other island province besides Newfoundland, Prince Edward Island, covers 5,660 sq km (2,186 sq miles), and is just over half the size of Cape Breton, which, at 10,311 sq km (3,981 sq miles), would be No. 18.

Did You Know? The volcanic island of Surtsey emerged from the sea to the south of Iceland in 1963. It was named after the Norse god Surtur.

UNDER THE VOLCANO

Volcanic Sumatra's tallest peak, Gunung Kerinici, is a 3,805-m (12,484-ft) active volcano that was first climbed in 1877. Southeast Asia has more active volcanoes than any other part of the world.

TOP 10 HIGHEST ISLANDS

(Island/location/highest elevation in m/ft)

1 **New Guinea**, Papua New Guinea/Indonesia, 5,030/16,503 **2** **Akutan**, Alaska, 4,275/14,026 **3** **Borneo**, Indonesia/Malaysia/Brunei, 4,175/13,698 **4** **Hawaii**, 4,169/13,678 **5** **Formosa**, China, 3,997/13,114 **6** **Sumatra**, Indonesia, 3,804/12,480 **7** **Ross**, Antarctica, 3,794/12,448 **8** **Honshu**, Japan, 3,776/12,388 **9** **South Island**, New Zealand, 3,764/12,349 **10** **Lombok**, Lesser Sunda Islands, Indonesia, 3,726/12,224

Source: *United Nations*

TOP 10 ★
LARGEST LAKE ISLANDS

	ISLAND	LAKE/LOCATION	AREA SQ KM	SQ MILES
1	Manitoulin	Huron, Ontario, Canada	2,766	1,068
2	Vozrozhdeniya	Aral Sea, Uzbekistan/ Kazakhstan	2,300	888
3	René-Lavasseur	Manicouagan Reservoir, Quebec, Canada	2,020	780
4	Olkhon	Baikal, Russia	730	282
5	Samosir	Toba, Sumatra, Indonesia	630	243
6	Isle Royale	Superior, Michigan	541	209
7	Ukerewe	Victoria, Tanzania	530	205
8	St. Joseph	Huron, Ontario, Canada	365	141
9	Drummond	Huron, Michigan	347	134
10	Idjwi	Kivu, Dem. Rep. of Congo	285	110

Not all islands are surrounded by sea: many sizable islands are situated in lakes. The second largest in this list, Vozrozhdeniya, is growing as the Aral Sea contracts, and is set to link up with the surrounding land as a peninsula.

TOP 10 LARGEST ISLANDS IN THE US

(Island/location/area in sq km/sq miles)

1 **Hawaii**, Hawaii, 10,456/4,037 **2** **Kodiak**, Alaska, 9,510/3,672 **3** **Prince of Wales**, Alaska, 6,700/2,587 **4** **Chicagof**, Alaska, 5,400/2,085 **5** **Saint Lawrence**, Alaska, 4,430/1,710 **6** **Admiralty**, Alaska, 4,270/1,649 **7** **Baranof**, Alaska, 4,237/1,636 **8** **Nunivak**, Alaska, 4,210/1,625 **9** **Unimak**, Alaska, 4,160/1,606 **10** **Long Island**, New York, 3,269/1,401

MALTESE SQUEEZE

Close-packed high-rise housing in the capital, Valletta, exemplifies Malta's status as the world's most densely populated island country. Over 383,000 people are packed into just 316 sq km (122 sq miles).

TOP 10 ★
MOST DENSELY POPULATED ISLAND COUNTRIES

	ISLAND	AREA SQ KM	SQ MILES	POPULATION*	POPULATION PER SQ KM	SQ MILE
1	Malta	316	122	383,285	1,213	3,142
2	Bermuda	53	21	62,912	1,187	2,996
3	Maldives	298	115	310,425	1,042	2,699
4	Bahrain	694	268	641,539	924	2,394
5	Mauritius	1,865	720	1,196,172	642	1,661
6	Taiwan	35,742	13,800	22,319,222	624	1,617
7	Barbados	430	166	259,248	603	1,562
8	Tuvalu	25	10	10,730	429	1,073
9	Marshall Islands	181	70	68,088	376	973
10	Japan	372,801	143,939	126,434,470	339	878

* *Estimated for the year 2000*   Source: *United Nations*

The Face of the Earth

TOP 10 ★
HIGHEST ACTIVE VOLCANOES

	VOLCANO	LOCATION	LATEST ACTIVITY	HEIGHT M	FT
1	Guallatiri	Chile	1987	6,060	19,882
2	Lascar	Chile	1991	5,990	19,652
3	Cotopaxi	Ecuador	1975	5,897	19,347
4	Tupungatito	Chile	1986	5,640	18,504
5	Popocatépetl	Mexico	1995	5,452	17,887
6	Ruiz	Colombia	1992	5,400	17,716
7	Sangay	Ecuador	1988	5,230	17,159
8	Guagua Pichincha	Ecuador	1988	4,784	15,696
9	Puracé	Colombia	1977	4,755	15,601
10	Kliuchevskoi	Russia	1995	4,750	15,584

This list includes all volcanoes that have been active at some time during the 20th century. The tallest currently active volcano in Europe is Mt. Etna.

TOP 10 ★
LARGEST DESERTS

	DESERT	LOCATION	APPROX. AREA SQ KM	SQ MILES
1	Sahara	North Africa	9,000,000	3,500,000
2	Australian	Australia	3,800,000	1,470,000
3	Arabian	Southwest Asia	1,300,000	502,000
4	Gobi	Central Asia	1,036,000	400,000
5	Kalahari	Southern Africa	520,000	201,000
6	Turkestan	Central Asia	450,000	174,000
7	Takla Makan	China	327,000	125,000
8 =	Namib	Southwest Africa	310,000	120,000
8 =	Sonoran	US/Mexico	310,000	120,000
10 =	Somali	Somalia	260,000	100,000
10 =	Thar	Northwest India/Pakistan	260,000	100,000

Did You Know? Analysis of the latest data concerning Everest indicates that the mountain is growing higher and moving northeast at a rate of 6 cm (2.4 in) per year.

TOP 10 ★
LONGEST CAVES

CAVE/LOCATION	TOTAL KNOWN LENGTH KM	MILES
1 **Mammoth cave system**, Kentucky	567	352
2 **Optimisticeskaja**, Ukraine	201	125
3 **Jewel Cave**, South Dakota	174	108
4 **Hölloch**, Switzerland	166	103
5 **Lechuguilla Cave**, New Mexico	161	100
6 **Siebenhengsteholen-system**, Switzerland	140	87
7= **Fisher Ridge cave system**, Kentucky	126	78
7= **Wind Cave**, South Dakota	126	78
9 **Ozernay**, Ukraine	111	69
10 **Gua Air Jernih**, Malaysia	109	68

Source: *Tony Waltham, BCRA, 1999*

TOP 10 ★
COUNTRIES WITH THE HIGHEST ELEVATIONS*

COUNTRY/PEAK	HEIGHT M	FT
1 **Nepal#**, Everest	8,846	29,022
2 **Pakistan**, K2	8,611	28,250
3 **India**, Kangchenjunga	8,598	28,208
4 **Bhutan**, Khula Kangri	7,554	24,784
5 **Tajikistan**, Mt. Garmo (formerly Kommunizma)	7,495	24,590
6 **Afghanistan**, Noshaq	7,490	24,581
7 **Kyrgystan**, Pik Pobedy	7,439	24,406
8 **Kazakhstan**, Khan Tengri	6,995	22,949
9 **Argentina**, Cerro Aconcagua	6,960	22,834
10 **Chile**, Ojos del Salado	6,885	22,588

* *Based on the tallest peak in each country*

\# *Everest straddles Nepal and Tibet, which, now known as Xizang, is a province of China*

TOP 10 ★
DEEPEST CAVES

CAVE SYSTEM/ LOCATION	TOTAL KNOWN DEPTH M	FT
1 **Lamprechtsofen**, Austria	1,632	5,354
2 **Gouffre Mirolda**, France	1,610	5,282
3 **Réseau Jean Bernard**, France	1,602	5,256
4 **Shakta Pantjukhina**, Georgia	1,508	4,948
5 **Sistema Huautla**, Mexico	1,475	4,839
6 **Sistema del Trave**, Spain	1,444	4,737
7 **Boj Bulok**, Uzbekistan	1,415	4,642
8 **Puerto di Illamina**, Spain	1,408	4,619
9 **Lukina Jama**, Croatia	1,392	4,567
10 **Sistema Cheve**, Mexico	1,386	4,547

Source: *Tony Waltham, BCRA, 1999*

TOP 10 ★
HIGHEST MOUNTAINS

MOUNTAIN/LOCATION	HEIGHT* M	FT
1 **Everest**, Nepal/Tibet	8,846	29,022
2 **K2**, Kashmir/China	8,611	28,250
3 **Kangchenjunga**, Nepal/Sikkim	8,598	28,208
4 **Lhotse**, Nepal/Tibet	8,501	27,890
5 **Makalu I**, Nepal/Tibet	8,470	27,790
6 **Dhaulagiri I**, Nepal	8,172	26,810
7 **Manaslu I**, Nepal	8,156	26,760
8 **Cho Oyu**, Nepal	8,153	26,750
9 **Nanga Parbat**, Kashmir	8,126	26,660
10 **Annapurna I**, Nepal	8,078	26,504

* *Height of principal peak; lower peaks of the same mountain are excluded*

In November 1999 it was announced that an analysis of data beamed from sensors on Everest's summit to GPS satellites had claimed a new height of 8,850 m (29,035 ft). This height has been accepted by the National Geographic Society but awaits confirmation as the official figure.

TOP 10 LARGEST METEORITE CRATERS

(Crater/location/diameter in km/miles)

1 = **Sudbury**, Ontario, Canada; = **Vredefort**, South Africa, 140/87 **3 Manicouagan**, Quebec, Canada; = **Popigai**, Russia, 100/62 **5 Puchezh-Katunki**, Russia, 80/50 **6 Kara**, Russia, 60/37 **7 Siljan**, Sweden, 52/32 **8 Charlevoix**, Quebec, Canada, 46/29 **9 Araguainha Dome**, Brazil, 40/25 **10 Carswell**, Saskatchewan, Canada, 37/23

METEORITE CRATERS

Unlike on the Solar System's other planets and moons, many astroblemes (collision sites) on the Earth have been weathered over time. Geologists are thus unsure whether or not certain craterlike structures are of meteoric origin or are the remnants of extinct volcanoes. The Vredefort Ring, for example, was thought to be volcanic but has since been claimed as a definite meteor crater. Barringer Crater in Arizona (1.265 km/0.79 miles) is, however, the largest that all scientists agree is an astrobleme. The original diameter of many craters, such as Manicouagan (seen from a space shuttle), has been reduced by erosion.

SNAP SHOTS

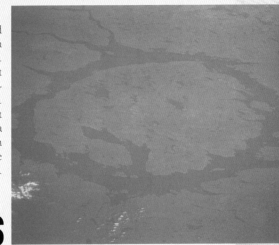

Background image: **NAMIB DESERT**

World Weather

COLDEST PLACES IN CANADA

CITY	AVERAGE NIGHTTIME TEMPERATURE DURING DECEMBER, JANUARY, AND FEBRUARY	
	°C	°F
1 Yellowknife, NWT	−29.9	−21.8
2 Thompson, Man.	−28.6	−19.5
3 Prince Albert, Sask.	−23.8	−10.8
4 Fort McMurray, Alta.	−22.9	−9.2
5 Brandon, Man.	−21.8	−7.2
6 Timmins, Ont.	−21.7	−7.1
7 Yorkton, Sask.	−21.6	−6.9
8 Val-d'Or, Que.	−21.3	−6.3
9 Winnipeg, Man.	−21.2	−6.2
10 Saskatoon, Sask.	−20.7	−5.3

WARMEST PLACES IN CANADA

CITY	AVERAGE DAYTIME TEMPERATURE DURING JUNE, JULY, AND AUGUST	
	°C	°F
1 Kamloops, B.C.	27.2	81.0
2 Penticton, B.C.	26.9	80.4
3 Windsor, Ont.	26.5	79.7
4 Kelowna, B.C.	26.4	79.5
5 Medicine Hat, Alta.	26.0	78.8
6 =St. Catharines, Ont.	25.7	78.3
6 =Estevan, Sask.	25.7	78.3
8 Moose Jaw, Sask.	25.6	78.1
9 Chateauguay, Que.	25.5	77.9
10 Sorel, Que.	25.3	77.5

COLDEST INHABITED PLACES

WEATHER STATION/LOCATION	AVERAGE TEMPERATURE	
	°C	°F
1 Norilsk, Russia	−10.9	12.4
2 Yakutsk, Russia	−10.1	13.8
3 Yellowknife, Canada	−5.4	22.3
4 Ulan-Bator, Mongolia	−4.5	23.9
5 Fairbanks, Alaska	−3.4	25.9
6 Surgut, Russia	−3.1	26.4
7 Chita, Russia	−2.7	27.1
8 Nizhnevartovsk, Russia	−2.6	27.3
9 Hailar, Mongolia	−2.4	27.7
10 Bratsk, Russia	−2.2	28.0

WETTEST CITIES IN CANADA

CITY	TOTAL ANNUAL PRECIPITATION	
	MM	IN
1 Prince Rupert	2,552	100.47
2 St. John's	1,482	58.35
3 Sydney	1,480	58.27
4 Halifax	1,474	58.03
5 Saint John	1,433	56.42
6 Moncton	1,229	48.39
7 Quebec	1,208	47.56
8 Charlottetown	1,201	47.28
9 Corner Brook	1,186	46.69
10 Vancouver	1,167	45.94

Source: *Environment Canada*

🍁 TOP 10 DRIEST CITIES IN CANADA

(City/number of days per year without measurable precipitation)

❶ **Medicine Hat**, Alta., 271 ❷ **Lethbridge**, Alta., 265 ❸ **Kamloops**, B.C., 263
❹ **Moose Jaw**, Sask., 260 ❺ **Brandon**, Man., 258 ❻ = **Penticton**, B.C.;
= **Saskatoon**, Sask., 257 ❽ **Regina**, Sask., 256
❾ **Calgary**, Alta., 254 ❿ **Swift Current**, Sask., 253

Source: *National Climatic Data Center*

COLD COMFORT

Yakutsk, Siberia, a port with a population of 200,000, experiences some of the world's coldest winters, but receives surprisingly little precipitation – just 213 mm (8.39 in) a year.

TOP 10 ★
HOTTEST INHABITED PLACES

WEATHER STATION/LOCATION	AVERAGE TEMPERATURE °C	°F
1 Djibouti, Djibouti	30.0	86.0
2 =Timbuktu, Mali	29.3	84.7
2 =Tirunelevi, India	29.3	84.7
2 =Tuticorin, India	29.3	84.7
5 =Nellore, India	29.2	84.6
5 =Santa Marta, Colombia	29.2	84.6
7 =Aden, South Yemen	28.9	84.0
7 =Madurai, India	28.9	84.0
7 =Niamey, Niger	28.9	84.0
10 =Hudaydah, North Yemen	28.8	83.8
10 =Ouagadougou, Burkina Faso	28.8	83.8
10 =Thanjavur, India	28.8	83.8
10 =Tiruchirapalli, India	28.8	83.8

HOT SPOT

A small town at the end of a Saharan caravan route, Timbuktu in Mali is one of the world's hottest places, coming second only to Djibouti.

TOP 10 ★
WETTEST INHABITED PLACES

WEATHER STATION/LOCATION	AVERAGE ANNUAL RAINFALL MM	IN
1 Buenaventura, Colombia	6,743	265.47
2 Monrovia, Liberia	5,131	202.01
3 Pago Pago, American Samoa	4,990	196.46
4 Moulmein, Myanmar	4,852	191.02
5 Lae, Papua New Guinea	4,645	182.87
6 Baguio, Luzon Island, Philippines	4,573	180.04
7 Sylhet, Bangladesh	4,457	175.47
8 Conakry, Guinea	4,341	170.91
9 =Padang, Sumatra Island, Indonesia	4,225	166.34
9 =Bogor, Java, Indonesia	4,225	166.34

The total annual rainfall of the Top 10 wettest locations is equivalent to over 26 1.83-m (6-ft) adults standing on top of each other. The greatest rainfall in a 12-month period was 26,461 mm (1,041.75 in) at Cherrapunji, India.

TOP 10 ★
DRIEST INHABITED PLACES

WEATHER STATION/LOCATION	AVERAGE ANNUAL RAINFALL MM	IN
1 Aswan, Egypt	0.5	0.02
2 Luxor, Egypt	0.7	0.03
3 Arica, Chile	1.1	0.04
4 Ica, Peru	2.3	0.09
5 Antofagasta, Chile	4.9	0.19
6 Minya, Egypt	5.1	0.20
7 Asyut, Egypt	5.2	0.21
8 Callao, Peru	12.0	0.47
9 Trujillo, Peru	14.0	0.54
10 Fayyum, Egypt	19.0	0.75

The total annual rainfall of the Top 10 driest inhabited places, as recorded over long periods, is just 64.8 mm (2½ in) – the average length of an adult little finger. The Atacama Desert often receives virtually no rain for years on end.

Did You Know? The highest temperature recorded in Canada was 45°C (113°F) (Midale, Sask.). The lowest on record is –63°C (–81.4°F) (Snag, Yukon).

Out of This World

HEAVIEST ELEMENTS

	ELEMENT	DISCOVERER/COUNTRY	YEAR DISCOVERED	DENSITY*
1	Osmium	S. Tennant, UK	1804	22.59
2	Iridium	S. Tennant	1804	22.56
3	Platinum	J. C. Scaliger #, Italy/France	1557	21.45
4	Rhenium	W. Noddack et al., Germany	1925	21.01
5	Neptunium	Edwin M. McMillan/ Philip H. Abelson, US	1940	20.47
6	Plutonium	G. T. Seaborg et al., US	1940	20.26
7	Gold	–	Prehistoric	19.29
8	Tungsten	J. J. and F. Elhuijar, Spain	1783	19.26
9	Uranium	M. J. Klaproth, Germany	1789	19.05
10	Tantalum	A. G. Ekeberg, Sweden	1802	16.67

* Grams per cu cm at 20°C
\# Earliest reference to this element

LIGHTEST ELEMENTS*

	ELEMENT	DISCOVERER/COUNTRY	YEAR DISCOVERED	DENSITY#
1	Lithium	J. A. Arfvedson, Sweden	1817	0.533
2	Potassium	Sir Humphry Davy, UK	1807	0.859
3	Sodium	Sir Humphry Davy	1807	0.969
4	Calcium	Sir Humphry Davy	1808	1.526
5	Rubidium	R. W. Bunsen/G. Kirchoff, Germany	1861	1.534
6	Magnesium	Sir Humphry Davy	1808+	1.737
7	Phosphorus	Hennig Brandt, Germany	1669	1.825
8	Beryllium	F. Wöhler, Germany/ A. A. B. Bussy, France	1828★	1.846
9	Cesium	R. W. Bunsen/G. Kirchoff	1860	1.896
10	Sulfur	–	Prehistoric	2.070

* Solids only   \# Grams per cu cm at 20°C   + Recognized by Joseph Black, 1755, but not isolated   ★ Recognized by Nicholas Vauquelin, 1797, but not isolated

TOP 10 MOST EXTRACTED METALLIC ELEMENTS

(Element/estimated annual extraction in tonnes)

1 Iron, 716,000,000   **2** Aluminum, 15,000,000   **3** Copper, 6,540,000
4 Manganese, 6,220,000   **5** Zinc, 5,020,000   **6** Lead, 2,800,000   **7** Nickel, 510,000
8 Magnesium, 325,000   **9** Sodium, 200,000   **10** Tin, 165,000

Certain metallic minerals are extracted in relatively small quantities, whereas compounds containing these elements are major industries: contrasting with 200,000 tonnes of metallic sodium, 168 million tonnes of salt are extracted annually; metallic calcium is represented by about 2,000 tonnes, contrasting with some 112 million tonnes of lime (calcium carbonate), and 200 tonnes of the metal potassium contrast with 51 million tonnes of potassium salts.

METALLIC ELEMENTS WITH THE GREATEST RESERVES

	ELEMENT	ESTIMATED GLOBAL RESERVES (TONNES)
1	Iron	110,000,000,000
2	Magnesium	20,000,000,000
3	Potassium	10,000,000,000
4	Aluminum	6,000,000,000
5	Manganese	3,600,000,000
6	Zirconium	>1,000,000,000
7	Chromium	1,000,000,000
8	Barium	450,000,000
9	Titanium	440,000,000
10	Copper	310,000,000

This list includes accessible reserves of commercially mined metallic elements, but excludes two, calcium and sodium, that exist in such vast quantities that their reserves are considered "unlimited" and unquantifiable.

COPPER TO SPARE

Copper is among the world's most extracted elements. Bingham Copper Mine, Utah, is the largest manmade excavation in the world.

TOP 10 ★
MOST COMMON ELEMENTS IN THE EARTH'S CRUST

	ELEMENT	PARTS PER MILLION*
1	Oxygen	474,000
2	Silicon	277,100
3	Aluminum	82,000
4 =	Iron	41,000
4 =	Calcium	41,000
6 =	Magnesium	23,000
6 =	Sodium	23,000
8	Potassium	21,000
9	Titanium	5,600
10	Hydrogen	1,520

* mg per kg

TOP 10 ★
MOST COMMON ELEMENTS IN THE UNIVERSE

	ELEMENT	PARTS PER MILLION
1	Hydrogen	739,000
2	Helium	240,000
3	Oxygen	10,700
4	Carbon	4,600
5	Neon	1,340
6	Iron	1,090
7	Nitrogen	970
8	Silicon	650
9	Magnesium	580
10	Sulfur	440

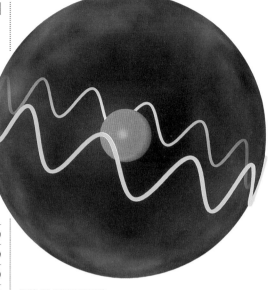

IT'S ELEMENTARY

The gas hydrogen is the simplest and most abundant element. This computer-generated image shows a hydrogen atom with a nucleus and orbiting electron.

TOP 10 PRINCIPAL COMPONENTS OF AIR
(Component/volume percent)

1 Nitrogen, 78.110 **2** Oxygen, 20.953 **3** Argon, 0.934 **4** Carbon dioxide, 0.01–0.10 **5** Neon, 0.001818 **6** Helium, 0.000524 **7** Methane, 0.0002 **8** Krypton, 0.000114 **9** = Hydrogen; = Nitrous oxide, 0.00005

THE 10 DEGREES OF HARDNESS*
(Substance)

1 Talc **2** Gypsum **3** Calcite **4** Fluorite **5** Apatite **6** Orthoclase **7** Quartz **8** Topaz **9** Corundum **10** Diamond

* According to the Mohs Scale, in which No. 1 is the softest mineral and No. 10 is the hardest

TOP 10 ★
MOST EXTRACTED NON-METALLIC ELEMENTS

	ELEMENT	ESTIMATED ANNUAL EXTRACTION (TONNES)
1	Hydrogen	350,000,000,000
2	Carbon*	16,200,000,000
3	Chlorine	167,795,000
4	Phosphorus	152,376,000
5	Oxygen	99,770,000
6	Sulfur	53,513,000
7	Nitrogen	43,536,000
8	Silicon#	3,885,000
9	Boron	1,000,000
10	Argon	700,000

* Carbon, natural gas, oil, and coal
# Various forms

THE GOLD RUSH

In August 1896, 35-year-old George Washington Carmack struck gold while panning the Rabbit (later Bonanza) Creek, south of the Yukon at Klondike near the Canadian/Alaskan border. When news of his discovery reached the outside world, it sparked the world's biggest gold rush since the California stampede of 1849. More than 100,000 prospectors traveled to the inhospitable region to seek their fortunes, and in the first year alone over $30 million worth of Klondike gold was shipped out. Most of the gold-seekers failed, however, with many dying from the freezing winter conditions or else returning home empty-handed. In 1976 much of the area was designated as the Klondike Gold Rush Historical Park.

SNAP SHOTS

CRYSTAL BOMB

Known since ancient times, sulfur is extracted in large quantities for use in many industrial and chemical processes, including making explosives.

After Toronto, what is Canada's largest megacity?
see p.84 for the answer
A Hamilton, ON
B Halifax, NS
C Laval, QC

THE 10 ★
WORST EARTHQUAKES OF THE 20TH CENTURY

	LOCATION	DATE	ESTIMATED NO. KILLED
1	**Tang-shan**, China	Jul 28, 1976	242,419
2	**Nan-Shan**, China	May 22, 1927	200,000
3	**Kansu**, China	Dec 16, 1920	180,000
4	**Messina**, Italy	Dec 28, 1908	160,000
5	**Tokyo/Yokohama**, Japan	Sep 1, 1923	142,807
6	**Kansu**, China	Dec 25, 1932	70,000
7	**Yungay**, Peru	May 31, 1970	66,800
8	**Quetta**, India*	May 30, 1935	50–60,000
9	**Armenia**	Dec 7, 1988	over 55,000
10	**Iran**	Jun 21, 1990	over 40,000

* *Now Pakistan*

Reaching 7.2 on the Richter scale, the earthquake that struck Kobe, Japan, on January 17, 1995 was exceptionally precisely monitored by the rescue authorities. It left a total of 3,842 dead and 14,679 injured.

THE 10 ★
WORST AVALANCHES AND LANDSLIDES OF THE 20TH CENTURY*

	LOCATION	INCIDENT	DATE	ESTIMATED NO. KILLED
1	**Yungay**, Peru	Landslide	May 31, 1970	17,500
2	**Italian Alps**	Avalanche	Dec 13, 1916	10,000
3	**Huarás**, Peru	Avalanche	Dec 13, 1941	5,000
4	**Nevada Huascaran**, Peru	Avalanche	Jan 10, 1962	3,500
5	**Medellin**, Colombia	Landslide	Sep 27, 1987	683
6	**Chungar**, Peru	Avalanche	Mar 19, 1971	600
7	**Rio de Janeiro**, Brazil	Landslide	Jan 11, 1966	550
8 =	**Northern Assam**, India	Landslide	Feb 15, 1949	500
8 =	**Grand Rivière du Nord**, Haiti	Landslide	Nov 13/14, 1963	500
10	**Blons**, Austria	Avalanche	Jan 11, 1954	411

* *Excluding those where most deaths resulted from flooding, earthquakes, etc., associated with landslides*

The worst incident of all, the destruction of Yungay, Peru, in May 1970, was only part of a much larger cataclysm that left a total of up to 70,000 dead. Following an earthquake and flooding, the town was wiped out by an avalanche that left just 2,500 survivors out of a population of 20,000. Among the most tragic landslide disasters of this century occurred at Aberfan, Wales, on October 20, 1966. Weakened by the presence of a spring, a huge volume of slurry from a 244-m (800-ft) high heap of coal-mine waste suddenly flowed down and engulfed the local school, killing 144 people.

TURKISH EARTHQUAKE

The earthquake that occurred in Turkey on August 17, 1999 was the second worst of the decade, resulting in a death toll unofficially estimated at between 30,000 and 40,000. It lasted only 45 seconds but measured 7.4 on the Richter scale. Its epicenter was 11 km (7 miles) southeast of Izmit, an industrial area 90 km (50 miles) east of Istanbul, where many multistory concrete apartment buildings collapsed into rubble. Most had been poorly constructed with inferior materials and little regard for the area's known vulnerability to earthquakes. In this and the surrounding area, some 20,000 structures were destroyed or damaged, while the country's industrial infrastructure was severely damaged. The Tüpras oil refinery in Korfez was set ablaze, Turkey's electricity supply cut, and water and road networks disrupted.

SNAP SHOTS

THE 10 ★
COSTLIEST HURRICANES TO STRIKE THE US

	HURRICANE	YEAR	DAMAGE (US$)*
1	Andrew	1992	30,475,000,000
2	Hugo	1989	8,491,561,181
3	Agnes	1972	7,500,000,000
4	Betsy	1965	7,425,340,909
5	Camille	1969	6,096,287,313
6	Diane	1955	4,830,580,808
7	Frederic	1979	4,328,968,903
8	New England	1938	4,140,000,000
9	Fran	1996	3,200,000,000
10	Opal	1995	3,069,395,018

* Adjusted to 1996 dollars

Source: *The National Hurricane Center*

THE 10 WORST EPIDEMICS OF ALL TIME

	EPIDEMIC	LOCATION	DATE	ESTIMATED NO. KILLED
1	Black Death	Europe/Asia	1347–51	75,000,000
2	Influenza	Worldwide	1918–20	21,640,000
3	Plague	India	1896–1948	12,000,000
4	AIDS	Worldwide	1981–	11,700,000
5	Typhus	Eastern Europe	1914–15	3,000,000
6 =	"Plague of Justinian"	Europe/Asia	541–90	millions*
6 =	Cholera	Worldwide	1846–60	millions*
6 =	Cholera	Europe	1826–37	millions*
6 =	Cholera	Worldwide	1893–94	millions*
10	Smallpox	Mexico	1530–45	>1,000,000

* No precise figures available

THE 10 ★
WORST VOLCANIC ERUPTIONS OF ALL TIME

LOCATION/DATE/INCIDENT	EST. NO. KILLED

1 Tambora, Indonesia, Apr 5–12, 1815 — 92,000
The eruption on the island of Sumbawa killed about 10,000 islanders immediately, with a further 82,000 dying subsequently from disease and famine resulting from crops being destroyed. An estimated 1,530,000 tonnes of ash was hurled into the atmosphere, blocking out the sunlight.

2 Miyi-Yama, Java, 1793 — 53,000
The volcano dominating the island of Kiousiou erupted, engulfing all the local villages in mudslides and killing most of the rural population.

3 Mont Pelée, Martinique, May 8, 1902 — 40,000
After lying dormant for centuries, Mont Pelée began to erupt in April 1902.

4 Krakatoa, Sumatra/Java, Aug 26–27, 1883 — 36,380
Krakatoa exploded with what may have been the biggest bang ever heard by humans, audible up to 4,800 km (3,000 miles) away.

5 Nevado del Ruiz, Colombia, Nov 13, 1985 — 22,940
The hot steam, rocks, and ash ejected from Nevado del Ruiz melted its icecap, resulting in a mudslide that completely engulfed the town of Armero.

6 Mount Etna, Sicily, Mar 11, 1669 — over 20,000
Europe's largest volcano has erupted frequently, but the worst instance occurred in 1669, when the lava flow engulfed the town of Catania.

7 Laki, Iceland, Jan–Jun 1783 — 20,000
An eruption on the Laki volcanic ridge culminated on June 11, with the largest ever recorded lava flow. It engulfed many villages in a river of lava up to 80 km (50 miles) long and 30 m (100 ft) deep, releasing poisonous gases that killed those who escaped.

8 Vesuvius, Italy, Aug 24, 79 — 16–20,000
The Roman city of Herculaneum was engulfed by a mud flow, while Pompeii was buried under a vast and preserving layer of pumice and volcanic ash.

9 Vesuvius, Italy, Dec 16–17, 1631 — up to 18,000
The next major cataclysm was almost as disastrous, when lava and mudflows gushed down onto the surrounding towns, including Naples.

10 Mount Etna, Sicily, 1169 — over 15,000
Large numbers died in Catania cathedral, where they believed they would be safe, and more were killed when a tidal wave caused by the eruption hit the port of Messina.

THE 10 ★
WORST FLOODS AND STORMS OF THE 20TH CENTURY

	LOCATION	DATE	ESTIMATED NO. KILLED
1	Huang He River, China	Aug 1931	3,700,000
2	Bangladesh	13 Nov 1970	300–500,000
3	Henan, China	Sep 1939	over 200,000
4	Bangladesh	30 Apr 1991	131,000
5	Chang Jiang River, China	Sep 1911	100,000
6	Bengal, India	15–16 Nov 1942	40,000
7	Bangladesh	1–2 Jun 1965	30,000
8	Bangladesh	28–29 May 1963	22,000
9	Bangladesh	11–12 May 1965	17,000
10	Morvi, India	11 Aug 1979	5–15,000

No. 4 was omitted previously because the total number of fatalities combines the effects of storm, flood and tidal wave, and it is impossible to isolate the figures for just those deaths attributable to the storm and flood aspects of the disaster.

Background image: INFLUENZA VIRUSES

What is the highest public observatory in the world?
see p.91 for the answer

A World Trade Center
B CN Tower
C Oriental Pearl Broadcasting Tower

Life on Earth

Extinct & Endangered

COME INTO MY PARLOR ...

Listed as "vulnerable" by the International Union for the Conservation of Nature, the distinctive Dolomedes Great raft or Fishing spider can sit on water as it awaits its prey.

THE 10 ★
MOST ENDANGERED BIG CATS*

1	Amur leopard
2	Anatolian leopard
3	Asiatic cheetah
4	Eastern puma
5	Florida cougar
6	North African leopard
7	Siberian tiger
8	South Arabian leopard
9	South China tiger
10	Sumatran tiger

* In alphabetical order

Source: *International Union for the Conservation of Nature*

All 10 of these big cats are classed by the International Union for Conservation of Nature as being "critically endangered," that is, facing an extremely high risk of extinction in the wild in the immediate future.

THE 10 ★
MOST ENDANGERED SPIDERS

	SPIDER	COUNTRY
1	Kauai cave wolf spider	US
2	Doloff cave spider	US
3	Empire cave pseudoscorpion	US
4	Glacier Bay wolf spider	US
5	Great raft spider	Europe
6	Kocevje subterranean spider (*Troglohyphantes gracilis*)	Slovenia
7	Kocevje subterranean spider (*Troglohyphantes similis*)	Slovenia
8	Kocevje subterranean spider (*Troglohyphantes spinipes*)	Slovenia
9	Lake Placid funnel wolf spider	US
10	Melones cave harvestman	US

Source: *International Union for the Conservation of Nature*

The first spider on this list is considered by the IUCN as "endangered" (facing a very high risk of extinction in the wild in the near future), and the others as "vulnerable" (facing a high risk of extinction in the wild in the medium-term future). Some exist exclusively in one habitat, making them especially susceptible to environmental threats.

THE 10 ★
RAREST BIRDS

	BIRD/COUNTRY	ESTIMATED NO.*
1=	Spix's macaw, Brazil	1
1=	Cebu flower pecker, Philippines	1
3	Hawaiian crow, Hawaii	5
4	Black stilt, New Zealand	12
5	Echo parakeet, Mauritius	13
6	Imperial Amazon parrot, Dominica	15
7	Magpie robin, Seychelles	20
8	Kakapo, New Zealand	24
9	Pink pigeon, Mauritius	70
10	Mauritius kestrel, Mauritius	100

* Of breeding pairs reported since 1986

Several rare bird species are known from old records or from only one specimen but, in the absence of recent sightings or records of breeding pairs, must be assumed to be extinct. With nowhere to seek refuge, rare birds come under most pressure on islands like Mauritius, where the dodo notoriously met its fate in the 17th century. Two birds that have recently escaped from the tail end of the relegation zone are the Pink pigeon and the Mauritius kestrel – formerly joint second rarest – which have made a remarkable recovery to over 100 pairs.

THE 10 ★
MOST RECENTLY EXTINCT ANIMAL SPECIES

1	Partula tree snails from Hawaii
2	Palos Verdes blue butterfly
3	Canary Islands blackfly
4	Lord Howe Islands phasmid fly
5	Dusky seaside sparrow
6	Colombian grebe and Atitlan grebe
7	Glaucous macaw
8	Hawaiian honey creeper
9	Pohmpei (Caroline Island bird)
10	Bali tiger

The saddest thing about this list is that by the time you read it, it will be out of date because yet another species will have become extinct, usually as a direct result of human intervention.

Did You Know? Once thought extinct but later rediscovered, the Kakapo parrot cannot fly, but instead climbs trees and glides down to the ground.

"AS DEAD AS A DODO"

When Portuguese sailors first encountered a large, flightless bird on the island of Mauritius, they were struck by its ludicrous clumsy appearance and the ease with which they were able to catch it; so they christened it the "doudo," the Portuguese word for "stupid." Even its Latin name emphasizes its silliness – *Didus ineptus*. As doudos, or dodos, tasted delicious, they were hunted down; and by 1681, when the last was seen by English naturalist Benjamin Harry, they were completely extinct – hence the expression, "as dead as a dodo." **WHY DO WE SAY?**

THE 10 ★
MOST ENDANGERED MAMMALS

	MAMMAL	ESTIMATED NO.
1=	Tasmanian wolf	?
1=	Halcon fruit bat	?
1=	Ghana fat mouse	?
4	Javan rhinoceros	50
5	Iriomote cat	60
6	Black lion tamarin	130
7	Pygmy hog	150
8	Kouprey	100–200
9	Tamaraw	200
10	Indus dolphin	400

The first three mammals on the list have not been seen for many years and may well be extinct.

THE 10 ★
COUNTRIES WITH THE MOST THREATENED SPECIES

	COUNTRY	MAMMALS	BIRDS	REPTILES	AMPHIBIANS	FISH	INVERTEBRATES	TOTAL
1	US	35	50	28	24	123	594	854
2	Australia	58	45	37	25	37	281	483
3	Indonesia	128	104	19	0	60	29	340
4	Mexico	64	36	18	3	86	40	247
5	Brazil	71	103	15	5	12	34	240
6	China	75	90	15	1	28	4	213
7	South Africa	33	16	19	9	27	101	205
8	Philippines	49	86	7	2	26	18	188
9	India	75	73	16	3	4	22	193
10=	Japan	29	33	8	10	7	45	132
10=	Tanzania	33	30	4	0	19	46	132

TOP 10 COUNTRIES WITH THE MOST AFRICAN ELEPHANTS

(Country/elephants)

❶ Tanzania, 73,459* ❷ Dem. Rep. of Congo, 65,974# ❸ Botswana, 62,998*
❹ Gabon, 61,794+ ❺ Zimbabwe, 56,297* ❻ Congo, 32,563# ❼ Zambia, 19,701*
❽ Kenya, 13,834* ❾ South Africa, 9,990* ❿ Cameroon, 8,824#

*Definite #Possible +Probable

Source: *International Union for the Conservation of Nature*

LONE WOLF

Although officially declared extinct in 1936, the marsupial Thylacine, or Tasmanian wolf, remains the subject of frequent alleged sightings.

Land Animals

HEAVIEST TERRESTRIAL MAMMALS

MAMMAL	LENGTH* M	FT	WEIGHT KG	LB
1 African elephant	7.3	24	7,000	14,432
2 White rhinoceros	4.2	14	3,600	7,937
3 Hippopotamus	4.0	13	2,500	5,512
4 Giraffe	5.8	19	1,600	3,527
5 American bison	3.9	13	1,000	2,205
6 Arabian camel (dromedary)	3.5	12	690	1,521
7 Polar bear	2.6	8	600	1,323
8 Moose	3.0	10	550	1,213
9 Siberian tiger	3.3	11	300	661
10 Gorilla	2.0	7	220	485

* From head to toe or head to tail

The list excludes domesticated cattle and horses. It also avoids comparing close kin, such as the African and Indian elephants.

SLEEPIEST ANIMALS*

ANIMAL	AVERAGE HOURS OF SLEEP PER DAY
1 Koala	22
2 Sloth	20
3 =Armadillo	19
3 =Opossum	19
5 Lemur	16
6 =Hamster	14
6 =Squirrel	14
8 =Cat	13
8 =Pig	13
10 Spiny anteater	12

* Excluding periods of hibernation

SLEEPYHEAD

The eastern Australian koala (which is actually a marsupial, not a bear), sleeps almost constantly to conserve the little energy it has.

HEAVIEST PRIMATES

PRIMATE	LENGTH* CM	IN	WEIGHT KG	LB
1 Gorilla	200	79	220	485
2 Man	177	70	77	170
3 Orangutan	137	54	75	165
4 Chimpanzee	92	36	50	110
5 =Baboon	100	39	45	99
5 =Mandrill	95	37	45	99
7 Gelada baboon	75	30	25	55
8 Proboscis monkey	76	30	24	53
9 Hanuman langur	107	42	20	44
10 Siamung gibbon	90	35	13	29

* Excluding tail

The longer, leaner, and lighter forms of the langurs, gibbons, and monkeys – evolved for serious monkeying around in trees – contrast sharply with their heavier great ape cousins.

GENTLE GIANT

The largest of all primates, the gorilla has a menacing appearance that has been exploited in such films as King Kong. In fact, gorillas are usually docile.

TOP 10 ★

HEAVIEST CARNIVORES

CARNIVORE	LENGTH M	FT	WEIGHT KG	LB
1 Southern elephant seal	6.5	21	3,500	7,716
2 Walrus	3.8	12	1,200	2,646
3 Steller sea lion	3.0	9	1,100	2,425
4 Grizzly bear	3.0	9	780	1,720
5 Polar bear	2.6	8	600	1,323
6 Tiger	2.8	9	300	661
7 Lion	1.9	6	250	551
8 American black bear	1.8	6	227	500
9 Giant panda	1.5	5	160	353
10 Spectacled bear	1.8	6	140	309

Of the 273 mammal species in the order Carnivora, or meat-eaters, many (including its largest representatives on land, the bears) are in fact omnivorous, and around 40 specialize in eating fish or insects. All, however, share a common ancestry indicated by the butcher's-knife form of their canine teeth. As the Top 10 would otherwise consist exclusively of seals and related marine carnivores, only three have been included in order to enable the terrestrial heavyweight division to make an appearance. The polar bear is probably the largest land carnivore if shoulder height (when the animal is on all fours) is taken into account: it tops an awesome 1.6 m (5.3 ft), compared with the 1.2 m (4 ft) of its nearest rival, the grizzly.

TOP BEAR

Although among the heaviest carnivores, many records of giant grizzlies have been exaggerated by hunters and showmen for prestige.

"GORILLA"

"Gorilla" was adopted in 1847 as part of the original scientific name for the large ape, *Troglodytes gorilla*. The word was coined by Dr. Thomas Staughton Savage, an American missionary in Africa, who had heard of the Gorillai, a mythical African tribe of hairy women, imaginatively described in a 5th- or 6th-century BC Greek account of the voyages of Hanno the Carthaginian.

WHY DO WE SAY?

Did You Know? Giant pandas spend up to 15 hours a day eating, consuming as much as 45 kg (99 lb) of bamboo shoots a day.

37

Land Animals

TOP 10 MOST INTELLIGENT MAMMALS

1 Human **2** Chimpanzee **3** Gorilla
4 Orangutan **5** Baboon **6** Gibbon
7 Monkey **8** Smaller-toothed whale **9** Dolphin **10** Elephant

This list is based on research conducted by Edward O. Wilson, Professor of Zoology at Harvard University, who defined intelligence as speed and extent of learning performance over a wide range of tasks, also taking account of the ratio of the animal's brain size to its body bulk.

TOP 10 ★ MOST PROLIFIC WILD MAMMALS

	ANIMAL	AVERAGE LITTER
1	Malagasy tenrec	25.0
2	Virginian opossum	22.0
3	Golden hamster	11.0
4	Ermine	10.0
5	Prairie vole	9.0
6	Coypu	8.5
7=	European hedgehog	7.0
7=	African hunting dog	7.0
9=	Meadow vole	6.5
9=	Wild boar	6.5

DEADLY CHARM
Traditionally used by Indian snake charmers, the menacingly hooded Indian cobra has venom that is sufficiently powerful to kill an elephant.

TOP 10 ★ MOST VENOMOUS CREATURES

	CREATURE*	FATAL AMOUNT TOXIN	MG#
1	Indian cobra	Peak V	0.009
2	Mamba	Toxin 1	0.02
3	Brown snake	Texilotoxin	0.05
4=	Inland taipan	Paradotoxin	0.10
4=	Mamba	Dendrotoxin	0.10
6	Taipan	Taipoxin	0.11
7=	Indian cobra	Peak X	0.12
7=	Poison arrow frog	Batrachotoxin	0.12
9	Indian cobra	Peak 1X	0.17
10	Krait	Bungarotoxin	0.50

* *Excluding bacteria*
\# *Quantity required to kill one average-sized human adult*

The venom of these creatures is almost unbelievably powerful: 1 milligram of Mamba Toxin 1 would be sufficient to kill 50 people. Such creatures as scorpions (0.5 mg) and black widow spiders (1.0 mg) fall just outside the Top 10.

PENSIVE PRIMATE
Numbered among the most intelligent mammals, and noted for its use of tools, the forest-dwelling orangutan's name derives from the Malay words for "man of the woods."

LONGEST LAND ANIMALS

	ANIMAL*	LENGTH# M	LENGTH# FT
1	Royal python	10.7	35
2	Tapeworm	10.0	33
3	African elephant	7.3	24
4	Estuarine crocodile	5.9	19
5	Giraffe	5.8	19
6	White rhinoceros	4.2	14
7	Hippopotamus	4.0	13
8	American bison	3.9	13
9	Arabian camel (dromedary)	3.5	12
10	Siberian tiger	3.3	11

* Longest representative of each species

Head to toe or head to tail

GROWING FAST

The giraffe is the tallest of all living animals. In 1937 a calf giraffe that measured 1.58 m (5 ft 2 in) at birth was found to be growing at an astonishing 1.3 cm (0.5 in) per hour.

FASTEST MAMMALS

	MAMMAL	MAXIMUM RECORDED SPEED KM/H	MAXIMUM RECORDED SPEED MPH
1	Cheetah	105	65
2	Pronghorn antelope	89	55
3 =	Mongolian gazelle	80	50
3 =	Springbok	80	50
5 =	Grant's gazelle	76	47
5 =	Thomson's gazelle	76	47
7	Brown hare	72	45
8	Horse	69	43
9 =	Greyhound	68	42
9 =	Red deer	68	42

QUICK OFF THE MARK

The speedy cheetah can accelerate to 96 km/h (60 mph) in just three seconds.

TOP 10 ★

DEADLIEST SNAKES

	SNAKE	MAXIMUM DEATHS PER BITE	MORTALITY RATE RANGE (PERCENT)
1	Black mamba	200	75–100
2	Forest cobra	50	70–95
3	Russell's viper	150	40–92
4	Taipan	26	10–90
5	Common krait	60	70–80
6	Jararacussa	100	60–80
7	Terciopelo	40	Not known
8	Egyptian cobra	35	50
9	Indian cobra	40	30–35
10	Jararaca	30	25–35

What is the most stolen car in Canada?
see p.228 for the answer

A Toyota 4Runner
B Acura Integra
C Volkswagen Golf

Marine Animals

TOP 10 HEAVIEST MARINE MAMMALS

	MAMMAL	LENGTH M	FT	WEIGHT TONNES
1	Blue whale	33.5	110.0	130.0
2	Fin whale	25.0	82.0	45.0
3	Right whale	17.5	57.4	40.0
4	Sperm whale	18.0	59.0	36.0
5	Gray whale	14.0	46.0	32.7
6	Humpback whale	15.0	49.2	26.5
7	Baird's whale	5.5	18.0	11.0
8	Southern elephant seal	6.5	21.3	3.6
9	Northern elephant seal	5.8	19.0	3.4
10	Pilot whale	6.4	21.0	2.9

Probably the largest animal that ever lived, the blue whale dwarfs even the other whales listed here, all but one of which far outweigh an elephant. Among the mammals that frequent inland waters, the dugong, a type of sea cow, is largest at 907 kg/2,000 lb and 4.1 m/13.5 ft.

TOP 10 ★ HEAVIEST SHARKS

	SHARK	WEIGHT KG	LB
1	Whale shark	21,000	46,297
2	Basking shark	14,515	32,000
3	Great white shark	3,314	7,300
4	Greenland shark	1,020	2,250
5	Tiger shark	939	2,070
6	Great hammerhead shark	844	1,860
7	Six-gill shark	590	1,300
8	Gray nurse shark	556	1,225
9	Mako shark	544	1,200
10	Thresher shark	500	1,100

As well as specimens that have been caught, estimates have been made of beached examples, but such is the notoriety of sharks that many accounts of their size are exaggerated, and this list should be taken as an approximate ranking based on the best available evidence.

TOP 10 ★ HEAVIEST TURTLES

	TURTLE	WEIGHT KG	LB
1	Pacific leatherback turtle	865	1,908
2	Atlantic leatherback turtle	454	1,000
3	Green sea turtle	408	900
4	Loggerhead turtle	386	850
5	Alligator snapping turtle	183	403
6	Black sea turtle	126	278
7	Flatback turtle	84	185
8	Hawksbill turtle	68	150
9 =	Kemps ridley turtle	50	110
9 =	Olive ridley turtle	50	110

TOP 10 FISHING COUNTRIES
(Country/annual catch in tonnes)

1. China, 33,166,640
2. Peru, 9,521,960
3. Chile, 7,590,947
4. Japan, 6,758,829
5. USA, 5,614,534
6. India, 5,260,420
7. Indonesia, 4,401,940
8. Russia, 4,373,827
9. Thailand, 3,647,900
10. Norway, 2,807,551

MARINE MONSTER
There are several species of right whale, with exceptional specimens reputedly exceeding 63 tonnes.

Background image: **SCHOOL OF MACKEREL**

TOP 10 ★
HEAVIEST SPECIES
OF FRESHWATER FISH CAUGHT

	SPECIES	ANGLER/LOCATION/DATE	KG	LB	OZ
1	White sturgeon	Joey Pallotta III, Benicia, California, Jul 9, 1983	212.28	468	0
2	Alligator gar	Bill Valverde, Rio Grande, Texas, Dec 2, 1951	126.55	279	0
3	Beluga sturgeon	Merete Lehne, Guryev, Kazakhstan, May 3, 1993	101.97	224	1
4	Nile perch	Adrian Brayshaw, Lake Nasser, Egypt, Dec 18, 1997	96.62	213	0
5	Flathead catfish	Ken Paulie, Withlacoochee River, Florida, May 14, 1998	56.05	123	9
6	Blue catfish	William P. McKinley, Wheeler Reservoir, Tennessee, Jul 5, 1996	50.35	111	0
7	Chinook salmon	Les Anderson, Kenai River, Alaska, May 17, 1985	44.11	97	4
8	Giant tigerfish	Raymond Houtmans, Zaire River, Zaire, Jul 9, 1988	44.00	97	0
9	Smallmouth buffalo	Randy Collins, Athens Lake, Arkansas, Jun 6, 1993	37.28	82	3
10	Atlantic salmon	Henrik Henrikson, Tana River, Norway (date unknown) 1928	35.89	79	2

TOP 10 ★
HEAVIEST SPECIES
OF SALTWATER FISH CAUGHT

	SPECIES	ANGLER/LOCATION/DATE	KG	LB	OZ
1	Great white shark	Alfred Dean, Ceduna, South Australia, Apr 21, 1959	1,208.39	2,664	0
2	Tiger shark	Walter Maxwell, Cherry Grove, California, Jun 14, 1964	807.4	1,780	0
3	Greenland shark	Terje Nordtvedt, Trondheims-fjord, Norway, Oct 18, 1987	775.00	1,708	9
4	Black marlin	A. C. Glassell, Jr., Cabo Blanco, Peru, Aug 4, 1953	707.62	1,560	0
5	Bluefin tuna	Ken Fraser, Aulds Cove, Nova Scotia, Canada, Oct 26, 1979	678.59	1,496	0
6	Atlantic blue marlin	Paulo Amorim, Vitoria, Brazil, Feb 29, 1992	635.99	1,402	2
7	Pacific blue marlin	Jay W. de Beaubien, Kaaiwi Point, Kona, May 31, 1982	624.15	1,376	0
8	Swordfish	L. Marron, Iquique, Chile, May 7, 1953	536.16	1,182	0
9	Mako shark	Patrick Guillanton, Black River, Mauritius, Nov 16, 1988	505.76	1,115	0
10	Hammerhead shark	Allen Ogle, Sarasota, Florida, May 20, 1982	449.52	991	0

Source: *International Game Fish Association*

TOP 10 ★
SPECIES OF FISH MOST
CAUGHT

	SPECIES	TONNES CAUGHT PER ANNUM
1	Anchoveta	11,896,808
2	Alaska pollock	4,298,619
3	Chilean jack mackerel	4,254,629
4	Silver carp	2,333,669
5	Atlantic herring	1,886,105
6	Grass carp	1,821,606
7	South American pilchard	1,793,425
8	Common carp	1,627,198
9	Chubb mackerel	1,507,497
10	Skipjack tuna	1,462,637

Among broader groupings of fish, some 3,000,000 tonnes of shrimps and prawns, and a similar tonnage of squids, cuttlefish, and octopuses, is caught annually.

SPEEDY SWIMMER
The highly streamlined sailfish is acknowledged as the fastest over short distances, with anglers reporting them capable of unreeling 91 m (300 ft) of line in three seconds.

TOP 10 FASTEST FISH
(Fish/recorded speed in km/h/mph)

1 Sailfish, 110/68 2 Marlin, 80/50 3 Bluefin tuna, 74/46 4 Yellowfin tuna, 70/44 5 Blue shark, 69/43 6 Wahoo, 66/41 7 = Bonefish; = Swordfish, 64/40 9 Tarpon, 56/35 10 Tiger shark, 53/33

Flying fish have a top speed in the water of only 37 km/h (23 mph), but airborne they can reach 56 km/h (35 mph). Many sharks qualify for the list; only two are listed here to prevent the list becoming overly shark-infested.

What is the busiest day of the year at Pearson International Airport?
see p.239 for the answer

A July 23
B July 30
C August 23

TOP 10 ISLANDS WITH THE MOST ENDEMIC BIRD SPECIES*

(Island/species)

1 New Guinea, 195 **2** Jamaica, 26 **3** Cuba, 23 **4** New Caledonia, 20 **5** Rennell Solomon Islands, 15 **6** São Tomé, 14 **7** = Aldabra, Seychelles; = Grand Cayman, Cayman Islands, 13 **9** Puerto Rico, 12 **10** New Britain, Papua New Guinea, 11

* Birds that are found uniquely on these islands.
Source: *United Nations*

TOP 10 MOST COMMON NORTH AMERICAN GARDEN BIRDS

(Bird/percentage of feeders visited)

1 Dark-eyed junco, 83 **2** House finch, 70 **3** = American goldfinch; = Downy woodpecker, 69 **5** Blue jay, 67 **6** Mourning dove, 65 **7** Black-capped chickadee, 60 **8** House sparrow, 59 **9** Northern cardinal, 56 **10** European starling, 52

Source: *Project FeederWatch/ Cornell Lab of Ornithology*

These are the birds that watchers are most likely to see at their feeders in North America.

TINSELTOWN BIRD

One of the most common garden birds, finches were spread from the western American states in the 1940s by dealers who sold them as "Hollywood Finches."

TOP 10 ★ LIGHTEST BATS

BAT/HABITAT	LENGTH CM	IN	WEIGHT G	OZ
1 Kitti's hognosed bat (*Craseonycteris thonglongyai*), Thailand	2.9	1.10	2.0	0.07
2 Proboscis bat (*Rhynchonycteris naso*), Central and South America	3.8	1.50	2.5	0.09
3 = Banana bat (*Pipistrellus nanus*), Africa	3.8	1.50	3.0	0.11
3 = Smoky bat (*Furiptera horrens*), Central and South America	3.8	1.50	3.0	0.11
5 = Little yellow bat (*Rhogeessa mira*), Central America	4.0	1.57	3.5	0.12
5 = Lesser bamboo bat (*Tylonycteris pachypus*), Southeast Asia	4.0	1.57	3.5	0.12
7 Disc-winged bat (*Thyroptera tricolor*), Central and South America	3.6	1.42	4.0	0.14
8 = Lesser horseshoe bat (*Rhynolophus hipposideros*), Europe and Western Asia	3.7	1.46	5.0	0.18
8 = California myotis (*Myotis californienses*), North America	4.3	1.69	5.0	0.18
10 Northern blossom bat (*Macroglossus minimus*), Southeast Asia to Australia	6.4	2.52	15.0	0.53

This list focuses on the smallest example of 10 different bat families. The weights shown are typical, rather than extreme – and since a bat can eat more than half its own weight, the weights of individual examples may vary considerably. The smallest of all weighs less than a table-tennis ball, and even the heaviest listed here weighs less than an empty aluminum drink can. Length is of head and body only, since tail lengths vary from zero (as in Kitti's hognosed bat and the Northern blossom bat) to long (as in the Proboscis bat and Lesser horseshoe bat).

TOP 10 ★ FASTEST BIRDS

BIRD	RECORDED SPEED KM/H	MPH
1 Spine-tailed swift	171	106
2 Frigate bird	153	95
3 Spur-winged goose	142	88
4 Red-breasted merganser	129	80
5 White-rumped swift	124	77
6 Canvasback duck	116	72
7 Eider duck	113	70
8 Teal	109	68
9 = Mallard	105	65
9 = Pintail	105	65

This list picks out star performers among the medium- to large-sized birds that can hit their top speed without help from wind or gravity. Fastest among swimming birds is the gentoo penguin at 35 km/h (22.3 mph), while the speediest of flightless birds is the ostrich at 72 km/h (45 mph).

TOP 10 ★ RAREST BIRDS

BIRD/COUNTRY	ESTIMATED NO.*
1 = Spix's macaw, Brazil	1
1 = Cebu flower pecker, Philippines	1
3 Hawaiian crow, Hawaii	5
4 Black stilt, New Zealand	12
5 Echo parakeet, Mauritius	13
6 Imperial Amazon parrot, Dominica	15
7 Magpie robin, Seychelles	20
8 Kakapo, New Zealand	24
9 Pink pigeon, Mauritius	70
10 Mauritius kestrel, Mauritius	100

* Of breeding pairs reported since 1986

Several rare bird species are known from old records or from only one specimen, but must be assumed to be extinct in the absence of recent sightings or records of breeding pairs. Rare birds come under most pressure on islands like Mauritius, where the dodo met its fate.

Where is Canada's longest running peace-keeping effort located?
see p.75 for the answer
A Kosovo
B Cyprus
C Bosnia-Herzegovina

OCEAN FLYER

Featuring in Coleridge's poem The Rime of the Ancient Mariner, *the albatross has a massive wingspan and can soar over the oceans for days at a time.*

TOP 10 BIRDS WITH THE LARGEST WINGSPANS

(Bird/wingspan in m/ft)

1 Marabou stork, 4.0/13 **2** Albatross, 3.7/12 **3** Trumpeter swan, 3.4 /11
4 = Mute swan; = Whooper swan; = Grey pelican;
= California condor; = Black vulture, 3.1/10
9 = Great bustard; = Kori bustard, 2.7/9

TOP 10 ★
HEAVIEST FLIGHTED BIRDS

BIRD	WINGSPAN		WEIGHT		
	M	FT	KG	LB	OZ
1 Great bustard	2.7	9	20.9	46	1
2 Trumpeter swan	3.4	11	16.8	37	1
3 Mute swan	3.1	10	16.3	35	15
4 =Albatross	3.7	12	15.8	34	13
4 =Whooper swan	3.1	10	15.8	34	13
6 Manchurian crane	2.1	7	14.9	32	14
7 Kori bustard	2.7	9	13.6	30	0
8 Grey pelican	3.1	10	13.0	28	11
9 Black vulture	3.1	10	12.5	27	8
10 Griffon vulture	2.1	7	12.0	26	7

Wing size does not necessarily correspond to weight in flighted birds. The 4-m (13-ft) wingspan of the marabou stork beats all the birds listed here, yet its body weight is normally no heavier than any of these. When laden with a meal of carrion, however, the marabou can double its weight and may fail to take off.

"A LITTLE BIRD TOLD ME"

This phrase is often used to announce that one has information but may not be willing to reveal the source of it. Birds as messengers are legendary, but this expression, like so many others, has its origin in the Bible. In the Book of Ecclesiastes (9:20), the writer warns those who complain against kings and the rich and powerful that "a bird of the air shall carry the voice, and that which hath wings shall tell the matter."

WHY DO WE SAY?

TOP 10 🍁
MOST COMMON BREEDING BIRDS IN CANADA

1. Red-winged blackbird
2. European starling
3. American robin
4. American crow
5. House sparrow
6. Song sparrow
7. White-throated sparrow
8. Savannah sparrow
9. Common grackle
10. Barn swallow

SWANNING AROUND

A heavyweight among flighted birds, exceptional specimens of the mute swan may top 22.5 kg (49 lb 10 oz) and have wingspans of up to 3.7 m (12 ft).

Cats, Dogs & Pets

TOP 10 ★
FILMS STARRING DOGS

FILM	YEAR
1 101 Dalmatians	1996
2 One Hundred and One Dalmatians*	1961
3 Lady and the Tramp*	1955
4 Oliver & Company*	1988
5 Turner & Hooch	1989
6 The Fox and the Hound*	1981
7 Beethoven	1992
8 Homeward Bound II: Lost in San Francisco	1996
9 Beethoven's 2nd	1993
10 K-9	1991

* Animated

Man's best friend has been stealing scenes since the earliest years of filmmaking, with the 1905 low-budget *Rescued by Rover* standing as one of the most successful productions of the pioneer period. The numerous silent era films starring Rin Tin Tin, an ex-German army dog who emigrated to the US, and his successor, Lassie, whose long series of feature and TV films date from the 1940s onward, are among the most enduring in cinematic history.

TOP 10 DOGS' NAMES IN THE US

❶ Max ❷ Buddy ❸ Molly ❹ Maggie
❺ Bailey ❻ Jake ❼ Lucy ❽ Sam
❾ Bear ❿ Shadow

Based on a database of 117,000 I.D. tag records.
Source: American Pet Classics

TOP DOGS

Labrador retrievers are the most popular pedigree dogs in both Canada and the US.

TOP 10 🍁
DOG BREEDS IN CANADA

BREED	NO. REGISTERED*
1 Labrador retriever	10,129
2 Golden retriever	6,916
3 German shepherd	5,016
4 Poodle	3,008
5 Shetland sheepdog	2,969
6 Yorkshire terrier	2,369
7 Miniature schnauzer	2,168
8 Shih tzu	1,770
9 Boxer	1,695
10 Bichon frise	1,670

* Registered with the Canadian Kennel Club in 1999

Source: *Canadian Kennel Club*

TOP 10 🍁
CAT BREEDS IN CANADA

BREED	NO. REGISTERED*
1 Himalayan	787
2 Persian	526
3 Himalayan non-pointed	239
4 = Exotic longhair	161
4 = Ragdoll	161
6 Exotic shorthair	97
7 Maine coon	91
8 Birman	87
9 Siamese	78
10 Abyssinian	75

* Cats registered with Canadian Cat Association

Source: *Canadian Cat Association*

TOP 10 ★
MOST INTELLIGENT DOG BREEDS

1 Border collie
2 Poodle
3 German shepherd (Alsatian)
4 Golden retriever
5 Doberman pinscher
6 Shetland sheepdog
7 Labrador retriever
8 Papillon
9 Rottweiler
10 Australian cattle dog

Source: *Stanley Coren*, The Intelligence of Dogs

Background image: **GUINEA PIGS**

TOP 10 CATS' NAMES IN THE US
① Tiger ② Max ③ Tigger ④ Sam ⑤ Kitty
⑥ Sammy ⑦ Smokey ⑧ Shadow
⑨ Misty ⑩ Fluffy

Based on a database of
117,000 I.D. tag records.
Source: American Pet Classics

WHAT'S NEW, PUSSYCAT?
*Although their role as household mouse
exterminators is less significant today, cats
maintain their place among the world's
favorite animals.*

TOP 10 ★

PETS IN THE US

	PET	ESTIMATED NO.*
1	Cat	66,150,000
2	Dog	58,200,000
3	Small animal pet#	12,740,000
4	Parakeet	11,000,000
5	Freshwater fish	10,800,000
6	Reptile	7,540,000
7	Finch	7,350,000
8	Cockatiel	6,320,000
9	Canary	2,580,000
10	Parrot	1,550,000

Source: *Pet Industry Joint Advisory Council*

** Number of households owning, rather
than individual specimens*

*# Includes small rodents: rabbits, ferrets,
hamsters, guinea pigs, and gerbils*

"IN THE DOGHOUSE"
In J. M. Barrie's famous children's play *Peter Pan* (1904), irascible Mr. Darling mistreats the dog-nursemaid, Nana, as a result of which the Darling children – Wendy, John, and Michael – leave home. As a penance, Mr. Darling lives in the doghouse until the children return. Mr. Darling was based on Arthur Llewelyn Davies, the real-life father of the boys on whom **WHY DO** Barrie based the story, and Nana was Barrie's **WE SAY?** own dog, Luath.

TOP 10 RABBITS' NAMES IN THE US
① Thumper ② Flopsy ③ Charlie ④ Fudge
⑤ Rosie ⑥ Smokey ⑦ Snowy
⑧ Daisy ⑨ George ⑩ Molly

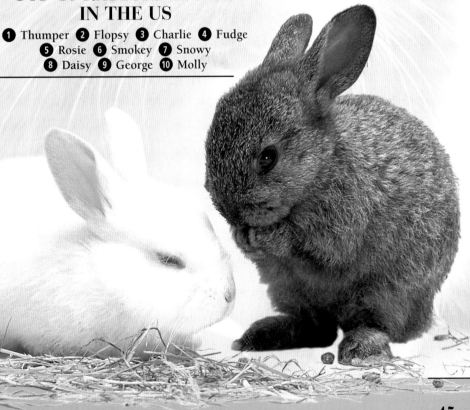

FURRY FAVORITES
*Although Flopsy is second choice,
Beatrix Potter's more famous creations of
Peter and Benjamin are surprisingly absent
from the Top 10 rabbits' names.*

Creepy Crawlies

FASTEST FLYING INSECTS

	SPECIES	KM/H	MPH
1	Hawkmoth (Sphingidae)	53.6	33.3
2=	West Indian butterfly (Nymphalidae prepona)	48.0	30.0
2=	Deer bot fly (Cephenemyia pratti)	48.0	30.0
4	Deer bot fly (Chrysops)	40.0	25.0
5	West Indian butterfly (Hesperiidae sp.)	30.0	18.6
6	Dragonfly (Anax parthenope)	28.6	17.8
7	Hornet (Vespa crabro)	21.4	13.3
8	Bumblebee (Bombus lapidarius)	17.9	11.1
9	Horsefly (Tabanus bovinus)	14.3	8.9
10	Honeybee (Apis millefera)	11.6	7.2

Few accurate assessments of these speeds have been attempted, and this list reflects only the results of those scientific studies recognized by entomologists.

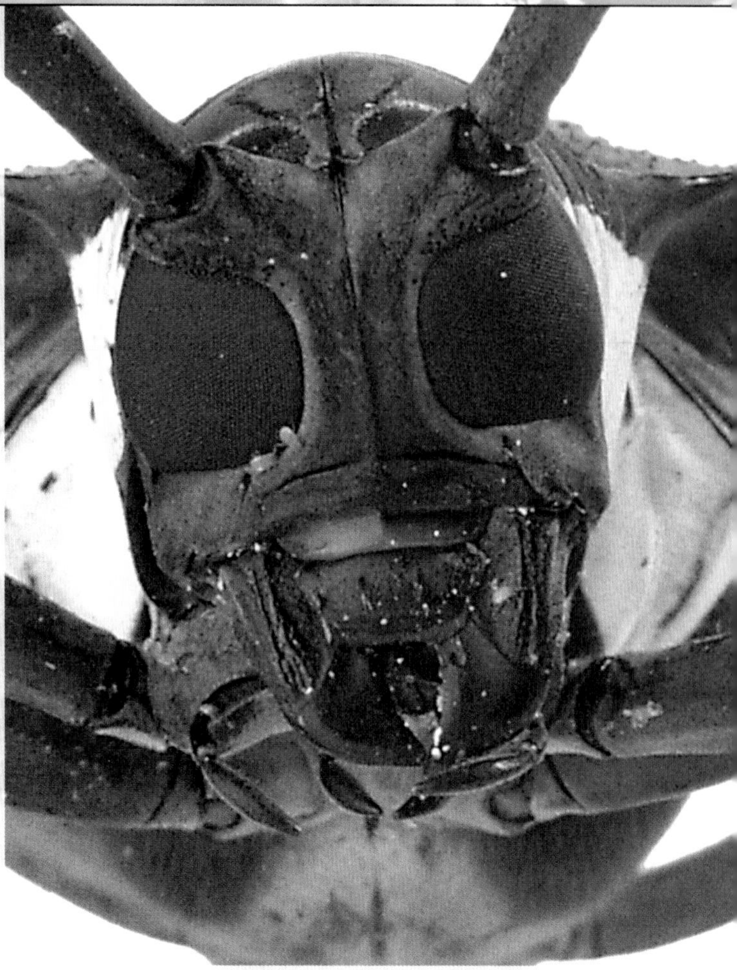

BEETLE BEATS ALL

This red-spotted longhorn beetle is one of about 400,000 beetles identified so far. This makes the beetle the most common known species of insect.

LARGEST MOTHS

	MOTH	WINGSPAN MM	IN
1	Atlas moth (Attacus atlas)	300	11.8
2	Owlet moth (Thysania agrippina)*	290	11.4
3	Haematopis grataria	260	10.2
4	Hercules emperor moth (Coscinocera hercules)	210	8.3
5	Malagasy silk moth (Argema mitraei)	180	7.1
6	Eacles imperialis	175	6.9
7=	Common emperor moth (Bunaea alcinoe)	160	6.3
7=	Giant peacock moth (Saturnia pyri)	160	6.3
9	Gray moth (Brahmaea wallichii)	155	6.1
10=	Black witch (Ascalapha odorata)	150	5.9
10=	Regal moth (Citheronia regalis)	150	5.9
10=	Polyphemus moth (Antheraea polyphemus)	150	5.9

* Exceptional specimen measured at 308 mm (12¼ in)

MOST COMMON INSECTS*

	SPECIES	APPROXIMATE NO. OF KNOWN SPECIES
1	Beetles (Coleoptera)	400,000
2	Butterflies and moths (Lepidoptera)	165,000
3	Ants, bees, and wasps (Hymenoptera)	140,000
4	True flies (Diptera)	120,000
5	Bugs (Hemiptera)	90,000
6	Crickets, grasshoppers, and locusts (Orthoptera)	20,000
7	Caddisflies (Trichoptera)	10,000
8	Lice (Phthiraptera/Psocoptera)	7,000
9	Dragonflies and damselflies (Odonata)	5,500
10	Lacewings (Neuroptera)	4,700

* By number of known species

This list includes only species that have been discovered and named: it is surmised that many thousands of species still await discovery.

Did You Know? The heaviest of all insects is the Goliath beetle, which can weigh up to 100 g (3½ oz), or more than twice the weight of a golf ball.

LEGGING IT TO THE TOP

The Haplophilus subterraneus *centipede measures up to 70 mm (2¾ in) and has 89 pairs of legs. It is interesting to note that all centipedes always have an odd number of body segments (although the number of legs is, of course, always even!).*

TOP 10 ★
CREATURES WITH THE MOST LEGS

	CREATURE	AVERAGE NO. OF LEGS
1	Millipede *Illacme plenipes*	750
2	Centipede *Himantarum gabrielis*	354
3	Centipede *Haplophilus subterraneus*	178
4	Millipedes*	30
5	Symphylans	24
6	Caterpillars*	16
7	Woodlice	14
8	Crabs, shrimps	10
9	Spiders	8
10	Insects	6

* *Most species*

Because "centipede" means 100 feet and "millipede" 1,000 feet, many people believe that centipedes have 100 legs and millipedes 1,000. However, despite their names and depending on their species, centipedes have anything from 28 to 354 legs and millipedes up to 400, with the record standing at more than 700. The other principal difference between them is that each body segment of a centipede has two legs, while that of a millipede has four.

BIG WING

Male African giant swallowtails, Papilio antimachus, *are Africa's largest butterflies, with wingspans of up to an impressive 230 mm (9⅛ in).*

TOP 10 ★
LARGEST BUTTERFLIES

	BUTTERFLY	WINGSPAN MM	IN
1	Queen Alexandra's birdwing	280	11.0
2	African giant swallowtail	230	9.1
3	Goliath birdwing	210	8.3
4 =	*Trogonoptera trojana*	200	7.9
4 =	Buru opalescent birdwing	200	7.9
4 =	*Troides hypolitus*	200	7.9
7 =	*Ornithoptera lydius*	190	7.5
7 =	Chimaera birdwing	190	7.5
7 =	*Troides magellanus*	190	7.5
7 =	*Troides miranda*	190	7.5

Creepy Crawlies

TOP 10 LARGEST SNAILS
(Species/length in mm/in)

1 Australian trumpet *(Syrinx aruanus)*, 770/30¼ **2** Horse conch *(Pleuroploc filamentosa)*, 580/22¾ **3** = Baler shell *(Voluta amphora)*; = Triton's trumpet *(Charonia tritonis)*, 480/18¾ **5** Beck's volute *(Voluta becki)*, 470/18½ **6** Umbilicate volute *(Voluta umbilicalis)*, 420/16½ **7** Madagascar helmet *(Cassis madagascariensis)*, 409/16 **8** Spider conch *(Lambis truncata)*, 400/15¼ **9** Knobbly trumpet *(Charonia nodifera)*, 390/15¼ **10** Goliath conch *(Strombus goliath)*, 380/15

TOP 10 ⭐
DEADLIEST SPIDERS

	SPIDER/LOCATION
1	**Banana spider** *(Phonenutria nigriventer)*, Central and South America
2	**Sydney funnel web** *(Atrax robustus)*, Australia
3	**Wolf spider** *(Lycosa raptoria/erythrognatha)*, Central and South America
4	**Black widow** (Latrodectus species), worldwide
5	**Violin spider/Recluse spider**, worldwide
6	**Sac spider**, Southern Europe
7	**Tarantula** *(Eurypelma rubropilosum)*, Neotropics
8	**Tarantula** *(Acanthoscurria atrox)*, Neotropics
9	**Tarantula** *(Lasiodora klugi)*, Neotropics
10	**Tarantula** *(Pamphobeteus species)*, Neotropics

This list ranks spiders according to their "lethal potential" – their venom yield divided by their venom potency. The Banana spider, for example, yields 6 mg of venom, with 1 mg the estimated lethal dose in man. However, few spiders are capable of killing humans – there were just 14 recorded deaths caused by black widows in the US in the whole of the 19th century.

READY TO STRIKE
Found only in New South Wales, male Sydney funnel web spiders are, unusually, more dangerous than the females.

TOP 10
MOST COMMON INSECTS IN CANADA

	INSECT ORDER	NUMBER OF SPECIES KNOWN IN CANADA
1	**Diptera** (true flies)	7,058
2	**Coleoptera** (beetles)	6,748
3	**Hymenoptera** (sawflies, ants, wasps, bees)	6,028
4	**Lepidoptera** (butterflies, moths)	4,692
5	**Hemiptera** (bugs, aphids, cicadas, leafhoppers)	3,079
6	**Acari** (mites, ticks)	1,915
7	**Araneae** (spiders)	1,256
8	**Trichoptera** (caddisflies)	546
9	**Phthiraptera** (lice)	362
10	**Ephemeroptera** (mayflies)	301

Source: *Census of Canadian Terrestrial Arthropods*

If this Top 10 were to take into account the estimated number of unrecorded Canadian species, the Hymenoptera order of insects comprising sawflies, ants, wasps, and bees would be No. 1, with 16,665 species, followed by the Diptera order, with 14,464 species.

THE 10 MOST POPULAR US STATE INSECTS
(Insect/No. of States with State Insect)

1 Honeybee, 15 **2** Swallowtail butterfly, 8 **3** Ladybird beetle/ladybug, 7 **4** Monarch butterfly, 5 **5** Firefly, 2 **6** = Baltimore checkerspot butterfly; = California dogface butterfly; = Carolina mantis; = Colorado hairstreak butterfly; = European praying mantis, 1

SNAIL'S PACE

Although exceeded by marine species, the Giant African snail is the largest terrestrial mollusk. Exceptional specimens may reach almost 400 mm (15.5 in) in length and weigh 900 g (2 lb).

THE 10 COUNTRIES WITH THE MOST THREATENED INVERTEBRATES

(Country/threatened invertebrate species)

1 US, 594 **2** Australia, 281 **3** South Africa, 101 **4** Portugal, 67 **5** France, 61 **6** Spain, 57 **7** Tanzania, 46 **8** = Japan; = Dem. Rep. of Congo, 45 **10** = Austria; = Italy, 41

Source: *International Union for the Conservation of Nature*

TOP 10 ★
LARGEST MOLLUSKS*

	SPECIES	CLASS	LENGTH MM	IN
1	**Giant squid** (*Architeuthis sp.*)	Cephalopod	16,764	660#
2	**Giant clam** (*Tridacna gigas*)	Marine bivalve	1,300	51
3	**Australian trumpet**	Marine snail	770	30
4	*Hexabranchus sanguineus*	Sea slug	520	20
5	*Carinaria cristata*	Heteropod	500	19
6	**Steller's coat of mail shell** (*Cryptochiton stelleri*)	Chiton	470	18
7	**Freshwater mussel** (*Cristaria plicata*)	Freshwater bivalve	300	11
8	**Giant African snail** (*Achatina achatina*)	Land snail	200	7
9	**Tusk shell** (*Dentalium vernedi*)	Scaphopod	138	5
10	**Apple snail** (*Pila werneri*)	Freshwater snail	125	4

* *Largest species within each class*
# *Estimated; actual length unknown*

Which province spends the most per capita on candy?
see p.218 for the answer
A Nova Scotia
B Manitoba
C British Columbia

Trees & Forests

10 TALLEST TREES IN NORTH AMERICA*

	TREE	LOCATION	HEIGHT M	FT
1	Coast Douglas fir	Coos County, Oregon	100.3	329
2	Sitka spruce	Carmanah Pacific Provincial Park, B.C.	95.7	314
3	Coast redwood	Prairie Creek Redwoods State Park, California	95.4	313
4	Coast Douglas fir	Meach Creek, Coquitlam Watershed, B.C.	94.5	310
5	General Sherman (giant sequoia)	Sequoia National Park, California	83.8	275
6 =	Coast Douglas fir	Strathcona Provincial Park, B.C.	82.9	272
6 =	Noble fir	Mount St. Helens National Monument, Washington	82.9	272
8	Sitka spruce	West Walbran Creek, Vancouver Island, B.C.	78.0	256
9	Grand fir	Olympic National Park, Washington	76.5	251
10	Western hemlock	Tahsish River, B.C.	75.6	248

* Based on data supplied by American Forests and Canada's British Columbia Register of Great Trees

ON TAP

In the 20th century, annual world demand for natural rubber, especially from the automotive industry, increased from under 50,000 to over 6 million tons.

TOP 10 ★
RUBBER-PRODUCING COUNTRIES

	COUNTRY	1998 PRODUCTION TONNES
1	Thailand	2,162,266
2	Indonesia	1,563,564
3	Malaysia	1,081,873
4	India	541,737
5	China	449,781
6	Philippines	199,903
7	Vietnam	180,612
8	Côte d'Ivoire	115,612
9	Sri Lanka	105,731
10	Nigeria	89,956
	World total	6,776,794

Source: *Food and Agriculture Organization of the United Nations*

TOP 10 ★
TIMBER-PRODUCING COUNTRIES

	COUNTRY	1998 PRODUCTION CU M	CU FT
1	US	494,937,000	17,478,536,826
2	China	313,017,000	11,054,092,059
3	India	306,455,000	10,822,357,195
4	Brazil	220,313,000	7,780,280,892
5	Indonesia	202,988,500	7,168,471,891
6	Canada	191,178,000	6,751,387,981
7	Nigeria	117,387,000	4,145,483,167
8	Russia	83,968,000	2,965,302,211
9	Sweden	60,224,000	2,126,790,686
10	Ethiopia	52,310,000	1,847,310,388
	World total	3,385,623,000	119,562,158,989

Source: *Food and Agriculture Organization of the United Nations*

TOP 10 🍁
MOST COMMON TREES IN CANADA

	TREE*	RANGE AREA (SQ KM)
1	Bebb willow	598,448,264.9
2	White spruce	584,828,363.5
3	White birch	575,653,762.6
4	Black spruce	571,891,662.1
5	Trembling aspen	515,389,155.9
6	Balsam poplar	504,270,554.7
7	Tamarack	496,913,053.9
8	Speckled alder	486,541,552.8
9	Pin cherry	354,370,638.4
10	Water birch	349,905,938.0

* A woody perennial plant that grows to at least 4.5 m/15 ft in height

Source: *Canadian Forest Service*

Surprisingly, Canada's national emblem doesn't make the Top 10. In fact, Canada's most common maple tree, the mountain maple (*Acer spicatum*), sits at No. 20! The majority of Canadian forest is boreal, and maples just aren't as widespread.

TOP 10 ⭐
COUNTRIES WITH THE LARGEST AREAS OF FOREST

	COUNTRY	AREA SQ KM	AREA SQ MILES
1	Russia	7,659,120	2,957,203
2	Canada	4,940,000	1,907,345
3	Brazil	4,880,000	1,884,179
4	US	2,959,900	1,142,824
5	Dem. Rep. of Congo	1,738,000	671,046
6	Australia	1,450,000	559,848
7	China	1,304,960	503,848
8	Indonesia	1,117,740	431,562
9	Peru	848,000	327,415
10	India	685,000	264,480
	World total	41,380,090	15,976,944

NATURAL BEAUTY

The largest National Forest in the US, the Tongass in Alaska, is a magnificent wilderness that encompasses mountains, rivers, glaciers, and islands. This vast forest is over three times the size of the next forest in the Top 10.

TOP 10 ⭐
LARGEST NATIONAL FORESTS IN THE US

	FOREST	LOCATION	AREA SQ KM	AREA SQ MILES
1	Tongass National Forest	Sitka, Alaska	67,177	25,937
2	Chugach National Forest	Anchorage, Alaska	21,448	8,281
3	Toiyabe National Forest	Sparks, Nevada	12,950	5,000
4	Tonto National Forest	Phoenix, Arizona	11,735	4,531
5=	Boise National Forest	Boise, Idaho	10,925	4,218
5=	Gila National Forest	Silver City, New Mexico	10,925	4,218
7=	Humboldt National Forest	Elko, Nevada	10,116	3,906
7=	Challis National Forest	Challis, Idaho	10,116	3,906
9=	Shoshone National Forest	Cody, Wyoming	9,712	3,750
9=	Flathead National Forest	Kalispell, Montana	9,712	3,750

Source: *Land Areas of the National Forest System*

Did You Know? A vast area of the Tunguska Forest of Siberia was flattened in an instant on June 30, 1908, when a meteorite – or perhaps part of Encke's comet – exploded in the sky above it.

TOP 10 ★

The Human World

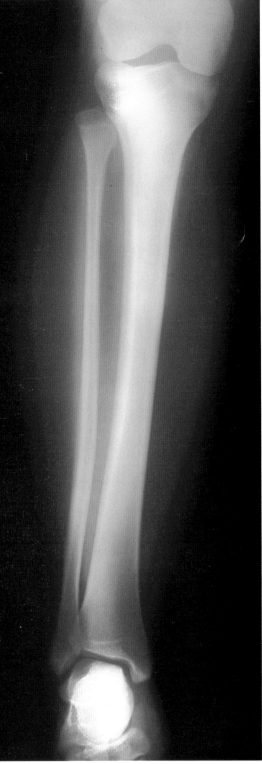

THE WINNING LEG

The second longest bone, the tibia is named after the Latin word for a flute, which it resembles in shape and length. The three longest bones are all in the leg.

TOP 10 ★
COUNTRIES THAT SPEND THE MOST ON HEALTH CARE

COUNTRY	HEALTH SPENDING PER CAPITA (US$)
1 US	4,093
2 Switzerland	3,603
3 Germany	2,677
4 Norway	2,622
5 Japan	2,442
6 Denmark	2,388
7 France	2,349
8 Sweden	2,222
9 Austria	2,012
10 Netherlands	1,978

Source: *World Bank*, World Development Indicators 1999

TOP 10 🍁
ALTERNATIVE THERAPIES IN CANADA

THERAPY USED	% OF SURVEY RESPONDENTS
1 Chiropractic	60
2 Herbology	25
3 Acupuncture	23
4 Homeopathy	18
5 Massage therapy	6
6 Naturopathy	3
7 =Vitamin therapy	2
7 =Osteopathy	2
9 =Reflexology	1
9 =Macrobiotics	1

Source: *Angus Reid poll* Use and Dangers of Alternative Medicines and Practises, *1997*

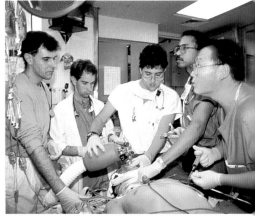

ER, US

The world's hospital emergency rooms have to be equipped to treat victims of everything from minor injuries to major traumas.

TOP 10 ★
LONGEST BONES IN THE HUMAN BODY

BONE	AVERAGE LENGTH CM	IN
1 **Femur** (thighbone)	50.50	19.88
2 **Tibia** (shinbone)	43.03	16.94
3 **Fibula** (outer lower leg)	40.50	15.94
4 **Humerus** (upper arm)	36.46	14.35
5 **Ulna** (inner lower arm)	28.20	11.10
6 **Radius** (outer lower arm)	26.42	10.40
7 **7th rib**	24.00	9.45
8 **8th rib**	23.00	9.06
9 **Innominate bone** (hipbone)	18.50	7.28
10 **Sternum** (breastbone)	17.00	6.69

THE 10 MOST COMMON ER CASES IN THE US
(Reason for visit/visits, 1997)

1 Stomach and abdominal pain, 5,527,000 **2** Chest pain and related symptoms, 5,315,000 **3** Fever, 4,212,000 **4** Headache, 2,518,000 **5** Injury – upper extremity, 2,383,000 **6** Shortness of breath, 2,242,000 **7** Cough, 2,220,000 **8** Back symptoms, 2,073,000 **9** Pain, nonspecific site, 2,040,000 **10** Symptoms referable to throat, 1,953,000

Source: *Center for Disease Control/ National Center for Health Statistics*

THE 10 ★
MOST COMMON TYPES OF ILLNESS

	TYPE	NEW CASES ANNUALLY
1	Diarrhea (including dysentery)	4,002,000,000
2	Malaria	up to 500,000,000
3	Acute lower respiratory infections	395,000,000
4	Occupational injuries	350,000,000
5	Occupational diseases	217,000,000
6	Trichomoniasis	170,000,000
7	Mood (affective) disorders	122,865,000
8	Chlamydial infections	89,000,000
9	Alcohol dependence syndrome	75,000,000
10	Gonococcal (bacterial) infections	62,000,000

Source: *World Health Organization*

TOP 10 🍁
DRUGS MOST PRESCRIBED IN CANADA

	DRUG	PRESCRIPTIONS IN 1999
1	Synthroid (Knoll)	5,052,000
2	Premarin (Wyeth-Ayerst)	4,872,000
3	Tylenol with Codeine #3 (Janssen-Ortho)	4,867,000
4	Novasen (Novapharm)	3,329,000
5	Losec (Astra Pharma)	3,229,000
6	Novamoxin (Novapharm)	2,640,000
7	Lipitor (Parke-Davis)	2,627,000
8	Paxil (SmithKline Beecham)	2,538,000
9	Vasotec (Merck Frosst)	2,489,000
10	Norvasc (Pfizer)	2,351,000

Source: *IMS Health, Canada*

TOP 10 ★
MOST COMMON PHOBIAS

	OBJECT OF PHOBIA	MEDICAL TERM
1	Spiders	Arachnephobia or arachnophobia
2	People and social situations	Anthropophobia or sociophobia
3	Flying	Aerophobia or aviatophobia
4	Open spaces	Agoraphobia, cenophobia or kenophobia
5	Confined spaces	Claustrophobia, cleisiophobia, cleithrophobia, or clithrophobia
6 =	Vomiting	Emetophobia or emitophobia
6 =	Heights	Acrophobia, altophobia, hypsophobia, or hypsiphobia
8	Cancer	Carcinomaphobia, carcinophobia, carcinomatophobia, cancerphobia, or cancerophobia
9	Thunderstorms	Brontophobia or keraunophobia
10 =	Death	Necrophobia or thanatophobia
10 =	Heart disease	Cardiophobia

WEIGHTY MATTER

The modern technique of Magnetic Resonance Imaging (MRI) enables us to view the human brain, the human body's third-largest organ.

TOP 10 ★
LARGEST HUMAN ORGANS

	ORGAN		AVERAGE WEIGHT G	OZ
1	Skin		10,886	384.0
2	Liver		1,560	55.0
3	Brain	male	1,408	49.7
		female	1,263	44.6
4	Lungs	right	580	20.5
		left	510	18.0
		total	1,090	38.5
5	Heart	male	315	11.1
		female	265	9.3
6	Kidneys	right	140	4.9
		left	150	5.3
		total	290	10.2
7	Spleen		170	6.0
8	Pancreas		98	3.5
9	Thyroid		35	1.2
10	Prostate (male only)		20	0.7

This list is based on average immediate post-mortem weights, as recorded by St. Bartholemew's Hospital, London, and other sources during a 10-year period. Various instances of organs far in excess of the average have been recorded, including male brains of over 2,000 g (70.6 oz). The Victorians believed that the heavier the brain, the greater the intelligence, and were impressed by the recorded weights of 1,658 g (58 oz) for author William Makepeace Thackeray.

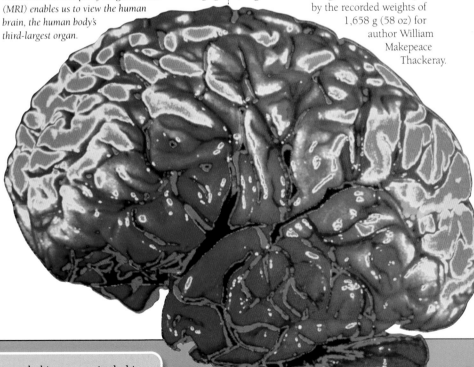

Did You Know? Among the least-common phobias are geniophobia (fear of eggshells), barophobia (gravity), apeirophobia (infinity), and linonophobia (string).

Diet & Fitness

TOP 10 🍁
CANADIAN PROVINCES WITH THE MOST OVERWEIGHT PERSONS

	PROVINCE	PERCENTAGE OF OVERWEIGHT PERSONS*
1	New Brunswick	42
2	Newfoundland	39
3	Nova Scotia	38
4	Prince Edward Island	37
5	Saskatchewan	36
6	Manitoba	35
7	Alberta	30
8	Ontario	29
9 =	British Columbia	27
9 =	Quebec	27

* Persons with a body mass index (BMI) of 27 or greater

Source: *Statistics Canada*

While overweight and obesity are best measured with special equipment, the Body Mass Index (BMI) is an acceptable indicator of relative weight. It is calculated by dividing a person's weight in kilograms by their height in meters, squared. A person with a BMI of over 30 is considered obese.

TOP 10 ACTIVITIES FOR WEIGHT MANAGEMENT

1 Walking 2 Cycling 3 Swimming
4 Active hobbies (gardening, DIY, etc.)
5 Low-impact aerobics
6 Jogging 7 Weight training
8 Vigorous sports 9 Housework
10 Switching off the television

Source: Slimming World

TOP 10 ★
PROTEIN CONSUMERS

	COUNTRY	PROTEIN CONSUMPTION PER CAPITA PER DAY G	OZ
1	Greece	114.9	4.05
2	Portugal	113.5	4.00
3	Iceland	113.3	3.99
4	France	113.1	3.98
5	US	112.3	3.96
6	Ireland	110.6	3.90
7	Malta	110.0	3.88
8	Cyprus	109.3	3.85
9	Italy	108.6	3.83
10	New Zealand	108.1	3.81
	World average	73.9	2.60

Source: *Food and Agricultural Organization of the UN*

TOP 10 ★
LEAST PROTEIN CONSUMERS

	COUNTRY	PROTEIN CONSUMPTION PER CAPITA PER DAY G	OZ
1	Dem. Rep. of Congo	28.1	0.99
2	Mozambique	34.9	1.23
3	Liberia	36.5	1.28
4	Angola	40.5	1.42
5	Haiti	41.0	1.44
6	Comoros	42.9	1.51
7	Republic of Congo	43.1	1.52
8	Sierra Leone	43.6	1.53
9	Djibouti	43.7	1.54
10	Central African Republic	43.8	1.54

Source: *Food and Agricultural Organization of the UN*

THE 10 ★
US CITIES WITH THE MOST OBESE PERSONS

	CITY/STATE	PERCENTAGE OBESE
1	New Orleans, Louisiana	37.55
2	Norfolk, Virginia	33.94
3	San Antonio, Texas	32.96
4	Kansas City, Kansas	31.66
5	Cleveland, Ohio	31.50
6	Detroit, Michigan	31.01
7	Columbus, Georgia	30.75
8	Cincinnati, Ohio	30.71
9	Pittsburgh, Pennsylvania	29.99
10	Houston, Texas	29.19

Source: *National Center for Health Statistics*

A 1997 NCHS interview considered the weights of people in the US's 33 largest metropolitan areas. "Obesity" was defined as 20 percent over the weight recommended by standard health charts, or a Body Mass Index greater than 30. Health officials consider that as many as 280,000 US deaths a year result from obesity-related disabilities.

TOP 10 ★
LEAST FAT CONSUMERS

	COUNTRY	FAT CONSUMPTION PER CAPITA PER DAY G	OZ
1	Burundi	11.0	0.38
2	Eritrea	19.5	0.68
3	Bangladesh	22.0	0.77
4	Rwanda	22.4	0.79
5	Ethiopia	22.7	0.80
6	Afghanistan	24.0	0.84
7	Laos	25.7	0.90
8	Dem. Rep. of Congo	27.7	0.95
9	Uganda	28.0	0.98
10	Zambia	29.7	1.04

Source: *Food and Agricultural Organization of the UN*

SINK OR SWIM

Swimming promotes all-around fitness with reduced danger of muscle strain, and is thus considered one of the most valuable activities for dieters.

Background image: LETTUCE

TOP 10 ★
MOST FATTENING FOODS*

FOOD	ENERGY DENSITY KCALS PER 100G
1 Cooking oils/fats#	891–899
2 Butter/margarine+	739
3 Hollandaise sauce	707
4 Mayonnaise	691
5 Creamed coconut	669
6 French dressing	651
7 Nuts★	630
8 Peanut butter	623
9 Tahini paste	607
10 Pork rinds	606

* Based on most concentrated source of Calories

\# Including coconut, cod liver, olive, lard, and dripping

\+ Margarine 737 kcals

★ Average

Source: Slimming World

TOP 10 ★
LEAST FATTENING FOODS*

FOOD	ENERGY DENSITY KCALS PER 100G
1 =Celery	7
1 =Rhubarb	7
1 =Chicory, boiled	7
4 =Globe artichoke, boiled	8
4 =Oyster mushrooms	8
6 Marrow, boiled	9
7 =Cucumber	10
7 =Canned bean sprouts, drained	10
9 =Mushrooms, boiled	11
9 =Fennel, boiled	11
9 =Rutabaga, boiled	11
9 =Canned bamboo shoots	11

* Based on least concentrated source of Calories

Source: Slimming World

TOP 10 ★
FAT CONSUMERS

COUNTRY	FAT CONSUMPTION PER CAPITA PER DAY G	OZ
1 France	164.0	5.78
2 Austria	161.4	5.69
3 Belgium and Luxembourg	159.6	5.63
4 Greece	153.4	5.41
5 Italy	146.8	5.18
6 Cyprus	146.7	5.17
7 Spain	144.7	5.10
8 Germany	144.4	5.09
9 Switzerland	143.6	5.06
10 US	142.8	5.03
World average	71.7	2.53

Source: *Food and Agricultural Organization of the UN*

PORTUGUESE PLATTER

This traditional beef, egg, and fried potato dish is a component of Portugal's high per capita Calorie consumption.

TOP 10 ★
CALORIE CONSUMERS

COUNTRY	AVERAGE DAILY PER CAPITA CONSUMPTION
1 US	3,699.1
2 Portugal	3,667.0
3 Greece	3,648.6
4 Belgium and Luxembourg	3,619.2
5 Ireland	3,565.1
6 Austria	3,535.8
7 Turkey	3,524.7
8 France	3,518.4
9 Italy	3,506.9
10 Cyprus	3,429.2

Source: *Food and Agricultural Organization of the UN*

The Calorie requirement of the average man is 2,700 and that of the average woman is 2,500. Inactive people need less, while those engaged in heavy labor might require to increase, perhaps even to double, these figures. Calories that are not consumed as energy turn to fat.

TOP 10

COUNTRIES WITH THE HIGHEST FEMALE LIFE EXPECTANCY

	COUNTRY	LIFE EXPECTANCY AT BIRTH (YEARS), 1998
1	Japan	83.59
2	Switzerland	81.90
3	France	81.86
4	Sweden	81.53
5	Norway	81.07
6	Australia	81.05
7	Canada	80.89
8	Italy	80.74
9	Belgium	80.61
10	Iceland	80.59
	US	78.9

Source: UN Demographic Yearbook

YOUNG AT HEART

In the past century, female life expectancy in Japan has increased by almost 40 years, from 44.3 years in 1900 to its present 83.59.

COUNTRIES WITH THE LOWEST BIRTH RATE

	COUNTRY	1998 LIVE BIRTHS PER 1,000
1	Bulgaria	7.4
2	Latvia	7.9
3	Estonia	8.6
4	Ukraine	8.7
5=	Belarus	8.8
5=	Czech Republic	8.8
7	Spain	9.0
8	Russia	9.2
9	Hong Kong	9.3
10=	Italy	9.4
10=	Slovenia	9.4
	US	14.8

Source: UN Demographic Yearbook

COUNTRIES WITH THE HIGHEST MALE LIFE EXPECTANCY

	COUNTRY	LIFE EXPECTANCY AT BIRTH (YEARS), 1998
1	Luxembourg	77.87
2	Japan	77.01
3	Sweden	76.51
4	Iceland	76.20
5	Switzerland	75.70
6	Greece	75.62
7	Norway	75.37
8	Israel	75.30
9	Australia	75.22
10	Malta	74.94
	US	72.5

Source: UN Demographic Yearbook

Half a century ago, the vast majority of the global population died before the age of 50. Today, the great majority survive well beyond that age. Between 1980 and 1995, global average life expectancy increased by an average of 4.6 years and is now 64 years for men, 67 for women.

♣ TOP 10 PROVINCES AND TERRITORIES WITH THE HIGHEST BIRTH RATE

(Province/birth rate per 1,000 1998–99)

1 Nunavut, 27.2 **2** Northwest Territories, 17.0 **3** Yukon, 13.9 **4** Alberta, 12.9 **5** Manitoba, 12.6 **6** Saskatchewan, 12.4 **7** Ontario, 11.5 **8** Prince Edward Island, 11.3 **9** British Columbia, 11.0 **10** Nova Scotia, 10.3

Canada, 11.2

Source: *Statistics Canada*

♣ TOP 10 MONTHS WITH THE MOST BIRTHS IN CANADA

(Month/number of births in 1997)

1 May, 31,735 **2** July, 31,033 **3** April, 30,678 **4** March, 30,018 **5** June, 29,982 **6** August, 29,235 **7** September, 29,232 **8** January, 28,408 **9** October, 28,284 **10** December, 27,185

Source: *Statistics Canada*

COUNTRIES WITH THE HIGHEST BIRTH RATE

	COUNTRY	1998 LIVE BIRTHS PER 1,000
1	Niger	52.5
2=	Angola	50.8
2=	Mali	50.8
2=	Uganda	50.8
5=	Guinea	50.6
5=	Malawi	50.6
7	Afghanistan	49.7
8	Sierra Leone	49.0
9	Ethiopia	48.9
10	Yemen	48.7
	Canada	12.1

Source: UN Demographic Yearbook

The countries with the highest birth rates are among the poorest countries in the world. In these countries, people often want to have large families so that the children can help to earn income for the family when they are older. The 10 countries with the highest birth rate therefore correspond very closely with those countries with the highest fertility rate.

THE 10 ★
MOST COMMON CAUSES OF DEATH

	CAUSE	APPROXIMATE NO. OF DEATHS PER ANNUM
1	Ischaemic heart disease	7,375,000
2	Cancers*	7,229,000
3	Cerebrovascular disease	5,106,000
4	Acute lower respiratory infection	3,452,000
5	HIV/AIDS	2,285,000
6	Chronic obstructive pulmonary disease	2,249,000
7	Diarrhea (including dysentery)	2,219,000
8	Childhood diseases#	1,651,000
9	Tuberculosis	1,498,000
10	Road traffic accidents	1,171,000

* Lung cancer deaths alone number 1,244,000

Including pertussis, polio, diphtheria, measles, and tetanus

Source: WHO World Health Report 1999

TOP 10 ★
COUNTRIES WITH THE HIGHEST DIVORCE RATE

	COUNTRY	1998 DIVORCE RATE PER 1,000
1	Maldives	10.75
2 =	Belarus	4.63
2 =	China	4.63
4	Russia	4.51
5	US	4.33
6	Surinam	4.26
7	Estonia	3.85
8	Cuba	3.72
9	Ukraine	3.71
10	Puerto Rico	3.49

Source: UN Demographic Yearbook

TOP 10 ★
PROFESSIONS OF COMPUTER-DATING MEMBERS IN THE US

WOMEN'S PROFESSIONS	PERCENTAGE OF THOSE REGISTERED		PERCENTAGE OF THOSE REGISTERED	MEN'S PROFESSIONS
Teachers/lecturers	7.8	1	6.1	Engineers
Nurses	5.2	2	5.3	Computer professionals
Women at home	4.8	3	4.8	Teachers/lecturers
Secretaries	4.5	4	4.5	Company directors
Civil servants	3.9	5	4.3	Accountants
Social workers	3.8	6	4.2	Doctors
Lawyers	3.5	7	4.0	Managers
Accountants	3.1	8	3.7	Civil servants
Doctors	2.8	9	2.5	Architects
Students	1.3	10	1.4	Farmers

Source: *Dateline International*

TOP 10 COUNTRIES WITH THE HIGHEST MARRIAGE RATE
(Country/1998 marriages per 1,000)

1 Antigua and Barbuda, 21.0 **2** Maldives, 19.7 **3** Bermuda, 15.7 **4** Barbados, 13.5 **5** Liechtenstein, 12.9 **6** Seychelles, 11.4 **7** Bangladesh, 9.7 **8** Mauritius, 9.5 **9** = Bahamas; = Sri Lanka, 9.3

Canada, 5.4   Source: UN Demographic Yearbook

The highest marriage rates in the world are actually recorded in places that are not independent countries. Gibraltar, for example, has a marriage rate of 26.7 per 1,000.

WEDDED BLISS?
Cuba once featured prominently among countries with a high marriage rate, but today ranks among the world's foremost countries for divorce.

Did You Know? In Rwanda, the death rate at 44.6 per 1,000 people is actually greater than the birth rate, which is 43.9 per 1,000 people.

What's in a Name?

TOP 10
FIRST NAMES IN CANADA

GIRLS		BOYS
Emily	1	Matthew
Sarah	2	Joshua
Emma	3	Nicholas
Jessica	4	Ryan
Taylor	5	Alexander
Hannah	6	Tyler
Megan	7	Michael
Samantha	8	Brandon
Ashley	9	Jacob
Nicole	10	Kyle

TOP 10 MOST COMMON SURNAMES IN QUEBEC, 1996

1 Tremblay 2 Gagnon 3 Roy 4 Côté 5 Bouchard 6 Morin 7 Gauthier 8 Pelletier 9 Fortin 10 Lavoie

Source: *Louis Duchesne*, Le choix du nom de famille en 1996, *Données sociodémographiques en bref, vol 3, no 2. p. 7., 1999*

TOP 10
FIRST NAMES IN ENGLAND & WALES

GIRLS		BOYS
Chloe	1	Jack
Emily	2	Thomas
Megan	3	James
Olivia	4	Joshua
Sophie	5	Daniel
Charlotte	6	Matthew
Lauren	7	Samuel
Jessica	8	Joseph
Rebecca	9	Callum
Hannah	10	William

TOP 10
FIRST NAMES IN IRELAND

GIRLS		BOYS
Chloe	1	Conor
Ciara	2	Sean
Sarah	3	Jack
Aoife	4	James
Emma	5	Adam
Niamh	6	Aaron
Rachel	7	Dylan
Megan	8	David
Rebecca	9	Michael
Lauren	10	Daniel

TOP 10
FIRST NAMES IN NORTHERN IRELAND

GIRLS		BOYS
Chloe	1	Matthew
Emma	2	Ryan
Rebecca	3	James
Amy	4	Jack
Lauren	5	Conor
Hannah	6	Adam
Shannon	7	Jordan
Sarah	8	Michael
Rachel	9	David
Megan	10	Christopher

A comparative survey of names recorded in both 1975 and 1998 showed that none of the Top 10 1998 girls' names appeared in the earlier list, while three boys' names (James, Michael, and David) were in both.

TOP 10 SURNAMES IN SCOTLAND*

1 Smith 2 Brown 3 Wilson 4 Thomson 5 Robertson 6 Campbell 7 Stewart 8 Anderson 9 Macdonald 10 Scott

* Based on a survey of names appearing on birth and death registers, and both names on marriage registers

TOP 10 SURNAMES IN THE UK
(Surname/number)

1 Smith, 538,369 2 Jones, 402,489 3 Williams, 279,150 4 Brown, 260,652 5 Taylor, 251,058 6 Davies/Davis, 209,584 7 Wilson, 191,006 8 Evans, 170,391 9 Thomas, 152,945 10 Johnson, 146,535

This survey of British surnames is based on an analysis of almost 50 million names appearing on the British electoral rolls.

TOP 10
FIRST NAMES IN WALES

GIRLS		BOYS
Chloe	1	Thomas
Megan	2	Jack
Emily	3	Joshua
Sophie	4	Daniel
Lauren	5	Callum
Jessica	6	James
Georgina	7	Liam
Ffion	8	Samuel
Hannah	9	Ryan
Rebecca	10	Matthew

TOP 10
FIRST NAMES IN SCOTLAND

BOYS		GIRLS
Jack	1	Chloe
Lewis	2	Rebecca
Ryan	3	Lauren
Cameron	4	Emma
Ross	5	Amy
James	6	Megan
Andrew	7	Caitlin
Liam	8	Rachel
Scott	9	Erin
Connor	10	Sophie

"WENDY"

Like Pamela, Lorna, Thelma, and Mavis, Wendy is one of a group of girls' names invented by authors. Margaret, the infant daughter of writer W. E. Henley, called family friend J. M. Barrie her "friendy," pronouncing it as "wendy." Margaret died aged 5 in 1894, but her name lived on as Wendy Darling in Barrie's 1904 play *Peter Pan*. The popularity of the play and 1911 book ensured that Wendy became a common first name in both the UK and North America.

WHY DO WE SAY?

TOP 10
FIRST NAMES IN AUSTRALIA*

GIRLS		BOYS
Emily	1	Joshua
Jessica	2	Matthew
Sarah	3	Daniel
Emma	4	James
Hannah	5	Jake
Samantha	6	Benjamin
Georgia	7	Lachlan
Rebecca	8	Nicholas
Amy	9	Jack
Sophie	10	Thomas

* Based on births registered in New South Wales

TOP 10
FIRST NAMES IN NORWAY

GIRLS		BOYS
Ingrid	1	Andreas
Ida	2	Markus
Marte	3	Kristian
Karoline	4	Martin
Silje	5	Kristoffer
Julie	6	Thomas
Camila	7	Jonas
Kristine	8	Fredrik
Maria	9	Daniel
Vilde	10	Marius

TOP 10 SURNAMES IN THE MANHATTAN TELEPHONE DIRECTORY

1 Smith **2** Brown **3** Williams **4** Cohen **5** Lee **6** Johnson **7** Rodriguez **8** Green **9** Davis **10** Jones

TOP 10
MOST COMMON SURNAMES IN THE US

	NAME	% OF ALL US NAMES
1	Smith	1.006
2	Johnson	0.810
3	Williams	0.699
4 =	Brown	0.621
4 =	Jones	0.621
6	Davis	0.480
7	Miller	0.424
8	Wilson	0.339
9	Moore	0.312
10 =	Anderson	0.311
10 =	Taylor	0.311
10 =	Thomas	0.311

The Top 10 (or, in view of those in equal 10th place, 12) US surnames together make up over 6 percent of the entire US population – in other words, one American in every 16 bears one of these names. Extending the list, some 28 different names make up 10 percent of the entire population, 115 names 20 percent, 315 names 30 percent, 755 names 40 percent, 1,712 names 50 percent, and 3,820 names 60 percent.

TOP 10 TERMS OF ENDEARMENT USED IN THE US

1 Honey **2** Baby **3** Sweetheart
4 Dear **5** Lover **6** Darling **7** Sugar
8 = Angel; = Pumpkin **10** = Beautiful; = Precious

A survey of romance conducted by a US champagne company concluded that 26 percent of American adults favored "honey" as their most frequently used term of endearment. Curiously, identical numbers were undecided whether to call their loved one an angel or a pumpkin....

TOP 10
BOYS' NAMES IN THE US, 1989–99

1989		1999
Michael	1	Jacob
Christopher	2	Michael
Joshua	3	Matthew
Matthew	4	Nicholas
David	5	Christopher
Daniel	6	Joshua
Andrew	7	Austin
Joseph	8	Tyler
Justin	9	Brandon
John	10	Joseph

TOP 10
GIRLS' NAMES IN THE US, 1989–99

1989		1999
Jessica	1	Emily
Ashley	2	Sarah
Amanda	= 3	Brianna
Brittany	= 3	
	4	Samantha
Sarah	5	Hailey
Jennifer	6	Ashley
Stephanie	7	Kaitlyn
Samantha	8	Madison
Elizabeth	9	Hannah
Lauren	10	Alexis

TOP 10 SURNAMES IN CHINA

1 Zhang **2** Whang **3** Li **4** Zhao
5 Chen **6** Yang **7** Wu **8** Liu
9 Huang **10** Zhou

Who was the last Canadian to win an Oscar?
see p.173 for the answer
A James Cameron
B Mary Pickford
C Norman Jewison

61

World Royalty

LONGEST-REIGNING BRITISH MONARCHS

	MONARCH	REIGN	AGE AT ACCESSION	AGE AT DEATH	REIGN YEARS
1	Queen Victoria	1837–1901	18	81	63
2	King George III	1760–1820	22	81	59
3	King Henry III	1216–72	9	64	56
4	King Edward III	1327–77	14	64	50
5	Queen Elizabeth II	1952–	25	—	48
6	Queen Elizabeth I	1558–1603	25	69	44
7	King Henry VI	1422–61*	8 months	49	38
8	King Henry VIII	1509–47	17	55	37
9	King Charles II	1649–85	19	54	36
10	King Henry I	1100–35	31–32#	66–67#	35

* Henry VI was deposed; he died in 1471

\# Henry I's birthdate is unknown, so his age at accession and death are uncertain

This list excludes the reigns of monarchs before 1066, so excludes such rulers as Ethelred II, who reigned for 37 years.

FIRST IN LINE TO THE BRITISH THRONE

	SUCCESSOR	BORN
1	HRH The Prince of Wales (Prince Charles Philip Arthur George)	Nov 14, 1948
2	HRH Prince William of Wales (Prince William Arthur Philip Louis)	Jun 21, 1982
3	HRH Prince Henry of Wales (Prince Henry Charles Albert David)	Sep 15, 1984
4	HRH The Duke of York (Prince Andrew Albert Christian Edward)	Feb 19, 1960
5	HRH Princess Beatrice of York (Princess Beatrice Elizabeth Mary)	Aug 8, 1988
6	HRH Princess Eugenie of York (Princess Eugenie Victoria Helena)	Mar 23, 1990
7	HRH Prince Edward (Prince Edward Antony Richard Louis)	Mar 10, 1964
8	HRH The Princess Royal (Princess Anne Elizabeth Alice Louise)	Aug 15, 1950
9	Master Peter Mark Andrew Phillips	Nov 15, 1977
10	Miss Zara Anne Elizabeth Phillips	May 15, 1981

LONGEST-REIGNING QUEENS*

	QUEEN	COUNTRY	REIGN	REIGN YEARS
1	Victoria	Great Britain	1837–1901	63
2	Wilhelmina	Netherlands	1890–1948	58
3	Wu Chao	China	655–705	50
4	Elizabeth II	UK	1952–	48
5	Salote Tubou	Tonga	1918–65	47
6	Elizabeth I	England	1558–1603	44
7	Maria Theresa	Hungary	1740–80	40
8	Maria I	Portugal	1777–1816	39
9	Joanna I	Italy	1343–81	38
10=	Suiko Tenno	Japan	593–628	35
10=	Isabella II	Spain	1833–68	35

* Queens and empresses who rule (or ruled) in their own right, not as consorts of kings or emperors

LONG TO REIGN OVER US

If Queen Elizabeth II is on the throne on September 11, 2015, she will have beaten Queen Victoria's record by one day and will become the world's longest-reigning queen.

THE 10 ★
LATEST WORLD MONARCHS TO COME TO POWER

	MONARCH/COUNTRY	ACCESSION
1	**King Sayyidi Muhammad VI ibn al-Hasan**, Morocco	Jul 23, 1999
2	**Sultan Tuanku Salehuddin Abdul Aziz Shah ibni al-Marhum Hisamuddin Alam Shah**, Malaysia	Apr 26, 1999
3	**Emir Sheikh Hamad ibn 'Isa al-Khalifah**, Bahrain	Mar 6, 1999
4	**King Abdallah (II) ibn al-Hussein al-Hashimi**, Jordan	Feb 7, 1999
5	**King Letsie III**, Lesotho	Feb 7, 1996
6	**Emir Sheikh Ahmad ibn Khalifa al-Thani**, Qatar	Jun 27, 1995
7	**King Albert II**, Belgium	Aug 9, 1993
8	**King Preah Baht Samdach Preah Norodom Sihanuk Varmn**, Cambodia	Sep 24, 1993*
9	**King Harald V**, Norway	Jan 17, 1991
10	**Prince Hans Adam II**, Liechtenstein	Nov 13, 1989

* Elected king

TOP 10 ★
LONGEST-REIGNING LIVING MONARCHS*

	MONARCH/COUNTRY	DATE OF BIRTH	ACCESSION
1	**King Bhumibol Adulyadej**, Thailand	Dec 5, 1927	Jun 9, 1946
2	**Prince Rainier III**, Monaco	May 31, 1923	May 9, 1949
3	**Queen Elizabeth II**, UK	Apr 21, 1926	Feb 6, 1952
4	**King Malietoa Tanumafili II**, Western Samoa	Jan 4, 1913	Jan 1, 1962#
5	**Grand Duke Jean**, Luxembourg	Jan 5, 1921	Nov 12, 1964
6	**King Taufa'ahau Tupou IV**, Tonga	Jul 4, 1918	Dec 16, 1965
7	**King Haji Hassanal Bolkiah**, Brunei	Jul 15, 1946	Oct 5, 1967
8	**Sultan Sayyid Qaboos ibn Said al-Said**, Oman	Nov 18, 1942	Jul 23, 1970
9	**Queen Margrethe II**, Denmark	Apr 16, 1940	Jan 14, 1972
10	**King Birendra Bir Bikram Shah Dev**, Nepal	Dec 28, 1945	Jan 31, 1972

* Including hereditary rulers of principalities, dukedoms, etc.

 # Sole ruler since April 15, 1963

There are 29 countries that have emperors, kings, queens, princes, dukes, sultans, or other hereditary rulers as their heads of state. The current Sultan of Oman took control of the country by ousting his own father in a palace coup.

THE 10 ★
LATEST WORLD MONARCHS TO BE ASSASSINATED

	MONARCH/COUNTRY	DATE OF DEATH
1	**King Faisal ibn Abdul Aziz**, Saudi Arabia *Murdered by his nephew during an audience with the Kuwaiti oil minister.*	Mar 25, 1975
2	**King Faisal II**, Iraq *Murdered with his entire household; their bodies were paraded through Baghdad as part of a military coup.*	Jul 14, 1958
3	**King Abdullah ibn al-Hussein**, Jordan *Gunned down on a visit to his father's tomb in Jerusalem by Mustafa Ashu, a young Palestinian nationalist.*	Jul 20, 1951
4	**King Ananda Mahidol, Rama VIII**, Thailand *Assassinated in the palace, having been conspired against by his personal secretary and others.*	Jun 9, 1946
5	**King Alexander I**, Yugoslavia *Shot in Marseilles by an assassin sent by Croat leader Ante Paveilic.*	Oct 9, 1934
6	**King Sardar Mohammad Nadir Khan**, Afghanistan *Shot while giving out prizes at a school.*	Nov 8, 1933
7	**King George I**, Greece *Killed in Salonika by Schinas, a Greek revolutionary.*	Mar 18, 1913
8	**King Carlos I**, Portugal *Ambushed and murdered, together with Luis Philippe, the crown prince, by anti-royalists.*	Feb 1, 1908
9	**King Alexander Obrenovich**, Serbia *Shot to death and hacked with sabers, together with his wife, Draga, by military conspirators.*	Jul 11, 1903
10	**King Umberto I**, Italy *Murdered in Monza by anarchist Gaetano Bresci.*	Jul 29, 1900

TOP 10 ★
LONGEST-REIGNING MONARCHS

	MONARCH/COUNTRY	REIGN	AGE AT ACCESSION	REIGN YEARS
1	**King Louis XIV**, France	1643–1715	5	72
2	**King John II**, Liechtenstein	1858–1929	18	71
3	**Emperor Franz-Josef**, Austria-Hungary	1848–1916	18	67
4	**Queen Victoria**, Great Britain	1837–1901	18	63
5	**Emperor Hirohito**, Japan	1926–89	25	62
6	**Emperor Kangxi**, China	1662–1722	8	61
7	**Emperor Qianlong**, China	1736–96	25	60
8=	**King Christian IV**, Denmark	1588–1648	11	59*
8=	**King George III**, Great Britain	1760–1820	22	59*
8=	**Prince Honore III**, Monaco	1733–93	13	59*

* Those with the same number of reign years are ranked according to days

Background image: **EMPEROR AND EMPRESS HIROHITO**

Did You Know? Despite being pregnant 17 times, British Queen Anne produced only one child – William, Duke of Gloucester – who survived infancy, although he died at the age of 11.

The Political World

FIRST COUNTRIES TO RATIFY THE UN CHARTER

	COUNTRY	DATE
1	Nicaragua	Jul 6, 1945
2	US	Aug 8, 1945
3	France	Aug 31, 1945
4	Dominican Republic	Sep 4, 1945
5	New Zealand	Sep 19, 1945
6	Brazil	Sep 21, 1945
7	Argentina	Sep 24, 1945
8	China	Sep 28, 1945
9	Denmark	Oct 9, 1945
10	Chile	Oct 11, 1945

In New York on June 26, 1945, barely weeks after the end of World War II in Europe (the Japanese did not surrender until September 3), 50 nations signed the World Security Charter, thereby establishing the United Nations as an international peacekeeping organization. The UN came into effect on October 24, which has since been celebrated as United Nations Day.

KEEPING THE PEACE

Since its formation in 1945, the United Nations has deployed forces to maintain the peace in the world's troublespots. Here, peacekeeping troops enter East Timor in September 1999.

FIRST COUNTRIES TO GIVE WOMEN THE VOTE

	COUNTRY	YEAR
1	New Zealand	1893
2	Australia, (South Australia, 1894; Western Australia, 1898; Australia united, 1901)	1902
3	Finland (a Grand Duchy under the Russian Crown)	1906
4	Norway (restricted franchise; all women over 25 in 1913)	1907
5	Denmark and Iceland (a Danish dependency until 1918)	1915
6 =	Netherlands	1917
6 =	USSR	1917
8 =	Austria	1918
8 =	Canada	1918
8 =	Germany	1918
8 =	Great Britain and Ireland (Ireland part of the United Kingdom until 1921; women over 30 – lowered to 21 in 1928)	1918
8 =	Poland	1918

WOMEN TO SERVE IN CANADA'S HOUSE OF COMMONS

	NAME	TERM SERVED	PARTY
1	Agnes MacPhail	1921–1940	Progressive, later United Farmers of Ontario
2	Martha Louise Black	1935–1940	Independent Conservative
3	Cora Casselman	1941–1945	Liberal
4	Gladys Strum	1945–1949	Co-operative Commonwealth Federation
5	Hon. Ellen Fairclough*	1950–1963	Progressive Conservative
6 =	Margaret Anne Aitken	1953–1962	Progressive Conservative
6 =	Sybil Bennett	1953–1956	Progressive Conservative
6 =	Ann Shipley	1953–1957	Liberal
9	Jean Casselman Wadds	1958–1968	Progressive Conservative
10	Hon. Julia ("Judy") LaMarsh#	1960–1968	Liberal

* First woman to hold a federal cabinet position. Fairclough was appointed Secretary of State in 1957, and she was Minister of Citizenship and Immigration from 1958 to 1962

\# Appointed Minister of National Health and Welfare in 1963; Secretary of State from 1965 to 1968

Source: Women in Federal Politics: A Bio-Bibliography, National Library of Canada, 1975

TOP 10 ★
LONGEST-SERVING PRESIDENTS TODAY

	PRESIDENT	COUNTRY	TOOK OFFICE
1	General Gnassingbé Eyadéma	Togo	Apr 14, 1967
2	El Hadj Omar Bongo	Gabon	Dec 2, 1967
3	Colonel Mu'ammar Gadhafi*	Libya	Sep 1, 1969
4	Lt.-General Hafiz al-Asad	Syria	Feb 22, 1971
5	Zayid ibn Sultan al-Nuhayyan	United Arab Emirates	Dec 2, 1971
6	Fidel Castro	Cuba	Nov 2, 1976
7	France-Albert René	Seychelles	Jun 5, 1977
8	Daniel Teroitich arap Moi	Kenya	Oct 14, 1978
9	Saddam Hussein	Iraq	Jul 16, 1979
10	Teodoro Obiang Nguema Mbasogo	Equatorial Guinea	Aug 3, 1979

* Since a reorganization in 1979, Colonel Gadhafi has held no formal position but continues to rule under the ceremonial title of "Leader of the Revolution."

TOP 10 🍁
LONGEST-SERVING PARLIAMENTARIANS IN CANADA*

	PARLIAMENTARIAN	TERM SERVED	TIME SERVED
1	Azellus Denis #	1935–1991	55 years, 10 months, 19 days
2	Hippolyte Montplaisir +	1874–1927	53 years, 4 months, 25 days
3	Charles Gavan Power #	1917–1968	50 years, 5 months, 12 days
4	Mackenzie Boswell ★	1867–1917	50 years, 2 months, 18 days
5	John Costigan +	1867–1916	49 years, 8 days
6	Pascal Poirier #	1885–1933	48 years, 6 months, 16 days
7	Rufus Henry Pope +	1889–1944	47 years, 11 months, 18 days
8	Joseph Bolduc ★	1876–1924	47 years, 9 months, 23 days
9	George Gerald King #	1878–1928	46 years, 5 months, 21 days
10	David Arnold Croll #	1945–1991	45 years, 11 months, 28 days

* As of March 30, 2000   # Liberal   + Liberal Conservative   ★ Conservative

Source: *Elections Canada*

The highest-ranking MP on this list still sitting in Parliament is Herb Gray (Liberal), with 37 years, 9 months, and 11 days.

THE 10 ★
FIRST FEMALE PRIME MINISTERS AND PRESIDENTS

	PRIME MINISTER OR PRESIDENT/COUNTRY	PERIOD IN OFFICE
1	Sirimavo Bandaranaike, (PM), Sri Lanka	1960–65/ 1970–77/ 1994–
2	Indira Gandhi (PM), India	1966–77/ 1980–84
3	Golda Meir (PM), Israel	1969–74
4	Maria Estela Perón (P), Argentina	1974–76
5	Elisabeth Domitien (PM), Central African Republic	1975–76
6	Margaret Thatcher (PM), UK	1979–90
7	Dr. Maria Lurdes Pintasilgo (PM), Portugal	1979–80
8	Vigdís Finnbogadóttir (P), Iceland	1980–
9	Mary Eugenia Charles (PM), Dominica	1980–95
10	Gro Harlem Brundtland (PM), Norway	Feb–Oct 1981/ 1986–89/ 1990–96

WOMEN IN POWER

The Swedish parliament has a high proportion of women members. Worldwide, women legislators today comprise 13 percent of all legislators.

TOP 10 ★
PARLIAMENTS WITH THE HIGHEST PERCENTAGE OF WOMEN MEMBERS*

	PARLIAMENT/ ELECTION	WOMEN MEMBERS	TOTAL MEMBERS	% WOMEN
1	Sweden, 1998	149	349	42.7
2	Denmark, 1998	67	179	37.4
3	Finland, 1999	74	200	37.0
4	Norway, 1997	60	165	36.4
5	Netherlands, 1998	54	150	36.0
6	Iceland, 1999	22	63	34.9
7	Germany, 1998	207	669	30.9
8	South Africa, 1999	120	400	30.0
9	New Zealand, 1999	35	120	29.2
10	Cuba, 1998	166	601	27.6
	Canada, 1997	62	301	20.6

* As of December 25, 1999

Source: *Inter-Parliamentary Union*

This information is based on the most recent general election results available for all democratic countries.

Did You Know? Félix Houhouët-Boigny, President of the Côte d'Ivoire until his death in 1993 at the age of 88, was the world's oldest president.

Human Achievements

THE 10 ★
NORTH POLE FIRSTS

1 First to reach the Pole?
American adventurer Frederick Albert Cook claimed that he had reached the Pole, accompanied by two Inuits, on April 21, 1908, but his claim is disputed. It is more likely that Robert Edwin Peary, Matthew Alexander Henson (both Americans), and four Inuits were first at the Pole on April 6, 1909.

2 First to fly over the Pole in an airship
A team of 16, led by Roald Amundsen, the Norwegian explorer who first reached the South Pole in 1911, flew across the North Pole on May 12, 1926 in the Italian-built airship Norge.

3 First to land at the Pole in an aircraft
Soviets Pavel Afanaseyevich Geordiyenko, Mikhail Yemel'yenovich Ostrekin, Pavel Kononovich Sen'ko, and Mikhail Mikhaylovich Somov arrived at and departed from the Pole by air on April 23, 1948.

4 First solo flight over the Pole in a single-engined aircraft
Capt. Charles Francis Blair, Jr. of the US flew a single-engined Mustang fighter, Excalibur III, on May 29, 1951, crossing from Bardufoss, Norway, to Fairbanks, Alaska.

5 First submarine to surface at the Pole
USS Skate surfaced at the Pole on March 17, 1959.

6 First confirmed overland journey to the Pole
American Ralph S. Plaisted, with companions Walter Pederson, Gerald Pitzel, and Jean Luc Bombardier, reached the Pole on April 18, 1968, using snowmobiles.

7 First solo overland journey to the Pole
Japanese explorer Naomi Uemura reached the Pole on May 1, 1978, traveling by dog sled, and was then picked up by an airplane.

8 First to reach the Pole on skis
A team of seven, led by Dimitry Shparo (USSR), was the first to reach the North Pole on May 31, 1979.

9 First crossing on a Pole-to-Pole expedition
Sir Ranulph Fiennes and Charles Burton walked over the North Pole on April 10, 1982, having crossed the South Pole on December 15, 1980.

10 First woman to walk to the Pole
Along with five male companions, American physical education teacher Ann Bancroft reached the Pole on May 1, 1986.

Lt.-Cdr. Richard Byrd and Floyd Bennett claimed to have traversed the Pole on May 9, 1926 in an aircraft, but recent analysis of Byrd's diary indicates that they turned back some 241 km (150 miles) short of the Pole, thereby disqualifying their entry.

POLE TO POLE
The 1979–82 Transglobe Expedition led by Sir Ranulph Fiennes, here at Scott Base, South Pole, was the first to traverse both Poles.

THE 10 ★
CIRCUMNAVIGATION FIRSTS

CIRCUMNAVIGATION/CRAFT	VOYAGER(S)	RETURN DATE
1 First, *Vittoria*	Juan Sebastian de Elcano*	Sep 6, 1522
2 First in less than 80 days, *various*	"Nellie Bly"#	Jan 25, 1890
3 First solo, *Spray*	Capt. Joshua Slocum	Jul 3, 1898
4 First by air, *Chicago, New Orleans*	Lt. Lowell Smith, Lt. Leslie P. Arnold	Sep 28, 1924
5 First nonstop by air, *Lucky Lady II*	Capt. James Gallagher	Mar 2, 1949
6 First underwater, *Triton*	Capt. Edward L. Beach	Apr 25, 1960
7 First nonstop solo, *Suhaili*	Robin Knox-Johnston	Apr 22, 1969
8 First helicopter, *Spirit of Texas*	H. Ross Perot, Jr. and Jay Coburn	Sep 30, 1982
9 First air without refueling, *Voyager*	Richard Rutan and Jeana Yeager	Dec 23, 1986
10 First by balloon, *Breitling Orbiter 3*	Brian Jones and Bertrand Piccard	Mar 21, 1999

* The expedition was led by Ferdinand Magellan, but he did not survive the voyage.

 # Real name Elizabeth Cochrane. This US journalist set out to beat the fictitious "record" established in Jules Verne's novel Around the World in 80 Days.

THE 10 FIRST MOUNTAINEERS TO CLIMB EVEREST

(Mountaineer/nationality/date)

❶ Edmund Hillary, New Zealander, May 29, 1953 **❷ Tenzing Norgay**, Nepalese, May 29, 1953 **❸ Jürg Marmet**, Swiss, May 23, 1956 **❹ Ernst Schmied**, Swiss, May 23, 1956 **❺ Hans-Rudolf von Gunten**, Swiss, May 24, 1956 **❻ Adolf Reist**, Swiss, May 24, 1956 **❼ Wang Fu-chou**, Chinese, May 25, 1960 **❽ Chu Ying-hua**, Chinese, May 25, 1960 **❾ Konbu**, Tibetan, May 25, 1960 **❿ = Nawang Gombu**, Indian; = **James Whittaker**, American, May 1, 1963

Nawang Gombu and James Whittaker are 10th equally because they ascended the last feet to the summit side by side.

What is the largest sports stadium in Canada?
see p.92 for the answer
A Olympic Stadium
B Commonwealth Stadium
C Toronto SkyDome

THE 10 ★
FIRST SUCCESSFUL HUMAN DESCENTS OVER NIAGARA FALLS

NAME/METHOD	DATE
1 **Annie Edson Taylor,** Wooden barrel	Oct 24, 1901
2 **Bobby Leach,** Steel barrel	Jul 25, 1911
3 **Jean Lussier,** Steel and rubber ball fitted with oxygen cylinders	Jul 4, 1928
4 **William Fitzgerald** (a.k.a. Nathan Boya), Steel and rubber ball fitted with oxygen cylinders	Jul 15, 1961
5 **Karel Soucek,** Barrel	Jul 3, 1984
6 **Steven Trotter,** Barrel	Aug 18, 1985
7 **Dave Mundy,** Barrel	Oct 5, 1985
8 = **Peter deBernardi,** Metal container	Sep 28, 1989
8 = **Jeffrey Petkovich,** Metal container	Sep 28, 1989
10 **Dave Mundy,** Diving bell	Sep 26, 1993

Source: *Niagara Falls Museum*

TOP 10 ★
FASTEST CROSS-CHANNEL SWIMMERS

SWIMMER/NATIONALITY	YEAR	TIME HRS:MINS
1 **Chad Hundeby,** American	1994	7:17
2 **Penny Lee Dean,** American	1978	7:40
3 **Tamara Bruce,** Australian	1994	7:53
4 **Philip Rush,** New Zealander	1987	7:55
5 **Hans van Goor,** Dutch	1995	8:02
6 **Richard Davey,** British	1988	8:05
7 **Irene van der Laan,** Dutch	1982	8:06
8 **Paul Asmuth,** American	1985	8:12
9 **Anita Sood,** Indian	1987	8:15
10 **John van Wisse,** Australian	1994	8:17

Source: *Channel Swimming Association*

The first person to swim the Channel was Matthew Webb (British), who on August 24–25, 1875 made the crossing in what now seems the rather leisurely time of 21 hours 45 minutes.

NIAGARA FALLS

Annie Edson Taylor, a Michigan schoolteacher, celebrated her 43rd birthday in 1901 by being the first to plunge over Niagara Falls and survive. She was followed in 1911 by 69-year-old Bobby Leach (who later died when he slipped on a piece of orange peel!). On July 4, 1928, watched by an excited crowd of 100,000, Jean Lussier (seen here), a circus acrobat from Springfield, Massachusetts, traveled over the Falls in a 344-kg (758-lb) steel-reinforced rubber sphere. In 1920, barber Charles Stephens became one of many killed in the attempt. Other failed efforts include those of George Stathakis (1930) and William Hill, Jr. (1951).

SNAP SHOTS

THE 10 LATEST WINNERS OF *TIME* MAGAZINE'S "PERSON OF THE YEAR" AWARD
(Year/recipient)

1 1999, **Jeffrey T. Bezos,** founder of Amazon.com **2** 1998, **Bill Clinton,** US President/**Kenneth Starr,** Independent Counsel **3** 1997, **Andrew S. Grove,** CEO of Intel, microchip company **4** 1996, **David Ho,** AIDS researcher **5** 1995, **Newt Gingrich,** US politician **6** 1994, **Pope John Paul II** **7** 1993, **Yasser Arafat, F. W. de Klerk, Nelson Mandela, Yitzhak Rabin,** "peacemakers" **8** 1992, **Bill Clinton,** US President **9** 1991, **George Bush,** US President **10** 1990, **Ted Turner,** US businessman

CHANNEL NO. 3

In 1994, 17-year-old Australian Tamara Bruce achieved the third-fastest Channel swim of all time, becoming the 487th person to swim from England to France.

The Nobel Century

LATEST WINNERS OF THE NOBEL PRIZE FOR PHYSICS

	WINNER	COUNTRY	YEAR
1=	Gerardus 't Hooft	Netherlands	1999
1=	Martinus J. G. Veltman	Netherlands	1999
3=	Robert B. Laughlin	US	1998
3=	Horst L. Störmer	Germany	1998
3=	Daniel C. Tsui	US	1998
6=	Steven Chu	US	1997
6=	William D. Phillips	US	1997
6=	Professor Claude Cohen-Tannoudji	France	1997
9=	David M. Lee	US	1996
9=	Douglas D. Osheroff	US	1996
9=	Robert C. Richardson	US	1996

NOBEL PRIZE-WINNING COUNTRIES*

	COUNTRY	PHY	CHE	PH/MED	LIT	PCE	ECO	TOTAL
1	US	67	43	78	10	18	25	241
2	UK	21	25	24	8	13	7	98
3	Germany	20	27	16	7	4	1	75
4	France	12	7	7	12	9	1	48
5	Sweden	4	4	7	7	5	2	29
6	Switzerland	2	5	6	2	3	–	18
7	USSR	7	1	2	3	2	1	16
8	Netherlands	8	3	2	–	1	1	15
9	Italy	3	1	3	6	1	–	14
10	Denmark	3	–	5	3	1	–	12

Phy – Physics; Che – Chemistry; Ph/Med – Physiology or Medicine; Lit – Literature; Pce – Peace; Eco – Economic Sciences. Germany includes the united country before 1948, West Germany to 1990 and the united country since 1990

In addition, institutions including the Red Cross have been awarded 17 Nobel Peace Prizes

LATEST WINNERS OF THE NOBEL PEACE PRIZE

	WINNER	COUNTRY	YEAR
1	Médecins Sans Frontières	Belgium	1999
2=	John Hume	UK	1998
2=	David Trimble	UK	1998
4=	International Campaign to Ban Landmines	–	1997
4=	Jody Williams	US	1997
6=	Carlos Filipe Ximenes Belo	East Timor	1996
6=	José Ramos-Horta	East Timor	1996
8	Joseph Rotblat	UK	1995
9=	Yasir Arafat	Palestine	1994
9=	Shimon Peres	Israel	1994
9=	Itzhak Rabin	Israel	1994

COMPASSION WITHOUT LIMITS

Brussels-based Médecins Sans Frontières, which has provided emergency medical aid worldwide since 1971, won the Peace Prize in 1999. International organizations have been awarded the prize 17 times.

LATEST WINNERS OF THE NOBEL PRIZE FOR PHYSIOLOGY OR MEDICINE

	WINNER	COUNTRY	YEAR
1	Günter Blobel	Germany	1999
2=	Robert F. Furchgott	US	1998
2=	Louis J. Ignarro	US	1998
2=	Ferid Murad	US	1998
5	Stanley B. Prusiner	US	1997
6=	Peter C. Doherty	Australia	1996
6=	Rolf M. Zinkernagel	Switzerland	1996
8=	Christiane Nüsslein-Volhard	Germany	1995
8=	Eric F. Wieschaus	US	1995
8=	Edward B. Lewis	US	1995

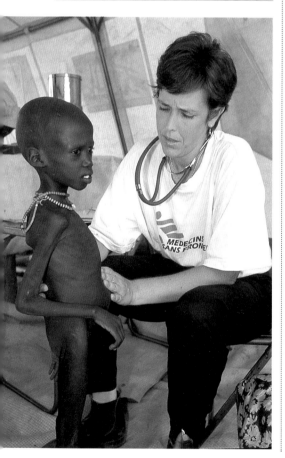

What is the most popular Canadian Internet Site?
see p.209 for the answer
A chapters.ca
B msn.ca
C sympatico.ca

THE 10 ★
LATEST WINNERS OF THE NOBEL PRIZE FOR LITERATURE

	WINNER	COUNTRY	YEAR
1	Günter Grass	Germany	1999
2	José Saramago	Portugal	1998
3	Dario Fo	Italy	1997
4	Wislawa Szymborska	Poland	1996
5	Seamus Heaney	Ireland	1995
6	Kenzaburo Oe	Japan	1994
7	Toni Morrison	US	1993
8	Derek Walcott	Saint Lucia	1992
9	Nadine Gordimer	South Africa	1991
10	Octavio Paz	Mexico	1990

TOP 10 NOBEL LITERATURE PRIZE-WINNING COUNTRIES
(Country/prizes)

1 France, 12 **2** US, 10 **3** UK, 8
4 = Sweden; = Germany, 7 **6** Italy, 6
7 Spain, 5 **8** = Denmark; = Ireland;
= Norway; = Poland; = USSR, 3

THE 10 🍁
LAST NOBEL PRIZES WON BY CANADIANS

YEAR	PRIZE	WINNER
1997	Economic Sciences	Myron S. Scholes (1941–)
1996	Economic Sciences	William Vickrey (1914–1996)*
1994	Physics	Bertram Neville Brockhouse (1918–)
1993	Chemistry	Michael Smith (1932–)
1992	Chemistry#	Rudolph A. Marcus (1923–)
1990	Physics	Richard E. Taylor (1929–)
1989	Chemistry	Sidney Altman (1939–)
1986	Chemistry	John Polanyi (1929–)
1971	Chemistry#	Gerhard Herzberg (1904–1999)
1957	Peace#	Lester B. Pearson (1897–1972)

* According to the World Almanac, Vickrey died on October 11, 1996, three days after winning the prize. Scholes, Vickrey, and Marcus are Americans who were born in Canada. Smith, on the other hand, is a British-born Canadian, while Altman is a Montreal-born citizen of both Canada and the US. John J. R. Macleod (1876–1935), who shared Sir Frederick G. Banting's prize for medicine in 1923, is sometimes cited as Canadian, although he was actually Scottish; Canada was, however, his adopted country, where he was professor of physiology at the University of Toronto for some years

\# These are the only three prizes on the list which were not shared with other recipients

Source: *The Nobel Foundation*

TOP 10 NOBEL PEACE PRIZE-WINNING COUNTRIES
(Country/prizes)

1 US, 18 **2** International Institutions, 17 **3** UK, 13 **4** France, 9 **5** Sweden, 5
6 = Belgium; = Germany; = South Africa, 4 **9** = Israel; = Switzerland, 3

LITERARY LAUREATE

German novelist Günter Grass, the most famous of whose darkly humorous stories is The Tin Drum, won the 1999 Nobel Prize for Literature.

TOP 10 ★
LATEST WINNERS OF THE NOBEL PRIZE FOR CHEMISTRY

	WINNER/COUNTRY	YEAR
1	Ahmed Zewail, Egypt	1999
2 =	Walter Kohn, US	1998
2 =	John A. Pople, UK	1998
4 =	Paul D. Boyer, US	1997
4 =	John E. Walker, UK	1997
4 =	Jens C. Skou, Denmark	1997
7 =	Sir Harold W. Kroto, UK	1996
7 =	Richard E. Smalley, US	1996
9 =	Paul Crutzen, Netherlands	1995
9 =	Mario Molina, Mexico	1995
9 =	Frank Sherwood Rowland, US	1995

Criminal Records

The US ranks second in the world for its total prison population. Here inmates move through the cell blocks of the Ellis II prison unit at Huntsville Prison, Texas.

TOP 10 ★
COUNTRIES WITH THE HIGHEST PRISON POPULATION RATES

COUNTRY	TOTAL PRISON POPULATION*	PRISONERS PER 100,000
1 Russia	1,009,863	685
2 US	1,725,842	645
3 Belarus	52,033	505
4 Kazakhstan	82,945	495
5 Belize	1,118	490
6 Bahamas	1,401	485
7 Singapore	15,746#	465
8 Kyrgyzstan	19,857	440
9 Ukraine	211,568	415
10 Latvia	10,070	410

* Including pre-trial detainees

\# Almost half the detainees are held in drug rehabilitation centers

Source: *Home Office*

THE 10 ★
STATES WITH THE MOST PRISONERS ON DEATH ROW

STATE	PRISONERS UNDER DEATH SENTENCE*
1 California	561
2 Texas	462
3 Florida	389
4 Pennsylvania	232
5 North Carolina	224
6 Ohio	199
7 Alabama	185
8 Illinois	160
9 Oklahoma	149
10 Georgia	134

* As of January 1, 2000

Source: *Death Penalty Information Center*

A total of 3,652 prisoners were on death row at the start of 2000, some having been sentenced in more than one state, causing a higher total to be arrived at by adding individual state figures together.

TOP 10 ★
COUNTRIES WITH THE MOST POLICE OFFICERS

COUNTRY	POPULATION PER POLICE OFFICER
1 Russia	81
2 Singapore	93
3 Uruguay	120
4 Kazakhstan	128
5 Bahamas	134
6 Croatia	149
7 Saint Vincent and Grenadines	167
8 Lithuania	183
9 Cyprus	191
10 Malta	197

Did You Know? Marie-Augustin, the 22-year-old Marquis de Pélier, was jailed in 1786 for whistling at Queen Marie Antoinette. Forgotten, he was not released until 1832.

TOP 10
FASTEST-DECLINING CRIMES IN CANADA

	CRIME	% CHANGE IN RATE 1997–98*
1	Failure to stop/remain (traffic violation)	−22.3
2	Aggravated sexual assault	−19.4
3	Abduction	−17.4
4	Attempted murder	−15.5
5	Sexual assault involving a weapon	−13.0
6	Break and enter, business	−9.2
7	Motor vehicle theft	−7.3
8	Robbery, no weapons	−7.1
9	Theft ($5,000 and under)	−6.9
10	Break and enter, residential	−6.4

* Rates calculated per 100,000 population

Source: Canadian Centre for Justice Statistics

Canada's police-reported crime rate decreased for the seventh year in a row in 1998, falling 4 percent. The 1998 rate was the lowest rate since 1979.

TOP 10
MOST COMMON CRIMES IN CANADA

	CRIME	NUMBER OF INCIDENTS (1998)*
1	Theft ($5,000 and under)	712,764
2	Break and enter	350,176
3	Mischief	325,884
4	Assault	223,260
5	Motor vehicle theft	165,799
6	Fraud	94,575
7	Impaired driving	87,385
8	Bail violation	72,451
9	Drugs	71,293
10	Disturbing the peace	64,995

* Federal statute incidents reported to police

Source: Statistics Canada

THE 10
FIRST COUNTRIES TO ABOLISH CAPITAL PUNISHMENT

	COUNTRY	DATE ABOLISHED
1	Russia	1826
2	Venezuela	1863
3	Portugal	1867
4 =	Brazil	1882
4 =	Costa Rica	1882
6	Ecuador	1897
7	Panama	1903
8	Norway	1905
9	Uruguay	1907
10	Colombia	1910

Some countries abolished capital punishment in peacetime only, or for all crimes except treason, generally abolishing it totally at a more recent date, although several later reinstated it. Some countries retained capital punishment on their statute books but effectively abolished it.

THE 10
COUNTRIES WITH THE HIGHEST CRIME RATES

	COUNTRY	RATE*
1	Gibraltar	18,316
2	Surinam	17,819
3	St. Kitts and Nevis	15,468
4	Finland	14,799
5	Rwanda	14,550
6	New Zealand	13,854
7	Sweden	12,982
8	Denmark	10,525
9	Canada	10,451
10	US Virgin Islands	10,441

* Reported crime per 100,000 population

WE STAND ON GUARD FOR THEE

Originally founded in 1873 to "bring law, order and Canadian authority to the North-West Territories," today the RCMP takes an active role in policing airports, drug enforcement, economic crime, and international police duties.

Murder File

MOTIVES FOR MURDER IN CANADA

MOTIVE	PERCENT OF TOTAL CASES*
1 Anger	16.3
2 Altercation	11.1
3 Drug-related	10.6
4 Revenge	10.4
5 Alcohol	7.7
6 Domestic murder	6.3
7 Financial gain	5.4
8 Robbery	4.7
9 Jealousy	3.8
10 Sexual	3.4

* Based on cases entered into the national Violent Crime Linkage Analysis System (ViCLAS) from January 1, 1999 to December 31, 1999

CITIES IN CANADA WITH THE HIGHEST MURDER RATES

CITY (100,00 + POPULATION)	MURDERS IN 1998 (PER 100,000 POPULATION)
1 Regina, Sask.	4.51
2 Halifax, N.S.	3.45
3 Victoria, B.C.	3.14
4 Saskatoon, Sask.	3.05
5 Windsor, Ont.	2.70
6 Winnipeg, Man.	2.66
7 Edmonton, Alta.	2.40
8 Thunder Bay, Ont.	2.33
9 Vancouver, B.C.	2.25
10 Quebec City, Que.	2.18

Source: Statistics Canada

RELATIONSHIPS OF PRINCIPAL SUSPECTS TO MURDER VICTIMS IN CANADA

SUSPECT'S RELATIONSHIP TO VICTIM	PERCENT OF SOLVED HOMICIDES, 1998*
1 Casual acquaintance	22.5
2 Stranger	15.1
3 Husband (legal and common law)	10.7
4 Father	7.9
5 Criminal relationships#	6.5
6 Close acquaintance	6.0
7 Other family relationship	4.9
8 Child	4.6
9 Mother	3.9
10 Neighbour	3.5

* Includes only incidents in which there are known suspects

Includes prostitutes, drug dealers, and their clients

Source: Homicide Survey, Canadian Centre for Justice Statistics, October 1998

MOST PROLIFIC SERIAL KILLERS OF THE 20TH CENTURY

NAME/COUNTRY/CRIMES AND PUNISHMENT	VICTIMS*
1 Pedro Alonso López, Colombia	300

Captured in 1980, López, nicknamed the "Monster of the Andes," led police to 53 graves, but probably murdered at least 300 in Colombia, Ecuador, and Peru. He was sentenced to life.

2 Henry Lee Lucas, US	200

Lucas admitted in 1983 to 360 murders. He remains on Death Row in Huntsville Prison, Texas.

3 Luis Alfredo Gavarito, Colombia	140

Gavarito confessed in 1999 to a spate of murders, which are still the subject of investigation.

4 Dr. Harold Shipman, UK	131

In January 2000, Manchester doctor Shipman was found guilty of the murder of 15 women patients, but police believe his total number of victims to be at least 131, and perhaps over 150.

5 =Donald Henry "Pee Wee" Gaskins, US	100

Gaskins was executed in 1991 for a series of murders that may have reached 200.

5 =Javed Iqbal, Pakistan	100

Iqbal and two accomplices were found guilty in March 2000 of murdering boys in Lahore. He was sentenced to be publicly strangled, dismembered, and his body dissolved in acid.

7 Delfina and Maria de Jesús Gonzales, Mexico	91

In 1964 the Gonzales sisters were sentenced to 40 years' imprisonment for killing 80 women and 11 men.

8 Bruno Lüdke, Germany	86

Lüdke confessed to murdering 86 women in 1928–43. He died in a hospital after a lethal injection.

9 Daniel Camargo Barbosa, Ecuador	71

Barbosa was sentenced to just 16 years in prison for a catalog of crimes.

10 Kampatimar Shankariya, India	70

Caught after a two-year killing spree, Shankariya was hanged in Jaipur, India, in 1979.

* Estimated minimum; includes individual and partnership murderers; excludes mercy killings by doctors, murders by bandits and by groups, such as political and military atrocities, and gangland slayings.

WORST CITIES FOR MURDER IN THE US

CITY	MURDERS (1998)*
1 Chicago	703
2 New York	633
3 Detroit	430
4 Los Angeles	426
5 Philadelphia	338
6 Baltimore	312
7 Washington, DC	260
8 Houston	254
9 Dallas	252
10 New Orleans	230

* Murders and non-negligent manslaughter

Source: FBI Uniform Crime Reports

THE 10 ★
COUNTRIES WITH THE HIGHEST MURDER RATES

COUNTRY	ANNUAL MURDERS PER 100,000 POPULATION
1 Swaziland	88.1
2 Colombia	81.9
3 Namibia	72.4
4 South Africa	56.9
5 Lesotho	33.9
6 Belize	33.2
7 Philippines	30.1
8 Jamaica	27.6
9 Guatemala	27.4
10 French Guiana	27.2
Canada	*2.7*

TOP 10 ★
COUNTRIES WITH THE LOWEST MURDER RATES

COUNTRY	ANNUAL MURDERS PER 100,000 POPULATION
1 = Argentina	0.1
1 = Brunei	0.1
3 = Burkina Faso	0.2
3 = Niger	0.2
5 = Guinea	0.5
5 = Guinea-Bissau	0.5
5 = Iran	0.5
8 = Finland	0.6
8 = Saudi Arabia	0.6
10 = Cameroon	0.7
10 = Ireland	0.7
10 = Mongolia	0.7

Among countries that report to international monitoring organizations, some 18 record murder rates of fewer than one per 100,000. It should be borne in mind, however, that some countries do not report, and there are a number of places that, having had no murders in recent years, could claim a murder rate of zero.

FIREPOWER

While handguns are the most common murder weapons in the US and certain other countries, restrictions on their use elsewhere relegates them to a less significant position.

TOP 10 ★
CIRCUMSTANCES FOR MURDER IN THE US

REASON	MURDERS (1998)
1 Argument (unspecified)	4,080
2 Robbery	1,232
3 Narcotic drug laws violation	679
4 Juvenile gang killing	627
5 Felony (unspecified)	268
6 Argument over money or property	240
7 Brawl due to influence of alcohol	206
8 Romantic triangle	184
9 Brawl due to influence of narcotics	116
10 Suspected felony	104

Source: FBI Uniform Crime Reports

A total of 14,088 murders were reported in 1998, including 1,560 without a specified reason, and 4,358 for which the reasons were unknown.

TOP 10 ★
MOST COMMON MURDER WEAPONS AND METHODS IN THE US

WEAPON OR METHOD	VICTIMS (1998)
1 Handguns	7,361
2 Knives or cutting instruments	1,877
3 Firearms (type not stated)	609
4 "Personal weapons" (hands, feet, fists, etc.)	949
5 Blunt objects (hammers, clubs, etc.)	741
6 Shotguns	619
7 Rifles	538
8 Strangulation	211
9 Fire	130
10 Asphyxiation	99

Source: FBI Uniform Crime Reports

Military Matters

"BAZOOKA"

American radio comedian Bob Burns (1893–1956) invented a bizarre trombone-like musical instrument to which he gave the name "bazooka." Bazoo was a slang word for the mouth, and Burns added the *ka* suffix to make it sound like an instrument, such as a harmonica. When the antitank rocket-launcher was demonstrated during World War II, a soldier commented that it "looks just like Bob Burns' bazooka."

WHY DO WE SAY ?

THE 10 YEARS WITH THE MOST NUCLEAR EXPLOSIONS
(Year/explosions)

1 1962, 178   **2** 1958, 116   **3** 1968, 79
4 1966, 76   **5** 1961, 71   **6** 1969, 67
7 1978, 66   **8** = 1967; = 1970, 64
10 1964, 60

TOP 10 ★ COUNTRIES WITH THE LARGEST DEFENSE BUDGETS

	COUNTRY	BUDGET (US$ MILLION)
1	US	270,200
2	Japan	41,100
3	UK	34,600
4	Russia	31,000
5	France	29,500
6	Germany	24,700
7	Saudi Arabia	18,400
8	Italy	16,200
9	China	12,600
10	South Korea	11,600

The so-called "peace dividend" – the savings made as a consequence of the end of the Cold War between the West and the former Soviet Union – means that both the numbers of personnel and the defense budgets of many countries have been cut.

TOP 10 LARGEST ARMED FORCES

	COUNTRY	ARMY	NAVY	AIR	TOTAL
		ESTIMATED ACTIVE FORCES			
1	China	1,830,000	230,000	420,000	2,480,000
2	US	469,300	369,800	361,400	1,371,500*
3	India	980,000	53,000	140,000	1,173,000
4	North Korea	950,000	46,000	86,000	1,082,000
4	Russia	348,000	171,500	184,600	1,004,100#
6	South Korea	560,000	60,000	52,000	672,000
7	Turkey	525,000	51,000	63,000	639,000
8	Pakistan	520,000	22,000	45,000	587,000
9	Iran	350,000	20,600	50,000	545,600+
10	Vietnam	412,000	42,000	30,000★	484,000

* Includes 171,000 Marine Corps personnel
# Includes Strategic Deterrent Forces, Paramilitary, National Guard, etc.
+ Includes 125,000 Revolutionary Guards
★ 15,000 air force/15,000 air defense

TOP 10 SMALLEST ARMED FORCES*
(Country/estimated total active forces)

1 Antigua and Barbuda, 150 **2** Seychelles, 450 **3** Barbados, 610
4 Luxembourg, 768 **5** The Gambia, 800 **6** Bahamas, 860 **7** Belize, 1,050
8 Cape Verde, 1,100 **9** Equatorial Guinea, 1,320 **10** Guyana, 1,600
* Excluding countries not declaring a defense budget

TOP 10 ★ COUNTRIES WITH THE MOST SUBMARINES

COUNTRY	SUBMARINES
1 US	76
2 China	71
3 Russia (and associated states)	over 70
4 North Korea	26
5 South Korea	19
6 =India	16
6 =Japan	16
8 =Turkey	15
8 =UK	15
10 Germany	14

TOP 10 ★ COUNTRIES WITH THE LARGEST NAVIES

COUNTRY	MANPOWER (1999)*
1 US	369,800
2 China	230,000
3 Russia	171,500
4 Taiwan	68,000
5 France	62,600
6 South Korea	60,000
7 India	53,000
8 Turkey	51,000
9 Indonesia	47,000
10 North Korea	46,000

* Including naval air forces and marines

CRUISE SHIP
The US Navy is the world's largest. Here, the destroyer USS Merrill launches a Tomahawk cruise missile.

THE 10 ★ 20TH-CENTURY WARS WITH THE MOST MILITARY FATALITIES

WAR	YEARS	MILITARY FATALITIES
1 World War II	1939–45	15,843,000
2 World War I	1914–18	8,545,800
3 Korean War	1950–53	1,893,100
4 =Sino-Japanese War	1937–41	1,000,000
4 =Biafra–Nigeria Civil War	1967–70	1,000,000
6 Spanish Civil War	1936–39	611,000
7 Vietnam War	1961–73	546,000
8 =India–Pakistan War	1947	200,000
8 =USSR invasion of Afghanistan	1979–89	200,000
8 =Iran–Iraq War	1980–88	200,000

The statistics of warfare have always been an imperfect science. Not only are battle deaths seldom recorded accurately, but figures are often deliberately inflated by both sides in a conflict. These figures thus represent military historians' "best guesses" – and fail to take into account civilian deaths.

TOP 10 🍁 LARGEST CANADIAN PEACE-KEEPING EFFORTS

PLACE/DATES	FORCE/MISSION	NO. OF TROOPS*
1 Bosnia–Herzegovina, 1996–present	NATO	1,399
2 Kosovo, 1999–present	KFOR	1,374
3 Somalia, 1992–1993	UNITAF	1,250
4 Egypt (Suez, Sinai), 1973–1979	UNEF II	1,145
5 Cyprus, 1964–present	UNFICYP	1,100
6 Bosnia–Herzegovina, 1995–1996	IFOR (NATO)	1,029
7 Egypt (Sinai), 1956–1967	UNEF I	1,007
8 Croatia, 1992–1995	UNPROFOR I	860
9 Former Yugoslavia, 1992–1995	UNPROFOR	826
10 Haiti (UN), 1996–1997	NSMIH (UN)	750

* Indicates peak participation in particular missions at any one time
Source: Department of National Defense

Did You Know? The first submarine attack to destroy a warship took place on February 17, 1864, when the Confederate submarine *H.L. Hunley* sunk the Union sloop *Housatonic* off Charleston, South Carolina.

Air Wars

AREAS OF EUROPE MOST BOMBED BY ALLIED AIRCRAFT* IN WORLD WAR II

	AREA	BOMBS DROPPED (IMPERIAL TONS)
1	Germany	1,350,321
2	France	583,318
3	Italy	366,524
4	Austria, Hungary, and the Balkans	180,828
5	Belgium and Netherlands	88,739
6	Southern Europe and Mediterranean	76,505
7	Czechoslovakia and Poland	21,419
8	Norway and Denmark	5,297
9	Sea targets	564
10	British Channel Islands	93

* British and US

Between Aug 1942 and May 1945 alone, Allied air forces (Bomber Command plus 8 and 15 US Air Forces) flew 731,969 night sorties (and Bomber Command a further 67,598 day sorties), dropping a total of 1,850,919 imperial tons of bombs.

COUNTRIES SUFFERING THE GREATEST AIRCRAFT LOSSES IN WORLD WAR II

	COUNTRY	AIRCRAFT LOST
1	Germany	116,584
2	USSR	106,652
3	US	59,296
4	Japan	49,485
5	UK	33,090
6	Australia	7,160
7	Italy	5,272
8	Canada	2,389
9	France	2,100
10	New Zealand	684

Reports of aircraft losses vary considerably from country to country, some of them including aircraft damaged, lost due to accidents, or scrapped, as well as those destroyed during combat. Very precise combat loss figures exist for the Battle of Britain: during the period July 10 to Oct 31, 1940, 1,065 RAF aircraft were destroyed, compared with 1,922 Luftwaffe fighters, bombers, and other aircraft.

CITIES MOST BOMBED BY THE RAF AND USAF IN WORLD WAR II

	CITY	ESTIMATED CIVILIAN FATALITIES
1	Dresden	over 100,000
2	Hamburg	55,000
3	Berlin	49,000
4	Cologne	20,000
5	Magdeburg	15,000
6	Kassel	13,000
7	Darmstadt	12,300
8 =	Heilbronn	7,500
8 =	Essen	7,500
10 =	Dortmund	6,000
10 =	Wuppertal	6,000

The high level of casualties in Dresden resulted principally from the saturation bombing and the firestorm that ensued after Allied raids on the lightly defended city. Although the main objective was to destroy the railway marshaling yards, the scale of the raids was massive: 775 British bombers took part in the first night's raid on Feb 13, 1945, followed the next day by 450 US bombers, with a final attack by 200 US bombers on Feb 15.

GERMAN AIR ACES OF WORLD WAR II

	PILOT	KILLS CLAIMED
1	Major Eric Hartmann	352
2	Major Gerhard Barkhorn	301
3	Major Günther Rall	275
4	Oberlt. Otto Kittel	267
5	Major Walther Nowotny	258
6	Major Wilhelm Batz	237
7	Major Erich Rudorffer	222
8	Oberst. Heinz Bär	220
9	Oberst. Hermann Graf	212
10	Major Heinrich Ehrler	209

Many of these figures relate to kills on the Eastern Front, where the Luftwaffe was undoubtedly superior to its Soviet opponents.

JAPANESE AIR ACES OF WORLD WAR II

	PILOT	KILLS CLAIMED
1	W. O. Hiroyoshi Nishizawa	87
2	Lt. Tetsuzo Iwamoto	80
3	Petty Officer 1st Class Shoichi Sugita	70
4	Lt. Saburo Sakai	64
5	Petty Officer 1st Class Takeo Okumura	54
6	Petty Officer 1st Class Toshio Ohta	34
7	W. O. Kazuo Sugino	32
8	Petty Officer 1st Class Shizuo Ishii	29
9	Ensign Kaeneyoshi Muto	28
10 =	Lt. Sadaaki Akamatsu	27
10 =	Lt. Junichi Sasai	27

US AIR ACES OF THE KOREAN WAR

	PILOT	KILLS CLAIMED*
1	Capt. Joseph McConnell, Jr.	16
2	Major James Jabara	15
3	Capt. Manuel J. Fernandez	14.5
4	Major George A. Davis, Jr.	14
5	Col. Royal N. Baker	13
6 =	Major Frederick C. Blesse	10
6 =	Lt. Harold H. Fischer	10
6 =	Lt. Col. Vermont Garrison	10
6 =	Col. James K. Johnson	10
6 =	Capt. Lonnie R. Moore	10
6 =	Capt. Ralph S. Parr, Jr.	10

* Decimals refer to kills shared across groups such as flying squadrons

Background image: BOMB-DAMAGED DRESDEN

TOP GUNS

Majors Richard I. Bong (left) and Thomas B. McGuire (right), the leading US air aces of World War II, are shown here in Leyte, the Philippines, in 1944. After achieving a total of 78 kills between them, they were both killed in crashes the following year.

TOP 10 US AIR ACES OF WORLD WAR II

(Pilot/kills claimed*)

1 Major Richard I. Bong, 40 **2** Major Thomas B. McGuire, 38 **3** Cdr. David S. McCampbell, 34 **4** = Col. Francis S. Gabreski#; = Lt-Col. Gregory Boyington, 28 **6** = Major Robert S. Johnson; = Col. Charles H. MacDonald, 27 **8** = Major George E. Preddy; = Major Joseph J. Foss, 26 **10** Lt. Robert M. Hanson, 25

* Decimals refer to kills shared across groups such as flying squadrons
 # Also 6.5 kills in Korean War

TOP 10 COUNTRIES WITH THE MOST COMBAT AIRCRAFT*

(Country/combat aircraft)

1 Russia, 3,966 **2** China, 3,520 **3** US, 2,598 **4** India, 774 **5** Taiwan, 598 **6** North Korea, 593 **7** Egypt, 583 **8** France, 531 **9** Ukraine, 521 **10** South Korea, 488

* Air force only, exluding long-range strike/attack aircraft

TOP 10 BRITISH AND COMMONWEALTH AIR ACES OF WORLD WAR II

PILOT/COUNTRY	KILLS CLAIMED*
1 Sqd. Ldr. Marmaduke Thomas St. John Pattle, South Africa	over 40
2 Gp. Capt. James Edgar "Johnny" Johnson, Great Britain	33.91
3 Wing Cdr. Brendan "Paddy" Finucane, Ireland	32
4 Flt. Lt. George Frederick Beurling, Canada	31.33
5 Wing Cdr. John Randall Daniel Braham, Great Britain	29
6 Gp. Capt. Adolf Gysbert "Sailor" Malan, South Africa	28.66
7 Wing Cdr. Clive Robert Caldwell, Australia	28.5
8 Sqd. Ldr. James Harry "Ginger" Lacey, Great Britain	28
9 Sqd. Ldr. Neville Frederick Duke, Great Britain	27.83
10 Wing Cdr. Colin F. Gray, New Zealand	27.7

* Decimals refer to kills shared across groups such as flying squadrons

TOP COMBAT AIRCRAFT

Following its debut in 1976, the F-16 Fighting Falcon proved to be one of the most versatile fighter aircraft of the 20th century. Although designed for air-to-air fighting, it is equally valued for air-to-ground attack, and is available in both one- and two-seater versions. In military terms, it has a relatively low cost (some US$20 million each), a considerable range of some 3,220 km (2,000 miles), and is strongly built. It is highly maneuverable, has a top speed of 2,170 km/h (1,350 mph), and is capable of achieving Mach 2.05 at 12,190 m (40,000 ft), with a ceiling of 15,240 m (50,000 ft). Its US makers, Lockheed Martin, have produced over 2,000 F-16s, while a similar number are on order, making it the world's most extensively flown combat aircraft.

SNAP SHOTS

TOP 10 FASTEST FIGHTER AIRCRAFT OF WORLD WAR II

AIRCRAFT/COUNTRY	MAXIMUM SPEED	
	KM/H	MPH
1 Messerschmitt Me 163, Germany	959	596
2 Messerschmitt Me 262, Germany	901	560
3 Heinkel He 162A, Germany	890	553
4 P-51-H Mustang, US	784	487
5 Lavochkin La-11, USSR	740	460
6 Spitfire XIV, UK	721	448
7 Yakovlev Yak-3, USSR	719	447
8 P-51-D Mustang, US	708	440
9 Tempest VI, UK	705	438
10 Focke-Wulf Fw 190D, Germany	700	435

Also known as the Komet, the Messerschmitt Me 163 was a short-range rocket-powered interceptor brought into service in 1944–45, during which time this aircraft scored a number of victories over its slower Allied rivals. The Messerschmitt Me 262 was the first jet in operational service. The jet engine of the Soviet Yakovlev Yak-3 was mounted centrally under the cockpit. To avoid the danger of setting the tail-wheel tire on fire, it was replaced with an all-steel wheel, making landings a somewhat noisy affair.

Did You Know? The highest "score" by a night-fighter pilot was the total of 121 kills credited to World War II pilot Major Heinz-Wolfgang Schnauffer.

World Religions

LARGEST JEWISH POPULATIONS

	COUNTRY	TOTAL JEWISH POPULATION
1	US	6,122,462
2	Israel	4,354,900
3	France	640,156
4	Russia	460,266
5	Ukraine	424,136
6	UK	345,054
7	Canada	342,096
8	Argentina	253,666
9	Brazil	107,692
10	Belarus	107,350
	World total	15,050,000

The Diaspora – the scattering of the Jewish people – has been in progress for nearly 2,000 years, and Jewish communities are found in virtually every country in the world. In 1939 the total world Jewish population was around 17 million. Some 6 million fell victim to Nazi persecution, but numbers have now topped 15 million.

JEWISH PRAYERS

The Wailing Wall, Jerusalem, was part of the temple erected by King Herod. Jews traditionally pray here, lamenting the destruction of the temple in AD 70.

LARGEST CHRISTIAN DENOMINATIONS

	DENOMINATION	MEMBERS
1	Roman Catholic	912,636,000
2	Orthodox	139,544,000
3	Pentecostal	105,756,000
4	Lutheran	84,521,000
5	Baptist	67,146,000
6	Anglican	53,217,000
7	Presbyterian	47,972,000
8	Methodist	25,599,000
9	Seventh Day Adventist	10,650,000
10	Churches of Christ	6,400,000

Source: *Christian Research*

Although Christian communities are found in almost every country in the world, it is difficult to put a precise figure on nominal membership (a declared religious persuasion) rather than active participation (regular attendance at a place of worship). In the US, Roman Catholicism is the largest single denomination in a total of 36 states, and the Southern Baptist Convention in 10 states. However, the latter has the most churches nationwide: a total of 37,893.

LARGEST HINDU POPULATIONS

	COUNTRY	TOTAL HINDU POPULATION
1	India	814,632,942
2	Nepal	21,136,118
3	Bangladesh	14,802,899
4	Indonesia	3,974,895
5	Sri Lanka	2,713,900
6	Pakistan	2,112,071
7	Malaysia	1,043,500
8	US	798,582
9	South Africa	649,980
10	Mauritius	587,884
	World total	865,000,000

More than 99 percent of the world's Hindu population lives in Asia, with 94 percent in India.

RELIGIOUS BELIEFS

	RELIGION	MEMBERS*
1	Christianity	2,015,743,000
2	Islam	1,215,693,000
3	Hinduism	865,000,000
4	Non-religions	774,693,000
5	Buddhism	362,245,000
6	Tribal religions	255,950,000
7	Atheism	151,430,000
8	New religions	102,174,000
9	Sikhism	23,102,000
10	Judaism	15,050,000

* Estimated total projections to mid-1998

Outside the Top 10, several other religions have members numbering in millions, among them some 7 million Baha'is, 6 million Confucians, 4 million Jains, and 3 million Shintoists.

RELIGIONS IN CANADA

	DENOMINATION	MEMBERS
1	Roman Catholic	10,339,110
2	United Church	2,174,870
3	Anglican	1,570,400
4	Eastern non-Christian	658,430
5	Presbyterian	520,610
6	Lutheran	518,420
7	Baptist	502,590
8	Pentecostal	351,150
9	Islam	241,740
10	Jewish	236,550

Source: *Statistics Canada, 1996 General Survey*

Did You Know? A Holocaust Memorial Museum in Washington, D.C. honors the millions of Jews killed during the Holocaust.

TOP 10 ★

LARGEST MUSLIM POPULATIONS

	COUNTRY	TOTAL MUSLIM POPULATION
1	Pakistan	157,349,290
2	Indonesia	156,213,374
3	Bangladesh	133,873,621
4	India	130,316,250
5	Iran	74,087,700
6	Turkey	66,462,107
7	Russia	64,624,770
8	Egypt	57,624,098
9	Nigeria	46,384,120
10	Morocco	33,542,780
	World total	1,215,693,000

Historically, Islam spread as a result of conquest, missionary activity, and through contacts with Muslim traders. In such countries as Indonesia, its appeal lay in part in its opposition to Western colonial influences, which, along with the concept of Islamic community and other tenets, has attracted followers worldwide.

BOWING TO MECCA

Islam places many strictures on its female members but is nonetheless the world's fastest-growing religion. Here, hundreds of Muslim women unite in prayer.

TOP 10 ★

LARGEST BUDDHIST POPULATIONS

	COUNTRY	TOTAL BUDDHIST POPULATION
1	China	104,000,000
2	Japan	90,510,000
3	Thailand	57,450,000
4	Vietnam	50,080,000
5	Myanmar (Burma)	41,880,000
6	Sri Lanka	12,540,000
7	South Korea	11,110,000
8	Cambodia	9,870,000
9	India	7,000,000
10	Malaysia	3,770,000
	World total	362,245,000

HEAD OF THE FAITH

Although India now features in ninth place among countries with high Buddhist populations, the religion originated there in the 6th century BC.

Town & Country

Countries of the World

LARGEST COUNTRIES

| | COUNTRY | AREA | |
		SQ KM	SQ MILES
1	Russia	17,070,289	6,590,876
2	Canada	9,970,599	3,849,670
3	China	9,596,961	3,705,408
4	US	9,169,389	3,540,321
5	Brazil	8,511,965	3,286,488
6	Australia	7,686,848	2,967,909
7	India	3,287,590	1,269,346
8	Argentina	2,780,400	1,073,512
9	Kazakhstan	2,717,300	1,049,156
10	Sudan	2,505,813	967,500
	World total	135,807,000	52,435,381

TOP 10 COUNTRIES IN WHICH WOMEN MOST OUTNUMBER MEN

(Country/women per 100 men)

1 Latvia, 120 **2** = Cape Verdi; = Ukraine, 115
4 Russia, 114 **5** = Belarus; = Estonia; = Lithuania, 112
8 = Hungary; = Antigua and Barbuda; = Georgia;
= Moldova, 109

Source: *United Nations*

SMALLEST COUNTRIES

| | COUNTRY | AREA | |
		SQ KM	SQ MILES
1	Vatican City	0.44	0.17
2	Monaco	1.95	0.77
3	Gibraltar	6.47	2.50
4	Macao	16.06	6.20
5	Nauru	21.23	8.20
6	Tuvalu	25.90	10.00
7	Bermuda	53.35	20.60
8	San Marino	59.57	23.00
9	Liechtenstein	157.99	61.00
10	Antigua	279.72	108.00

The "country" status of several of these microstates is questionable, since their government, defense, currency, and other features are often intricately linked with those of larger countries, such as the Vatican City with Italy's.

LONGEST BORDERS

| | COUNTRY | BORDERS | |
		KM	MILES
1	China	22,143	13,759
2	Russia	20,139	12,514
3	Brazil	14,691	9,129
4	India	14,103	8,763
5	US	12,248	7,611
6	Dem. Rep. of Congo	10,271	6,382
7	Argentina	9,665	6,006
8	Canada	8,893	5,526
9	Mongolia	8,114	5,042
10	Sudan	7,697	4,783

This list represents the total length of borders, compiled by adding together the lengths of individual land borders.

RUSSJAN SURVIVORS

The disproportionately high number of women in Russia and other former Soviet countries is the result of high mortality rates among the region's men, caused in part by poor diet and excessive consumption of alcohol and tobacco.

TOP 10 COUNTRIES IN WHICH MEN MOST OUTNUMBER WOMEN

(Country/men per 100 women)

1 Qatar, 189 **2** United Arab Emirates, 174 **3** Bahrain, 133
4 Saudi Arabia, 124 **5** = Oman; = Andorra, 113
7 = Guam; = Hong Kong, 112 **9** Brunei, 110 **10** Kuwait, 109

Source: *United Nations*

Did You Know? The US's 6,416-km (3,987-mile) frontier with Canada is the longest continuous frontier in the world.

TOP 10 MOST DENSELY POPULATED COUNTRIES

	COUNTRY	AREA (SQ KM)	ESTIMATED POPULATION*	POPULATION PER SQ KM
1	Monaco	1.95	32,231	16,528.7
2	Singapore	618	3,571,710	5,779.5
3	Malta	316	383,285	1,212.9
4	Maldives	298	310,425	1,041.7
5	Bahrain	694	641,539	924.4
6	Bangladesh	143,998	129,146,695	896.9
7	Mauritius	1,865	1,196,172	641.4
8	Barbados	430	259,248	602.9
9	South Korea	99,274	47,350,529	476.9
10	San Marino	61	25,215	413.4
	Canada	9,970,599	29,942,000	3.0
	World	135,807,000	6,073,098,801	44.7

* For the year 2000

Source: *US Bureau of the Census/United Nations*

LARGEST COUNTRIES IN EUROPE

	COUNTRY	AREA SQ KM	AREA SQ MILES
1	**Russia** (in Europe)	4,710,227	1,818,629
2	Ukraine	603,700	233,090
3	France	547,026	211,208
4	Spain*	504,781	194,897
5	Sweden	449,964	173,732
6	Germany	356,999	137,838
7	Finland	337,007	130,119
8	Norway	324,220	125,182
9	Poland	312,676	120,725
10	Italy	301,226	116,304

* *Including offshore islands*

The UK falls just outside the Top 10 at 244,101 sq km (94,247 sq miles). Excluding the Isle of Man and the Channel Islands, its area comprises England (130,410 sq km/50,351 sq miles), Scotland (78,789 sq km/30,420 sq miles), Wales (20,758 sq km/8,015 sq miles), and Northern Ireland (14,144 sq km/5,461 sq miles).

TOP 10 COUNTRIES WITH THE OLDEST POPULATIONS

(Country/percentage over 65)

1 Sweden, 17.3 **2** = Italy; = Greece, 16.6 **4** Portugal, 16.1 **5** Belgium, 16.0 **6** Spain, 15.9 **7** UK, 15.8 **8** Norway, 15.7 **9** = Germany; = Japan, 15.5

Source: *World Bank*

Nine of the ten countries with the oldest populations are in western Europe, implying that this region has lower death rates and a higher life expectancy than the rest of the world.

LOOKING TO THE FUTURE

Soaring birth rates in many African countries have created broad-based population pyramids, with up to half their populations aged under 15.

TOP 10 COUNTRIES WITH THE YOUNGEST POPULATIONS

(Country/percentage under 15)

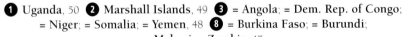

1 Uganda, 50 **2** Marshall Islands, 49 **3** = Angola; = Dem. Rep. of Congo; = Niger; = Somalia; = Yemen, 48 **8** = Burkina Faso; = Burundi; = Malawi; = Zambia, 47

Source: *United Nations*

Countries with high proportions of their people under the age of 15 are usually characterized by high birth rates and high death rates.

83

World Cities

MOST DENSELY POPULATED CITIES*

CITY/COUNTRY	POPULATION PER SQ KM	POPULATION PER SQ MILE
1 Hong Kong, China	98,053	253,957
2 Lagos, Nigeria	67,561	174,982
3 Dhaka, Bangladesh	63,900	165,500
4 Jakarta, Indonesia	56,650	146,724
5 Bombay, India	54,997	142,442
6 Ahmadabad, India	50,676	131,250
7 Ho Chi Minh City (Saigon), Vietnam	50,617	131,097
8 Shenyang, China	44,125	114,282
9 Bangalore, India	43,583	112,880
10 Cairo, Egypt	41,413	107,260

* Includes only cities with populations of over 2 million

Source: *US Bureau of the Census*

RUSH HOUR – NIGERIAN STYLE

Nigeria's former capital and still its most important city, Lagos, is also one of the world's densest and fastest-growing cities, as a result of which it suffers from traffic congestion, overcrowding, and slum dwellings.

TOP 10 ★

FASTEST-GROWING CITIES

CITY/COUNTRY	EST. INCREASE, 1995–2010 (%)*
1 Hangzhou, China	171.1
2 Addis Ababa, Ethiopia	170.7
3 Kabul, Afghanistan	156.3
4 Handan, China	141.6
5 Isfahan, Iran	141.3
6 Maputo, Mozambique	139.9
7 Lagos, Nigeria	139.5
8 Luanda, Angola	138.8
9 Nairobi, Kenya	133.6
10 Qingdao, China	132.4

* Urban agglomerations of over 1 million population only

Source: *United Nations*

TOP 10 🍁

CANADIAN MEGACITIES*

CITY	POP. AFTER MERGER	EFFECTIVE DATE
1 City of Toronto, ON	2,385,421	Jan 1, 1998
2 Ottawa, ON#	747,650	Jan 1, 2001
3 Hamilton, ON#	467,799	Jan 1, 2001
4 Halifax, NS (Halifax Regional Municipality)	342,966	Apr 1, 1996
5 Laval, QC	330,393+	1965
6 City of Greater Sudbury, ON#	161,945	Jan 1, 2001
7 Sydney, NS (Cape Breton Regional Municipality)	117,849	Aug 1, 1995
8 City of Abbotsford, BC	116,000	Jan 1, 1995
9 City of Kingston, ON	113,000	Jan 1, 1998
10 City of Chatham–Kent, ON	109,500	Jan 1, 1998

* Largest existing and proposed municipal mergers
\# proposed municipal mergers
\+ present-day population

Source: *Federation of Canadian Municipalities*

Did You Know? Ein Bokek, beside the Dead Sea, is the world's lowest inhabited place at 393.5 m (1,291 ft) below sea level.

TOP 10 ★
LARGEST CITIES

	CITY/COUNTRY	EST. POPULATION, 2015*
1	**Tokyo**, Japan	28,900,000
2	**Bombay**, India	26,200,000
3	**Lagos**, Nigeria	24,600,000
4	**São Paulo**, Brazil	20,300,000
5	**Dhaka**, Bangladesh	19,500,000
6	**Karachi**, Pakistan	19,400,000
7	**Mexico City**, Mexico	19,200,000
8	**Shanghai**, China	18,000,000
9	**New York**, USA	17,600,000
10	**Calcutta**, India	17,300,000

* Of urban agglomeration

Source: *United Nations*

The definition taken in the above and other city lists is the United Nations definition of "urban agglomeration," which comprises the city or town proper and also the suburban fringe or thickly settled territory lying outside of, but adjacent to, the city boundaries.

TOP 10 ★
LARGEST CITIES IN NORTH AMERICA

	CITY/COUNTRY	EST. POPULATION, 2015*
1	**Mexico City**, Mexico	19,200,000
2	**New York**, US	17,600,000
3	**Los Angeles**, US	14,200,000
4	**Chicago**, US	7,500,000
5	**Toronto**, Canada	5,200,000
6	**Philadelphia**, US	4,800,000
7	**Santa Domingo**, Dominican Republic	4,700,000
8 =	**Guadalajara**, Mexico	4,500,000
8 =	**San Francisco**, US	4,500,000
10 =	**Dallas**, US	4,400,000
10 =	**Washington, DC**, US	4,400,000

* Of urban agglomeration

Source: *United Nations*

TOP 10 ★
LARGEST CITIES IN EUROPE

	CITY/COUNTRY	EST. POPULATION, 2015*
1	**Paris**, France	9,700,000
2	**Moscow**, Russia	9,300,000
3	**London**, UK	7,600,000
4	**Essen**, Germany	6,600,000
5	**St. Petersburg**, Russia	5,100,000
6	**Milan**, Italy	4,300,000
7	**Madrid**, Spain	4,100,000
8 =	**Frankfurt**, Germany	3,700,000
8 =	**Katowice**, Poland	3,700,000
10	**Dusseldorf**, Germany	3,400,000

* Of urban agglomeration

Source: *United Nations*

PARISIAN GRANDEUR

A population of 9.5 million, a central location, and cultural and other attractions have led to the inexorable growth of Paris to its present rank as Europe's largest city.

TOP 10 ★
LARGEST NONCAPITAL CITIES

	CITY/COUNTRY/CAPITAL CITY	POPULATION
1	**Shanghai**, China *Beijing*	13,584,000 *11,299,000*
2	**Bombay**, India *New Delhi*	15,138,000 *8,419,000*
3	**Calcutta***, India *New Delhi*	11,923,000 *8,419,000*
4	**Lagos**, Nigeria *Abuja*	10,287,000 *378,671*
5	**São Paulo**, Brazil *Brasília*	10,017,821 *1,864,000*
6	**Karachi***, Pakistan *Islamabad*	9,733,000 *350,000*
7	**Tianjin**, China *Beijing*	9,415,000 *11,299,000*
8	**Istanbul***, Turkey *Ankara*	8,274,921 *2,937,524*
9	**New York**, USA *Washington, DC*	7,420,166 *523,124*
10	**Madras**, India *New Delhi*	6,002,000 *8,419,000*

* *Former capital*

TOP 10 ★
MOST POPULATED FORMER CAPITAL CITIES

	CITY/COUNTRY	CEASED TO BE CAPITAL	POPULATION*
1	**Calcutta**, India	1912	11,021,918
2	**Istanbul**, Turkey	1923	7,774,169
3	**Karachi**, Pakistan	1968	7,183,000
4	**Rio de Janeiro**, Brazil	1960	5,547,033
5	**St. Petersburg**, Russia	1980	4,273,001
6	**Berlin**, Germany	1949	3,472,009
7	**Alexandria**, Egypt	c.641	3,380,000
8	**Melbourne**, Australia	1927	3,189,200
9	**Nanjiang**, China	1949	2,610,594
10	**Philadelphia**, US	1800	1,524,249

* *Within administrative boundaries*

Canadian Places & Peoples

☘ TOP 10 LARGEST PROVINCES & TERRITORIES

	PROVINCE/TERRITORY	LAND (SQ KM)	WATER (SQ KM)	TOTAL
1	Nunavut	1,936,113	157,077	2,093,190
2	Quebec	1,365,128	176,928	1,542,056
3	Northwest Territories	1,183,085	163,021	1,346,106
4	Ontario	917,741	158,654	1,076,395
5	British Columbia	925,186	19,549	944,735
6	Alberta	642,317	19,531	661,848
7	Saskatchewan	591,670	59,366	651,036
8	Manitoba	553,556	94,241	647,797
9	Yukon Territory	474,391	8,052	482,443
10	Newfoundland	373,872	31,340	405,212

Source: *Statistics Canada*

TOP 10 ☘ PROVINCES & TERRITORIES WITH THE LONGEST COASTLINES

	PROVINCE/TERRITORY	TOTAL COASTLINE (KM)
1	Nunavut	153,365*
2	Newfoundland	28,956
3	British Columbia	25,725
4	Quebec	13,773
5	Northwest Territories	12,591*
6	Nova Scotia	7,579
7	New Brunswick	2,269
8	Prince Edward Island	1,260
9	Ontario	1,210
10	Manitoba	917

* Estimated

Source: *Canadian Hydrographic Service, Fisheries and Oceans Canada*

TOP 10 ☘ BEST-SELLING MILLENNIUM QUARTERS OF 1999

	COIN	ARTIST	MONTH ISSUED	NUMBER SOLD
1	From Coast to Coast	Gordon Ho	June	11,004
2	The Voyageurs	Sergiy Mineok	May	9,315
3	A Country Unfolds	Peter Ka-Kin Poon	January	9,190
4	Canada Through a Child's Eye	Claudia Bertrand	September	9,169
5	Our Northern Heritage	Kenojuak Ashevak	April	9,040
6	A Nation of People	Maria H. Sarkany	July	8,899
7	The Airplane Opens the North	Brian R. Bacon	November	8,813
8	The Log Drive	Marjolaine Lavoie	March	8,765
9	Etched in Stone	Lonnie Springer	February	8,691
10	The Pioneer Spirit	Alzira Botelho	August	8,570

Source: *Royal Canadian Mint*

Minting THE MILLENNIUM

The Royal Canadian Mint invited Canadians to design a coin for the Millennium in 1998. Over 50,000 designs later, the Mint released twelve commemorative 25-cent coins in 1999 with designs from Canadians across the country. The most popular coin was Gordon Ho's From Coast to Coast. Twelve more quarters will be issued in 2000.

☘ THE FIRST 10 PROVINCES JOINING CONFEDERATION

(Province/year joining Confederation)

1 = Ontario*; = Quebec#; = Nova Scotia; = New Brunswick, 1867 **5** Manitoba, 1870 **6** British Columbia, 1871 **7** Prince Edward Island, 1873 **8** = Alberta; = Saskatchewan, 1905 **10** Newfoundland, 1949

* Formerly Canada West # Formerly Canada East

TOP 10
PROVINCES & TERRITORIES WITH THE MOST FIRST NATIONS LAND

	PROVINCE/TERRITORY	LAND AREA (HECTARES)
1	Saskatchewan	797,205.3
2	Ontario	748,979.8
3	Alberta	697,526.5
4	British Columbia	347,701.2
5	Manitoba	265,389.7
6	Quebec	77,897.4
7	New Brunswick	17,500.4
8	Northwest Territories	13,562.0
9	Nova Scotia	11,344.5
10	Yukon	1,154.5

Source: *Indian and Northern Affairs Canada*

TOP 10
ETHNIC ORIGINS REPORTED BY CANADIANS*

	ETHNIC ORIGIN	NO. OF RESPONDENTS
1	Canadian	8,806,275
2	English	6,832,095
3	French	5,597,845
4	Scottish	4,260,840
5	Irish	3,767,610
6	German	2,757,140
7	Italian	1,207,475
8	Aboriginal origins	1,101,955
9	Ukranian	1,026,475
10	Chinese	921,585

* In the 1996 census
Source: *Statistics Canada*

The 1996 Census question on ethnic origin was changed over previous years and included "Canadian" among the examples of ethnic origins.

TOP 10
LARGEST NATIVE BANDS IN CANADA 1999

	FIRST NATIONS	REGION	POPULATION
1	Mohawks of Akwesasne	Ontario	9,260
2	Kahnawake	Quebec	8.793
3	Saddle Lake	Alberta	7,466
4	Lac La Ronge	Saskatchewan	6,955
5	Peguis	Manitoba	6,948
6	Mohawks of Bay of Quinte	Ontario	6,921
7	Peter Ballantyne Cree Nation	Saskatchewan	6,601
8	Wikwemikong	Manitoba	6,347
9	Fort Alexander	Manitoba	5,799
10	Cross Lake First Nation	Manitoba	5,508

Source: *Indian and Northern Affairs Canada*

CanStats

On April 1, 1999, the new territory of Nunavut was created from Canada's central and eastern Arctic, in what was once the Northwest Territories. Nunavut means "our land" in Inuktitut, the language spoken by more than four-fifths of Nunavut's 25,000 inhabitants.

• Comprising the former Keewatin and Franklin districts of the Northwest Territories, Nunavut covers 1.9 million sq km/735,000 sq mi, making it one-fifth the size of Canada.

• Nunavut spans four time zones: Atlantic, Central, Eastern, and Mountain.

• Nunavut's capital is Iqaluit, or "place of many fish" in Inuktitut.

• Nunavut's coat of arms features a narwhal and a caribou, as well as the motto "Sanginivut," which means "our strength" in Inuktitut.

• Nunavut's online newspaper, the *Nunatsiaq News*, can be found at www.nunatsiaq.com.

• Nunavut will share the same polar bear-shaped license plate (the only non-rectangular license plate in North America) as the Northwest Territories, but it will say "Nunavut" instead of "NWT."

• On February 15, 1999, Nunavut elected 19 MLAs (members of legislative assembly). Inuktituk is to be the official language of government, which will rely on Inuit *Qaujimajatuqangit* (traditional knowledge) in government policy making. Nunavut's civil service will also have flexible hours to accommodate hunting schedules.

Source: *www.nunavut.com*

THE FIRST 10 GOVERNORS GENERAL OF CANADA

1 Viscount Monck (1867–68) 2 Baron Lisgar (1868–72)
3 The Earl of Dufferin (1872–78) 4 The Marquess of Lorne (1878–83)
5 The Marquess of Lansdowne (1883–88) 6 Baron Stanley of Preston (1888–93)
7 The Earl of Aberdeen (1893–98) 8 The Earl of Minto (1898–1904)
9 Earl Grey (1904–11) 10 The Duke of Connaught (1911–16)

Did You Know? The original name for Regina – assigned August 23, 1882, by the Governor General, the Marquess of Lorne, in honor of his wife's mother, Queen Victoria – was "Pile O'Bones"?

Place Names

LONGEST PLACE NAMES IN THE US*

NAME/LOCATION	LETTERS
1 Chargoggagoggmanchauggagoggchaubunagungamaugg (see Top 10 Longest Place Names)	45
2 Nunathloogagamiutbingoi, Dunes, Alaska	23
3 Winchester-on-the-Severn, Maryland	21
4 Scraper-Moechereville, Illinois	20
5 Linstead-on-the-Severn, Maryland	19
6 =Kentwood-in-the-Pines, California	18
6 =Lauderdale-by-the-Sea, Florida	18
6 =Vermilion-on-the-Lake, Ohio	18
9 =Chippewa-on-the-Lake, Ohio	17
9 =Fairhaven-on-the-Bay, Maryland	17
9 =Highland-on-the-Lake, New York	17
9 =Kleinfeltersville, Pennsylvania	17
9 =Mooselookmeguntic, Maine	17
9 =Palermo-by-the-Lakes, Ohio	17
9 =Saybrook-on-the-Lake, Ohio	17

* Single and hyphenated names only   Source: US Geological Survey

COUNTRIES WITH THE LONGEST OFFICIAL NAMES

OFFICIAL NAME*	COMMON ENGLISH NAME	LETTERS
1 al-Jamāhīrīyah al-Arabīya al-Lībīyah ash-Sha bīyah al-Ishtirākīyah	Libya	56
2 al-Jumhūrīyah al-Jazā'irīyah ad-Dīmuqrātīyah ash-Sha bīyah	Algeria	49
3 United Kingdom of Great Britain and Northern Ireland	United Kingdom	45
4 Sri Lankā Prajathanthrika Samajavadi Janarajaya	Sri Lanka	43
5 Jumhurīyat al-Qumur al-Ittihādīyah al-Islāmīyah	The Comoros	41
6 =al-Jumhūrīyah al-Islāmīyah al-Mūritānīyah	Mauritania	36
6 =The Federation of St. Christopher and Nevis	St. Kitts and Nevis	36
8 Jamhuuriyadda Dimuqraadiga Soomaaliya	Somalia	35
9 al-Mamlakah al-Urdunnīyah al-Hāshimīyah	Jordan	34
10 Repoblika Demokratika n'i Madagaskar	Madagascar	32

* Some official names have been transliterated from languages that do not use the Roman alphabet; their length may vary according to the method used.

♣ TOP 10 MOST COMMON PLACE NAMES IN CANADA

(Name/occurrences)

❶ Mount Pleasant, 16 ❷ = Centreville; = Lakeview, 15 ❹ = Fairview; = Pleasant Valley, 13 ❻ = Bellevue; = Glenwood; = Richmond; = Riverside; = Rosedale; = Salem; = Springfield; = Victoria; = Westmount, 10

♣ TOP 10 MOST COMMON STREET NAMES IN QUEBEC

(Street name/occurrences)

❶ Principale, 435 ❷ Église, 380
❸ Érables, 363 ❹ Pins, 311
❺ Parc, 285 ❻ Saint-Joseph, 281
❼ = Bouleaux; = Cèdres, 259
❾ Moulin, 217 ❿ Montagne, 212

Source: Commission de toponymie, Quebec

MOST COMMON GEOGRAPHICAL FEATURE NAMES IN ONTARIO

FEATURE NAME	NUMBER IN ONTARIO
1 Mud Lake	75
2 Long Lake	66
3 =Birch Lake	48
3 =Burnt Island	48
5 Otter Lake	47
6 Big Island	46
7 =Clear Lake	45
7 =Green Island	45
9 Lost Lake	41
10 Black Creek	39

Source: Office of the Surveyor General, Ontario Ministry of Natural Resources

MOST COMMONLY NAMED GEOGRAPHICAL FEATURES IN ONTARIO

FEATURE	NUMBER IN ONTARIO
1 Lake	22,251
2 Island	5,909
3 Creek	5,472
4 Bay	2,769
5 Point	2,278
6 River	1,272
7 Rock	669
8 Rapids	419
9 Hill	387
10 Falls	366

Source: Office of the Surveyor General, Ontario Ministry of Natural Resources

Did You Know? 1st/First Street is the third most common street name in the US only because many streets that would be so designated are instead called Main Street.

TOP 10 ⭐
LONGEST PLACE NAMES*

NAME	LETTERS

1 Krung thep mahanakhon bovorn ratanakosin mahintharayutthaya mahadilok pop noparatratchathani burirom udomratchanivetmahasathan amornpiman avatarnsathit sakkathattiyavisnukarmprasit — 167

When the poetic name of Bangkok, capital of Thailand, is used, it is usually abbreviated to "Krung Thep" (city of angels).

2 Taumatawhakatangihangakoauauotamateaturipukakapikimaungahoronu-kupokaiwhenuakitanatahu — 85

This is the longer version (the other has a mere 83 letters) of the Maori name of a hill in New Zealand. It translates as "The place where Tamatea, the man with the big knees, who slid, climbed, and swallowed mountains, known as land-eater, played on the flute to his loved one."

3 Gorsafawddacha'idraigodanheddogleddollônpenrhynareurdraethceredigion — 67

A name contrived by the Fairbourne Steam Railway, Gwynedd, North Wales, for publicity purposes and in order to outdo its rival, No. 4. It means "The Mawddach station and its dragon teeth at the Northern Penrhyn Road on the golden beach of Cardigan Bay."

4 Cape St. George-Petit Jardin-Grand Jardin-De Grau-Marches Point-Loretto — 59

Canada's longest place name belongs to an isolated cape in Newfoundland that faces St-George's Bay and the Gulf of St. Lawrence.

5 Llanfairpwllgwyngyllgogerychwyrndrobwllllantysiliogogogoch — 58

This is the place in Gwynedd famed especially for the length of its train tickets. It means "St. Mary's Church in the hollow of the white hazel near to the rapid whirlpool of Llantysilio of the Red Cave." Questions have been raised about its authenticity, since its official name comprises only the first 20 letters, and the full name appears to have been invented as a hoax in the 19th century by a local poet, John Evans, known as Y Bardd Cocos. It also has Britain's longest Internet site name: http://www.llanfairpwllgwyngyllgogerychwyrndrobwllllantysilio-gogogoch.-wales.com/llanfair

6 El Pueblo de Nuestra Señora la Reina de los Angeles de la Porciuncula — 57

The site of a Franciscan mission and the full Spanish name of Los Angeles; it means "The town of Our Lady the Queen of the Angels of the Little Portion." Nowadays it is customarily known by its initial letters, "LA," making it also one of the shortest-named cities in the world.

7 Cours d'eau du Cordon des Terres des Sixième et Septième Rangs — 51

When translated from French, this Quebec waterway indicates its location on "the lands of the sixth and seventh rows" – a name that harks back to the seigneurial days of New France, when farmland was settled in very narrow strips facing a river or stream.

8 Ruisseau Katakuschuwepaishit Kachikuschikepaisham — 47

This 47-letter stream is located in Quebec.

9 Décharge des Neuvième, Dixième et Onzième Concessions — 46

This Quebec place name, loosely translated from French, means "the stream from the ninth, tenth, and eleventh rural row."

10 Chargoggagoggmanchauggagoggchaubunagungamaugg — 45

America's longest place name, a lake near Webster, Massachusetts. Its Native American name, loosely translated, means "You fish on your side, I'll fish on mine, and no one fishes in the middle." It is said to be pronounced "Char-gogg-a-gogg (pause) man-chaugg-a-gogg (pause) chau-bun-a-gung-amaugg." It is, however, an invented extension of its real name (Chagungungamaug Pond, or "boundary fishing place"), devised in the 1920s by Larry Daly, the editor of the Webster Times.

* Including single-word, hyphenated, and multiple-word names

CITY OF ANGELS
The original 57-letter Spanish name of Los Angeles contrasts dramatically with its more common designation as "LA."

Tallest Buildings

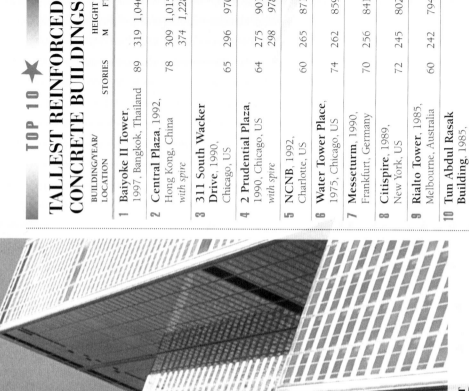

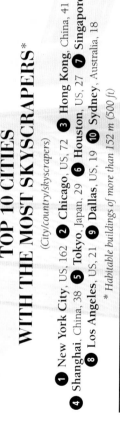

TOP 10 ★ TALLEST HABITABLE BUILDINGS

BUILDING/YEAR/ LOCATION	STORIES	HEIGHT M	FT
1 Petronas Towers, 1996, Kuala Lumpur, Malaysia	96	452	1,482
2 Sears Tower, 1974, Chicago, US with spires	110	443 520	1,454 1,707
3 World Trade Center*, 1972, New York, US	110	417	1,368
4 World Finance Center, 2001, Hong Kong, China	88	400	1,312
5 Jin Mao Building, 1997, Shanghai, China with spire	93	382 420	1,255 1,378
6 Empire State Building, 1931, New York, US with spire	102	381 449	1,250 1,472
7 T & C Tower, 1997, Kao-hsiung, Taiwan	85	348	1,142
8 Amoco Building, 1973, Chicago, US	80	346	1,136
9 John Hancock Center, 1969, Chicago, US with spires	100	343 449	1,127 1,470
10 Shun Hing Square, 1996, Shenzen, China with spires	80	330 384	1,082 1,260

* Twin towers; the second tower, completed in 1973, has the same number of stories but is slightly smaller at 415 m (1,360 ft), although its spire takes it up to 521 m (1,710 ft).

TOP 10 ★ TALLEST REINFORCED CONCRETE BUILDINGS

BUILDING/YEAR/ LOCATION	STORIES	HEIGHT M	FT
1 Baiyoke II Tower, 1997, Bangkok, Thailand	89	319	1,046
2 Central Plaza, 1992, Hong Kong, China with spire	78	309 374	1,015 1,228
3 311 South Wacker Drive, 1990, Chicago, US	65	296	970
4 2 Prudential Plaza, 1990, Chicago, US with spire	64	275 298	901 978
5 NCNB, 1992, Charlotte, US	60	265	871
6 Water Tower Place, 1975, Chicago, US	74	262	859
7 Messeturm, 1990, Frankfurt, Germany	70	256	841
8 Citispire, 1989, New York, US	72	245	802
9 Rialto Tower, 1985, Melbourne, Australia	60	242	794
10 Tun Abdul Rasak Building, 1985, Penang, Malaysia	61	232	761

Reinforced concrete was patented in France on March 16, 1867 by Joseph Monier (1823–1906) and was later developed by another Frenchman, François Hennebique (1842–1921). The first North American buildings constructed from it date from a century ago, and since then it has become one of the most important of all building materials. It is constructed from concrete slabs containing steel bars which expand and contract at the same rate as the concrete. This provides great tensile strength and fire resistance. These qualities make it the ideal construction material for bridge spans and skyscrapers.

CHICAGO GIANT

Chicago's tallest skyscraper weighs 201,848 tonnes. It has 16,100 windows and contains 69,000 km (43,000 miles) of telephone cable.

TOP 10 CITIES WITH THE MOST SKYSCRAPERS*
(City/country/skyscrapers)

❶ New York City, US, 162 ❷ Chicago, US, 72 ❸ Hong Kong, China, 41 ❹ Shanghai, China, 38 ❺ Tokyo, Japan, 29 ❻ Houston, US, 27 ❼ Singapore, 25 ❽ Los Angeles, US, 21 ❾ Dallas, US, 19 ❿ Sydney, Australia, 18

* Habitable buildings of more than 152 m (500 ft)

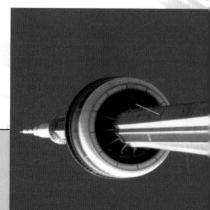

TOP 10 ★ TALLEST TELECOMMUNICATIONS TOWERS

TOWER/YEAR/LOCATION	HEIGHT M	FT
1 CN Tower, 1975, Toronto, Canada	555	1,821
2 Ostankino Tower, 1967, Moscow, Russia	537	1,762
3 Oriental Pearl Broadcasting Tower, 1995, Shanghai, China	468	1,535
4 Menara Telecom Tower, 1996, Kuala Lumpur, Malaysia	421	1,381
5 Tianjin TV and Radio Tower, 1991, Tianjin, China	415	1,362
6 Central Radio and TV Tower, 1994, Beijing, China	405	1,328
7 TV Tower, 1983, Tashkent, Uzbekistan	375	1,230
8 Liberation Tower, 1998, Kuwait City, Kuwait	372	1,220
9 Alma-Ata Tower, 1983, Kazakhstan	370	1,214
10 TV Tower, 1969, Berlin, Germany	365	1,198

TOP 10 ★ TALLEST MASTS

MAST/LOCATION	HEIGHT M	FT
1 KVLY Channel 11 TV Tower (formerly KTHI-TV), Blanchard/Fargo, North Dakota	629	2,063
2 KSLA-TV Mast, Shreveport, Louisiana	579	1,898
3 = WBIR-TV Mast, Knoxville, Tennessee	533	1,749
3 = WTVM & WRBL TV Mast, Columbus, Georgia	533	1,749
5 KFVS-TV Mast, Cape Girardeau, Missouri	511	1,676
6 WPSD-TV Mast, Paducah, Kentucky	499	1,638
7 WGAN-TV Mast, Portland, Maine	493	1,619
8 KWTV-TV Mast, Oklahoma City, Oklahoma	479	1,572
9 BREN Tower, Area 25, Nevada Test Site, Nevada	465	1,530
10 Omega Base Navigational Mast, Gippsland, Victoria, Australia	426	1,400

TOP 10 HIGHEST PUBLIC OBSERVATORIES

BUILDING/LOCATION	OBSERVATORY	YEAR	HEIGHT M	FT
1 CN Tower, Toronto, Canada	Space deck	1975	447	1,465
2 World Trade Center, New York, NY	Rooftop Tower B	1973	415	1,360
3 Sears Tower, Chicago, IL	103rd floor	1974	412	1,353
4 Empire State Building, New York, NY	102nd floor / Outdoor observatory	1931	381 / 320	1,250 / 1,050
5 Ostankino Tower, Moscow, Russia	5th floor turret	1967	360	1,181
6 Oriental Pearl Broadcasting Tower, Shanghai, China	VIP observation level / Public observation level	1995	350 / 263	1,148 / 863
7 Jin Mao Building, Shanghai, China	88th floor	1997	340	1,115
8 John Hancock Center, Chicago, IL	94th floor	1968	314	1,030
9 Sky Central Plaza, Guanghshou, China	90th floor	1996	310	1,016
10 KL Tower, Kuala Lumpur, Malaysia	Revolving restaurant / Public observation level	1995	282 / 276	925 / 907

TALLEST BY FAR
The world's tallest free-standing structure, the CN Tower in Toronto, Canada, attracts almost 2 million visitors a year to its space deck level at 447 m (1,465 ft).

Bridges & Other Structures

TOP 10 ★
LONGEST ROAD TUNNELS

	TUNNEL/YEAR	LOCATION	LENGTH KM	MILES
1	**Laerdal**, 2000	Norway	24.50	15.22
2	**St. Gotthard**, 1980	Switzerland	16.32	10.14
3	**Arlberg**, 1978	Austria	13.98	8.69
4=	**Fréjus**, 1980	France/Italy	12.90	8.02
4=	**Pinglin Highway**, U/C	Taiwan	12.90	8.02
6	**Mont-Blanc**, 1965	France/Italy	11.60	7.21
7	**Gudvangen**, 1992	Norway	11.43	7.08
8	**Folgefonn**, 2001	Norway	11.10	6.90
9	**Kan-Etsu II**, 1991	Japan	11.06	6.87
10	**Kan-Etsu I**, 1986	Japan	10.93	6.79

U/C = under construction

TOP 10 ★
LONGEST CABLE-STAYED BRIDGES

	BRIDGE/YEAR/LOCATION	LENGTH OF MAIN SPAN M	FT
1	**Tatara**, 1999, Onomichi–Imabari, Japan	890	2,920
2	**Pont de Normandie**, 1994, Le Havre, France	856	2,808
3	**Qinghzhou Minjiang**, 1996, Fozhou, China	605	1,985
4	**Yang Pu**, 1993, Shanghai, China	602	1,975
5=	**Meiko–Chuo**, 1997, Nagoya, Japan	590	1,936
5=	**Xu Pu**, 1997, Shanghai, China	590	1,936
7	**Skarnsundet**, 1991, Trondheim Fjord, Norway	530	1,739
8	**Tsurumi Tsubasa**, Yokohama, Japan	510	1,673
9=	**Ikuchi**, 1994, Onomichi–Imabari, Japan	490	1,608
9=	**Öresund**, 2000, Copenhagen–Malmö, Denmark/Sweden)	490	1,608

SHANGHAI SURPRISE

One of the world's longest cable-stayed bridges, Shanghai's Yang Pu was built to ease traffic congestion on the city's busy inner ring road.

TOP 10 ★
LARGEST SPORTS STADIUMS

	STADIUM/LOCATION	CAPACITY
1	**Strahov Stadium**, Prague, Czech Republic	240,000
2	**Maracaña Municipal Stadium**, Rio de Janeiro, Brazil	220,000
3	**Rungnado Stadium**, Pyongyang, South Korea	150,000
4	**National Stadium of Iran**, Azadi, Iran	128,000
5	**Estádio Maghalaes Pinto**, Belo Horizonte, Brazil	125,000
6=	**Estádio Morumbi**, São Paulo, Brazil	120,000
6=	**Estádio da Luz**, Lisbon, Portugal	120,000
6=	**Senayan Main Stadium**, Jakarta, Indonesia	120,000
6=	**Yuba Bharati Krirangan**, Nr. Calcutta, India	120,000
10	**Estádio Castelão**, Fortaleza, Brazil	119,000

These figures represent maximum capacities. In fact, new safety regulations introduced in many countries mean that actual audiences for most events are smaller. The New Orleans Superdome is the largest indoor stadium, with a capacity of 97,365.

THE 10 🍁
BIGGEST SPORTS STADIUMS IN CANADA

	STADIUM/LOCATION	PERMANENT SEATS
1	**Commonwealth Stadium**, Edmonton	60,081
2	**BC Place Stadium**, Vancouver	59,478
3	**Olympic Stadium**, Montreal	56,245 *
4	**SkyDome Stadium**, Toronto	52,595
5	**McMahon Stadium**, Calgary	37,317 #
6	**Labbatt Park Stadium**, Montreal	36,287 +
7	**Winnipeg Stadium**, Winnipeg	29,544 ★
8	**Ivor Wynne Stadium**, Hamilton	28,830
9	**Frank Clair Stadium**, Ottawa	28,826
10	**Taylor Field Stadium**, Regina	27,732 #

* 64,000 with extra floor seats
 # upcoming construction is expected to reduce overall number of seats
+ plus 257 club seats and 66 loges, planned opening in 2002
★ down from 33,551 due to construction
Sources: Canadian Football League, Olympic Stadium, 1999 Audarena Stadium Guide

TOP 10 ★
LONGEST CANTILEVER BRIDGES

BRIDGE/YEAR/LOCATION	LONGEST SPAN M	FT
1 Pont de Québec, 1917, Canada	549	1,800
2 Firth of Forth, 1890, Scotland	521	1,710
3 Minato, 1974, Osako, Japan	510	1,673
4 Commodore John Barry, 1974, New Jersey/Pennsylvania	494	1,622
5 =Greater New Orleans 1, 1958, Louisiana	480	1,575
5 =Greater New Orleans 2, 1988, Louisiana	480	1,575
7 Howrah, 1943, Calcutta, India	457	1,500
8 Gramercy, 1995, Louisiana	445	1,460
9 Transbay, 1936, San Francisco	427	1,400
10 Baton Rouge, 1969, Louisiana	376	1,235

TOP 10 ★
LONGEST UNDERWATER TUNNELS

TUNNEL/YEAR/LOCATION	LENGTH KM	MILES
1 Seikan, 1988, Japan	53.90	33.49
2 Channel Tunnel, 1994, France/England	49.94	31.03
3 Dai–Shimizu, 1982, Japan	22.17	13.78
4 Shin–Kanmon, 1975, Japan	18.68	11.61
5 Great Belt Fixed Link (Eastern Tunnel), 1997, Denmark	8.00	4.97
6 Bømlafjord*, 2000, Norway	7.82	4.86
7 Oslofjord*, 2000, Norway	7.39	4.59
8 Severn, 1886, UK	7.01	4.36
9 Magerøysund*, 1999, Norway	6.87	4.27
10 Haneda, 1971, Japan	5.98	3.72

* Road; others rail

The need to connect the Japanese islands of Honshu, Kyushu, and Hokkaido has resulted in a wave of undersea tunnel building in recent years, with the Seikan the most ambitious project of all. Connecting Honshu and Hokkaido, 23.3 km (14.4 miles) of the tunnel is 100 m (328 ft) below the seabed. It took 24 years to complete.

TOP 10 ★
HIGHEST DAMS

DAM/RIVER/LOCATION	YEAR	HEIGHT M	FT
1 Rogun, Vakhsh, Tajikistan	U/C	335	1,099
2 Nurek, Vakhsh, Tajikistan	1980	300	984
3 Grande Dixence, Dixence, Switzerland	1961	285	935
4 Inguri, Inguri, Georgia	1980	272	892
5 Vajont, Vajont, Italy	1960	262	860
6 =Manuel M. Torres (Chicoasén), Grijalva, Mexico	1980	261	856
6 =Tehri, Bhagirathi, India	U/C	261	856
8 Alvaro Obregon (El Gallinero), Tenasco, Mexico	1946	260	853
9 Mauvoisin, Drance de Bagnes, Switzerland	1957	250	820
10 Alberto Lleras C., Guavio, Colombia	1989	243	797

U/C = under construction

Source: *International Commission on Large Dams (ICOLD)*

TOP 10 ★
LONGEST SUSPENSION BRIDGES

BRIDGE/YEAR/LOCATION	LENGTH OF MAIN SPAN M	FT
1 Akashi–Kaiko, 1998, Kobe–Naruto, Japan	1,990	6,529
2 Great Belt, 1997, Denmark	1,624	5,328
3 Humber Estuary, 1981, UK	1,410	4,626
4 Jiangyin, 1998, China	1,385	4,544
5 Tsing Ma, 1997, Hong Kong, China	1,377	4,518
6 Verrazano Narrows, 1964, New York	1,298	4,260
7 Golden Gate, 1937, San Francisco	1,280	4,200
8 Höga Kusten, 1997, Veda, Sweden	1,210	3,970
9 Mackinac Straits, 1957, Michigan	1,158	3,800
10 Minami Bisan-seto, 1988, Kojima–Sakaide, Japan	1,100	3,609

The Messina Strait Bridge between Sicily and Calabria, Italy, remains a speculative project but, if constructed according to plan, it will have by far the longest center span of any bridge at 3,320 m (10,892 ft). However, at 3,910 m (12,828 ft), Japan's Akashi–Kaiko bridge, completed in 1998 and with a main span of 1,990 m (6,528 ft), is the world's longest overall.

DAM RECORD BUSTER

An incongruous mural depicting Lenin celebrates this Soviet engineering accomplishment, the building of the world's second highest dam, the Nurek in Tajikistan.

Background image: **PONT DE QUÉBEC, CANADA**

What is the longest river in Canada?
see p.20 for the answer
A St. Lawrence
B Fraser
C Mackenzie

93

Culture & Learning

Word Power

TOP 10 ★

LONGEST WORDS IN THE ENGLISH LANGUAGE*

WORD/MEANING   LETTERS

1 Ornicopytheobibliopsychocrystarroscioaerogenethliometeoroaustrohiero-anthropoichthyopyrosiderochpnomyoalectryoophiobotanopegohydrorhab-docrithoaleuroalphitohalomolybdoclerobeloaxinocoscinodactyliogeolitho-pessopsephocatoptrotephraoneirochiroonychodactyloarithstichooxogelo-scogastrogyrocerobletonooenoscapulinaniac   310

Medieval scribes used this word to refer to "A deluded human who practices divination or forecasting by means of phenomena, interpretation of acts, or other manifestations related to the following animate or inanimate objects and appearances: birds, oracles, Bible, ghosts, crystal gazing, shadows, air appearances, birth stars, meteors, winds, sacrificial appearances, entrails of humans and fishes, fire, red-hot irons, altar smoke, mice, grain picking by rooster, snakes, herbs, fountains, water, wands, dough, meal, barley, salt, lead, dice, arrows, hatchet balance, sieve, ring suspension, random dots, precious stones, pebbles, pebble heaps, mirrors, ash writing, dreams, palmistry, nail rays, finger rings, numbers, book passages, name letterings, laughing manners, ventriloquism, circle walking, wax, susceptibility to hidden springs, wine, and shoulder blades."

2 Lopadotemachoselachogaleokranioleipsanodrimhypotrimmatosilphioparao-melitokatakechymenokichlepikossyphophattoperisteralektryonoptekephall-iokigklopeleiolagoiosiraiobaphetraganopterygon   182

The English transliteration of a 170-letter Greek word that appears in The Ecclesiazusae (a comedy by the Greek playwright Aristophanes, c.448–380 BC). It is used as a description of a 17-ingredient dish.

3 Aequeosalinocalcalinosetaceoaluminosocupreovitriolic   52

Invented by a medical writer, Dr. Edward Strother (1675–1737), to describe the spa waters at Bath.

4 Osseocarnisanguineoviscericartilaginonervomedullary   51

Coined by writer and East India Company official Thomas Love Peacock (1785–1866), and used in his satire Headlong Hall (1816) as a description of the structure of the human body.

5 Pneumonoultramicroscopicsilicovolcanoconiosis   45

It first appeared in print (though ending in "-koniosis") in F. Scully's Bedside Manna [sic] (1936), then found its way into Webster's Dictionary and is now in the Oxford English Dictionary. It is said to mean a lung disease caused by breathing fine dust.

6 Hepaticocholecystostcholecystenterostomies   42

Surgical operations to create channels of communication between gall bladders and hepatic ducts or intestines.

7 Praetertranssubstantiationalistically   37

The adverb describing the act of surpassing the act of transubstantiation; the word is found in Mark McShane's novel Untimely Ripped (1963).

8 = Pseudoantidisestablishmentarianism   34

A word meaning "false opposition to the withdrawal of state support from a Church," derived from that perennial favorite long word, antidisestablishmentarianism (a mere 28 letters).

8 = Supercalifragilisticexpialidocious   34

An invented word, but perhaps now eligible since it has appeared in the Oxford English Dictionary. It was popularized by the song of this title in the film Mary Poppins (1964), where it is used to mean "wonderful," but it was originally written in 1949 in an unpublished song by Parker and Young who spelled it "supercalafajalistickespialadojus" (32 letters).

10 = Encephalomyeloradiculoneuritis   30

A syndrome caused by a virus associated with encephalitis.

10 = Hippopotomonstrosesquipedalian   30

Appropriately, the word that means "pertaining to an extremely long word."

10 = Pseudopseudohypoparathyroidism   30

First used (hyphenated) in the US in 1952 and (unhyphenated) in Great Britain in The Lancet in 1962 to describe a medical case in which a patient appeared to have symptoms of pseudohypoparathyroidism, but with "no manifestations suggesting hypoparathyroidism."

* Excluding names of chemical compounds

TOP 10 ★

MOST USED LETTERS IN WRITTEN ENGLISH

SURVEY*		#MORSE
e	1	e
t	2	t
a	3	a
o	4	i
i	5	n
n	6	o
s	7	s
r	8	h
h	9	r
l	10	d

* The order as indicated by a survey across approximately 1 million words appearing in a wide variety of printed texts, ranging from newspapers to novels.

 # The order estimated by Samuel Morse, the inventor in the 1830s of Morse code, based on his calculations of the respective quantities of type used by a printer. The number of letters in the printer's type trays ranged from 12,000 for "e" to 4,400 for "d," with only 200 for "z."

TOP 10 ★

MOST COMMON WORDS IN ENGLISH

SPOKEN ENGLISH		WRITTEN ENGLISH
the	1	the
and	2	of
I	3	to
to	4	in
of	5	and
a	6	a
you	7	for
that	8	was
in	9	is
it	10	that

Various surveys have been conducted to establish the most common words in spoken English of various types, from telephone conversations to broadcast commentaries. Beyond the Top 10, words such as "yes" and "well" appear.

Did You Know? Honorificabilitudinitatibus (27 letters), which means "honorably," is the longest word used by Shakespeare; it appears in *Love's Labour's Lost* (Act V, Scene i).

TOP 10 ★
COUNTRIES WITH THE MOST ENGLISH-LANGUAGE SPEAKERS*

	COUNTRY	APPROXIMATE NO. OF SPEAKERS
1	US	232,910,000
2	UK	57,520,000
3	Canada	18,655,000
4	Australia	15,204,000
5	South Africa	3,900,000
6	Ireland	3,590,000
7	New Zealand	3,309,000
8	Jamaica	2,400,000
9	Trinidad and Tobago	1,199,000
10	Guyana	749,000

Inhabitants for whom English is their mother tongue

The Top 10 represents the countries with the greatest numbers of inhabitants who speak English as their mother tongue. After the 10th entry, the figures dive to around or under 260,000, in the case of the Bahamas, Barbados, and Zimbabwe. In addition to these and others that make up a world total that is probably in excess of 500 million, there are perhaps as many as 1 billion who speak English as a second language: a large proportion of the population of the Philippines, for example, speaks English, and there are many countries, such as India, Nigeria, and other former British colonies in Africa, where English is either an official language or is widely understood.

THE ROSETTA STONE

Made in Egypt in around 200 BC and discovered in 1799 during the French occupation of Egypt, the Rosetta Stone was taken to England in 1801 and is now in the British Museum, London. It has the same inscription in three different alphabets – Egyptian hieroglyphics at the top, demotic Egyptian in the middle, and Greek below. After a painstaking study of the relationship between the different alphabets, French scholar Jean François Champollion (1790–1832) was able to decipher the hieroglyphics, all knowledge of which had previously been lost. The Rosetta Stone thus provided the key to our understanding of this ancient language.

SNAP SHOTS ★

TOP 10 ★
MOST WIDELY SPOKEN LANGUAGES

	LANGUAGE	APPROXIMATE NO. OF SPEAKERS
1	Chinese (Mandarin)	1,075,000,000
2	English	514,000,000
3	Hindustani	496,000,000
4	Spanish	425,000,000
5	Russian	275,000,000
6	Arabic	256,000,000
7	Bengali	215,000,000
8	Portuguese	194,000,000
9	Malay-Indonesian	176,000,000
10	French	129,000,000

According to mid-1999 estimates by Sidney S. Culbert of the University of Washington, Seattle, in addition to those languages appearing in the Top 10, there are three further languages that are spoken by more than 100 million individuals: German (128 million), Japanese (126 million), and Urdu (105 million). A further 13 languages are spoken by 50–100 million: Punjabi (94), Korean (78), Telugu (76), Tamil (74), Marathi (71), Cantonese (71), Wu (70), Vietnamese (67), Javanese (64), Italian (63), Turkish (61), Tagalog (58), and Thai (52).

TOP 10 MOST STUDIED FOREIGN LANGUAGES IN THE US*

❶ Spanish ❷ French ❸ German
❹ Japanese ❺ Italian
❻ Chinese (Mandarin) ❼ Latin
❽ Russian
❾ Ancient Greek ❿ Hebrew

In US institutions of higher education
Source: *Modern Language Association of America*
These rankings are from the most recent survey conducted every five years, from colleges and universities in the fall of 1995.

TOP 10 🍁
FASTEST-GROWING LANGUAGE GROUPS IN CANADA*

	LANGUAGE GROUP	PERCENTAGE INCREASE 1991–96
1	Punjabi	78.2
2	Italian	77.5
3	Chinese	61.0
4	German	60.0
5	Tagalog	59.3
6	Arabic	56.6
7	Spanish	34.2
8	Polish	24.1
9	English	22.7
10	French	20.0

By mother tongue
Source: *Statistics Canada*

Back to School

China has the most children in school and the world's longest school year, but spends just 2 percent of its GNP on education – less than half that of Western countries.

TOP 10 ★
COUNTRIES SPENDING THE MOST ON EDUCATION

COUNTRY	EXPENDITURE AS PERCENTAGE OF GNP*
1 Kiribati	11.4
2 Moldova	9.4
3 Namibia	8.4
4 Botswana	7.8
5 Denmark	7.7
6 South Africa	7.5
7 Barbados	7.3
8 =Finland	7.2
8 =Zimbabwe	7.2
10 Sweden	7.1

* Gross National Product in latest year for which data available

Source: *UNESCO*

A number of other countries rank high in this list, but there are insufficient recent data to include them. In 1980, French Guyana spent 16.5 percent of its GNP on education, Martinique 14.5 percent, and Guadeloupe 13.6 percent. Canada and the US do not make it into the Top 20.

TOP 10 COUNTRIES WITH THE LONGEST SCHOOL YEARS

(Country/school year in days)

1 China, 251　**2** Japan, 243　**3** Korea, 220　**4** Israel, 215　**5** = Germany; = Russia, 210　**7** Switzerland, 207　**8** = Netherlands; = Scotland; = Thailand, 200

Canada, 186

TOP 10 🍁
PROVINCES WITH THE MOST PRIMARY/SECONDARY SCHOOL STUDENTS PER TEACHER

PROVINCE	STUDENTS PER TEACHER 1996–97
1 Nova Scotia	17.6
2 Alberta	17.5
3 =British Columbia	17.4
3 =New Brunswick	17.4
5 Saskatchewan	17.3
6 Prince Edward Island	17.1
7 Ontario	16.7
8 Manitoba	15.9
9 Quebec	14.7
10 Newfoundland	14.4

Source: *Statistics Canada*

TOP 10 🍁
PROVINCES WITH HIGHEST GRADUATION RATES

PROVINCE/TERRITORY	RATIO OF SECONDARY GRADUATES TO POPULATION AT AGE 18*
1 Quebec	86
2 New Brunswick	85
3 Nova Scotia	80
4 Newfoundland	79
5 Prince Edward Island	78
6 Manitoba	76
7 Ontario	75
8 Saskatchewan	74
9 British Columbia	67
10 Alberta	64

* Calculated as the number of graduates (irrespective of age) as a percentage of the total 18-year-old population

"ACADEMY"

Fabled queen Helen of Troy ("the face that launched a thousand ships") was kidnapped from Sparta by Theseus and later rescued by her brothers Castor and Pollux. They were assisted in their task by an Athenian named Academus. A grove or public garden called the Grove of Academus was planted in Athens to commemorate this event. It was here that the Greek philosopher Plato founded his school of philosophy, where like-minded scholars could gather to listen to his orations and discuss moral issues. This school was called the Academia, from which we have the word "academy."

WHY DO WE SAY?

EDUCATING THE MASSES
Indian culture places a high value on education, and consequently some 7 percent of the country's entire population attends secondary school.

TOP 10 ★

COUNTRIES WITH THE MOST SECONDARY SCHOOL STUDENTS

	COUNTRY	SECONDARY SCHOOL STUDENTS
1	China	69,155,538
2	India	68,872,393
3	US	21,473,692
4	Russia	13,732,000
5	Indonesia	12,223,753
6	Japan	9,878,568
7	Iran	8,776,792
8	Germany	8,260,674
9	Mexico	7,589,414
10	Egypt	6,726,738

In the US, about 8 percent of the population attends secondary school – a figure that shows how impressive India's rate of 7 percent is.

Source: *UNESCO*

THE 10 ★

COUNTRIES WITH THE HIGHEST ILLITERACY RATES*

COUNTRY	FEMALE ILLITERACY RATE (%)		MALE ILLITERACY RATE (%)	COUNTRY
Niger	93.4	1	79.1	Niger
Burkina Faso	90.8	2	71.7	Nepal
Guinea-Bissau	85.5	3	70.5	Burkina Faso
Afghanistan	85.0	4	60.6	Mali
Yemen	82.8	5	59.3	Guinea-Bissau
Sierra Leone	81.8	6	57.0	Senegal
= Central African Republic	79.7	7	54.6	Sierra Leone
= Nepal	79.7	8	54.5	Ethiopia
Guinea	78.1	9	52.8	Afghanistan
Liberia	77.6	10	52.0	Central African Republic

* Age over 15; figures estimated where no recent data available   Source: *UNESCO*

The United Nations defines an illiterate person as someone who cannot, with understanding, both read and write a short, simple statement on his or her daily life. Literacy is a good measure of educational achievement in developing regions, because it reflects successful schooling, not just attendance at school as is measured by enrollment figures. The Top 10 list shows that in some countries of the world, the majority of the population cannot read or write.

TOP 10 ★

COUNTRIES WITH THE MOST PRIMARY SCHOOL STUDENTS PER TEACHER

	COUNTRY	PRIMARY SCHOOL STUDENTS PER TEACHER*
1	Central African Republic	77
2	Congo	70
3	Mali	70
4	Chad	67
5	Malawi	59
6	Bangladesh	63
7 =	Afghanistan	58
7 =	Mozambique	58
7 =	Rwanda	58
7 =	Senegal	58

* In latest year for which figures available
Source: *UNESCO*

Who is Canada's richest person or family?
see p.202 for the answer
A Irving Family
B Charles Rosner Bronfman
C Kenneth Roy Thomson

CRÈME DE LA CRÈME
Between the late 1960s and 1970, the University of Paris was split into 13 separate establishments, which comprise the world's largest higher education body.

TOP 10 ★ LARGEST UNIVERSITIES

	UNIVERSITY/LOCATION	STUDENTS
1	University of Paris*, France	311,163
2	University of Calcutta, India	300,000
3	University of Mexico, Mexico	269,000
4	University of Bombay, India	262,350
5	University of Guadalajara, Mexico	214,986
6	University of Rome, Italy	189,000
7	University of Buenos Aires, Argentina	183,397
8	University of Rajasthan, India	175,000
9	University of California, US	157,331
10	Gujarat University, India	153,379

* *Divided into numerous separate centers; the figure is for the combined total of all the centers.*

The huge number of university institutions in India reflects not only the country's massive population and the high value placed on education in Indian culture, but also the inclusion of many "Affiliating and Teaching" colleges attached to universities.

THE 10 ★ COUNTRIES WITH THE LOWEST PERCENTAGE OF FEMALE UNIVERSITY STUDENTS

	COUNTRY	PERCENTAGE OF FEMALE STUDENTS*
1	Equatorial Guinea	4
2 =	Central African Republic	9
2 =	Guinea	9
4	Chad	12
5 =	Eritrea	13
5 =	Yemen	13
7	Mali	14
8	Mauritania	15
9	Cambodia	16
10 =	Ethiopia	17
10 =	Tanzania	17
10 =	Togo	17

* *In latest year for which data available*
Source: *UNESCO*

WOMAN'S WORK
Women study separately but in large numbers at the United Arab Emirates University in Al-Ain, which was founded in 1976.

TOP 10 ★ COUNTRIES WITH THE HIGHEST PERCENTAGE OF FEMALE UNIVERSITY STUDENTS

	COUNTRY	PERCENTAGE OF FEMALE STUDENTS*
1	Cyprus	75
2	US Virgin Islands	74
3	Qatar	73
4	United Arab Emirates	72
5	Kuwait	66
6	Namibia	65
7	Myanmar	64
8	Barbados	62
9	Mongolia	61
10 =	Bulgaria	60
10 =	Cuba	60
10 =	Panama	60

* *In latest year for which data available*
Source: *UNESCO*

TOP 10
COUNTRIES OF ORIGIN FOR STUDENTS STUDYING IN CANADA

	COUNTRY	NO. OF STUDENTS WITH VALID STUDENT VISAS*
1	Republic of Korea	11,264
2	US	11,125
3	Japan	10,215
4	China	7,768
5	Hong Kong	6,751#
6	France	5,908
7	Taiwan	5,870
8	Yugoslavia	3,402
9	Mexico	3,379
10	Germany	2,096

* As of December 1, 1999
\# Includes student visas granted to students prior to the Chinese takeover in 1997
Source: *Citizenship and Immigration Canada*

TOP 10
COUNTRIES WITH THE MOST UNIVERSITY STUDENTS

	COUNTRY	PERCENTAGE FEMALE	UNIVERSITY STUDENTS*
1	US	53	8,529,132
2	India	32	4,425,247
3	China	36	3,170,936
4	Russia	53	2,587,510
5	Japan	29	2,311,618
6	Philippines	57	2,017,972
7	Indonesia	31	1,889,408
8	Germany	42	1,857,906
9	Brazil	53	1,716,263
10	Korea	32	1,556,949

* In latest year for which data available
Source: *UNESCO*

GRADUATION DAY

Decked in their traditional tasseled mortar boards and gowns, more students graduate from US universities than from those of any other country.

TOP 10
MOST EXPENSIVE UNIVERSITIES IN CANADA

	INSTITUTION	TUITION FEES ($)*
1	Trinity Western University, B.C.	9,540
2	Redeemer College, Ont.	8,600
3	The King's University College, Alta.	5,208
4	Augustana University College, Alta.	4,695
5	University College of Concordia, Alta.	4,470
6	Acadia University,# N.S.	4,250
7	Mount Allison University, N.B.	4,220
8	St. Francis Xavier University, N.S.	4,160
9 =	University of King's College,# N.S.	4,050
9 =	Dalhousie University, N.S.	4,050

* For 1999/2000, Arts Faculty
\# A range of lower and upper fees was reported; the lower range was used
Source: *Statistics Canada Survey*

TOP 10
COUNTRIES WITH THE HIGHEST PROPORTION OF ADULTS IN HIGHER EDUCATION

	COUNTRY	TOTAL ADULT STUDENTS	ADULT STUDENTS PER 100,000*
1	Canada	1,763,105	5,997
2	Korea	2,541,659	5,609
3	Australia	1,002,476	5,552
4	US	14,261,778	5,339
5	New Zealand	162,350	4,508
6	Finland	213,995	4,190
7	Norway	180,383	4,164
8	Spain	1,591,863	4,017
9	Ireland	47,955	3,618
10	France	2,091,688	3,600

* In latest year for which data available
Source: *UNESCO*

What was the first single to debut at No. 1 in Canada?
see p.124 for the answer

A Shania Twain's *God Bless the Child*
B Band Aid's *Do They Know It's Christmas*
C U2's *Discotheque*

Book Firsts & Records

TOP 10 MOST CITED AUTHORS OF ALL TIME

(Author/country/dates)

1 William Shakespeare, UK, 1564–1616 **2** Charles Dickens, UK, 1812–70

3 Sir Walter Scott, UK, 1771–1832 **4** Johann Goethe, Germany, 1749–1832

5 Aristotle, Greece, 384–322 BC **6** Alexandre Dumas (père), France, 1802–70

7 Robert Louis Stevenson, UK, 1850–94 **8** Mark Twain, US, 1835–1910

9 Marcus Tullius Cicero, Italy, 106–43 BC **10** Honoré de Balzac, France, 1799–1850

This Top 10 is based on a search of a major US library computer database, Citations, which includes books both by and about the author, with a total of more than 15,000 for Shakespeare.

TOP 10 ★
LARGEST LIBRARIES

	LIBRARY	LOCATION	FOUNDED	BOOKS
1	Library of Congress	Washington, DC	1800	23,994,965
2	National Library of China	Beijing, China	1909	20,000,000
3	National Library of Canada	Ottawa, Canada	1953	16,000,000
4	Deutsche Bibliothek*	Frankfurt, Germany	1990	15,997,000
5	British Library#	London, UK	1753	15,000,000
6	Harvard University Library	Cambridge, Massachusetts	1638	13,617,133
7	Vernadsky Central Scientific Library of the National Academy of Sciences	Kiev, Ukraine	1919	13,000,000
8	Russian State Library+	Moscow, Russia	1862	11,750,000
9	New York Public Library★	New York	1895	11,445,971
10	Bibliotheque Nationale de Paris	Paris, France	1400	11,000,000

* *Formed in 1990 through the unification of the Deutsche Bibliothek, Frankfurt (founded 1947) and the Deutsche Bucherei, Leipzig*

\# *Founded as part of the British Museum, 1753; became an independent body in 1973*

\+ *Founded 1862 as Rumyantsev Library, formerly State V.I. Lenin Library*

★ *Astor Library founded 1848, consolidated with Lenox Library and Tilden Trust to form New York Public Library in 1895*

The figures for books in such vast collections as held by the libraries listed above represent only a fraction of the total collections, which include manuscripts, microfilms, maps, prints, and records. The Library of Congress has perhaps more than 100 million cataloged items and the New York Public Library more than 26 million manuscripts, maps, audio-visual, and other cataloged items in addition to books.

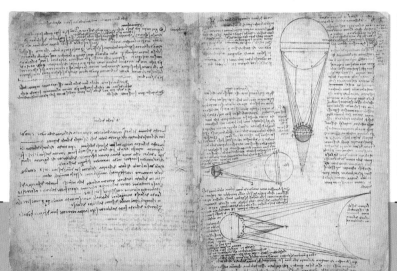

UNDER THE HAMMER

The Codex Hammer, *a collection of Leonardo da Vinci's scientific writings, was compiled in the early 16th century. It has over 350 drawings that illustrate the artist's scientific theories. In 1994 it achieved a record price at auction when bought by Bill Gates.*

TOP 10 ★
MOST EXPENSIVE BOOKS AND MANUSCRIPTS EVER SOLD AT AUCTION

BOOK OR MANUSCRIPT/SALE	PRICE (US$)*

1 *The Codex Hammer*, c.1508–10, Christie's, New York, Nov 11, 1994 — 30,800,000
This Leonardo da Vinci notebook was bought by Bill Gates, the billionaire founder of Microsoft.

2 *The Gospels of Henry the Lion*, c.1173–75, Sotheby's, London, Dec 6, 1983 — 10,846,000
At the time of its sale, this became the most expensive manuscript or book ever sold.

3 *The Birds of America*, John James Audubon, 1827–38, Christie's, New York, Mar 10, 2000 — 8,000,000
This holds the record for any natural history book.

4 *The Canterbury Tales*, Geoffrey Chaucer, c.1476–77, Christie's, London, Jul 8, 1998 — 7,406,000
This is the world's most expensive book.

5 *The Gutenberg Bible*, 1455, Christie's, New York, Oct 22, 1987 — 5,390,000
This is one of the first books ever printed, by Johann Gutenberg and Johann Fust in 1455.

6 *The Northumberland Bestiary*, c.1250–60, Sotheby's, London, Nov 29, 1990 — 5,049,000
This holds the record for an English manuscript.

7 *The Burdett Psalter and Hours*, 1282–86, Sotheby's, London, Jun 23, 1998 — 4,183,000
This is the third most expensive illustrated manuscript ever sold.

8 Autograph manuscript of nine symphonies by **Wolfgang Amadeus Mozart**, c.1773–74, Sotheby's, London, May 22, 1987 — 3,854,500
This holds the record for any music manuscript.

9 *The Birds of America*, John James Audubon, 1827–38, Sotheby's, New York, Jun 6, 1989 — 3,600,000
Resold 11 years later. See No. 3.

10 *The Hours of Saint-Lô*, 1470, Sotheby's, New York, Apr 21, 1998 — 3,300,000

* *Excluding premiums*

TOP 10 🍁
LARGEST PUBLIC CITY LIBRARIES IN CANADA

	LIBRARY/LOCATION	HOLDINGS (1998)*
1	**Toronto Public Library**, Ontario	12,083,075#
2	**Bibliothèque municipale de Montréal**, Quebec	2,708,681
3	**Vancouver Public Library**, British Columbia	2,252,040
4	**Calgary Public Library**, Alberta	2,078,838
5	**Mississauga Library System**, Ontario	1,675,443
6	**Winnipeg Public Library**, Manitoba	1,623,128
7	**Edmonton Public Library**, Alberta	1,541,737
8	**Halifax Regional Library**, Nova Scotia	1,203,481
9	**Hamilton Public Library**, Ontario	1,140,554
10	**Ottawa Public Library**, Ontario	1,103,057

* In addition to books, holdings include other printed material (magazines, newspapers, manuscripts), as well as audiovisual material (CDs, cassettes, videos) and miscellaneous items (games, toys, maps). Books represent the majority of total holdings

The huge holdings of the Toronto Public Library reflect the amalgamation of six Toronto municipalities – North York, Scarborough, East York, York, Etobicoke, and Toronto – in 1998. The merger of the libraries has resulted in the largest library system in Canada and the largest public library in North America

Source: *Council of Administrators of Large Urban Public Libraries*

"BLURB"

American humorist Frank Gelett Burgess (1866–1951), best known as the author of the nonsense poem *I Never Saw a Purple Cow*, was also the inventor of the word "blurb" – the effusive text used on book jackets to describe the book within. In his book *Are You a Bromide?*, Burgess claimed that its author was Miss Belinda Blurb, whose work was said to be the sensation of the year.

WHY DO WE SAY ?

BEST RED AUTHOR

During the Cultural Revolution, Chinese leader Mao Tse-tung (Zedong) became the subject of a personality cult, with his bestselling Quotations ... *(Little Red Book) its most potent symbol.*

THE 10 🍁
FIRST BOOKS PUBLISHED IN CANADA

	BOOK	YEAR
1	**Catholic Church Catechism** (French)	1765
2	**Quebec Primer** (French Alphabet)	1765
3	**Quebec Primer** (Latin Alphabet)	1766
4	**A devotional book in the Mohawk language by Jean Baptiste de la Brosse** (a Jesuit missionary)	1767
5	*Nova Scotia Almanac**	1769
6	*The Universal Prayer* (a prayer book and remarks) by William Doyle	1770
7	**Catholic Church Liturgy and Ritual** (French)	1772
8	*The Gospel of Christ Preached to the Poor* by Peter Delaroche, Missionary	1773
9	**Catholic Church Psalter** (French)	1773
10	**A three-volume treatise on the French laws of Quebec** by François Joseph Cugnet	1775

* Reprinted in 1772, 1773, and 1775. The 1775 edition of this almanac was apparently the first Canadian printed book with illustration

Source: *Bibliography of Canadian Imprints 1751–1800*

TOP 10 ★
BESTSELLING BOOKS OF ALL TIME

	BOOK/AUTHOR	FIRST PUBLISHED	APPROX. SALES
1	The Bible	c.1451–55	over 6,000,000,000
2	*Quotations from the Works of Mao Tse-tung* (dubbed *Little Red Book* by the Western press)	1966	900,000,000
3	*American Spelling Book* by Noah Webster	1783	up to 100,000,000
4	*The Guinness Book of Records*	1955	over 85,000,000*
5	World Almanac	1868	73,500,000*
6	*The McGuffey Readers* by William Holmes McGuffey	1836	60,000,000
7	*The Common Sense Book of Baby and Child Care* by Benjamin Spock	1946	over 50,000,000
8	*A Message to Garcia* by Elbert Hubbard	1899	up to 40,000,000
9=	*In His Steps: "What Would Jesus Do?"* by Rev. Charles Monroe Sheldon	1896	over 30,000,000
9=	*Valley of the Dolls* by Jacqueline Susann	1966	over 30,000,000

* Aggregate sales of annual publication

Which province has the most overweight people in Canada?
see p.56 for the answer

A Quebec
B New Brunswick
C Newfoundland

Bestsellers & Literary Awards

TOP 10 ★
CANADIAN FICTION BESTSELLERS OF 1999

	BOOK	AUTHOR*
1	Pilgrim	Timothy Findley
2	A Good House	Bonnie Burnard
3	No Great Mischief	Alistair MacLeod
4	Home from the Vinyl Cafe – A Year of Stories	Stuart McLean
5	The Love of a Good Woman	Alice Munro
6	Elizabeth and After	Matt Cohen
7	Summer Gone	David Macfarlane
8	A Recipe for Bees	Gail Anderson-Dargatz
9	The White Bone	Barbara Gowdy
10	Hitler Versus Me	Donald Jack

* Canadian authors only

Source: *Chapters*

THE WRITE STUFF

Michael Cunningham made his debut as a novelist in 1990 and rounded off the decade in 1999 by winning the Pulitzer Prize for Fiction.

THE 10 ★
LATEST WINNERS OF THE HUGO AWARDS FOR BEST SCIENCE FICTION NOVEL

YEAR	AUTHOR/TITLE
1999	Connie Willis, *To Say Nothing of the Dog*
1998	Joe Haldeman, *Forever Peace*
1997	Kim Stanley Robinson, *Blue Mars*
1996	Neal Stephenson, *The Diamond Age*
1995	Lois McMaster Bujold, *Mirror Dance*
1994	Kim Stanley Robinson, *Green Mars*
1993	Vernor Vinge, *A Fire Upon the Deep*
1992	Connie Willis, *Doomsday Book*
1991	Lois McMaster Bujold, *Barrayar*
1990	Lois McMaster Bujold, *The Vor Game*

Hugo Awards for science fiction novels, short stories, and other fiction and non-fiction works are presented by the World Science Fiction Society. They were established in 1953 as "Science Fiction Achievement Awards for the best science fiction writing." The prize in the Awards' inaugural year was presented to Alfred Bester for *The Demolished Man*.

THE 10 ★
LATEST WINNERS OF THE PULITZER PRIZE FOR FICTION

YEAR	AUTHOR/TITLE
1999	Michael Cunningham, *The Hours*
1998	Philip Roth, *American Pastoral*
1997	Steven Millhauser, *Martin Dressler: The Tale of an American Dreamer*
1996	Richard Ford, *Independence Day*
1995	Carol Shields, *The Stone Diaries*
1994	E. Annie Proulx, *The Shipping News*
1993	Robert Olen Butler, *A Good Scent from a Strange Mountain: Stories*
1992	Jane Smiley, *A Thousand Acres*
1991	John Updike, *Rabbit at Rest*
1990	Oscar Hijuelos, *The Mambo Kings Play Songs of Love*

THE 10 ★
LATEST WINNERS OF THE RANDOLPH CALDECOTT MEDAL

YEAR	AUTHOR/TITLE
2000	Simms Taback, *Joseph Had a Little Overcoat*
1999	Jacqueline Briggs Martin, *Snowflake Bentley*
1998	Paul O. Zelinsky, *Rapunzel*
1997	David Wisniewski, *Golem*
1996	Peggy Rathman, *Officer Buckle and Gloria*
1995	Eve Bunting, *Smoky Night*
1994	Allen Say, *Grandfather's Journey*
1993	Emily Arnold McCully, *Mirette on the High Wire*
1992	David Wiesner, *Tuesday*
1991	David Macauley, *Black and White*

THE 10 ★
LATEST WINNERS OF THE WHITBREAD "BOOK OF THE YEAR" AWARD

YEAR	AUTHOR/TITLE
1999	Seamus Heaney, *Beowulf*
1998	Ted Hughes, *Birthday Letters*
1997	Ted Hughes, *Tales from Ovid*
1996	Seamus Heaney, *The Spirit Level*
1995	Kate Atkinson, *Behind the Scenes at the Museum*
1994	William Trevor, *Felicia's Journey*
1993	Joan Brady, *Theory of War*
1992	Jeff Torrington, *Swing Hammer Swing!*
1991	John Richardson, *A Life of Picasso*
1990	Nicholas Mosley, *Hopeful Monsters*

Winning his second Whitbread Award, in 1999 for his translation of the Anglo Saxon poem *Beowulf*, Seamus Heaney controversially only narrowly defeated J. K. Rowling, whose *Harry Potter and the Prisoner of Azkaban* went on to win the "Children's Book of the Year" Award.

Did You Know? Before being filmed, *Gone with the Wind* was the bestselling US novel of both 1936 and 1937, in the latter year winning the Pulitzer prize for Fiction.

TOP 10 ★
CHILDREN'S BOOKS OF 1999 IN THE US

	TITLE	SALES
1	Harry Potter and the Prisoner of Azkaban	3,600,000
2	Harry Potter and the Chamber of Secrets	3,400,000
3	Harry Potter and the Sorcerer's Stone	3,100,000
4	Love You Forever	559,865
5	Goodnight Moon	515,877
6	The Cheerios Play Book	488,962
7	Green Eggs and Ham	452,504
8	Scholastic Children's Dictionary	444,000
9	Disney's Tarzan Read-Aloud Storybook	428,902
10	Guess How Much I Love You	420,936

Source: Publishers Weekly

TOP 10 🍁
CANADIAN NON-FICTION BESTSELLERS OF 1999

	BOOK*	AUTHOR
1	Crazy Plates	Janet and Greta Podleski
2	Ontario Driver's Handbook	Ontario Ministry of Transportation
3	Heart Smart Cooking for Family & Friends	Bonnie Stern
4	Lemon-Aid Used Cars 2000	Phil Edmonston
5	The Wealthy Barber: Special Gold Edition	David Chilton
6	Looneyspoons	Janet and Greta Podleski
7	Oxford Dictionary of Current English	Della Thompson
8	The Canadian Encyclopedia: Year 2000 Edition	James Marsh
9	Have You Made Your Will?	Self Counsel
10	Gordon Pape's 2000 Buyer's Guide to Mutual Funds	Gordon Pape

* Canadian titles only
Source: Chapters

THE 10 LATEST WINNERS OF THE BOOKER PRIZE
(Year/author/title)

1 1999 J. M. Coetzee, *Disgrace*
2 1998 Ian McEwan, *Amsterdam*
3 1997 Arundhati Roy, *The God of Small Things* 4 1996 Graham Swift, *Last Orders* 5 1995 Pat Barker, *The Ghost Road* 6 1994 James Kelman, *How Late It Was, How Late* 7 1993 Roddy Doyle, *Paddy Clarke Ha Ha Ha*
8 1992 = Michael Ondaatje, *The English Patient;* = Barry Unsworth, *Sacred Hunger* 10 1991 Ben Okri, *Famished Road*

The South African writer J. M. Coetzee is the only person to have won the Booker prize twice (*Life and Times of Michael K* in 1983).

FIRST THINGS FIRST
Bengal-born Arundhati Roy achieved fame and fortune with her Booker prize-winning The God of Small Things.

THE 10 🍁
LATEST WINNERS OF THE GOVERNOR GENERAL'S AWARD FOR FICTION

ENGLISH AUTHOR/BOOK	YEAR	FRENCH BOOK/AUTHOR
Matt Cohen, *Elizabeth and After*	1999	*La Danse juive*, **Lise Tremblay**
Diane Schoemperlen, *Forms of Devotion*	1998	*La Terre ferme*, **Christiane Frenette**
Jane Urquhart, *The Underpainter*	1997	*Cet imperceptible mouvement*, **Aude**
Guy Vanderhaeghe, *The Englishman's Boy*	1996	*Soifs*, **Marie-Claire Blais**
Greg Hollingshead, *The Roaring Girl*	1995	*Les Oiseaux de Saint-John Perse*, **Nicole Houde**
Rudy Wiebe, *A Discovery of Strangers*	1994	*Le Petit Aigle à tête blanche*, **Robert Lalonde**
Carol Shields, *The Stone Diaries*	1993	*Cantique des plaines*, **Nancy Huston**
Michael Ondaatje, *The English Patient*	1992	*L'enfant chargé de songes Andromède attendra*, **Anne Hébert**
Rohinton Mistry, *Such a Long Journey*	1991	*La Croix du Nord*, **André Brochu**
Nino Ricci, *Lives of the Saints*	1990	*La Mauvaise Foi*, **Gérald Tougas**

Source: Canadian Press

Canada's foremost literary prize, the Governor General's Award for Fiction is one of several awards, including non-fiction, poetry, and drama (children's literature was added as a category in 1987), first established in 1937. The first winner was Bertram Brooker, for his 1936 novel *Think of the Earth*.

The Press

TOP 10 LONGEST-RUNNING COMIC STRIPS IN THE US

(Comic strip/first published)

1 *Gasoline Alley*, 1918 **2** *Winnie Winkle*, 1920 **3** *Tarzan*, 1929 **4** *Blondie*, 1930 **5** *Dick Tracy*, 1931 **6** *Alley Oop*, 1933 **7** *L'il Abner*, 1934 **8** *The Phantom*, 1936 **9** *Prince Valliant*, 1937 **10** *Nancy*, 1938

TOP 10 ★ LONGEST-RUNNING MAGAZINES IN THE US

	MAGAZINE	FIRST PUBLISHED
1	*Scientific American*	1845
2	*Town & Country*	1846
3	*Harper's**	1850
4	*The Moravian*	1856
5	*The Atlantic*#	1857
6	*Armed Forces Journal*+	1863
7	*The Nation*	1865
8	*American Naturalist*	1867
9	*Harper's Bazaar*	1867
10	*Animals*★	1868

* Originally Harper's New Monthly Magazine

Originally The Atlantic Monthly

+ Originally Army and Navy Journal

★ Originally Our Dumb Animals

Source: *Magazine Publishers of America*

TOP 10 🍁 MAGAZINES IN CANADA

	MAGAZINE	CIRCULATION*
1	*Reader's Digest* (Canada)	1,012,346
2	*Chatelaine* (English edition)	763,778
3	*TV Guide*	630,739
4	*Canadian Living*	551,884
5	*Maclean's*	503,369
6	*Sélection du Reader's Digest*	226,533
7	*Canadian Geographic*	205,488
8	*Style at Home*	201,616
9	*TV Hebdo*	200,672
10	*Chatelaine* (French edition)	183,114

* Average paid circulation per issue for six months ending December 31, 1999

Source: *Audit Bureau of Circulations*

TOP 10 MAGAZINES IN THE US

(Magazine/no. of issues a year/circulation*)

1 NRTA/AARP Bulletin (10), 20,444,791 **2** Modern Maturity (36), 20,369,590 **3** Reader's Digest (12), 13,368,327 **4** TV Guide (52), 11,807,043 **5** National Geographic (12), 8,618,632 **6** Better Homes and Gardens (12), 7,600,667 **7** Family Circle (17), 5,002,255 **8** Good Housekeeping (12), 4,626,346 **9** Ladies Home Journal (12), 4,500,404 **10** McCall's (17), 4,202,995

* Average for first six months of 1999
Source: *Magazine Publishers of America*

"TABLOID"

The British drug company Burroughs, Wellcome & Co. registered "tabloid" as a trade name on March 14, 1884. Derived from the word "tablet," it was applied to concentrated types of drugs marketed by the firm. By the end of the 19th century, "tabloid" was used to describe anything compressed and small. The phrase "tabloid journalism," which described the content of small-format newspapers, soon became so established in the language that the company could no longer claim the word as their trademark. **WHY DO WE SAY ?**

TOP 10 ★ DAILY NEWSPAPERS IN THE US

	NEWSPAPER	AVERAGE DAILY CIRCULATION*
1	*Wall Street Journal*	1,752,693
2	*USA Today*	1,671,539
3	*New York Times*	1,086,293
4	*Los Angeles Times*	1,078,186
5	*Washington Post*	763,305
6	*New York Daily News*	701,831
7	*Chicago Tribune*	657,690
8	*Long Island Newsday*	574,941
9	*Houston Chronicle*	542,414
10	*Dallas Morning News*	490,249

* Through September 30, 1999

Source: *Audit Bureau of Circulations*

Apart from the *Wall Street Journal*, which focuses mainly on financial news, *USA Today* remains the United States' only true national daily newspaper. Historically, America's press has been regionally based, and, in consequence, the top four listed are the only newspapers with million-plus circulations. This contrasts with, for example, the UK, where, despite its comparatively small population, nationwide newspapers dominate the market, five of them achieving sales in excess of 1 million.

SNAP HAPPY

Despite the growth of television, newspaper photographers continue to provide images to feed the insatiable demands of the world's press, often going to extraordinarily intrusive lengths to gain their shots.

Launched in 1964 as a revamped Daily Herald, *British tabloid* The Sun *has become the world's bestselling English-language daily newspaper.*

THE 10 🍁
OLDEST CANADIAN MAGAZINES STILL PUBLISHING*

	NAME	FIRST YEAR PUBLISHED
1	The United Church Observer #	1829
2 =	The Canadian Entomologist	1868
2 =	Canadian Pharmaceutical Journal	1868
4 =	Canadian Mining Journal	1879
4 =	The Watchtower	1879
6	Canadian Forest Industries	1880
7	Canadian Textile Journal	1883
8	Canadian Grocer	1886
9	Saturday Night+	1887
10	Hardware Merchandising	1888

* *Magazines with no initial publication dates excluded*

Originally The New Outlook; *then* The Christian Guardian

+ *Originally* Toronto Saturday Night, *1887–1889*

Source: *Canadian Serials Index*

The 1999 *Canadian Encyclopedia* states the oldest magazine in Canada was *The Nova Scotia Magazine and Comprehensive Review of Literature, Politics, and News*, which ran for three years starting in 1789.

TOP 10 NEWSPAPER-READING COUNTRIES

(Country/daily newspapers per 1,000 people)

1 Norway, 593   **2** Japan, 580
3 Finland, 455   **4** Sweden, 446
5 South Korea, 394   **6** Kuwait, 376
7 UK, 332   **8** Switzerland, 330
9 Singapore, 324   **10** Denmark, 311

Source: *World Bank*

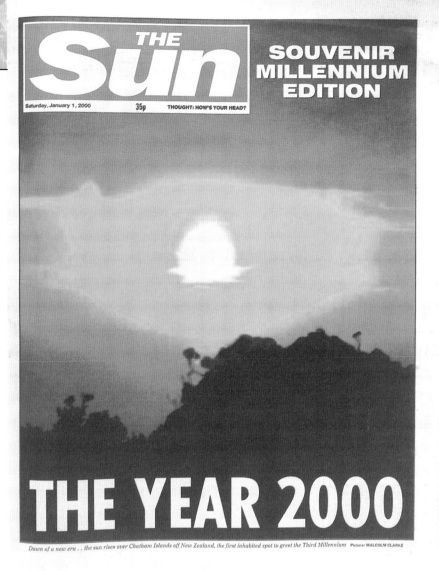

Dawn of a new era . . the sun rises over Chatham Islands off New Zealand, the first inhabited spot to greet the Third Millennium   Picture: MALCOLM CLARKE

TOP 10 🍁
DAILY NEWSPAPERS IN CANADA, 1999

	NEWSPAPER	COPIES SOLD WEEKLY
1	The Toronto Star	3,415,235
2	The Globe and Mail	1,984,083
3	Le Journal de Montréal	1,970,462
4	The Toronto Sun	1,824,755
5	The National Post	1,658,120
6	La Presse, Montreal	1,360,995
7	The Vancouver Sun	1,231,154
8	The Gazette, Montreal	1,052,178
9	The Edmonton Journal	1,032,809
10	Ottawa Citizen	1,012,934

Source: *Canadian Newspaper Association*

TOP 10 ⭐
DAILY NEWSPAPERS

	NEWSPAPER	COUNTRY	AVERAGE DAILY CIRCULATION
1	Yomiuri Shimbun	Japan	14,533,000
2	Asahi Shimbun	Japan	12,601,000
3	Mainichi Shimbun	Japan	5,846,000
4	Chunichi Shimbun	Japan	4,704,000
5	Bild-Zeitung	Germany	4,409,000
6	The Sun	UK	3,592,000
7	Daily Mail	UK	2,300,000
8	The Mirror	UK	2,290,000
9	Wall Street Journal	US	1,740,000
10	USA Today	US	1,653,000

Source: *World Association of Newspapers*

What was Canada's population in 1901?
see p.8 for the answer

A Over 5 million
B Over 7 million
C Over 8 million

Toys & Games

TOP 10 TOYS OF 1999 IN THE US*

1. Furbys 2. Hot Wheels basic cars 3. Star Wars Episode 1 Figure #1 4. Barbie Millennium 5. Pokémon booster packs 6. Furby Babies 7. Barbie Sun Jammer 4x4 8. Pokémon deck assistant 9. Sesame Street rock 'n' roll assistant 10. Pokémon Fossil booster packs

By value of sales
Source: *Toy Manufacturers of America, Inc.*

TOP 10 ★ BOARD GAMES IN THE US, 1999

	GAME	MANUFACTURER
1	Pokémon Monopoly	Parker Brothers
2	Monopoly	Parker Brothers
3	Trouble	Milton Bradley
4	Pokémon Master Trainer	Milton Bradley
5	Operation	Milton Bradley
6	Connect Four	Milton Bradley
7	Twister	Milton Bradley
8	Disney Wonderful World of Trivia	Mattel
9	Standard Scrabble	Milton Bradley
10	The Game of Life	Milton Bradley

Source: *NPD TRSTS Toys Tracking Service*

TOP 10 INTERACTIVE ENTERTAINMENT SOFTWARE TITLES IN THE US, 1999*

(Game/format)

1. Pokémon Blue, Gameboy# 2. Pokémon Red, Gameboy# 3. Pokémon Yellow, Gameboy# 4. Pokémon Pinball, Gameboy# 5. Pokémon Snap, Nintendo 64# 6. Donkey Kong 64, Nintendo 64# 7. Gran Turismo Racing, Sony PlayStation+ 8. Super Smash Brothers, Nintendo 64# 9. Driver, Sony PlayStation+ 10. Spyro the Dragon, Sony PlayStation+

*Ranked by units sold   # Published by Nintendo
+ Published by Sony*
Source: *NPD TRSTS Toys Tracking Service*

TOP 10 ★ TOYS INTRODUCED IN THE US IN 1999

	TOY	MANUFACTURER
1	Star Wars Episode 1 Figure #1	Hasbro
2	Barbie Millennium	Mattel
3	Pokémon booster packs	Wizards of the Coast
4	Furby Babies	Tiger Electronics
5	Sesame Street rock 'n' roll assistant	Tyco Preschool
6	Pokémon Fossil booster packs	Wizards of the Coast
7	Disney Walk 'n' Wag Pluto	Mattel
8	Star Wars Episode 1 Figure #2	Hasbro
9	Kawasaki New Ninja	Fisher-Price
10	Harley Davidson motorcycle	Fisher-Price

Source: *Toy Manufacturers of America, Inc.*

TOP 10 ★ MOST LANDED-ON SQUARES IN MONOPOLY®*

US GAME		UK GAME
Illinois Avenue	1	Trafalgar Square
Go	2	Go
B. & O. Railroad	3	Fenchurch Street Station
Free Parking	4	Free Parking
Tennessee Avenue	5	Marlborough Street
New York Avenue	6	Vine Street
Reading Railroad	7	King's Cross Station
St. James Place	8	Bow Street
Water Works	9	Water Works
Pennsylvania Railroad	10	Marylebone Station

Based on a computer analysis of the probability of landing on each square

Monopoly® is a registered trademark of Parker Brothers division of Tonka Corporation, US.

TOP 10 ★ HIGHEST-SCORING SCRABBLE® WORDS

WORD/PLAY	SCORE
1 QUARTZY	164/162

(i) Play across a triple-word-score (red) square with the Z on a double-letter-score (light blue) square
(ii) Play across two double-word-score (pink) squares with Q and Y on pink squares

2 =BEZIQUE	161/158

(i) Play across a red square with either the Z or the Q on a light blue square
(ii) Play across two pink squares with the B and second E on two pink squares

2 =CAZIQUE	161/158

(i) Play across a red square with either the Z or the Q on a light blue square
(ii) Play across two pink squares with the C and E on two pink squares

4 ZINKIFY	158

Play across a red square with the Z on a light blue square

5 =QUETZAL	155

Play across a red square with either the Q or the Z on a light blue square

5 =JAZZILY	155

(Using a blank as one of the Zs) Play across a red square with the non-blank Z on a light blue square

5 =QUIZZED	155

(Using a blank as one of the Zs) Play across a red square with the non-blank Z or the Q on a light blue square

8 =ZEPHYRS	152

Play across a red square with the Z on a light blue square

8 =ZINCIFY	152

Play across a red square with the Z on a light blue square

8 =ZYTHUMS	152

Play across a red square with the Z on a light blue square

All the Top 10 words contain seven letters and therefore earn the premium of 50 for using all the letters in the rack. Being able to play them depends on there already being suitable words on the board to which they can be added. In an actual game, the face values of the perpendicular words to which they are joined would also be counted, but these are discounted here as the total score variations would be infinite. Scrabble was invented in the US during the Depression by an unemployed architect, Alfred Butts, and developed in the 1940s by James Brunot.

TOP 10 ★
MOST EXPENSIVE TOYS EVER SOLD AT AUCTION BY CHRISTIE'S EAST, NY

TOY/SALE	PRICE (US$)*
1 "The Charles," a fire-hose reel made by American manufacturer George Brown and Co., c.1875, Dec 1991	231,000
2 Märklin fire station, Dec 1991	79,200
3 Horse-drawn double-decker tram, Dec 1991	71,500
4 Mikado mechanical bank, Dec 1993	63,000
5 Märklin Ferris wheel, Jun 1994	55,200
6 Girl skipping rope mechanical bank, Jun 1994	48,300
7 Märklin battleship, Jun 1994	33,350
8 Märklin battleship, Jun 1994	32,200
9 = Bing keywind open phaeton tinplate automobile, Dec 1992	24,200
9 = Märklin fire pumper, Dec 1991	24,200

* Including 10 percent buyer's premium

Source: Christie's East

The fire-hose reel at #1 in this list is the record price paid at auction for a toy other than a doll. Models by the German tinplate maker Märklin, regarded by collectors as the Rolls-Royce of toys, similarly feature among the record prices of auction houses in the UK and other countries, where high prices have also been attained. On both sides of the Atlantic, pristine examples of high-quality mechanical toys (ideally in their original boxes, and unplayed with by the children for whom they were designed) command top dollar prices.

TOP 10 🍁
CHILDREN'S CHOICE TOYS FOR 1999

TOY/MANUFACTURER	AGES
1 **Dog Dice**, Gamewright	3–5
A bingo-style board game for two to four players.	
2 **I Dig the Past: Dig & Grow Ancient Pet Triops**, Earth Lore	6+
A digging kit where budding paleontologists can hatch and grow dinosaur eggs.	
3 **I Spy Spooky Mansion CD-ROM**, Scholastic	5+
An interactive computer puzzle game adapted from the I Spy books.	
4 **Lego Star Wars Series**, Lego	5+
Various model sets based on the hit movie The Phantom Menace.	
5 **Les Bebes–Nourrisson Love**, Corolle	3+
A lifelike 42 cm (17 in) soft doll that was a huge hit with nurturing children.	
6 **My Life According to Me**, Klutz	8+
A compact, humorous, spiral-bound diary with its own silver gel roller pen.	
7 **Noris Club Thick Triangular Coloured Pencils**, Staedtler-Mars	4+
Unique, non-toxic triangular colored pencils that made grasping easy for little fingers.	
8 **Play-Doh Seaside Playworld**, Hasbro	3+
A molding compound play set with textures, colors and scents of the ocean.	
9 **Radio Go Race Car**, Little Tikes Co.	3+
A brightly colored and durable sporty remote controlled car.	
10 = **Rat a Tat Cat**, Gamewright	6+
An engaging numbers and memory card game.	
10 = **Small Miracles Dress-Up Clothes**, Learning Curve	3–6
Fun costumes with easy-to-use Velcro fasteners.	
10 = **Tendre Calin**, Corolle	1+
A small, sweet baby doll with a flexible beanbag body.	

Source: The Canadian Toy Testing Council

"TEDDY BEAR"

While on a hunting trip, US President Theodore ("Teddy") Roosevelt refused to shoot a young bear. This became the subject of a famous cartoon by Clifford K. Berryman, published in the *Washington Post*. Immediately afterward, Morris Michtom, a New York shopkeeper, made stuffed bears and, with Roosevelt's permission, advertised them as "Teddy's Bears". Margarete Steiff, a German toymaker, soon began making her toy bears, exporting them to the US to meet demand.

WHY DO WE SAY?

TOP 10 ★
MOST EXPENSIVE DOLLS SOLD AT AUCTION

DOLL/SALE	PRICE (US$)
1 **Kämmer and Reinhardt doll**, Sotheby's, London, Feb 8, 1994	282,750
2 **Kämmer and Reinhardt bisque character doll**, German, c.1909, Sotheby's, London, Oct 17, 1996 *(Previously sold at Sotheby's, London, February 16, 1989, for $140,171)*	169,117
3 **Kämmer and Reinhardt bisque character doll**, German, c.1909, Sotheby's, London, Oct 17, 1996	143,327
4 **Albert Marque bisque character doll**, Sotheby's, London, Oct 17, 1996	112,380
5 **William and Mary wooden doll**, English, c.1690, Sotheby's, London, Mar 24, 1987	110,396
6 **Wooden doll, Charles II**, 17th century, Christie's, London, May 18, 1989	103,850
7 **Albert Marque bisque character doll**, Sotheby's, London, Oct 17, 1996	91,748
8 = **Albert Marque bisque character doll**, Christie's, London, May 23, 1997	89,581
8 = **Pressed bisque swivel-head Madagascar doll**, Sotheby's, London, Oct 17, 1996	88,310
10 **Shellacked pressed bisque swivel-head doll**, Sotheby's, London, Oct 17, 1996	71,117

TOP 10 TOY RETAIL OUTLETS IN THE US, 1999*
(Outlet type/percentage of market share)

1 Discount stores, 41.5 **2** National toy stores, 21.7 **3** Other outlets (not toy stores), 12.8 **4** Mail order, 5.3 **5** Department stores, 4.1 **6** Other toy stores, 3.7 **7** Food/drug stores, 3.6 **8** Card/gift/stationery stores, 3.1 **9** Hobby/craft stores, 2.7 **10** Variety stores, 1.5

* Ranked by dollar share perentage in 1998   Soure: Toy Manufacturers of America Inc.

What is the bestselling Sarah McLachlan single in Canada?
see p.139 for the answer

A *Building a Mystery*
B *Sweet Surrender*
C *Adia*

TOP 10 ★
TALLEST FREESTANDING STATUES

STATUE/LOCATION	HEIGHT M	FT
1 Chief Crazy Horse, Thunderhead Mountain, South Dakota	172	563
Started in 1948 by Polish-American sculptor Korczak Ziolkowski, and continued after his death in 1982 by his widow and eight of his children, this gigantic equestrian statue is even longer than it is high (195 m/641 ft). It is being carved out of the granite mountain by dynamiting and drilling.		
2 Buddha, Tokyo, Japan	120	394
This Japanese–Taiwanese project, unveiled in 1993, took seven years to complete and weighs 998 tonnes.		
3 The Indian Rope Trick, Riddersberg Säteri, Jönköping, Sweden	103	337
Sculptor Calle Örnemark's 145-tonne wooden sculpture depicts a long strand of "rope" held by a fakir, while another figure ascends.		
4 Motherland, 1967, Volgograd (formerly Stalingrad), Russia	82	270
This concrete statue of a woman with a raised sword, designed by Yevgeniy Vuchetich, commemorates the Soviet victory at the Battle of Stalingrad (1942–43).		
5 Buddha, Bamian, Afghanistan	53	173
This dates from the 3rd–4th centuries AD.		
6 Kannon, Otsubo-yama, near Tokyo, Japan	52	170
The vast statue of the goddess of mercy was unveiled in 1961 in honor of the dead of World War II.		
7 Statue of Liberty, New York	46	151
Designed by Auguste Bartholdi and presented to the US by the people of France, the statue was shipped in sections to Liberty (formerly Bedloes) Island, where it was assembled before being unveiled on October 28, 1886, and restored on July 4, 1986.		
8 Christ, Rio de Janeiro, Brazil	38	125
The work of sculptor Paul Landowski and engineer Heitor da Silva Costa, the figure of Christ was unveiled in 1931.		
9 Tian Tan (Temple of Heaven) Buddha, Po Lin Monastery, Lantau Island, Hong Kong	34	112
This was completed after 20 years' work and was unveiled on December 29, 1993.		
10 Quantum Cloud, Greenwich, London, UK	29	95
This gigantic steel human figure surrounded by a matrix of steel struts was created in 1999.		

❖ TOP 10 MOST-VISITED MUSEUMS AND GALLERIES IN CANADA

(Museum or gallery/Total attendance 1997)

1 Canadian Museum of Civilization, Hull, 1,373,542 **2 Montreal Biodome**, Montreal, 869,602 **3 Richmond Museum**, Richmond, BC, 846,902 **4 Musée de la civilisation**, Quebec, 770,650 **5 Royal Ontario Museum**, Toronto, 694,198 **6 National Museum of Science and Technology**, Ottawa, 694,294 **7 Royal British Columbia Museum**, Victoria, 641,260 **8 National Gallery of Canada**, Ottawa, 537,900 **9 Nova Scotia Museum**, Halifax, 499,988 **10 Montreal Museum of Fine Arts**, Montreal, 477,774

Source: The Council for Business and the Arts in Canada

HIGH AND MIGHTY
The statue of Christ the Redeemer, Rio de Janeiro, Brazil, is 30 m (100 ft) tall and stands on a 7-m (22-ft) pedestal with a chapel inside. It was unveiled in 1931 by the radio pioneer Guglielmo Marconi.

TOP 10 ★

LARGEST PAINTINGS IN THE LOUVRE MUSEUM, PARIS

PAINTING/ARTIST	SIZE (HEIGHT X WIDTH) M	FT
1 *Interior of Westminster Abbey*, Jean-Pierre Alaux	19.0 x 40.0	62 x 131
2 *Interior of St. Peter's, Rome*, Jean-Pierre Alaux	17.5 x 40.0	57 x 131
3 *Palace Ceiling*, Francesco Fontebasso	8.0 x 10.0	26 x 33
4 *The Marriage Feast at Cana*, Paolo Veronese	6.7 x 9.9	22 x 32
5 *The Coronation of Napoleon*, Jacques-Louis David	6.2 x 9.8	20 x 32
6 *The Battle of Arbela*, Charles Lebrun	4.7 x 12.7	15 x 42
7 *Alexander and Porus*, Charles Lebrun	4.7 x 12.6	15 x 41
8 *Crossing the Granicus*, Charles Lebrun	4.7 x 12.1	15 x 40
9 *The Battle of Eylau*, Antoine-Jean Gros	5.2 x 7.8	17 x 26
10 *Napoleon Visiting the Plague Victims of Jaffa*, Antoine-Jean Gros	5.2 x 7.2	17 x 24

TOP 10 ART EXHIBITIONS, 1999

(Exhibition/venue/total attendance)

1 *Van Gogh's van Goghs*, Los Angeles County Museum, 821,004
2 *Monet in the 20th Century*, The Royal Academy, London, 739,324
3 *The Maya*, Palazzo Grassi, Venice, 700,000 4 *Richard Serra*, Bilbao Guggenheim, 675,071 5 *Millet, van Gogh*, Musée d'Orsay, Paris, 661,568 6 *Eduardo Chillida*, Bilbao Guggenheim, 542,770 7 *Van Gogh's van Goghs*, National Gallery of Art, Washington, D.C., 480,496 8 *Egyptian Art in the Age of Pyramids*, Metropolitan Museum of Fine Art, New York City, 473,234 9 *John Singer Sargent*, National Gallery of Art, Washington, D.C., 453,937 10 *Cézanne to van Gogh: Doctor Gachet Collection*, Metropolitan Museum of Fine Art, New York City, 429,024

Source: The Art Newspaper

Art on Sale

TOP 10 ★
MOST EXPENSIVE PAINTINGS EVER SOLD AT AUCTION

PAINTING/ARTIST/SALE	PRICE (US$)
1 *Portrait of Dr. Gachet*, Vincent van Gogh (Dutch; 1853–90), Christie's, New York, May 15, 1990	75,000,000
2 *Au Moulin de la Galette*, Pierre-Auguste Renoir (French; 1841–1919), Sotheby's, New York, May 17, 1990	71,000,000
3 *Portrait de l'artiste sans barbe*, Vincent van Gogh, Christie's, New York, Nov 19, 1998	65,000,000
4 *Rideau, cruchon et compotier*, Paul Cézanne (French; 1839–1906), Sotheby's, New York, May 10, 1999	55,000,000
5 *Les Noces de Pierrette, 1905*, Pablo Picasso (Spanish; 1881–1973), Binoche et Godeau, Paris, Nov 30, 1989	51,672,000
6 *Irises*, Vincent van Gogh, Sotheby's, New York, Nov 11, 1987	49,000,000
7 *Femme assise dans un jardin*, Pablo Picasso, Sotheby's, New York, Nov 10, 1999	45,000,000
8 *Le Rêve*, Pablo Picasso, Christie's, New York, Nov 10, 1997	44,000,000
9 *Self Portrait: Yo Picasso*, Pablo Picasso, Sotheby's, New York, May 9, 1989	43,500,000
10 *Nu au fauteuil noir*, Pablo Picasso, Christie's, New York, Nov 9, 1999	41,000,000

TOP 10 ★
ARTISTS WITH MOST WORKS SOLD FOR MORE THAN ONE MILLION DOLLARS

ARTIST	TOTAL VALUE OF WORKS SOLD (US$)	NO. OF WORKS SOLD
1 Pablo Picasso (Spanish; 1881–1973)	1,187,184,808	257
2 Claude Monet (French; 1888–1926)	828,576,015	196
3 Pierre Auguste Renoir (French; 1841–1919)	607,167,714	183
4 Edgar Degas (French; 1834–1917)	324,757,303	99
5 Paul Cézanne (French; 1839–1906)	387,426,172	74
6 Marc Chagall (Russian; 1887–1985)	160,935,200	70
7=Henri Matisse (French; 1869–1954)	124,236,994	68
7=Camille Pissarro (French; 1830–1903)	238,671,445	68
9 Vincent van Gogh (Dutch; 1853–90)	535,560,639	54
10 Amedeo Modigliani (Italian; 1884–1920)	235,313,301	53

RAGS TO RICHES

The impoverished van Gogh painted this self-portrait, Portrait de l'artiste sans barbe, at Arles in September 1888. Just over a century later, it fetched US$65 million at auction, making it the third most expensive painting sold at auction.

TOP 10 ★
MOST EXPENSIVE PAINTINGS BY 20TH-CENTURY ARTISTS*

PAINTING/ARTIST/SALE	PRICE (US$)
1 *Paysage, Île de la Grande Jatte*, George Seurat, (French; 1859–91) Sotheby's, New York, May 10, 1999	32,000,000
2 *Fugue*, Wassily Kandinsky (Russian; 1866–1944), Sotheby's, New York, May 17, 1990	19,000,000
3 *Interchange*, Willem de Kooning (American/ Dutch; 1904–97), Sotheby's, New York, Nov 8, 1989	18,800,000
4 *Orange Marilyn*, Andy Warhol (American; 1928–87), Sotheby's, New York, May 14, 1998	15,750,000
5 *False Start*, Jasper Johns (American; b.1930), Sotheby's, New York, Nov 10, 1988	15,500,000
6 *Nu assis sur un divan*, Amedeo Modigliani (Italian; 1884–1920), Sotheby's, New York, Nov 11, 1999	15,250,000
7 *Woman*, Willem de Kooning, Christie's, New York, Nov 20, 1996	14,200,000
8 *Portrait de Jeanne Hebuterne*, Amedeo Modigliani, Sotheby's, New York, Nov 3, 1993	13,750,000
9=*Anniversaire*, Marc Chagall (French/Russian; 1887–1985), Sotheby's, New York, May 17, 1990	13,500,000
9=*La Pose hindoue*, Henri Matisse, Sotheby's, New York, May 8, 1995	13,500,000

* Excluding Picasso, who would otherwise completely dominate the list

Did You Know? Vincent van Gogh did not cut off his ear, as is popularly believed. He lopped off only part of his left ear lobe.

TOP 10 ⭐
MOST EXPENSIVE OLD MASTER PAINTINGS EVER SOLD AT AUCTION

PAINTING/ARTIST/SALE	PRICE (US$)
1 *Portrait of Duke Cosimo I de Medici*, **Jacopo Carrucci (Pontormo)** (Italian; 1493–1558), Christie's, New York, May 31, 1989	32,000,000
2 *The Old Horse Guards, London, from St. James's Park*, **Canaletto** (Italian; 1697–1768), Christie's, London, Apr 15, 1992	16,008,000
3 *View of the Giudecca and the Zattere, Venice*, **Francesco Guardi** (Italian; 1712–93), Sotheby's, Monaco, Dec 1, 1989	13,943,000
4 *Venus and Adonis*, **Titian** (Italian; *c*.1488–1576), Christie's, London, Dec 13, 1991	12,376,000
5 *Tieleman Roosterman in Black Doublet, White Ruff*, **Frans Hals** (elder, Dutch; *c*.1580–1666), Christie's, London, Jul 8, 1999	11,625,000
6 *Le Retour du Bucentaure le Jour de l'Ascension*, **Canaletto**, Ader Tajan, Paris, Dec 15, 1993	11,316,000
7 *View of Molo from Bacino di San Marco, Venice and View of the Grand Canal Facing East from Campo di Santi, Venice* (pair), **Canaletto**, Sotheby's, New York, Jun 1, 1990	10,000,000
8 *Adoration of the Magi*, **Andrea Mantegna** (Italian; 1431–1506), Christie's, London, Apr 18, 1985	9,525,000
9 *Portrait of a Girl Wearing a Gold-trimmed Cloak*, **Rembrandt** (Dutch; 1606–69), Sotheby's, London, Dec 10, 1986	9,372,000
10 *Portrait of Bearded Man in Red Coat*, **Rembrandt**, Sotheby's, New York, Jan 30, 1998	8,250,000

THERE'S SOMETHING ABOUT MARY

Six paintings by Mary Cassatt, such as her Mother, Sara, and the Baby, *are numbered among the 10 highest priced paintings by a woman.*

TOP 10 ⭐
MOST EXPENSIVE PAINTINGS BY WOMEN ARTISTS EVER SOLD AT AUCTION

PAINTING/ARTIST/SALE	PRICE (US$)
1 *The Conversation*, **Mary Cassatt** (American; 1844–1926), Christie's, New York, May 11, 1988	4,100,000
2 *In the Box*, **Mary Cassatt**, Christie's, New York, May 23, 1996	3,700,000
3 = *Cache-cache*, **Berthe Morisot** (French; 1841–95), Sotheby's, New York, May 10, 1999	3,500,000
3 = *Mother, Sara, and the Baby*, **Mary Cassatt**, Christie's, New York, May 10, 1989	3,500,000
5 *From the Plains*, **Georgia O'Keeffe** (American; 1887–1986), Sotheby's, New York, Dec 3, 1997	3,300,000
6 *Après le Déjeuner*, **Berthe Morisot**, Christie's, New York, May 14, 1997	3,250,000
7 *Autoretrato con Chango y Loro*, **Frida Kahlo** (Mexican; 1907–54), Sotheby's, New York, May 17, 1995	2,900,000
8 *Augusta Reading to Her Daughter*, **Mary Cassatt**, Sotheby's, New York, May 9, 1989	2,800,000
9 *Children Playing with Cat*, **Mary Cassatt**, Sotheby's, New York, Dec 3, 1998	2,700,000
10 *Sarah Holding Her Dog*, **Mary Cassatt**, Sotheby's, New York, Nov 11, 1999	2,500,000

TOP 10 ★

MOST EXPENSIVE PAINTINGS BY ANDY WARHOL

PAINTING*/SALE	PRICE (US$)
1 *Orange Marilyn*, Sotheby's, New York, May 14, 1998	15,750,000
2 *Shot Red Marilyn*, Sotheby's, New York, May 3, 1989	3,700,000
3 *Marilyn Monroe, Twenty Times*, Sotheby's, New York, Nov 10, 1988	3,600,000
4 *Marilyn X 100*, Sotheby's, New York, Nov 17, 1992	3,400,000
5 *Shot Red Marilyn*, Sotheby's, New York, Nov 2, 1994	3,300,000
6 *Big Torn Campbell's Soup Can*, Christie's, New York, May 7, 1997	3,200,000
7 *Orange Marilyn*, Christie's, New York, Nov 19, 1998	2,500,000
8 *Marion,* Sotheby's, New York, May 18, 1999	2,400,000
9 *Big Electric Chair*, Christie's, London, Jun 30, 1999	2,370,000
10 *Self Portrait*, Christie's, New York, May 12, 1998	2,200,000

* *Including silkscreen works*

"FAMOUS FOR 15 MINUTES"

Andy Warhol's own fame has outlived his famous phrase. His works continue to attain considerable prices at auction.

HIGH FIGURES
The distinctive elongated figures created by Swiss sculptor Alberto Giacometti (1901–66), shown at work in his studio in 1958, command high prices at auction.

TOP 10 ★

MOST EXPENSIVE SCULPTURES BY ALBERTO GIACOMETTI

SCULPTURE/SALE	PRICE (US$)	SCULPTURE/SALE	PRICE (US$)
1 *La Forêt – sept figures et une tête*, Sotheby's, New York, Nov 16, 1998	6,800,000	6 *Trois hommes qui marchent*, Christie's, New York, May 11, 1988	3,500,000
2 *L'Homme qui marche I*, Christie's, London Nov 28, 1988	6,358,000	7 *Grande femme debout II*, Christie's, New York, May 12, 1987	3,300,000
3 *Trois hommes qui marchent I*, Sotheby's, New York, Nov 11, 1999	5,200,000	8 *Trois hommes qui marchent II*, Christie's, New York, May 14, 1997	3,200,000
4 *Grande femme debout I*, Christie's, New York, Nov 14, 1989	4,500,000	9 *Grande femme debout I*, Christie's, New York, May 12, 1987	2,800,000
5 *Grande femme debout I*, Christie's, New York, Nov 14, 1990	3,600,000	10 *L'Homme qui marche III – Walking Man III*, Christie's, New York, May 12, 1998	2,700,000

Did You Know? Between October 18 and December 4, 1961, Henri Matisse's painting *Le Bateau* hung upside down in the Museum of Modern Art, New York. An estimated 116,000 people passed through the gallery before anyone noticed.

TOP 10 ★
MOST EXPENSIVE SCULPTURES BY HENRY MOORE

SCULPTURE/SALE	PRICE ($)
1 =*Reclining Figure*, Christie's, New York, May 13, 1999	3,700,000
1 =*Two-piece Reclining Figure, Points*, Christie's, New York, Nov 9, 1999	3,700,000
1 =*Working Model for UNESCO Reclining Figure*, Christie's, New York, May 15, 1990	3,700,000
4 *Reclining Figure, Angles*, Christie's, New York, Nov 13, 1996	2,400,000
5 *Draped Reclining Woman*, Sotheby's, New York, Nov 13, 1997	2,350,000
6 *Reclining Connected Forms*, Sotheby's, New York, May 17, 1990	2,200,000
7 =*Reclining Figure, Bone Skirt*, Sotheby's, New York, May 13, 1997	2,000,000
7 =*Working Model for Three Way Piece No. 3 Vertebrae*, Sotheby's, New York, May 17, 1990	2,000,000
9 =*Festival Reclining Figure*, Sotheby's, New York, May 11, 1994	1,850,000
9 =*Reclining Figure*, Sotheby's, New York, Nov 11, 1988	1,850,000

British sculptor Henry Spencer Moore (1898–1986) was a war artist before achieving international fame for his sculptures. Many of these were commissioned for public buildings, but those that have entered the marketplace have achieved consistently high prices.

SECOND KISS

Kiss II *by pop artist Roy Lichtenstein (1923–97) gained a record US$5.5 million at auction, followed closely at US$5 million by* Torpedo...Los. *His work was partly inspired by images from comic strips.*

TOP 10 ★
MOST EXPENSIVE PAINTINGS BY ROY LICHTENSTEIN

PAINTING/SALE	PRICE (US$)
1 *Kiss II*, Christie's, New York, May 7, 1990	5,500,000
2 *Torpedo...Los*, Christie's, New York, Nov 7, 1989	5,000,000
3 *Tex!*, Christie's, New York, Nov 20, 1996	3,600,000
4 *Blang!*, Christie's, New York, May 7, 1997	2,600,000
5 *Kiss II*, Christie's, New York, May 3, 1995	2,300,000
6 *I...I'm Sorry!*, Sotheby's, New York, Nov 1, 1994	2,250,000
7 *The Ring*, Sotheby's, New York, Nov 19, 1997	2,000,000
8 =*I Can See the Whole Room... And There's Nobody in It*, Christie's, New York, Nov 9, 1988	1,900,000
8 =*Forest Scene*, Sotheby's, New York, Nov 19, 1996	1,900,000
10 *Girl with Piano*, Sotheby's, New York, Nov 17, 1992	1,650,000

TOP 10 ★
MOST EXPENSIVE PAINTINGS BY JACKSON POLLOCK

PAINTING*/SALE	PRICE (US$)
1 *Number 8, 1950*, Sotheby's, New York, May 2, 1989	10,500,000
2 *Frieze*, Christie's, New York, Nov 9, 1988	5,200,000
3 *Search*, Sotheby's, New York, May 2, 1988	4,400,000
4 *Number 19, 1949*, Sotheby's, New York, May 2, 1989	3,600,000
5 *Number 31, 1949*, Christie's, New York, May 3, 1988	3,200,000
6 *Number 13*, Christie's, New York, Nov 7, 1990	2,800,000
7 *Number 26, 1950*, Sotheby's, New York, May 4, 1987	2,500,000
8 =*Number 20*, Sotheby's, New York, May 8, 1990	2,200,000
8 =*Number 19, 1948*, Christie's, New York, May 4, 1993	2,200,000
8 =*Something of the Past*, Christie's, New York, May 7, 1996	2,200,000

* Includes mixed media compositions

115

Collector's Corner

WATERCOLOR/ARTIST/SALE	PRICE (US$)
1 *La Moisson en Provence*, **Vincent van Gogh** (Dutch; 1853–90), Sotheby's, London, Jun 24, 1997	13,280,000
2 *Les Toits – 1882*, **Vincent van Gogh**, Ader Picard & Tajan, Paris, Mar 20, 1990	4,669,000
3 *Nature morte au melon vert*, **Paul Cézanne** (French; 1839–1906), Sotheby's, London, Apr 4, 1989	3,933,000
4 *Die Sangerin L. Ais Fiordiligi*, **Paul Klee** (Swiss; 1879–1940), Sotheby's, London, Nov 28, 1989	3,744,000
5 *John Biglin in Single Scull*, **Thomas Eakins** (American; 1844–1916), Christie's, New York, May 23, 1990	3,200,000
6 *Au Moulin Rouge, la fille du roi d'Egypte*, **Pablo Picasso** (Spanish; 1881–1973), Sotheby's, London, Nov 29, 1994	2,557,500
7 *Coral Divers*, **Winslow Homer** (American; 1836–1910), Christie's, New York, Dec 2, 1998	2,400,000
8 *Two Girls in Boat, Tynemouth, England*, **Winslow Homer**, Christie's, New York, Dec 2, 1998	2,300,000
9 *La Montagne Sainte-Victoire vue des Lauves*, **Paul Cézanne**, Christie's, London, Nov 30, 1992	2,054,000
10 *Selbstbildnis. Skizze eines mannlichen aktes*, **Egon Schiele** (Austrian; 1890–1918), Christie's, New York, Nov 19, 1998	2,000,000

PRINT/ARTIST/SALE	PRICE (US$)
1 *Diehard*, **Robert Rauschenberg** (American; b.1925), Sotheby's, New York, May 2, 1989	1,600,000
2 *Mao*, **Andy Warhol** (American; 1928–87), Sothebys, London, Jun 26, 1996	939,400
3 *Famille tahitienne*, **Paul Gauguin** (French; 1848–1903), Francis Briest, Paris, Dec 4, 1998	806,900
4 *Elles*, **Henri de Toulouse-Lautrec** (French; 1864–1901), Sotheby's, New York, May 10, 1999	800,000
5 *Glider*, **Robert Rauschenberg**, Christie's, New York, Nov 14, 1995	750,000
6 *Elles*, **Henri de Toulouse-Lautrec**, Sotheby's, New York, Nov 7, 1997	695,000
7 = *La Suite Vollard*, **Pablo Picasso** (Spanish; 1881–1973), Christie's, New York, Nov 2, 1999	650,000
7 = *Suicide*, **Andy Warhol**, Sotheby's, New York, May 18, 1999	650,000
9 *Head of Marilyn Monroe*, **Andy Warhol**, Beijers, Stockholm, May 21, 1990	640,500
10 *Les Saltimbanques*, **Pablo Picasso**, Sotheby's, New York, May 3, 1996	600,000

Included within the classification of prints are silkscreens, lithographs, monotypes, aquatints, woodcuts, engravings, and etchings.

TOP 10 ★
MOST EXPENSIVE DRAWINGS*

TITLE/ARTIST/SALE	PRICE (US$)
1 *Famille de l'Arlequin*, Pablo **Picasso** (Spanish; 1881–1973), Christie's, New York, Nov 14, 1989	14,000,000
2 *Study for Head and Hand of an Apostle*, **Raphael** (Italian; 1483–1520), Christie's, London, Dec 13, 1996	7,920,000
3 *Oliviers avec les Alpilles au fond*, Vincent **van Gogh** (Dutch; 1853–90), Sotheby's, London, Dec 7, 1999	7,776,000
4 =*Corpse and Mirror*, **Jasper Johns** (American: b.1930), Christie's, New York, Nov 10, 1997	7,600,000
4 =*Jardin de fleurs*, Vincent **van Gogh**, Christie's, New York, Nov 14, 1990	7,600,000
6 *Rebus*, Robert **Rauschenberg** (American, b.1925), Sotheby's, New York, Apr 30, 1991	6,600,000
7 *Rebus*, Robert **Rauschenberg**, Sotheby's, New York, Nov 10, 1988	5,750,000
8 Untitled oil crayon canvas, **Cy Twombly** (American; b.1929), Sotheby's, New York, May 8, 1990	5,000,000
9 *Bateaux de pêche sur la plage à Saintes-Maries-de-la-Mer, Mediterranée*, Vincent **van Gogh**, Christie's, New York, May 5, 1998	4,600,000
10 *La Toilette de Vénus*, Pablo **Picasso**, Sotheby's, New York, Nov 12, 1997	4,500,000

* Media include pencil, pen, ink, drawing, crayon

AHEAD OF THE FIELD

Van Gogh's harvest scene, La Moisson en Provence *(1888), sold for £8 million in 1997, making it the world's most expensive watercolor.*

TRIBAL RECORD

Edward S. Curtis's magnificent 20-volume set of photographs recording the life of North American Indians in the early twentieth century is the costliest ever sold at auction.

TOP 10 ★
MOST EXPENSIVE PHOTOGRAPHS

PHOTOGRAPH/PHOTOGRAPHER/SALE	PRICE (US$)
1 *Egypte et Nubie: Sites et monuments les plus intéressants pour l'étude de l'art et de l'histoire** (1858), **Félix Teynard** (French; 1817–92), Laurin Guilloux Buffetaud Tailleur, Paris, Dec 21, 1990	707,000
2 *Noire et Blanche* (1926), **Man Ray** (American; 1890–1976), Christie's, New York, Oct 4, 1998	607,500
3 *The North American Indian** (1907–30), **Edward S. Curtis** (American; 1868–1952), Sotheby's, New York, Oct 7, 1993	662,500
4 *The North American Indian** (1907–30), **Edward S. Curtis**, Christie's, New York, Apr 6, 1995	464,500
5 *Georgia O'Keeffe: A Portrait – Hands with Thimble* (1930), **Alfred Stieglitz** (American; 1864–1946), Christie's, New York, Oct 8, 1993	398,500
6 =*Equivalents (21)** (1920s), **Alfred Stieglitz**, Christie's, New York, Oct 30, 1989	396,000
6 =*The North American Indian** (1907–30), **Edward S. Curtis**, Christie's, New York, Oct 13, 1992	396,000
8 *Mondrian's Pipe and Glasses* (1926), **André Kertész** (Hungarian-American; 1894–1985), Christie's, New York, Apr 17, 1997	376,500
9 *Noire et Blanche* (1926), **Man Ray**, Christie's, New York, Apr 21, 1994	354,500
10 *Chez Mondrian, Paris* (1926), **André Kertész**, Christie's, New York, Apr 17, 1997	299,500

* Collections; all others are single prints

TOP 10 ★
MOST COLLECTED BEANIE BABIES*

BEANIE BABY
1 Bear
2 2000 Signature Bear #
3 Billionaire Bear
4 Billionaire Bear 2
5 Britannia
6 1998 Holiday Teddy Bear
7 1997 Holiday Teddy Bear
8 Chilly
9 Groovy #
10 Germania

* In April 2000

\# Beanie Buddy

Source: Ty Inc.

Beanie Babies were invented by Chicago toy designer H. Ty Warner, who introduced his first nine at a toy fair in 1993. They went on sale in Chicago the following year, and by 1995 – largely through word-of-mouth recommendation – had become one of the country's most popular and sought-after toys. The company's policy of constantly "retiring" selected lines and introducing new products has kept them at the forefront of collectibles. (Bronty the Brontosaurus, for example, was retired on April 6, 2000.)

Collector's Corner

TOP 10 ★
MOST EXPENSIVE ITEMS OF ENGLISH FURNITURE

ITEM/SALE	PRICE (US$)
1 The Dundas Armchairs, pair of George III giltwood armchairs, designed by Robert Adam and made by Thomas Chippendale, Christie's, London, Jul 3, 1997	2,855,000
2 The Warwick Tables, supplied to Queen Anne for St. James's Palace in 1704–05, by Gerrit Jensen, probably in association with Thomas Pelletier, Sotheby's, London, Jul 10, 1998	2,692,000
3 The Anglesey Desk, Regency bronze-mounted and brass-inlaid ebony and mahogany library desk, attributed to Marsh & Tatbam, Christie's, London, Jul 8, 1993	2,625,000
4 The Dundas Sofas, pair of George III giltwood sofas designed by Robert Adam and made by Thomas Chippendale, Christie's, London, Jul 3, 1997	2,579,000
5 The Lonsdale Langlois Commode, a George III ormolu-mounted rosewood, fruitwood, and marquetry bombe commode, Christie's, New York, Nov 24, 1998	2,532,500
6 The St. Giles's Dining-Chairs, set of 17 George II mahogany dining-chairs, attributed to William Hallett Senior, Christie's, London, Jul 8, 1999	1,890,000
7 A George II ormolu-mounted mahogany dressing and writing-commode, attributed to John Channon, Christie's, London, Jul 6, 1989	1,782,000
8 A George III mahogany commode, attributed to Thomas Chippendale, Christie's, London, Dec 5, 1991	1,655,000
9 The Stowe Apollo Tables, pair of George II gilt-gesso side tables, attributed to Benjamin Goodison, Christie's, London, Jul 9, 1998	1,531,000
10 The Raynham Commode, a George II ormolu-mounted mahogany commode, Christie's, New York, Nov 24, 1998	1,487,500

TOP 10 ★
MOST EXPENSIVE ITEMS OF AMERICAN FURNITURE

ITEM/SALE	PRICE (US$)
1 The Nicholas Brown Chippendale mahogany block and shell desk and bookcase, c.1760–70, attributed to John Goddard, Christie's, New York, Jun 3, 1989	12,100,000
2 Richard Edwards Chippendale carved mahogany pier table, by Thomas Tufft, c.1775–76, Christie's, New York, Jan 20, 1990	4,620,000
3 The Samuel Whitehorne Queen Anne block-and-shell carved mahogany kneehole desk, attributed to Edmund Townsend, c.1780, Sotheby's, New York, Jan 20, 1996	3,632,500
4 Chippendale carved mahogany tea-table, c.1760–80, Christie's, New York, May 28, 1987	2,422,500
5 The Edwards-Harrison family Chippendale carved mahogany high chest-of-drawers, dressing table and pair of side chairs, by Thomas Tufft, c.1775–76, Christie's, New York, May 28, 1987	1,760,000
6 The Edward Jackson parcel gilt inlaid and figured mahogany mirrored bonnet-top secretary bookcase, c.1738–48, Sotheby's, New York, Jan 20, 1996	1,432,500
7 Chippendale carved mahogany tea-table, c.1760–80, Christie's, New York, Jan 25, 1986	1,045,000
8 Cornelius Stevenson Chippendale carved mahogany tea-table, attributed to Thomas Affleck, carving attributed to Nicholas Bernard & Martin Jugiez, c.1760–80, Christie's, New York, Jan 20, 1990	1,210,000
9 Chipppendale carved mahogany tea-table, c.1770, Christie's, New York, Jan 26, 1995	695,500
10 Chippendale mahogany block front and shell-carved kneehole desk, c.1760–85, Christie's, New York, Jun 2, 1983	627,000

TOP 10 ★
MOST EXPENSIVE MINIATURES

MINIATURE/ARTIST/SALE	PRICE (US$)
1 *Two Orientals,* Francisco José de Goya y Lucientes (Spanish; 1746–1828), Christie's, London, Dec 3, 1997	580,000
2 *Maja and Celestina,* Francisco José de Goya y Lucientes, Sotheby's, New York, May 30, 1991	500,000
3 *Portrait of George Villiers, Duke of Buckingham,* Jean Petitot (French; 1607–91), Christie's, London, Apr 30, 1996	375,000
4 *Man Clasping Hand from Cloud,* possibly Lord Thomas Howard, Nicholas Hilliard, (British; 1547–1619), Christie's, London, Mar 3, 1993	230,400
5 *King George III when Prince of Wales Wearing Order of Garter,* Jean-Etienne Liotard, (Swiss; 1702–89), Christie's, London, Oct 21, 1997	187,450
6 *Portrait of Henry Stuart, Earl of Ross and 1st Duke of Albany,* attributed to Lievine Teerling-Bening (Flemish; 16th century), Bonhams, London, Nov 20, 1997	184,800
7 *Landscape with Saint Jerome,* Hans Bol (Dutch; 1534–93), Sotheby's, London, Feb 11, 1999	146,700
8 *Bacchic Scenes,* Jean Jacques de Gault (French; c.1738–1812), Sotheby's, Geneva, Nov 13, 1995	140,900
9 *Portrait of Tsar Nicholas II in Uniform with Orders,* Russian School (Russian; 20th century), Christie's, New York, Dec 1, 1995	140,000
10 *Lady Wearing Rust Coloured Dress with Lace Collar and Jewels,* Samuel Cooper (British; 1609–72), Sotheby's, London, Oct 11, 1994	127,000

Background image: **JIMI HENDRIX'S FENDER STRATOCASTER ELECTRIC GUITAR**

SUPER HERO

*Created by writer Jerry Siegel (American, 1914–96)
and artist Joe Shuster (Canadian, 1914–92), Superman
made his debut in the June 1938 first issue of* Action
Comics, *now the most prized of all comic books.*

TOP 10 ⭐
MOST VALUABLE
AMERICAN COMICS

COMIC	VALUE (US$)
1 **Action Comics** No. 1	185,000

*Published in June 1938, the first issue of Action
Comics marked the original appearance of Superman.*

2 **Detective Comics** No. 27	165,000

*Issued in May 1939, it is prized as the first
comic book to feature Batman.*

3 **Superman** No. 1	130,000

*The first comic book devoted to Superman,
reprinting the original Action Comics story,
was published in summer 1939.*

4 **Marvel Comics** No. 1	115,000

*The Human Torch and other heroes were first
introduced in the issue dated October 1939.*

5 **All American Comics** No. 16	65,000

*The Green Lantern made his debut in the
issue dated July 1940.*

6 =**Batman** No. 1	63,000

*Published in spring 1940, this was the first
comic book devoted to Batman.*

6 =**Whizz Comics** No. 2	63,000

*Published in February 1940 – and confusingly
numbered "2" when it was in fact the first issue –
it was the first comic book to feature Captain Marvel.*

8 **Flash Comics** No. 1	57,000

*Dated January 1940, and featuring The Flash,
it is rare because it was produced in small
numbers for promotional purposes, and was
unique since issue 2 was retitled Whizz Comics.*

9 **Captain America Comics** No. 1	56,000

*Published in March 1941, this was the original comic
book in which Captain America appeared.*

10 **Detective Comics** No. 1	50,000

*Published in March 1937, it was the first in a
long-running series.*

Source: The Overstreet Comic Book Price Guide,
#30, 2000. ©2000 Gemstone Publishing, Inc.
All rights reserved.

TOP 10 ⭐
MOST EXPENSIVE MUSICAL INSTRUMENTS

INSTRUMENT*/SALE	PRICE (US$)
1 "Kreutzer" violin by Antonio Stradivari, Christie's, London, Apr 1, 1998	1,582,800
2 "Cholmondeley" violoncello by Antonio Stradivari, Sotheby's, London, Jun 22, 1998	1,141,100
3 Steinway grand piano, decorated by Lawrence Alma-Tadema and Edward Poynter for Henry Marquand, 1884–87, Sotheby Parke Bernet, New York, Mar 26, 1980	390,000
4 Jimi Hendrix's Fender Stratocaster electric guitar, Sotheby's, London, Apr 25, 1990	370,800
5 Acoustic guitar owned by David Bowie, Paul McCartney, and George Michael, Christie's, London, May 18, 1994	339,800

INSTRUMENT*/SALE	PRICE (US$)
6 Double bass by Domenico Montagnana, Sotheby's, London, Mar 16, 1999	250,300
7 Verne Powell's platinum flute, Christie's, New York, Oct 18, 1986	187,000
8 English double-manual harpsichord by Burkat Shudi and John Broadwood, Sotheby's, London, Oct 27, 1999	170,600
9 Viola by Giovanni Paolo Maggini, Christie's, London, Nov 20, 1984	161,100
10 Seven-keyed bugle by Charles-Joseph Sax, Brussels, 1842, Sotheby's, London, Nov 18, 1993	7,800

* *Most expensive example only given per category of
instrument*

What was the most popular production ever at the shaw festival?
see p.156 for the answer

A *Hobson's Choice*
B *Cavalcade*
C *Pygmalion*

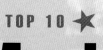

TOP 10 ★
Music

Chart Hits

TOP 10 ALBUMS OF ALL TIME
(Title/artist or group)

❶ *Thriller*, Michael Jackson ❷ *Dark Side of the Moon*, Pink Floyd
❸ *Their Greatest Hits 1971–1975*, The Eagles ❹ *The Bodyguard*, Soundtrack
❺ *Rumours*, Fleetwood Mac ❻ *Sgt. Pepper's Lonely Hearts Club Band*, The Beatles
❼ *Led Zeppelin IV*, Led Zeppelin ❽ *Greatest Hits*, Elton John ❾ *Jagged Little Pill*,
Alanis Morissette ❿ *Bat out of Hell*, Meat Loaf

Total worldwide sales of albums have traditionally been notoriously hard to gauge, but even with the huge expansion of the album market during the 1980s, and multiple million sales of many major releases, this Top 10 is still élite territory.

TOP 10 ALBUMS OF ALL TIME IN THE US
(Title/artist or group/sales)

❶ *Their Greatest Hits 1971–75*, The Eagles, 26,000,000 ❷ *Thriller*, Michael Jackson, 25,000,000 ❸ *Led Zeppelin IV*, Led Zeppelin, 22,000,000 ❹ *Rumours*, Fleetwood Mac, 18,000,000 ❺ = *The Beatles*, The Beatles; = *The Bodyguard*, Soundtrack, 17,000,000 ❼ = *Boston*, Boston; = *Back in Black*, AC/DC; = *No Fences*, Garth Brooks; = *Jagged Little Pill*, Alanis Morissette; = *Cracked Rear View*, Hootie & the Blowfish, 16,000,000

Source: *RIAA*

SOARING LIKE EAGLES

One of the world's best-selling albums of all time, the Eagles' Their Greatest Hits 1971–1975 was also the No. 2 album of the 1970s in Canada.

🍁 TOP 10 ARTISTS WITH MOST WEEKS ON THE CANADIAN SINGLES CHART*
(Artist/no. of weeks)

❶ Madonna, 709 ❷ Elton John, 595
❸ Mariah Carey, 429
❹ Michael Jackson, 387
❺ Rod Stewart, 380
❻ Janet Jackson, 370
❼ Bryan Adams, 369 ❽ Celine Dion, 344
❾ Bon Jovi, 319
❿ John Cougar Mellencamp, 313

* Top 40 only
Source: *Music Data Canada*

TOP 10 🍁 CANADIAN SINGLES OF ALL TIME IN CANADA

	SINGLE/ARTIST OR GROUP	YEAR
1	*Tears Are Not Enough*, Northern Lights	1985
2	*(Everything I Do) I Do It for You*, Bryan Adams	1991
3	*Never Surrender*, Corey Hart	1985
4	*Don't Forget Me (When I'm Gone)*, Glass Tiger	1986
5	*Crying Over You*, Platinum Blonde	1985
6	*(Boogie Woogie) Dancin' Shoes*, Claudja Barry	1979
7	*Christmas Time*, Bryan Adams	1985
8	*Life Is a Highway*, Tom Cochrane	1991
9	*My Girl (Gone, Gone, Gone)*, Chilliwack	1981
10	*Pop Goes the World*, Men Without Hats	1988

Source: *Music Data Canada*

TOP 10 🍁 SINGLES THAT STAYED LONGEST ON THE CANADIAN CHARTS*

	SINGLE/ARTIST/YEAR	NUMBER OF WEEKS
1	*Candle in the Wind 1997/ Something About the Way You Look Tonight*, Elton John, 1997	137
2	*Quit Playing Games (with My Heart)*, Backstreet Boys, 1997	85
3	*The Power of Love*, Celine Dion, 1994	70
4	=*Anytime, Anyplace*, Janet Jackson, 1994	59
4	=*God Bless the Child*, Shania Twain, 1996	59
6	=*Wild Night*, John Mellencamp, 1994	53
6	=*Get Down (You're the One for Me)*, Backstreet Boys, 1996	53
8	*Streets of Philadelphia*, Bruce Springsteen, 1994	52
9	*Perfect Drug*, Nine Inch Nails, 1997	51
10	=*Always*, Bon Jovi, 1995	49
10	=*Breathe*, Prodigy, 1997	49

* As of May 8, 2000

TOP 10 ★
SINGLES OF ALL TIME

#	TITLE/ARTIST OR GROUP/YEAR	SALES EXCEED
1	*Candle in the Wind (1997)/ Something About the Way You Look Tonight*, Elton John, 1997	37,000,000
2	*White Christmas*, Bing Crosby, 1943	30,000,000
3	*Rock Around the Clock*, Bill Haley and His Comets, 1954	17,000,000
4	*I Want to Hold Your Hand*, The Beatles, 1963	12,000,000
5=	*Hey Jude*, The Beatles, 1968	10,000,000
5=	*It's Now or Never*, Elvis Presley, 1960	10,000,000
5=	*I Will Always Love You*, Whitney Houston, 1993	10,000,000
8=	*Hound Dog/Don't Be Cruel*, Elvis Presley, 1956	9,000,000
8=	*Diana*, Paul Anka, 1957	9,000,000
10=	*I'm a Believer*, The Monkees, 1966	8,000,000
10=	*(Everything I Do) I Do it for You*, Bryan Adams, 1991	8,000,000

♣ TOP 10 SINGLES OF ALL TIME IN CANADA

(Single/artist/year)

1 *Candle in the Wind 1997/Something About the Way You Look Tonight*, Elton John, 1997 **2** *I Just Called to Say I Love You*, Stevie Wonder, 1984 **3** *Tears Are Not Enough*, Northern Lights, 1985 **4** *We Are the World*, USA for Africa, 1985 **5** *YMCA*, Village People, 1979 **6** *Le Freak*, Chic, 1979 **7** *(Everything I Do) I Do It for You*, Bryan Adams, 1991 **8** *Heart of Glass*, Blondie, 1979 **9** *Flashdance... What a Feelin'*, Irene Cara, 1983 **10** *Live Is Life*, Opus, 1986

Source: *Music Data Canada*

♣ TOP 10 CANADIAN ALBUMS OF ALL TIME

(Album/artist/year)

1 *Jagged Little Pill*, Alanis Morissette, 1996 **2** *The Woman in Me*, Shania Twain, 1995 **3** *Boy in the Box*, Corey Hart, 1985 **4** *Reckless*, Brian Adams, 1985 **5** *Come On Over*, Shania Twain, 1997 **6** *The Colour of My Love*, Celine Dion, 1994 **7** *Mad Mad World*, Tom Cochrane, 1991 **8** *Waking Up the Neighbours*, Bryan Adams, 1991 **9** *Alannah Myles*, Alannah Myles, 1990 **10** *Surfacing*, Sarah McLachlan, 1997

Source: *Music Data Canada*

TEEN TRIUMPH

Paul Anka's song Diana, released when he was just 16 years old, remains one of the bestselling singles of all time.

OLD BLUE EYES

Frank Sinatra charted from the 1940s right through the 1990s. His last album debuted on the Canadian albums chart just shortly before his death in 1998.

TOP 10 ★
OLDEST ARTISTS TO HAVE A NO. 1 HIT SINGLE IN THE US

		AGE*	
	ARTIST/TITLE	YRS	MTHS
1	**Louis Armstrong**, *Hello Dolly!*	63	10
2	**Lawrence Welk**, *Calcutta*	57	11
3	**Morris Stoloff**, *Moonglow and Theme from Picnic*	57	10
4	**Cher**, *Believe*	52	7
5	**Frank Sinatra**,# *Somethin' Stupid*	51	4
6	**Elton John**, *Candle in the Wind (1997)*	50	6
7	**Lorna Greene**, *Ringo*	49	9
8	**Dean Martin**, *Everybody Loves Somebody*	47	2
9	**Bill Medley**,+ *(I've Had) The Time of My Life*	47	2
10	**Sammy Davis, Jr.**, *The Candy Man*	46	6

* During first week of No. 1

Duet with Nancy Sinatra

+ Duet with Jennifer Warnes

Source: *The Popular Music Database*

The ages listed are those of the artists during the first week of their No. 1 US single.

Record Firsts

FIRST SINGLES TO DEBUT AT NO. 1 IN CANADA

	SINGLE/ARTIST	DATE AT NO. 1
1	*Do They Know It's Christmas*, Band Aid	Jan 14, 1985
2	*Can You Feel the Love Tonight*, Elton John	Aug 1, 1994
3	*God Bless the Child*, Shania Twain	Dec 8, 1996
4	*Discotheque*, U2	Feb 9, 1997
5	*Don't Cry for Me Argentina*, Madonna	Feb 16, 1997
6	*I'll Be Missing You*, Puff Daddy and Faith Evans*	Jun 22, 1997
7	*Candle in the Wind 1997/Something About the Way You Look Tonight*, Elton John	Sep 21, 1997
8	*The Boy Is Mine*, Brandy & Monica	May 24, 1998
9	*Sweetest Thing*, U2	Oct 25, 1998
10	*Goodbye*, Spice Girls	Dec 13, 1998

* Featuring 112   Source: *Music Data Canada*

FIRST ALBUMS TO DEBUT AT NO. 1 IN CANADA

	ALBUM/ARTIST	YEAR
1	*Zooropa*, U2	1993
2	*Superunknown*, Soundgarden	1994
3	*The Division Bell*, Pink Floyd	1994
4	*Voodoo Lounge*, The Rolling Stones	1994
5	*Day for Night*, Tragically Hip	1994
6	*MTV Unplugged in New York*, Nirvana	1994
7	*Live at the BBC*, The Beatles	1994
8	*Greatest Hits*, Bruce Springsteen	1995
9	*Pulse*, Pink Floyd	1995
10	*HIStory*, Michael Jackson	1995

Source: *The Record*

THE 10 FIRST US CHART SINGLES
(Single/artist)

❶ *I'll Never Smile Again*, Tommy Dorsey ❷ *The Breeze and I*, Jimmy Dorsey ❸ *Imagination*, Glenn Miller ❹ *Playmates*, Kay Kyser ❺ *Fools Rush in*, Glenn Miller ❻ *Where Was I*, Charlie Barnet ❼ *Pennsylvania 6-5000*, Glenn Miller ❽ *Imagination*, Tommy Dorsey ❾ *Sierra Sue*, Bing Crosby ❿ *Make-believe Island*, Mitchell Ayres

FIRST AMERICAN GROUPS TO HAVE A NO. 1 SINGLE IN THE UK

	GROUP/SINGLE	DATE AT NO. 1
1	**Bill Haley and His Comets,** *Rock Around the Clock*	Nov 25, 1955
2	**Dream Weavers,** *It's Almost Tomorrow*	Mar 16, 1956
3	**Teenagers featuring Frankie Lymon,** *Why Do Fools Fall in Love?*	Jul 20, 1956
4	**The Crickets,** *That'll Be the Day*	Nov 1, 1957
5	**Platters,** *Smoke Gets in your Eyes*	Mar 20, 1959
6	**Marcels,** *Blue Moon*	May 4, 1961
7	**Highwaymen,** *Michael*	Oct 12, 1961
8	**B. Bumble and the Stingers,** *Rocker*	May 17, 1962
9	**Supremes,** *Baby Love*	Nov 19, 1964
10	**Byrds,** *Mr. Tambourine Man*	Jul 22, 1965

Source: *The Popular Music Database*

SUPREME SUPREMES
Nine years after their first US No. 1, the Supremes became only the ninth US group to top the UK charts – the song was Baby Love.

THE 10 ⭐
FIRST BRITISH GROUPS TO HAVE A NO. 1 SINGLE IN THE US

	GROUP/SINGLE	DATE AT NO. 1
1	Tornados, *Telstar*	Dec 22, 1962
2	The Beatles, *I Want to Hold Your Hand*	Feb 1, 1964
3	The Animals, *House of the Rising Sun*	Sep 5, 1964
4	Manfred Mann, *Do Wah Diddy Diddy*	Oct 17, 1964
5	Freddie and the Dreamers, *I'm Telling You Now*	Apr 10,1965
6	Wayne Fontana and the Mindbenders, *The Game of Love*	Apr 24, 1965
7	Herman's Hermits, *Mrs. Brown You've Got a Lovely Daughter*	May 1, 1965
8	The Rolling Stones, *(I Can't Get No) Satisfaction*	Jul 10, 1965
9	Dave Clark Five, *Over and Over*	Dec 25, 1965
10	Troggs, *Wild Thing*	Jul 30, 1966

Source: *The Popular Music Database*

HIT MANN
Do Wah Diddy Diddy, a cover version of a US-written song, became British group Manfred Mann's debut No. 1 US chart hit.

THE 10 🍁
FIRST CANADIAN SONGS TO HIT NO. 1 IN THE US

	ARTIST/TITLE	DATE AT NO. 1
1	Paul Anka, *Diana*	Sep 9, 1957
2	Paul Anka, *Lonely Boy*	Jul 13, 1959
3	Percy Faith, theme from *A Summer Place*	Feb 22, 1960
4	Lorne Greene, *Ringo*	Dec 5, 1964
5 =	The Guess Who, *American Woman*	Mar 18, 1972
5 =	Neil Young, *Heart of Gold*	Mar 18, 1972
7	Terry Jacks, *Seasons in the Sun*	Mar 2, 1974
8	Gordon Lightfoot, *Sundown*	Jun 29, 1974
9	Paul Anka, *(You're) Having My Baby*	Aug 24, 1974
10	Andy Kim, *Rock Me Gently*	Sep 28, 1974

THE 10 ⭐
FIRST MILLION-SELLING US SINGLES

	SINGLE/ARTIST	CERTIFICATION DATE
1	*Catch a Falling Star*, Perry Como	Mar 14, 1958
2	*He's Got the Whole World in His Hands*, Laurie London	Jul 18, 1958
3	*Hard Headed Woman*, Elvis Presley	Aug 11, 1958
4	*Patricia*, Perez Prado	Aug 18, 1958
5	*Tom Dooley*, Kingston Trio	Jan 21, 1959
6	*Calcutta*, Lawrence Welk	Feb 14, 1961
7	*Big Bad John*, Jimmy Dean	Dec 14, 1961
8	*The Lion Sleeps Tonight*, The Tokens	Jan 19, 1962
9	*Can't Help Falling in Love*, Elvis Presley	Mar 30, 1962
10	*I Can't Stop Loving You*, Ray Charles	Jul 19, 1962

Source: *RIAA*

THE 10 🍁
FIRST CANADIAN TOP 10 SINGLES CHART

	ARTIST	TITLE
1	Elton John	*Pinball Wizard*
2	America	*Sister Golden Hair*
3	Ace	*How Long Ago*
4	Kay Kyser	*Playmates*
5	John Denver	*Thank God I'm a Country Boy*
6	Grand Funk Railroad	*Bad Time*
7	Ozark Mountain Daredevils	*Jackie Blue*
8	The Carpenters	*Only Yesterday*
9	Elton John	*Philadelphia Freedom*
10	Earth Wind & Fire	*Shining Star*

Source: The Steede Report

Even though earlier national charts exist, this was the first Top 10 list that was used for research purposes by Music Data Canada. It was a test chart published in the June 14, 1975 issue of *The Steede Report*, reflecting radio airplay for the week ending May 31, 1975.

Did You Know? The Tornados' *Telstar*, the first ever US No. 1 by a British group, was inspired by the July 10, 1962 launch of the first satellite to transmit TV signals between Europe and the US. It sold over 5 million copies worldwide.

TOP 10 ⭐
ALBUMS WITH THE MOST CONSECUTIVE WEEKS AT NO. 1 IN THE US

TITLE/ARTIST OR GROUP	WEEKS AT NO. 1
1 *Love Me or Leave Me*, soundtrack, Doris Day	25
2 =*Calypso*, Harry Belafonte	24
2 =*Saturday Night Fever*, soundtrack	24
2 =*Purple Rain*, soundtrack, Prince	24
5 *Blue Hawaii*, soundtrack, Elvis Presley	20
6 *Rumours*, Fleetwood Mac	19
7 =*More of the Monkees*, The Monkees	18
7 =*Please Hammer Don't Hurt 'Em*, MC Hammer	18
9 =*Thriller*, Michael Jackson (1st entry)	17
9 =*Thriller*, Michael Jackson (2nd entry)	17
9 =*Some Gave All*, Billy Ray Cyrus	17

* Based on Billboard charts, up to January 1, 2000

CHILD'S PLAY

Thirteen-year-old Donny Osmond's recording of *Go Away Little Girl* held the US No. 1 slot for three weeks in September 1971.

TOP 10 ⭐
YOUNGEST SOLO ARTISTS TO HAVE A NO. 1 SINGLE IN THE US*

	ARTIST/TITLE/YEAR	AGE[#] YRS	MTHS
1	**Jimmy Boyd**, *I Saw Mommy Kissing Santa Claus*, 1952	12	11
2	**Stevie Wonder** *Fingertips*, 1963	13	1
3	**Donny Osmond**, *Go Away Little Girl*, 1971	13	7
4	**Michael Jackson**, *Ben*, 1972	13	11
5	**Laurie London**, *He's Got the Whole World in His Hands*, 1958	14	2
6	**Little Peggy March**, *I Will Follow Him*, 1963	15	0
7	**Brenda Lee**, *I'm Sorry*, 1960	15	5
8	**Paul Anka**, *Diana*, 1957	16	0
9	**Tiffany**, *I Think We're Alone Now*, 1987	16	10
10	**Lesley Gore**, *It's My Party*, 1963	17	0

* To December 1999

During first week of debut No. 1 US single

Source: *The Popular Music Database*

🍁 TOP 10 CANADIAN ACTS WITH THE MOST WEEKS AT NO. 1

(Artist or group/no. of weeks)

- ❶ Bryan Adams, 27
- ❷ Celine Dion, 13
- ❸ = Corey Hart; = Shania Twain; = Los Del Mar, 9
- ❻ Tom Cochrane, 6
- ❼ Soul Decision, 5
- ❽ = Northern Lights; = Alanis Morissette; = Boomtang Boys, 4

Source: *Music Data Canada*

TOP 10 🍁
YOUNGEST ARTISTS TO HAVE A NO. 1 SINGLE IN CANADA*

	ARTIST/TITLE/YEAR	AGE[#] YRS	MTHS
1	**Britney Spears**, *...Baby One More Time*, 1998	16	11
2	**Monica**, *The Boy Is Mine*, 1998	17	7
3	**Shaun Cassidy**, *Da Doo Ron Ron*, 1977	17	10
4	**Debbie Gibson**, *Foolish Beat*, 1988	17	11
5	**Brandy**, *The Boy Is Mine*, 1998	19	3
6	**Andy Gibb**, *I Just Want to Be Your Everything*, 1977	19	6
7	**Mariah Carey**, *Vision of Love*, 1990	20	5
8	**Bobby Brown**, *On Our Own*, 1989	20	6
9	**Samantha Fox**, *Touch Me (I Want Your Body)*, 1987	20	10
10	**Debby Boone**, *You Light Up My Life*, 1977	21	1

* To May 2000

During first week of debut No. 1 single

Source: *Music Data Canada*

🍁 TOP 10 ALBUMS WITH THE MOST WEEKS AT NO. 1 IN CANADA

(Album/artist or group/year/weeks at No. 1)

- ❶ *Synchronicity*, The Police, 1983, 23
- ❷ *Jagged Little Pill*, Alanis Morissette, 1996, 20
- ❸ *Brothers In Arms*, Dire Straits, 1985, 18
- ❹ = *Whitney Houston*, Whitney Houston, 1986; *Unplugged*, Eric Clapton, 1992, 17
- ❻ *The Raw and the Cooked*, Fine Young Cannibals, 1989, 16
- ❼ = *I Do Not Want What I Haven't Got*, Sinead O'Connor, 1990; *True Blue*, Madonna, 1986; *The Joshua Tree*, U2, 1987; *Dirty Dancing* soundtrack, 1987; *Born in the U.S.A.*, Bruce Springsteen, 1984, 14

Source: *The Record*

SATCHMO SINGS

Four years after his chart-topping success in the US, Louis Armstrong topped the UK charts at the age of 67. His hit, What a Wonderful World, *sold over 1 million copies worldwide.*

TOP 10 ★

OLDEST ARTISTS TO HAVE A NO. 1 SINGLE IN THE US*

ARTIST OR GROUP/TITLE	AGE[#] YRS	MTHS
1 Louis Armstrong, *Hello Dolly!*	63	10
2 Lawrence Welk, *Calcutta*	57	11
3 Morris Stoloff, *Moonglow* and *Theme from Picnic*	57	10
4 Cher, *Believe*	52	9
5 Frank Sinatra,+ *Somethin' Stupid*	51	4
6 Elton John, *Candle in the Wind (1997)/ Something About the Way You Look Tonight*	50	6
7 Lorne Greene, *Ringo*	49	9
8 Dean Martin, *Everybody Loves Somebody*	47	2
9 Bill Medley,★ *(I've Had) The Time of My Life*	47	2
10 Sammy Davis, Jr., *The Candy Man*	46	6

* *To December 1999*

[#] *During first week of No. 1 single*

+ *Duet with Nancy Sinatra*

★ *Duet with Jennifer Warnes*

Source: *The Popular Music Database*

TOP 10 🍁

OLDEST ARTISTS TO HAVE A NO. 1 SINGLE IN CANADA

ARTIST/SINGLE/YEAR	AGE YRS	MTHS
1 Eric Clapton, *Change the World*, 1996	51	4
2 Willie Nelson, *To All the Girls I've Loved Before,** 1984	51	1
3 Elton John, *Candle in the Wind 1997*, 1997		
4 Tina Turner, *We Don't Need Another Hero*, 1985	45	9
5 Kenny Rogers, *Islands In the Stream*,[#] 1983	45	2
6 John Mellencamp, *Key West Intermezzo (I Saw You First)*, 1996	44	11
7 Bruce Springsteen, *Streets of Philadelphia*, 1994	44	7
8 Paul McCartney, *Say, Say, Say,*+ 1984	41	6
9 Michael Bolton, *Said I Loved You...But I Lied*, 1993	40	9
10 Steve Winwood, *Roll with It*, 1988	40	2

* *Duet with Julio Iglesias*

[#] *Duet with Dolly Parton*

+ *Duet with Michael Jackson*

🍁 TOP 10 CANADIAN COLLEGE/COMMUNITY RADIO ALBUMS OF 1999

(Album/artist)

1 *Clayton Park*, Thrush Hermit **2** *Sometimes I Cry*, Tricky Woo **3** *Keep It Like a Secret*, Built to Spill **4** *Mule Variations*, Tom Waits **5** *Stereotype A*, Cibo Matto **6** *Central Reservation*, Beth Orton **7** *The Sebadoh*, Sebadoh **8** *The Moon*, Wooden Stars; **=** *Throwing Copper*, Live, 52 **10** *Do the Collapse*, Guided by Voices

Source: *The Popular Music Database*

BROTHERS IN WAITING

A gap of almost a decade separates The Bee Gees' No. 1 hits: I've Gotta Get a Message to You in September 1968 and Tragedy in April 1978.

Hit Singles of the Decades

TOP 10 ⬥

SINGLES OF THE 1990s IN CANADA

	SINGLE/ARTIST	YEAR
1	*Candle in the Wind (1997)/Something About the Way You Look Tonight*, Elton John	1997
2	*Goodbye*, Spice Girls	1998
3	*(Everything I Do) I Do It for You*, Bryan Adams	1991
4	*I'll Be Missing You*, Puff Daddy and Faith Evans*	1997
5	*More Than Words*, Extreme	1991
6	*Step By Step*, New Kids On The Block	1990
7	*Swing the Mood*, Jive Bunny & The Mastermixers	1990
8	*Vogue*, Madonna	1990
9	*Strokin'*, Clarence Carter	1990
10	*Broken*, Nine Inch Nails	1997

* Featuring 112   Source: *Music Data Canada*

TOP 10 ⬥

CANADIAN SINGLES OF THE 1990s IN CANADA

	SINGLE/ARTIST	YEAR
1	*(Everything I Do) I Do It for You*, Bryan Adams	1991
2	*Life Is a Highway*, Tom Cochrane	1991
3	*Let Your Backbone Slide*, Maestro Fresh-Wes	1990
4	*Can't Stop This Thing*, Bryan Adams	1991
5	*The Power of Love*, Celine Dion	1994
6	*Have You Ever Really Loved a Woman*, Bryan Adams	1995
7	*God Bless the Child*, Shania Twain	1996
8	*Macarena*, Los Del Mar	1995
9	*Please Forgive Me*, Bryan Adams	1993
10	*Squeeze Toy*, Boomtang Boys	1999

⬥ TOP 10 SINGLES OF THE 1990s IN CANADA

(Single/artist/year)

1 *Tears Are Not Enough*, Northern Lights, 1985 **2** *Don't Forget Me (When I'm Gone)*, Glass Tiger, 1985 **3** *Crying Over You*, Platinum Blonde, 1985 **4** *Christmas Time*, Bryan Adams, 1985 **5** *My Girl (Gone, Gone, Gone)*, Chilliwack, 1981 **6** *Pop Goes the World*, Men Without Hats, 1988 **7** *Eyes of a Stranger*, The Payola$, 1982 **8** *Heat of the Night*, Bryan Adams, 1987 **9** *When a Man Loves a Woman*, Luba, 1988 **10** *Everything in My Heart*, Corey Hart, 1986

FANTASY FIGURE

Mariah Carey had six No. 1 hits during the 1990s. Her biggest hit, Fantasy, held the top spot for 12 weeks in 1995–96.

TOP 10 🍁
SINGLES OF EACH YEAR OF THE 1990s IN CANADA

YEAR	SINGLE/ARTIST
1990	*Vogue*, Madonna
1991	*More Than Words*, Extreme
1992	*Beauty and the Beast*, Celine Dion & Peabo Bryson
1993	*That's the Way Love Goes*, Janet Jackson
1994	*The Power of Love*, Celine Dion
1995	*Always*, Bon Jovi
1996	*Stayin' Alive*, N-Trance
1997	*Candle in the Wind (1997)/ Something About the Way You Look Tonight*, Elton John
1998	*Candle in the Wind (1997)/ Something About the Way You Look Tonight*, Elton John
1999	*Last Kiss*, Pearl Jam

Source: *Music Data Canada*

TOP 10 🍁
SINGLES OF EACH YEAR OF THE 1980s IN CANADA

YEAR	SINGLE/ARTIST
1980	*Rapper's Delight*, Sugarhill Gang
1981	*The Tide Is High*, Blondie
1982	*I Love Rock 'n' Roll*, Joan Jett and The Blackhearts
1983	*Total Eclipse of the Heart*, Bonnie Tyler
1984	*I Just Called to Say I Love You*, Stevie Wonder
1985	*Never Surrender*, Corey Hart
1986	*The Lady in Red*, Chris DeBurgh
1987	*Faith*, George Michael
1988	*Groovy Kind of Love*, Phil Collins
1989	*The Locomotion*, Kylie Minogue

Source: *Music Data Canada*

TOP 10 🍁
SINGLES OF THE 1970s IN CANADA*

	SINGLE/ARTIST	YEAR
1	*YMCA*, Village People	1979
2	*Le Freak*, Chic	1978
3	*Heart of Glass*, Blondie	1979
4	*You Light Up My Life*, Debby Boone	1977
5	*Stayin' Alive*, The Bee Gees	1978
6	*Born to Be Alive*, Patrick Hernandez	1979
7	*Boogie Oogie Oogie*, A Taste Of Honey	1978
8	*Star Wars Theme/Cantina Band*, Meco	1977
9	*Grease*, Frankie Valli	1978
10	*Night Fever*, The Bee Gees	1978

* 1975–79. The official Canadian charts and CRIA (Canadian Recording Industry Association) certification were introduced in 1975

Source: *Canadian Recording Industry Association (CRIA), Music Data Canada*

TOP 10 🍁
SINGLES OF THE 1980s IN CANADA

	SINGLE/ARTIST	YEAR
1	*I Just Called to Say I Love You*, Stevie Wonder	1984
2	*Tears Are Not Enough*, Northern Lights	1985
3	*We Are the World*, USA for Africa	1985
4	*Flashdance... What a Feeling*, Irene Cara	1983
5	*Live Is Life*, Opus	1986
6	*Billie Jean*, Michael Jackson	1983
7	*Karma Chameleon*, Culture Club	1984
8	*Girls Just Wanna Have Fun*, Cyndi Lauper	1984
9	*I Love Rock 'n' Roll*, Joan Jett and The Blackhearts	1982
10	*Funkytown*, Lipps Inc	1980

Source: *Music Data Canada*

QUEEN RULES

Queen's Bohemian Rhapsody was a hit twice. It hit No. 3 in 1976 and later reached at No. 13 in 1992 after it was featured in the film Wayne's World.

TOP 10 🍁
SINGLES OF THE 1960s IN CANADA

	SINGLE/ARTIST	YEAR
1	*Get Back*, The Beatles	1969
2	*Lady Willpower*, Gary Puckett & The Union Gap	1968
3	*Wichita Lineman*, Glen Campbell	1968
4	*Something/Come Together*, The Beatles	1969
5	*Hey Jude/Revolution*, The Beatles	1968
6	*Shakin' All Over*, The Guess Who	1965
7	*Aquarius/Let the Sunshine In*, Fifth Dimension	1969
8	*Sugar Sugar*, The Archies	1969
9	*Spinning Wheel*, Blood Sweat & Tears	1969
10	*A Little Bit Me/Girl I Knew Somewhere*, Monkees	1967

What is the fastest-growing language in Canada?
see p.97 for the answer

A Chinese
B Punjabi
C Italian

Hit Albums of the Decades

NO TROUBLE

Simon and Garfunkel's single and album Bridge over Troubled Water was the No. 1 album in Canada for the year 1970.

🍁 TOP 10 ALBUMS OF THE 1970s IN CANADA
(Album/artist/year)

1 *Rumours*, Fleetwood Mac, 1977   **2** *Their Greatest Hits 1971–1975*, The Eagles, 1976
3 *Led Zeppelin IV*, Led Zeppelin, 1971   **4** *Bat Out of Hell*, Meat Loaf, 1978
5 *Breakfast in America*, Supertramp, 1979   **6** *Saturday Night Fever*, Soundtrack, 1978
7 *Grease*, Soundtrack, 1978   **8** *The Dark Side of the Moon*, Pink Floyd, 1973
9 *Hotel California*, The Eagles, 1977   **10** *Crime of the Century*, Supertramp, 1977

Source: *Music Data Canada*

TOP 10 🍁
ALBUMS OF EACH YEAR IN THE 1970s IN CANADA

YEAR	ALBUM/ARTIST
1970	*Bridge Over Troubled Water*, Simon and Garfunkel
1971	*Tapestry*, Carole King
1972	*American Pie*, Don McLean
1973	*Dark Side of the Moon*, Pink Floyd
1974	*Band on the Run*, Paul McCartney & Wings
1975	*Captain Fantastic and the Brown Dirt Cowboy*, Elton John
1976	*Frampton Comes Alive*, Peter Frampton
1977	*Rumours*, Fleetwood Mac
1978	*Saturday Night Fever*, Soundtrack
1979	*Breakfast in America*, Supertramp

Source: RPM, *Music Data Canada*

TOP 10 🍁
ALBUMS OF EACH YEAR IN THE 1980s IN CANADA

YEAR	ALBUM/ARTIST
1980	*The Wall*, Pink Floyd
1981	*Double Fantasy*, John Lennon
1982	*Business As Usual*, Men At Work
1983	*Thriller*, Michael Jackson
1984	*Thriller*, Michael Jackson
1985	*Born in the USA*, Bruce Springsteen
1986	*Whitney Houston*, Whitney Houston
1987	*Slippery When Wet*, Bon Jovi
1988	*Kick*, INXS
1989	*The Raw and the Cooked*, Fine Young Cannibals

Source: The Record, RPM, *Music Data Canada*

TOP 10 🍁
ALBUMS OF THE 1980s IN CANADA

	ALBUM/ARTIST	YEAR
1	*Thriller*, Michael Jackson	1983
2	*The Wall*, Pink Floyd	1980
3	*Brothers in Arms*, Dire Straits	1985
4	*Whitney Houston*, Whitney Houston	1986
5	*True Blue*, Madonna	1986
6	*The Joshua Tree*, U2	1987
7	*Dirty Dancing*, Soundtrack	1987
8	*Born in the USA*, Bruce Springsteen	1984
9	*Colour by Numbers*, Culture Club	1983
10	*Girl You Know It's True*, Milli Vanilli	1989

Source: *Music Data Canada*

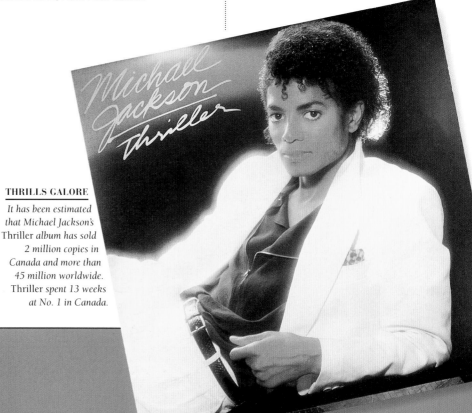

THRILLS GALORE

It has been estimated that Michael Jackson's Thriller album has sold 2 million copies in Canada and more than 45 million worldwide. Thriller spent 13 weeks at No. 1 in Canada.

130

TOP 10
CANADIAN ALBUMS OF THE 1980s IN CANADA

	ALBUM/ARTIST	YEAR
1	*Boy in the Box*, Corey Hart	1985
2	*Reckless*, Bryan Adams	1985
3	*Into the Fire*, Bryan Adams	1987
4	*Alien Shores*, Platinum Blonde	1985
5	*The Thin Red Line*, Glass Tiger	1986
6	*Fields of Fire*, Corey Hart	1986
7	*Great Dirty World*, Gowan	1987
8	*Grace Under Pressure*, Rush	1984
9	*Strange Animal*, Gowan	1985
10	*Cuts Like a Knife*, Bryan Adams	1983

TOP 10
CANADIAN ALBUMS OF THE 1990s IN CANADA

	ALBUM/ARTIST	YEAR
1	*Jagged Little Pill*, Alanis Morissette	1996
2	*The Woman in Me*, Shania Twain	1995
3	*Come on Over*, Shania Twain	1997
4	*The Colour of My Love*, Celine Dion	1994
5	*Mad Mad World*, Tom Cochrane	1991
6	*Waking Up the Neighbours*, Bryan Adams	1991
7	*Alannah Myles*, Alannah Myles	1990
8	*Surfacing*, Sarah McLachlan	1997
9	*Let's Talk About Love*, Celine Dion	1997
10	*Falling Into You*, Celine Dion	1997

❦ TOP 10 ALBUMS OF THE 1990s IN CANADA
(Album/artist/year)

1 *Jagged Little Pill*, Alanis Morissette, 1996 **2** *The Woman in Me*, Shania Twain, 1995 **3** *Come on Over*, Shania Twain, 1997 **4** *Unplugged*, Eric Clapton, 1992 **5** *Titanic*, Soundtrack, 1998 **6** *The Bodyguard*, Soundtrack, 1992 **7** *Big Shiny Tunes 2*, Various Artists, 1997 **8** *The Sign*, Ace of Base, 1994 **9** *Dookie*, Green Day, 1995 **10** *Spice*, Spice Girls, 1997

Source: *Music Data Canada*

BLUER THAN BLUE

Madonna's True Blue spent nine weeks at No. 1 in Canada during the summer of 1986 making it the No. 5 album of the 1980s and the Material Girl's biggest album to date.

❦ TOP 10 ALBUMS OF EACH YEAR IN THE 1990s IN CANADA*
(Year/album/artist)

1 1990 *...But Seriously*, Phil Collins **2** 1991 *To the Extreme*, Vanilla Ice **3** 1992 *Waking Up the Neighbours*, Bryan Adams **4** 1993 *Unplugged*, Eric Clapton **5** 1994 *The Sign*, Ace of Base **6** 1995 *No Need to Argue*, The Cranberries **7** 1996 *Jagged Little Pill*, Alanis Morissette **8** 1997 *Let's Talk About Love*, Celine Dion **9** 1998 *Titanic*, Soundtrack **10** 1999 *Millennium*, Backstreet Boys

* As of June 1999   Source: The Record

Did You Know? With 2 million copies sold in Canada, *Jagged Little Pill* by Ottawa's Alanis Morissette is this country's best-selling domestic release.

Women in the Charts

TOP 10
YOUNGEST FEMALE SINGERS TO HAVE A NO. 1 SINGLE IN CANADA

	SINGER/TITLE/YEAR	AGE YEARS	MONTHS
1	Britney Spears, *...Baby One More Time*, 1988	16	11
2	Monica, *The Boy Is Mine*, 1998	17	7
3	Debbie Gibson, *Foolish Beat*, 1988	17	11
4	Christina Aguilera, *Genie in a Bottle*, 1999	18	8
5	Brandy, *The Boy Is Mine*, 1998	19	3
6	Mariah Carey, *Vision of Love*, 1990	20	5
7	Kylie Minogue, *The Locomotion*, 1988	20	7
8	Samantha Fox, *Touch Me (I Want Your Body)* 1987	20	10
9	Debby Boone, *You Light Up My Life*, 1977	21	1
10	Anita Ward, *Ring My Bell*, 1979	21	7

Source: *Music Data Canada*

TOP 10
OLDEST FEMALE SINGERS TO HAVE A NO. 1 SINGLE IN CANADA

	SINGER/TITLE/YEAR	AGE YEARS	MONTHS
1	Tina Turner, *We Don't Need Another Hero*, 1985	45	9
2	Madonna, *American Pie*, 2000	42	6
3	Barbra Streisand, *Woman In Love*, 1980	38	6
4	Dolly Parton, *Islands in the Stream*, 1983	37	10
5	Diana Ross, *Endless Love*, 1981	37	5
6	Kim Carnes, *Bette Davis Eyes*, 1981	35	10
7	Cyndi Lauper, *True Colors*, 1986	33	5
8	Deniece Williams, *Let's Hear It for the Boy*, 1984	33	1
9	Tracy Chapman, *Give Me One Reason*, 1996	32	4
10	Donna Summer, *Hot Stuff*, 1979	30	5

Source: *Music Data Canada*

BRITNEY'S BEST

Her debut single ...Baby One More Time was a No. 1 hit for Louisiana-born Britney Spears, a former performer on Disney Channel's Mickey Mouse Club.

TOP 10 🍁
FEMALE SINGERS WITH THE MOST TOP 40 HITS IN CANADA

	SINGER	TOP 40 HITS*
1	Madonna	44
2	Janet Jackson	29
3	Whitney Houston	26
4=	Celine Dion	23
4=	Mariah Carey	23
6	Alanis Morissette	17
7	Tina Turner	16
8=	Gloria Estefan	15
8=	Olivia Newton-John	15
10	Donna Summer	14

* To May 2000

SINGING PHENOMENON

Born Cherilyn Sarkasian La Pier in El Centro, California, on May 20, 1946, Cher formed the singing double act of Sonny and Cher with her husband Sonny Bono. Their single *I Got You Babe* topped the charts worldwide in 1965, and Cher went on to achieve her first solo million-seller, *Bang Bang (My Baby Shot Me Down)* the following year. Television work with Sonny (from whom she was divorced in 1974) and later movie acting, for which she won an Oscar in 1988 (for *Moonstruck*), have since served as the backdrop to a quite phenomenal singing career that saw her score a No. 2 hit in Canada at the age of 52.

SNAP SHOTS

SAILING TO FAME
One of Canada's most successful singers, Celine Dion achieved worldwide fame with My Heart Will Go On *from the movie* Titanic.

TOP 10 🍁
ALBUMS BY FEMALE SINGERS IN CANADA

	TITLE/ARTIST	YEAR
1	*Jagged Little Pill*, Alanis Morissette	1996
2	*The Woman In Me*, Shania Twain	1995
3	*Come on Over*, Shania Twain	1997
4	*Whitney Houston*, Whitney Houston	1986
5	*I Do Not Want What I Haven't Got*, Sinead O'Connor	1990
6	*True Blue*, Madonna	1986
7	*The Bodyguard* soundtrack	1992
8	*Let's Talk About Love*, Celine Dion	1997
9	*The Colour of My Love*, Celine Dion	1994
10	*Alannah Myles*, Alannah Myles	1990

Source: *Music Data Canada*

TOP 10 🍁
SINGLES BY FEMALE SINGERS IN CANADA*

	SINGLE/ARTIST	YEAR
1	*The Power of Love*, Celine Dion	1994
2	*You Light Up My Life*, Debby Boone	1977
3	*Fantasy*, Mariah Carey	1995
4	*God Bless The Child*, Shania Twain	1996
5	*Secret*, Madonna	1994
6	*Touch Me (I Want Your Body)*, Samantha Fox	1987
7	*That's the Way Love Goes*, Janet Jackson	1993
8	*Don't Cry for Me Argentina*, Madonna	1997
9	*Girls Just Wanna Have Fun*, Cyndi Lauper	1984
10	*Love Theme from A Star Is Born (Evergreen)*, Barbra Streisand	1977

* Excludes duets between female solo singers

Source: *Music Data Canada*

Did You Know? Released in 1915, Romanian soprano Alma Gluck's *Carry Me Back to Old Virginny* was the first recording by a woman to sell over a million copies.

133

Girl Groups

❤ TOP 10 SINGLES BY FEMALE GROUPS IN CANADA*

(Single/group/year)

1 *Goodbye*, Spice Girls, 1998 **2** *I Love Rock'n'Roll*, Joan Jett & The Blackhearts, 1982 **3** *Funkytown*, Lipps Inc., 1980 **4** *Heart of Glass*, Blondie, 1979 **5** *Call Me*, Blondie, 1980 **6** *Release Me*, Wilson Phillips, 1990 **7** *Boogie Oogie Oogie*, A Taste of Honey, 1978 **8** *The Tide Is High*, Blondie, 1981 **9** *Walk Like an Egyptian*, Bangles, 1987 **10** *Take My Breath Away*, Berlin, 1986

* Includes groups led by a female

Source: Music Data Canada

TOP TRIO

The initial letters of the singers' nicknames – "T-Boz," "Left Eye," and "Chilli" – provided the name for the 1990s' singing sensation TLC.

TOP 10 🍁
FEMALE GROUPS IN CANADA*

GROUP	SINGLES AT NO. 1#	SINGLES IN TOP 10	TOP 40
1 Wilson Phillips	1	6	7
2 Spice Girls	1	5	8
3 Pointer Sisters	0	5	9
4 Expose	0	2	9
5 The Bangles	1	2	7
6 Salt-n-Pepa	0	3	7
7 West End Girls	1	1	7
8 Bananarama	1	2	5
9 All Saints	1	2	3
10 TLC	0	2	4

* To May 2000

 # Ranked by total number of hits. Where a tie exists, the groups are ranked according to No. 1 hits

Source: Music Data Canada

WORTH THEIR SALT

Formed as a duo in 1985 and joined by Spinderella in 1987, rap girl group Salt-n-Pepa have achieved huge success on both sides of the Atlantic.

TOP 10 ★
SINGLES BY FEMALE GROUPS IN THE US

	TITLE/GROUP	YEAR
1	*Don't Let Go*, En Vogue	1996
2	*Hold On*, En Vogue	1990
3	*Wannabe*, Spice Girls	1997
4	*Whatta Man*, Salt-n-Pepa	1994
5	*Expressions*, Salt-n-Pepa	1990
6	*Push It*, Salt-n-Pepa	1987
7	*Waterfall*, TLC	1995
8	*Creep*, TLC	1994
9	*Weak*, SWV	1993
10	*Baby, Baby, Baby*, TLC	1992

Source: *The Popular Music Database*

TOP 10 ★
SINGLES BY FEMALE GROUPS IN THE UK

	TITLE/GROUP	YEAR
1	*Wannabe*, Spice Girls	1996
2	*Say You'll Be There*, Spice Girls	1996
3	*2 Become 1*, Spice Girls	1996
4	*Never Ever*, All Saints	1997
5	*C'est La Vie*, B*Witched	1998
6	*Goodbye*, Spice Girls	1998
7	*Viva Forever*, Spice Girls	1998
8	*Spice Up Your Life*, Spice Girls	1997
9	*Too Much*, Spice Girls	1997
10	*Mama/Who Do You Think You Are*, Spice Girls	1997

Such has been the Spice Girls' impact on popular music that they have totally rewritten the record book as far as successful girl-group singles are concerned, snatching eight of the all-time bestsellers in the UK.

TOP 10 🍁
ALBUMS BY FEMALE GROUPS IN CANADA

	TITLE/GROUP	YEAR
1	*Spice*, Spice Girls	1998
2	*No Need to Argue*, The Cranberries	1995
3	*Joyride*, Roxette	1991
4	*Wilson Phillips*, Wilson Phillips	1990
5	*Spiceworld*, Spice Girls	1997
6	*Aquarium*, Aqua	1997
7	*Fanmail*, TLC	1999
8	*Crazysexycool*, TLC	1995
9	*All Saints*, All Saints	1998
10	*Breakout*, Pointer Sisters	1984

Source: *Music Data Canada*

As this list exemplifies, the 1990s saw a huge surge in the popularity of all-girl groups, with sales eclipsing those of such predecessors as The Supremes and Bangles.

GIRL POWER
The original lineup of five Spice Girls achieved unprecedented dominance of the singles charts during the late 1990s.

Who was the most recent Canadian astronaut in space?
see p.19 for the answer

A Dave Williams
B Julie Payette
C Chris Hadfield

Star Singles & Albums

BEAT ALL

In a lifespan of little over 10 years (1960–70), the Beatles revolutionized rock music, achieving worldwide sales of more than 1 billion recordings.

TOP 10 ★ ARTISTS WITH THE MOST ALBUM SALES IN THE US

	ARTIST OR GROUP	TOTAL ALBUM SALES*
1	The Beatles	106,530,000
2	Garth Brooks	92,000,000
3	Led Zeppelin	83,620,000
4	Elvis Presley	77,280,000
5	Eagles	65,000,000
6	Billy Joel	63,250,000
7	Barbra Streisand	62,750,000
8	Elton John	61,620,000
9	Aerosmith	54,370,000
10	Pink Floyd	52,600,000

* To January 2000

Source: *RIAA*

The RIAA, which certifies US record sales, has logged over 70 artists who have achieved total album sales of more than 20 million each.

TOP 10 🍁 ELVIS PRESLEY SINGLES IN CANADA

	SINGLE	YEAR
1	(Let Me Be Your) Teddy Bear	1957
2	Big Hunk O' Love/ My Wish Came True	1959
3	It's Now or Never	1960
4	Stuck on You/Fame and Fortune	1960
5	A Fool Such As I/ I Need Your Love Tonight	1959
6	Hard Headed Woman	1958
7	Return to Sender	1962
8	I Got Stung	1958
9	Suspicious Minds	1969
10	Don't	1958

Source: *Music Data Canada*

Elvis had dozens of million-selling singles throughout his career, but most of his monster hits were during his 1950s heyday.

KING OF ROCK

Elvis Presley's first singles were released in 1954, when he was 19. Baby, Let's Play House, released in 1955, became his first chart hit in the US.

TOP 10 🍁 BEATLES SINGLES IN CANADA

	SINGLE	YEAR
1	I Want to Hold Your Hand	1964
2	Get Back	1969
3	All My Lovin'	1964
4	Something	1969
5	She Loves You	1964
6	Hey Jude	1968
7	Let It Be	1970
8	Hello Goodbye	1967
9	A Hard Day's Night	1964
10	All You Need Is Love	1967

Source: *Music Data Canada*

🍁 TOP 10 MADONNA ALBUMS IN CANADA

(Album/year)

1 *True Blue*, 1986
2 *Like a Virgin*, 1985
3 *Like A Prayer*, 1989
4 *Ray of Light*, 1998
5 *The Immaculate Collection*, 1990
6 *I'm Breathless*, 1990
7 *Erotica*, 1992
8 *Songs to Remember*, 1995
9 *Bedtime Stories*, 1994
10 *Who's That Girl* soundtrack, 1987

Source: *Music Data Canada*

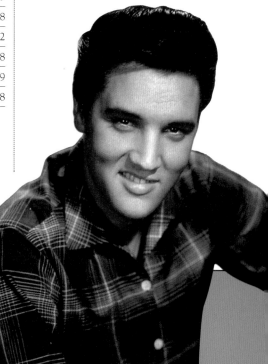

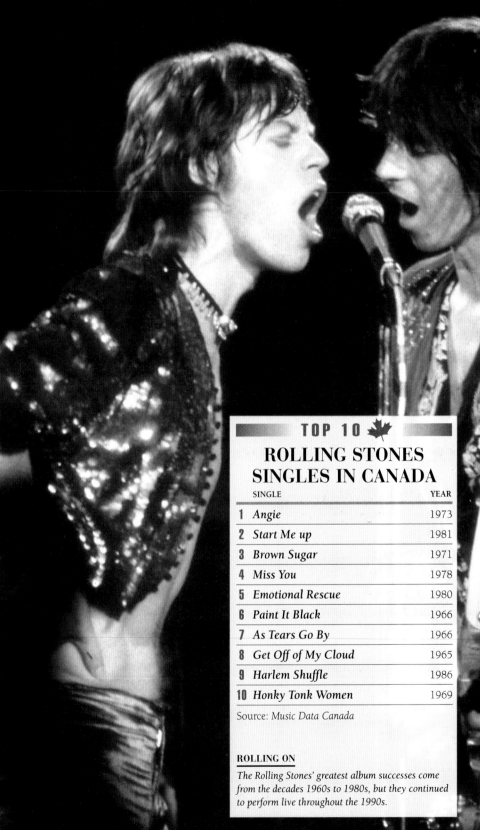

TOP 10
JOHN LENNON SINGLES IN CANADA

	SINGLE	YEAR
1	*(Just Like) Starting Over*	1980
2	*Woman*	1981
3	*Imagine*	1971
4	*Whatever Gets You Through the Night*	1974
5	*Instant Karma*	1970
6	*Power to the People*	1971
7	*Watching the Wheels*	1981
8	*Give Peace a Chance*	1969
9	*Nobody Told Me*	1984
10	*Mind Games*	1973

Source: *Music Data Canada*

John Lennon began his extracurricular recording projects during the year before the Beatles actually split up: *Give Peace a Chance* appeared in 1969, credited to the Plastic Ono Band. *Imagine* was a hit twice, the second occasion being immediately after Lennon's death. *Nobody Told Me* was a posthumous Top 20 chart entry just over four years after he died.

TOP 10
ELTON JOHN SINGLES IN CANADA

	SINGLE	YEAR
1	*Candle in the Wind 1997/ Something About the Way You Look Tonight*	1997
2	*Don't Go Breaking My Heart*	1976*
3	*Nikita*	1986
4	*Island Girl*	1975
5	*Little Jeannie*	1980
6	*Sorry Seems to Be the Hardest Word*	1977
7	*Can You Feel the Love Tonight*	1994
8	*I Don't Wanna Go On with You Like That*	1988
9	*Pinball Wizard*	1975
10	*Believe*	1995

* *Elton John/Kiki Dee*

Source: *Music Data Canada*

TOP 10
ROLLING STONES SINGLES IN CANADA

	SINGLE	YEAR
1	*Angie*	1973
2	*Start Me up*	1981
3	*Brown Sugar*	1971
4	*Miss You*	1978
5	*Emotional Rescue*	1980
6	*Paint It Black*	1966
7	*As Tears Go By*	1966
8	*Get Off of My Cloud*	1965
9	*Harlem Shuffle*	1986
10	*Honky Tonk Women*	1969

Source: *Music Data Canada*

ROLLING ON

The Rolling Stones' greatest album successes come from the decades 1960s to 1980s, but they continued to perform live throughout the 1990s.

Did You Know? *Come On*, the Rolling Stones' first single (1963), had to be re-recorded, altering the word "jerk" to "guy" in order to avoid a radio ban.

Pop Stars of the 90s

TOP 10 🍁
U2 SINGLES IN CANADA

	SINGLE	YEAR
1	Mysterious Ways	1992
2	One	1992
3	Hold Me, Thrill Me, Kiss Me, Kill Me	1995
4	Sweetest Thing	1998
5	Discotheque	1997
6	Staring at the Sun	1997
7	The Fly	1991
8	Even Better Than the Real Thing	1992
9	Last Night on Earth	1997
10	Please	1997

TOP 10 🍁
SPICE GIRLS SINGLES IN CANADA

	SINGLE	YEAR
1	Goodbye	1998
2	Spice Up Your Life	1997
3	Look At Me*	1999
4	Too Much	1998
5	Viva Forever	1998
6	Stop	1998
7	Wannabe	1997
8	Say You'll Be There	1997
9	When You're Gone#	1999
10	2 Become 1	1997

* Geri Halliwell
# Bryan Adams with Mel C.

TOP 10 🍁
BACKSTREET BOYS SINGLES IN CANADA

	SINGLE	YEAR
1	I Want It That Way	1999
2	Everybody (Backstreet's Back)	1997
3	Get Down (You're the One for Me)	1996
4	As Long As You Love Me	1997
5	Quit Playing Games (With My Heart)	1997
6	All I Have to Give	1998
7	Larger Than Life	1999
8	Anywhere for You	1997
9	We've Got It Goin' On	1997
10	Nick Shape CD	1998

TOP 10 🍁
SHERYL CROW SINGLES IN CANADA

	SINGLE	YEAR
1	Strong Enough	1995
2	All I Wanna Do	1994
3	Everyday Is a Winding Road	1997
4	A Change Would Do You Good	1997
5	My Favorite Mistake	1998
6	If It Makes You Happy	1996
7	Can't Cry Anymore	1995
8	Leaving Las Vegas	1994
9	Anything But Down	1999
10	Sweet Child O' Mine	1999

TOP 10 🍁
AEROSMITH SINGLES IN CANADA

	SINGLE	YEAR
1	I Don't Want to Miss a Thing	1998
2	Crazy	1994
3	Amazing	1994
4	Janie's Got a Gun	1990
5	Cryin'	1993
6	What It Takes	1990
7	Livin' on the Edge	1993
8	Blind Man	1995
9	Falling in Love (Is Hard on the Knees)	1997
10	Hole in My Soul	1997

🍁 TOP 10 MADONNA SINGLES IN CANADA
(Single/year)

❶ Secret, 1994 ❷ This Used to Be My Playground, 1992 ❸ Vogue, 1990 ❹ Deeper and Deeper, 1993 ❺ Take a Bow, 1995 ❻ Rain, 1993 ❼ Frozen, 1998 ❽ Justify My Love, 1990 ❾ Erotica, 1992 ❿ Hanky Panky, 1990

TOP 10 🍁
R.E.M. SINGLES IN CANADA

	SINGLE	YEAR
1	Losing My Religion	1991
2	Siny Happy People	1991
3	What's the Frequency, Kenneth?	1994
4	Bang and Blame	1995
5	Man on the Moon	1993
6	Drive	1992
7	E-Bow the Letter	1996
8	Everybody Hurts	1993
9	Strange Currencies	1995
10	Bittersweet Me	1996

🍁 TOP 10 SMASHING PUMPKINS SINGLES IN CANADA
(Single/year)

❶ 1979, 1996 ❷ Bullet with Butterfly Wings, 1995 ❸ Tonight Tonight, 1996 ❹ Ava Adore, 1998 ❺ Disarm, 1994 ❻ Perfect, 1998 ❼ Thirty-Three, 1997 ❽ Cherub Rock, 1997 ❾ Muzzle, 1996 ❿ Today, 1997

Source: Music Data Canada

TOP 10 🍁
SARAH McLACHLAN SINGLES IN CANADA

	SINGLE	YEAR
1	Building a Mystery	1997
2	Adia	1998
3	Sweet Surrender	1998
4	Angel	1999
5	I Will Remember You (Live)	1999
6	Good Enough	1994
7	I Will Remember You	1995
8	Possession	1993
9	Into the Fire	1991
10	Dear God	1995

Source: Music Data Canada

TOP 10 🍁
TRAGICALLY HIP SINGLES IN CANADA

	SINGLE	YEAR
1	Ahead by a Century	1996
2	Courage	1993
3	Little Bones	1991
4	Locked in the Trunk of a Car	1992
5	Grace, Too	1994
6	Greasy Jungle	1994
7	Boots or Hearts	1990
8	Poets	1998
9	Flamenco	1997
10	Gift Shop	1996

Source: Music Data Canada

🍁 TOP 10 JANN ARDEN SINGLES IN CANADA
(Single/year)

1 Insensitive, 1995 **2** Could I Be Your Girl, 1994
3 Wonderdrug, 1995 **4** The Sound Of..., 1997
5 Looking for It, 1996 **6** Good Mother, 1995
7 Wishing That, 1998 **8** I Know You, 1998
9 Will You Remember Me?, 1993 **10** Unloved, 1995

Source: Music Data Canada

GORGEOUS GEORGE

George Michael has achieved bestselling albums across two decades in both the UK and the US.

🍁 TOP 10 GEORGE MICHAEL SINGLES IN CANADA
(Single/year)

1 Fastlove, 1996 **2** Praying for Time, 1990
3 Too Funky, 1992 **4** Don't Let the Sun Go Down on Me*, 1992 **5** Freedom, 1991
6 Somebody to Love, 1993 **7** Jesus to a Child, 1996 **8** Waiting for That Day, 1991
9 Killer/Papa Was a Rolling Stone, 1993
10 Outside, 1998 *With Elton John

Did You Know? Whitney Houston's mother, Cissy Houston, born Drinkard, began her musical career in a group called The Drinkard Sisters, with her nieces Dionne and Dee Dee Warwick.

Roots Rock Reggae

TOP 10 — HEAVY METAL ALBUMS IN CANADA

	ALBUM	ARTIST
1	Slippery When Wet	Bon Jovi
2	Hysteria	Def Leppard
3	1984	Van Halen
4	Metallica	Metallica
5	Bat Out of Hell	Meat Loaf
6	Back in Black	AC/DC
7	Eliminator	ZZ Top
8	Appetite for Destruction	Guns 'N' Roses
9	Get a Grip	Aerosmith
10	Boston	Boston

Source: Music Data Canada

TOP 10 — REGGAE ALBUMS IN THE US, 1999

	TITLE	ARTIST
1	Reggae Gold 1999	Various
2	Strictly the Best 21	Various
3	Reggae Gold 1998	Various
4	Pure Reggae	Various
5	The Doctor	Beenie Man
6	Reggae Party	Various
7	DJ Reggae Mix	Various
8	Best of Bob Marley	Bob Marley
9	Everyone Falls in Love	Tantro Metro & Devonte
10	Labour of Love III	UB40

Source: Billboard

DIAMOND FOR HEAVY METAL
In 1999, Joe Elliot, Def Leppard's vocalist, received an RIAA Diamond award (for albums that have sold more than 10 million copies) for the band's 1987 Hysteria.

LEGEND

Bob Marley's posthumous compilation Legend became the all-time bestselling reggae album, residing at UK No. 1 for 12 weeks and in the charts for 129 weeks.

TOP 10 ★
REGGAE ALBUMS IN THE UK

	TITLE/ARTIST OR GROUP	YEAR
1	*Legend*, Bob Marley and the Wailers	1984
2	*The Best of UB40 Vol. 1*, UB40	1987
3	*Labour of Love II*, UB40	1989
4	*Labour of Love*, UB40	1983
5	*Promises and Lies*, UB40	1993
6	*Present Arms*, UB40	1981
7	*Signing Off*, UB40	1980
8	*Tease Me*, Chaka Demus and Pliers	1993
9	*Labour of Love III*, UB40	1998
10	*Exodus*, Bob Marley and the Wailers	1977

Source: The Popular Music Database

TOP 10 🍁
INSTRUMENTAL SINGLES IN CANADA

	SINGLE	ARTIST
1	*Star Wars Theme/Cantina Band*	Meco
2	*A Fifth of Beethoven*	Walter Murphey & The Big Apple Band
3	*The Hustle*	Van McCoy & The Soul City Symphony
4	*The Homecoming*	Hagood Hardy
5	*Music Box Dancer*	Frank Mills
6	*Axel F*	Harold Faltermeyer
7	*Peter Gunn*	Art of Noise
8	*Miami Vice Theme*	Jan Hammer
9	*Chariots of Fire*	Vangelis
10	*Love Theme from St. Elmo's Fire*	David Foster

Source: Music Data Canada

TOP 10 🍁
LATIN POP SINGLES IN CANADA, 1999

	SINGLE	ARTIST
1	*Livin La Vida Loca*	Ricky Martin
2	*Genie in a Bottle*	Christina Aguilera
3	*If You Had My Love*	Jennifer Lopez
4	*Balaimos*	Enrique Iglesias
5	*Waiting for Tonight*	Jennifer Lopez
6	*Smooth*	Santana featuring Rob Thomas
7	*I Need to Know*	Marc Anthony
8	*She's All I Ever Had*	Ricky Martin
9	*Shake Your Bon-Bon*	Ricky Martin
10	*The Cup of Life*	Ricky Martin

Source: Music Data Canada

TOP 10 — IRISH ALBUMS IN CANADA

	ALBUM/ARTIST	YEAR
1	*The Joshua Tree*, U2	1987
2	*I Do Not Want What I Haven't Got*, Sinead O'Connor	1990
3	*Rattle and Hum*, U2	1988
4	*Zooropa*, U2	1993
5	*No Need to Argue*, Cranberries	1995
6	*Achtung Baby!*, U2	1991
7	*Pop*, U2	1997
8	*The Best of 1980–1990*, U2	1998
9	*Watermark*, Enya	1988
10	*To the Faithful Departed*, Cranberries	1996

THE BOYS IN THE BAND

A string of UK No. 1 albums has secured Boyzone four of the Top 10 Irish albums of all time in the UK.

TOP 10 — WORLD MUSIC ALBUMS IN THE US, 1999

	ALBUM	ARTIST
1	*Sogno*	Andrea Bocelli
2	*Romanza*	Andrea Bocelli
3	*Buena Vista Social Club*	Buena Vista Social Club
4	*Tears of Stone*	Chieftains
5	*The Book of Secrets*	Loreena McKennitt
6	*Buena Vista Social Club*	Buena Vista Social Club Presents Ibrahim Ferrer
7	*The Irish Tenors*	John McDermott/ Anthony Kearns/Ronan Tynan
8	*Sueno (with Spanish tracks)*	Andrea Bocelli
9	*Romanza (with Spanish tracks)*	Andrea Bocelli
10	*Return To Pride Rock – Songs Inspired by Disney's The Lion King II*	Various Artists

Source: Billboard

THE 9 — LAST RECIPIENTS OF THE FREDDIE STONE AWARD

YEAR	ARTIST
1999	Bill Brennan, percussionist
1998	Lori Freedman, bass clarinetist
1997	Nic Gotham, saxophonist
1996	René Lussier, guitarist
1995	Paul Plimley, pianist
1994	Michele George, vocalist
1993	John Oswald, composer
1992	Jean Derome, saxophonist
1991	Lisle Ellis, bassist

The Freddie Stone award was established in 1991 in honor of the influential Toronto jazz trumpeter, flugelhorn player, teacher, and composer who died in 1986. The award honors Canadian musicians in the field of jazz and new music who reflect musical integrity and innovation.

Did You Know? The first-ever rap album to reach a mass audience and achieve gold status in the US was *Run D.M.C.*, on December 17, 1984.

TOP 10 🍁
COUNTRY ALBUMS IN CANADA, 1999
ALBUM/ARTIST

1	*Come On Over*, Shania Twain	
2	*Wide Open Spaces*, Dixie Chicks	
3	*Fly*, Dixie Chicks	
4	*Breathe*, Faith Hill	
5	*In the Life of Chris Gaines*, Garth Brooks	
6	*Place in the Sun*, Tim McGraw	
7	*Lonely Grill*, Lonestar	
8	*Double Live*, Garth Brooks	
9	*CMT 99*, various artists	
10	*Faith*, Faith Hill	

Source: *SoundScan*

TWAIN MAKES HER MARK
Having sold over 27 million copies to date, Come On Over by Canadian-born Shania Twain ranks as the bestselling country album in Canada and the US.

Shania Twain swept the music awards in 2000: she earned Junos for Songwriter of the Year and Best Country Female Artist, and Grammys for Best Female Country Vocal Performance and Best Country Song.

TOP 10 🍁
RAP SINGLES IN CANADA

	SINGLE/ARTIST	YEAR
1	*Rapper's Delight*, Sugarhill Gang	1980
2	*I'll Be Missing You*, Puff Daddy & Faith Evans (featuring 112)	1997
3	*Push It*, Salt'n'Pepa	1988
4	*Let Your Backbone Slide*, Maestro Fresh Wes	1990
5	*Wild Thing*, Tone Loc	1989
6	*U Can't Touch This*, M.C. Hammer	1990
7	*Bust a Move*, Young M.C.	1989
8	*Walk This Way*, Run D.M.C.	1986
9	*Insane in the Brain*, Cypress Hill	1993
10	*I'll Be There for You/You're All I Need (To Get By)*, Method Man Feat. Mary J. Blige	1995

Source: *Music Data Canada*

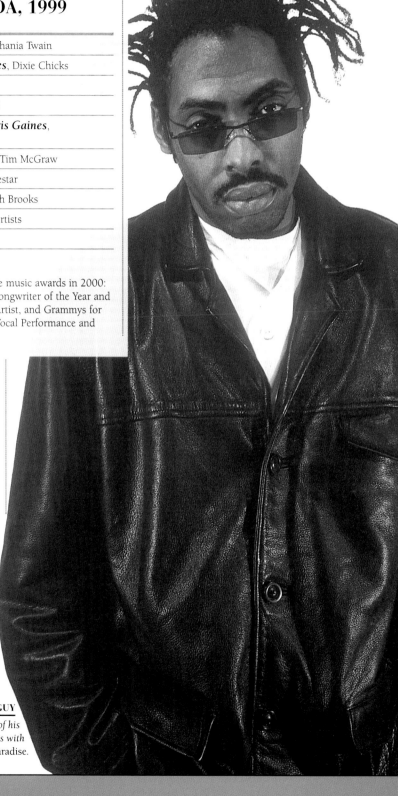

COOL GUY
Coolio (born Artis Ivey, 1963) sold over a million copies of his debut album, It Takes a Thief, achieving even greater success with his bestselling 1995 album, Gangsta's Paradise.

Gold, Platinum & Diamond Discs

COUNTRY GOLD

In a recording career of over 30 years, Kenny Rogers has gained an impressive 28 gold and 44 platinum albums in the US.

TOP 10 ★
MALE ARTISTS WITH THE MOST PLATINUM ALBUMS IN THE US

	ARTIST	PLATINUM ALBUMS
1	Garth Brooks	97
2	Elvis Presley	75
3	Billy Joel	74
4	Elton John	58
5=	Michael Jackson	53
5=	Bruce Springsteen	53
7	George Strait	46
8	Kenny Rogers	44
9	Kenny G	41
10	Neil Diamond	35

Source: *RIAA*

Platinum singles and albums in the US are those that have achieved sales of 1 million units.

THE 10 🍁
LAST SINGLES CERTIFIED IN CANADA*

	SINGLE/ARTIST	CERTIFICATION	DATE
1	*Blue (Da Ba Dee)*, Eiffel 65	Gold	Mar 2000
2	*Broken*, Nine Inch Nails	Platinum	Feb 1999
3	*Goodbye*, Spice Girls	2 x Platinum	Jan 1999
4	*Candle in the Wind 1997*, Elton John	19 x Platinum	Dec 1997
5	*I'll Be Missing You*, Puff Daddy & Faith Evans	Platinum	Oct 1997
6	*When Something Stands for Nothing*, Headstones	Platinum	Dec 1994
7	*The Lion King Read-Along*, soundtrack cast	Platinum	Nov 1994
8	*Praying for Rain*, Junkhouse	Platinum	Oct 1994
9	*Please Don't Go*, K.W.S.	Gold	Oct 1993
10=	*I'm Too Sexy*, Right Said Fred	Gold	Mar 1992
10=	*The Baby Record*, Bob McGrath/Katharine Smithrim	Gold	Mar 1992

* As of May 2000. Gold signifies sales of 50,000 in Canada, platinum sales of 100,000

Source: *Canadian Recording Industry Association (CRIA)*

THE 10 🍁
FIRST PLATINUM CANADIAN CONTENT SINGLES*

	SINGLE	ARTIST	DATE CERTIFIED
1	*The Unicorn*	The Irish Rovers	Feb 1978
2	*Tu t'en vas*	Alain Barrière	Jul 1978
3	*Boogie Woogie Dancin' Shoes*	Claudja Barry	Apr 1979
4	*Wasn't That a Party*	The Rovers	Feb 1981
5	*You Needed Me*	Anne Murray	Nov 1984
6	*Tears Are Not Enough*	Northern Lights	May 1985
7	*Never Surrender*	Corey Hart	Aug 1985
8	*Crying Over You*	Platinum Blonde	Jan 1986
9	*Christmas Time*	Bryan Adams	Jan 1986
10	*Don't Forget Me (When I'm Gone)*	Glass Tiger	Jul 1986

* Platinum signifies 100,000 copies sold in Canada   Source: *CRIA*

🍁 THE 10 LAST DIAMOND ALBUMS IN CANADA*

(Album & artist/date certified)

1 *Amanda Marshall*, Amanda Marshall, Apr 2000 **2** *...Baby One More Time*, Britney Spears, Dec 1999 **3** *Ricky Martin*, Ricky Martin, Dec 1999 **4** *Millennium*, Backstreet Boys, Oct 1999 **5** *Come On Over*, Shania Twain, Apr 1999 **6** *Romanza*, Andrea Bocelli, Mar 1999 **7** *Up to Here*, The Tragically Hip, Jan 1999 **8** *Spiceworld*, Spice Girls, Oct 1998 **9** *Surfacing*, Sarah McLachlan, Oct 1998 **10** *Savage Garden*, Savage Garden, Aug 1998

* As of May 2000. Diamond signifies 1 million copies sold in Canada

Source: *Music Data Canada*

Did You Know? In Canada, gold discs are those that have sold 50,000 copies, while platinum are for sales of 100,00 copies. Diamond signifies sales of 1 million.

ONE OF THE BEST
With eight gold and 17 platinum albums to her name in the US, Tina Turner has secured a place in the top echelons of music.

TOP 10 ★
GROUPS WITH THE MOST PLATINUM ALBUMS IN THE US

GROUP	PLATINUM ALBUMS
1 The Beatles	90
2 Led Zeppelin	80
3 Pink Floyd	66
4 The Eagles	62
5 Aerosmith	51
6 Van Halen	50
7 Fleetwood Mac	46
8 Alabama	44
9 = AC/DC	42
9 = U2	42

Source: *The Popular Music Database*

TOP 10 ★
FEMALE ARTISTS WITH THE MOST PLATINUM ALBUMS IN THE US

ARTIST	PLATINUM ALBUMS
1 Barbra Streisand	49
2 Madonna	47
3 = Whitney Houston	45
3 = Mariah Carey	45
5 Celine Dion	34
6 Reba McEntire	24
7 Linda Ronstadt	23
8 = Janet Jackson	19
8 = Shania Twain	19
10 = Sade	18
10 = Gloria Estefan	18

Source: *RIAA*

TOP 10 ★
GROUPS WITH THE MOST GOLD ALBUMS IN THE US

GROUP	GOLD ALBUMS
1 The Beatles	40
2 The Rolling Stones	37
3 Kiss	23
4 Rush	22
5 = Aerosmith	21
5 = Alabama	21
5 = Chicago	21
8 Jefferson Airplane/Starship	20
9 The Beach Boys	19
10 Santana	18

Source: *RIAA*

The RIAA's gold awards have been presented since 1958 to artists who have sold 500,000 of a single, album, or multidisc set.

GOLDEN SUMMER
Donna Summer has been making hit records for almost 30 years, during which time she has scored nine gold albums in the UK.

TOP 10 ★
FEMALE ARTISTS WITH THE MOST GOLD ALBUMS IN THE US

ARTIST	GOLD ALBUMS
1 Barbra Streisand	40
2 Reba McEntire	19
3 Linda Ronstadt	17
4 Olivia Newton-John	15
5 = Aretha Franklin	13
5 = Madonna	13
5 = Dolly Parton	13
8 = Gloria Estefan*	12
8 = Anne Murray	12
8 = Tanya Tucker	12

* Includes hits with Miami Sound Machine
Source: *RIAA*

Oscar-Winning Movie Music

THE 10 ★
"BEST SONG" OSCAR WINNERS OF THE 1940s

YEAR	TITLE/MOVIE
1940	*When You Wish Upon a Star*, Pinocchio
1941	*The Last Time I Saw Paris*, Lady Be Good
1942	*White Christmas*, Holiday Inn
1943	*You'll Never Know*, Hello, Frisco, Hello
1944	*Swinging on a Star*, Going My Way
1945	*It Might as Well Be Spring*, State Fair
1946	*On the Atchison, Topeka and Santa Fe*, The Harvey Girls
1947	*Zip-A-Dee-Doo-Dah*, Song of the South
1948	*Buttons and Bows*, The Pale Face
1949	*Baby, It's Cold Outside*, Neptune's Daughter

THE 10 ★
"BEST SONG" OSCAR WINNERS OF THE 1950s

YEAR	TITLE/MOVIE
1950	*Mona Lisa*, Captain Carey
1951	*In the Cool, Cool, Cool of the Evening*, Here Comes the Groom
1952	*High Noon (Do Not Forsake Me, Oh My Darling)*, High Noon
1953	*Secret Love*, Calamity Jane
1954	*Three Coins in the Fountain*, Three Coins in the Fountain
1955	*Love Is a Many-Splendored Thing*, Love Is a Many-Splendored Thing
1956	*Whatever Will Be, Will Be (Que Sera, Sera)*, The Man Who Knew Too Much
1957	*All the Way*, The Joker is Wild
1958	*Gigi*, Gigi
1959	*High Hopes*, A Hole in the Head

Doris Day benefited strongly from these Oscars, scoring million-selling singles with *Secret Love* and *Whatever Will Be, Will Be*.

THE 10 ★
"BEST SONG" OSCAR WINNERS OF THE 1960s

YEAR	TITLE/MOVIE
1960	*Never on Sunday*, Never on Sunday
1961	*Moon River*, Breakfast at Tiffany's
1962	*Days of Wine and Roses*, Days of Wine and Roses
1963	*Call Me Irresponsible*, Papa's Delicate Condition
1964	*Chim Chim Cheree*, Mary Poppins
1965	*The Shadow of Your Smile*, The Sandpiper
1966	*Born Free*, Born Free
1967	*Talk to the Animals*, Dr. Dolittle
1968	*The Windmills of Your Mind*, The Thomas Crown Affair
1969	*Raindrops Keep Fallin' on My Head*, Butch Cassidy and the Sundance Kid

Both *The Windmills of Your Mind* and *Raindrops Keep Fallin' on My Head* hit the US Top 10. Sacha Distel's cover version of the 1969 Oscar winner charted five times in the UK in 1970.

TOP 10 🍁
"BEST SONG" OSCAR-WINNING SINGLES IN CANADA

	TITLE/ARTIST	YEAR
1	*I Just Called to Say I Love You*, Stevie Wonder	1984
2	*Flashdance... What a Feeling*, Irene Cara	1983
3	*You Light Up My Life*, Debby Boone	1977
4	*Say You, Say Me*, Lionel Richie	1986
5	*Evergreen* (Love Theme from A Star Is Born), Barbra Streisand	1976
6	*Take My Breath Away*, Berlin	1986
7	*The Way We Were*, Barbra Streisand	1974
8	*Up Where We Belong*, Joe Cocker and Jennifer Warnes	1982
9	*(I've Had) The Time of My Life*, Bill Medley and Jennifer Warnes	1987
10	*Beauty and the Beast*, Celine Dion and Peabo Bryson	1992

Source: *Music Data Canada*

ALL IN A DAY'S WORK

Songs by Doris Day (real name Doris Kappelhoff), from films in which she also starred, produced a duo of Oscar winners in the 1950s.

OSCAR-WINNING PRINCE
A new phenomenon is that half the Oscar-winning songs of the past decade are from animated movies, such as the 1998 winner The Prince of Egypt.

THE 10 ★
"BEST SONG" OSCAR WINNERS OF THE 1970s

YEAR — TITLE/MOVIE

1970 *For All We Know*, Lovers and Other Strangers

1971 *Theme from "Shaft,"* Shaft

1972 *The Morning After*, The Poseidon Adventure

1973 *The Way We Were*, The Way We Were

1974 *We May Never Love Like This Again*, The Towering Inferno

1975 *I'm Easy*, Nashville

1976 *Evergreen*, A Star Is Born

1977 *You Light Up My Life*, You Light Up My Life

1978 *Last Dance*, Thank God It's Friday

1979 *It Goes Like It Goes*, Norma Rae

THE 10 ★
"BEST SONG" OSCAR WINNERS OF THE 1980s

YEAR — TITLE/MOVIE

1980 *Fame*, Fame

1981 *Up Where We Belong*, An Officer and a Gentleman

1982 *Arthur's Theme (Best That You Can Do)*, Arthur

1983 *Flashdance... What a Feeling*, Flashdance

1984 *I Just Called to Say I Love You*, The Woman in Red

1985 *Say You, Say Me*, White Nights

1986 *Take My Breath Away*, Top Gun

1987 *(I've Had) The Time of My Life*, Dirty Dancing

1988 *Let the River Run*, Working Girl

1989 *Under the Sea*, The Little Mermaid

THE 10 ★
"BEST SONG" OSCAR WINNERS OF THE 1990s

YEAR — TITLE/MOVIE

1990 *Sooner or Later (I Always Get My Man)*, Dick Tracy

1991 *Beauty and the Beast*, Beauty and the Beast

1992 *Whole New World*, Aladdin

1993 *Streets of Philadelphia*, Philadelphia

1994 *Can You Feel the Love Tonight*, The Lion King

1995 *Colors of the Wind*, Pocahontas

1996 *You Must Love Me*, Evita

1997 *My Heart Will Go On*, Titanic

1998 *When You Believe*, The Prince of Egypt

1999 *You'll Be in My Heart*, Tarzan

Which country boasts the most students coming to Canada to study? A Korea B France C US see p.149 for the answer

Soundtrack Successes

MUSICAL MOVIES*

	TITLE	YEAR
1	*Grease*	1978
2	*Saturday Night Fever*	1977
3	*The Sound of Music*	1965
4	*Footloose*	1984
5	*American Graffiti*	1973
6	*Mary Poppins*	1964
7	*Flashdance*	1983
8	*The Rocky Horror Picture Show*	1975
9	*Coal Miner's Daughter*	1980
10	*My Fair Lady*	1964

* *Traditional musicals (in which the cast actually sing) and movies in which a musical soundtrack is a major component of the movie are included*

MUSIC TO THE EARS

Despite being made over 35 years ago, The Sound of Music, starring British actress Julie Andrews, remains among the Top 10 highest-earning musicals of all time.

🍁 TOP 10 ORIGINAL SOUNDTRACK ALBUMS IN CANADA

(Movie soundtrack/year)

1 *Saturday Night Fever*, 1977 **2** *Grease*, 1978 **3** *Dirty Dancing*, 1987 **4** *Titanic*, 1998 **5** *The Bodyguard*, 1992 **6** *Forrest Gump*, 1994 **7** *Cocktail*, 1988 **8** *The Lion King*, 1994 **9** *Rattle and Hum*, 1988 **10** *Purple Rain*, 1984

Source: *Music Data Canada*

TOP 10 🍁

JAMES BOND SINGLES IN CANADA

	TITLE/ARTIST	YEAR
1	*A View to a Kill*, Duran Duran	1985
2	*Live and Let Die*, Paul McCartney and Wings	1973
3	*Nobody Does It Better*, Carly Simon	1977
4	*Goldfinger*, Shirley Bassey	1965
5	*Goldfinger*, John Barry	1965
6	*For Your Eyes Only*, Sheena Easton	1981
7	*Thunderball*, Tom Jones	1966
8	*All Time High*, Rita Coolidge	1983
9	*You Only Live Twice*, Nancy Sinatra	1967
10	*Diamonds Are Forever*, Shirley Bassey	1972

Source: *Music Data Canada*

NOBODY DOES IT BETTER

Written by Marvin Hamlisch and Carole Bayer Sager, Carly Simon's song from The Spy Who Loved Me was a worldwide hit.

TOP 10 ★
ARTISTS WITH THE MOST "BEST SONG" OSCAR NOMINATIONS

	ARTIST/WINS/YEARS	NOMINATIONS
1	Sammy Cahn, 4, 1942–75	26
2	Johnny Mercer, 4, 1938–71	18
3=	Paul Francis Webster, 3, 1944–76	16
3=	Alan and Marilyn Bergman, 2, 1968–95	16
5	James Van Heusen, 4, 1944–68	14
6=	Henry Warren, 3, 1935–57	11
6=	Henry Mancini, 2, 1961–86	11
6=	Ned Washington, 1, 1940–61	11
9=	Alan Menken, 4, 1986–97	10
9=	Sammy Fain, 2, 1937–77	10
9=	Leo Robin, 1, 1934–53	10
9=	Jule Styne, 1, 1940–68	10

It was not until 1934 that the category of "Best Song" was added to the many accolades bestowed on films. The awards are often multiple, including the writers of the music and the lyrics.

THE 10 ★
FIRST DISNEY "BEST SONG" OSCAR WINNERS

YEAR	TITLE/FILM
1940	When You Wish Upon a Star, Pinocchio
1947	Zip-a-Dee-Doo-Dah, Song of the South
1964	Chim Chim Cher-ee, Mary Poppins
1989	Under the Sea, The Little Mermaid
1990	Sooner or Later (I Always Get My Man), Dick Tracy
1991	Beauty and the Beast, Beauty and the Beast
1992	Whole New World, Aladdin
1994	Can You Feel the Love Tonight, The Lion King
1995	Colors of the Wind, Pocahontas
1996	You Must Love Me, Evita

TOP 10 ★
POP MUSIC FILMS

	TITLE	YEAR
1	The Blues Brothers	1980
2	Purple Rain	1984
3	La Bamba	1987
4	The Doors	1991
5	What's Love Got to Do With It?	1993
6	Xanadu	1980
7	The Jazz Singer	1980
8	Sgt. Pepper's Lonely Hearts Club Band	1978
9	Lady Sings the Blues	1972
10	Pink Floyd – The Wall	1982

RAINING PRINCE
Produced in 1984, Prince's semi-autobiographical film Purple Rain is one of the most successful pop music films ever released.

Music Awards

LATEST GRAMMY RECORDS OF THE YEAR

YEAR	RECORD/ARTIST
1999	*Smooth*, Santana featuring Rob Thomas
1998	*My Heart Will Go On*, Celine Dion
1997	*Sunny Came Home*, Shawn Colvin
1996	*Change the World*, Eric Clapton
1995	*Kiss from a Rose*, Seal
1994	*All I Wanna Do*, Sheryl Crow
1993	*I Will Always Love You*, Whitney Houston
1992	*Tears in Heaven*, Eric Clapton
1991	*Unforgettable*, Natalie Cole with Nat "King" Cole
1990	*Another Day in Paradise*, Phil Collins

THE 10 LATEST RECIPIENTS OF THE GRAMMY LIFETIME ACHIEVEMENT AWARD

(Year/artist*)

1 2000 Harry Belafonte **2** 2000 Sam Cooke **3** 2000 Woody Guthrie **4** 2000 John Lee Hooker **5** 2000 Mitch Miller **6** 2000 Willie Nelson **7** 1999 Johnny Cash **8** 1999 Otis Redding **9** 1999 William "Smokey" Robinson **10** 1999 Mel Tormé

* Listed alphabetically by year
Source: *NARAS*

ARTISTS WITH THE MOST GRAMMY AWARDS

	ARTIST	AWARDS
1	Sir Georg Solti	31
2	Quincy Jones	26
3	Vladimir Horowitz	25
4	Pierre Boulez	23
5	Stevie Wonder	21
6	Henry Mancini	20
7=	John T. Williams	17
7=	Leonard Bernstein	17
9=	Aretha Franklin	15
9=	Itzhak Perlman	15

The Grammy Awards ceremony has been held annually in the United States since its inauguration on May 4, 1959, and the awards are considered to be the most prestigious in the music industry.

FIRST GRAMMY RECORDS OF THE YEAR

YEAR	RECORD/ARTIST OR GROUP
1958	*Nel Blu Dipinto di Blu (Volare)*, Domenico Modugno
1959	*Mack the Knife*, Bobby Darin
1960	*Theme from a Summer Place*, Percy Faith
1961	*Moon River*, Henry Mancini
1962	*I Left My Heart in San Francisco*, Tony Bennett
1963	*The Days of Wine and Roses*, Henry Mancini
1964	*The Girl from Ipanema*, Stan Getz and Astrud Gilberto
1965	*A Taste of Honey*, Herb Alpert and the Tijuana Brass
1966	*Strangers in the Night*, Frank Sinatra
1967	*Up Up and Away*, 5th Dimension

CASHBACK

Johnny Cash was awarded the accolade of a Grammy Lifetime Achievement Award in 1999, 44 years after releasing his first single, Hey Porter/Cry Cry Cry.

THE 10 ★
LAST JUNO ALBUMS OF THE YEAR

YEAR	ALBUM	ARTIST
2000	*Supposed Former Infatuation Junkie*	Alanis Morissette
1999	*Let's Talk About Love*	Celine Dion
1998	*Surfacing*	Sarah McLachlan
1997	*Trouble at the Henhouse*	Tragically Hip
1996	*Jagged Little Pill*	Alanis Morissette
1995	*Colour of My Love*	Celine Dion
1994	*Harvest Moon*	Neil Young
1993	*Ingenue*	k.d. lang
1992	*Mad Mad World*	Tom Cochrane
1991	*Unison*	Celine Dion

Source: *Canadian Academy of Recording Arts & Sciences (CARAS)*

♣ THE 10 LAST CANADIAN COUNTRY MUSIC AWARDS SINGLES OF THE YEAR

(Year/single/artist)

1999, *26 Cents*, The Wilkinsons
1998, *You're Still the One*, Shania Twain
1997, *I Do*, Paul Brandt **1996**, *Better Things to Do*, Terri Clark **1995**, *Any Man of Mine*, Shania Twain **1994**, *I'm Gonna Drive You Out of My Mind*, Charlie Major
1993, *He Would Be Sixteen*, Michelle Wright
1992, *Take It Like a Man*, Michelle Wright
1991, *New Kind of Love*, Michelle Wright
1990, *Goodbye, So Long, Hello*, Prairie Oyster
Source: *Canadian Country Music Association*

THE 10 LAST GRAMMY NEW ARTISTS OF THE YEAR

1 1999 Christina Aguilera
2 1998 Lauryn Hill **3** 1997 Paula Cole
4 1996 LeeAnn Rimes **5** 1995 Hootie & The Blowfish **6** 1994 Sheryl Crow
7 1993 Toni Braxton **8** 1992 Arrested Development **9** 1991 Mark Cohn
10 1990 Mariah Carey

THE 10 ★
LAST JUNO RECORDS OF THE YEAR

YEAR	RECORD	ARTIST
2000	*Bobcaygeon*	The Tragically Hip
1999	*One Week*	Barenaked Ladies
1998	*Building a Mystery*	Sarah McLachlan
1997	*Ironic*	Alanis Morissette
1996	*You Oughta Know*	Alanis Morissette
1995	*Could I Be Your Girl*	Jann Arden
1994	*Fare Thee Well Love*	Rankin Family
1993	*Beauty and the Beast*	Celine Dion/ Peabo Bryson
1992	*Life Is a Highway*	Tom Cochrane
1991	*Just Came Back*	Colin James

THE 10 ★
LATEST RECIPIENTS OF THE SAMMY CAHN LIFETIME ACHIEVEMENT AWARD

YEAR	RECIPIENT
1999	Kenny Rogers
1998	Berry Gordy
1997	Vic Damone
1996	Frankie Laine
1995	Steve Lawrence and Eydie Gorme
1994	Lena Horne
1993	Ray Charles
1992	Nat "King" Cole
1991	Gene Autry
1990	B. B. King

Source: *Songwriter's Hall of Fame*

THE 10 LATEST INDUCTEES INTO THE ROCK 'N' ROLL HALL OF FAME

1 Eric Clapton
2 Earth, Wind & Fire **3** Lovin' Spoonful **4** Moonglows **5** Bonnie Raitt **6** James Taylor **7** Nat King Cole (Early influence category) **8** Billie Holiday (Early influence category) **9** King Curtis (Sideman) **10** = James Jamerson (Sideman); = Earl Palmer (Sideman); = Hal Blaine (Sideman); = Scotty Moore (Sideman)

THE 10 ★
LATEST INDUCTEES INTO THE COUNTRY MUSIC HALL OF FAME

YEAR	ARTIST*
1999	Johnny Bond
1999	Dolly Parton
1999	Conway Twitty
1998	George Morgan
1998	Elvis Presley
1998	E. W. "Bud" Wendell
1998	Tammy Wynette
1997	Harlan Howard
1997	Cindy Walker
1997	Brenda Lee

* *Listed alphabetically by year*

Source: *Country Music Association*

Founded in 1961 by the Country Music Association in Nashville, the Country Music Hall of Fame recognizes outstanding contributions to the world of Country. It inducted 72 members between 1961 and 1999.

THE 10 LATEST GRAMMY POP VOCAL PERFORMANCES OF THE YEAR, MALE

1 1999 Sting, *Brand New Day* **2** 1998 Eric Clapton, *My Father's Eyes* **3** 1997 Elton John, *Candle in the Wind 1997* **4** 1996 Eric Clapton, *Change the World* **5** 1995 Seal, *Kiss from a Rose* **6** 1994 Elton John, *Can You Feel the Love Tonight* **7** 1993 Sting, *If I Ever Lose My Faith in You* **8** 1992 Eric Clapton, *Tears in Heaven* **9** 1991 Michael Bolton, *When a Man Loves a Woman* **10** 1990 Roy Orbison, *Oh, Pretty Woman*

Did You Know? The first-ever Grammy Record of the Year, *Nel Blu Dipinto di Blu (Volare)*, was revived by David Bowie in the 1986 film *Absolute Beginners*.

Classical & Opera

TOP 10 ★
LONGEST OPERAS PERFORMED AT THE METROPOLITAN OPERA HOUSE, NEW YORK CITY*

	OPERA	COMPOSER	RUNNING TIME# HR:MIN
1	Götterdämmerung	Richard Wagner	4:27
2	Die Meistersinger von Nürnberg	Richard Wagner	4:21
3	Parsifal	Richard Wagner	4:17
4=	Les Troyens	Hector Berlioz	4:02
4=	Siegfried	Richard Wagner	4:02
6	Tristan und Isolde	Richard Wagner	4:00
7	Die Walküre	Richard Wagner	3:41
8	Don Carlo	Giuseppe Verdi	3:33
9	Semiramide	Gioacchino Rossini	3:30
10	Lohengrin	Richard Wagner	3:28

* In current repertory
\# Excluding intervals

Source: Metropolitan Opera House

THE 10 🍁
LATEST WINNERS OF "THE BEST CLASSICAL ALBUM"* JUNO AWARD

YEAR	COMPOSER/TITLE/ENSEMBLE OR ORCHESTRA & CONDUCTOR
2000	Schumann, String Quartets, St. Lawrence String Quartet
1999	Handel, Music for the Royal Fireworks, Tafelmusik
1998	Mozart, Horn Concertos, CBC Vancouver Orchestra/Mario Bernardi
1997	Ginastera/Villa-Lobos/Evangelista, I Musici de Montréal
1996	Shostakovich, Symphonies No. 9 and 5, L'Orchestre Symphonique de Montréal/Charles Dutoit
1995	J. S. Bach, Brandenburg Concertos No. 1–6, Tafelmusik
1994	Handel, Concerti Grossi, Op. 3 No. 1–6, Tafelmusik
1993	Handel, Excerpts from Floridante, Tafelmusik
1992	Debussy, Pelléas et Mélisande, L'Orchestre Symphonique de Montréal/ Charles Dutoit
1991	Debussy, Images, Nocturnes, L'Orchestre Symphonique de Montréal/ Charles Dutoit

*Large Ensemble or Soloist(s) with Large Ensemble Accompaniment
Source: CARAS

THE 10 ★
LATEST WINNERS OF THE "BEST CLASSICAL ALBUM" GRAMMY AWARD

YEAR	COMPOSER/TITLE	CONDUCTOR/SOLOIST/ORCHESTRA
1999	Stravinsky, Firebird; The Rite of Spring; Perséphone	Michael Tilson Thomas, Stuart Neill, San Francisco Symphony Orchestra
1998	Barber, Prayers of Kierkegaard/ Vaughan Williams, Dona Nobis Pacem/ Bartok, Cantata Profana	Robert Shaw, Richard Clement, Nathan Gunn, Atlanta Symphony Orchestra and Chorus
1997	Danielpour, Kirchner, Rouse, Premières – Cello Concertos	Yo-Yo Ma, David Zinman, Philadelphia Orchestra
1996	Corigliano, Of Rage and Remembrance	Leonard Slatkin, National Symphony Orchestra
1995	Claude Debussy, La Mer	Pierre Boulez, Cleveland Orchestra
1994	Béla Bartók, Concerto for Orchestra; Four Orchestral Pieces, Op. 12	Pierre Boulez, Chicago Symphony Orchestra
1993	Béla Bartók, The Wooden Prince	Pierre Boulez, Chicago Symphony Orchestra and Chorus
1992	Gustav Mahler, Symphony No. 9	Leonard Bernstein, Berlin Philharmonic Orchestra
1991	Leonard Bernstein, Candide	Leonard Bernstein, London Symphony Orchestra
1990	Charles Ives, Symphony No. 2 (and Three Short Works)	Leonard Bernstein, New York Philharmonic Orchestra

Source: NARAS

TOP 10 🍁
CLASSICAL ALBUMS OF ALL TIME IN CANADA

	ARTIST/ALBUM	YEAR
1	Carreras, Domingo, Pavarotti, Three Tenors 1994	1994
2	Luciano Pavarotti, Pavarotti & Friends 2	1995
3	Placido Domingo, Perhaps Love	1981
4	Luciano Pavarotti, Pavarotti & Friends 1	1993
5	Glenn Gould, The Goldberg Variations	1982
6	Walter Carlos, Switched-On Bach	1969
7	Luciano Pavarotti and Friends, Together for the Children of Bosnia	1996
8	Luciano Pavarotti, O Holy Night	1976
9	Carreras, Domingo, Pavarotti, The Three Tenors in Concert	1990
10	Luciano Pavarotti, Greatest Hits	1980

Source: Music Data Canada & Canadian Recording Industry Association

NORMAN CONQUEST

One of the world's leading opera divas, Georgia-born Jessye Norman on a recording of Bluebeard's Castle *contributed to its gaining the 1999 Grammy "Best Opera Recording" award.*

TOP 10 MOST PROLIFIC CLASSICAL COMPOSERS

(Composer/nationality/hours of music)

1 Joseph Haydn (1732–1809), Austrian, 340 **2** George Handel (1685–1759), German–English, 303 **3** Wolfgang Amadeus Mozart (1756–91), Austrian, 202 **4** Johann Sebastian Bach (1685–1750), German, 175 **5** Franz Schubert (1797–1828), German, 134 **6** Ludwig van Beethoven (1770–1827), German, 120 **7** Henry Purcell (1659–95), English, 116 **8** Giuseppe Verdi (1813–1901), Italian, 87 **9** Anton Dvořák (1841–1904), Czech, 79 **10** = Franz Liszt (1811–86), Hungarian; = Peter Tchaikovsky (1840–93), Russian, 76

This list is based on a survey conducted by *Classical Music*, which ranked classical composers by the total number of hours of music each composed.

THE 10 ★
LATEST WINNERS OF THE "BEST OPERA RECORDING" GRAMMY AWARD

YEAR	COMPOSER/TITLE	SOLOISTS/ORCHESTRA
1999	Stravinsky, *The Rake's Progress*	Ian Bostridge, Bryn Terfel, Anne Sofie van Otter, Deborah York, Monteverdi Choir, London Symphony Orchestra
1998	Bartok, *Bluebeard's Castle*	Jessye Norman, Laszlo Polgar, Karl-August Naegler, Chicago Symphony Orchestra
1997	Richard Wagner, *Die Meistersinger von Nürnberg*	Ben Heppner, Herbert Lippert, Karita Mattila, Alan Opie, Rene Pape, Jose van Dam, Iris Vermillion, Chicago Symphony Chorus, Chicago Symphony Orchestra
1996	Benjamin Britten, *Peter Grimes*	Philip Langridge, Alan Opie, Janice Watson, Opera London, London Symphony Chorus, City of London Sinfonia
1995	Hector Berlioz, *Les Troyens*	Gary Lakes, Françoise Pollet, Orchestre Symphonique de Montréal
1994	Carlisle Floyd, *Susannah*	Jerry Hadley, Samuel Ramey, Cheryl Studer, Kenn Chester
1993	George Handel, *Semele*	Kathleen Battle, Marilyn Horne, Samuel Ramey, Sylvia McNair, Michael Chance
1992	Richard Strauss, *Die Frau Ohne Schatten*	Placido Domingo, Jose Van Dam, Hildegard Behrens
1991	Richard Wagner, *Götterdämmerung*	Hildegard Behrens, Ekkehard Wlashiha
1990	Richard Wagner, *Das Rheingold*	James Morris, Kurt Moll, Christa Ludwig

Source: *NARAS*

TOP 10 LARGEST OPERA HOUSES

(Opera house/location/capacity*)

1 Arena di Verona,# Verona, Italy, 16,663 **2** Municipal Opera Theater,# St. Louis, MO, 11,745 **3** Music Hall, Cincinnati, OH, 3,417 **4** Teatro alla Scala, Milan, Italy, 3,600 **5** Civic Opera House, Chicago, IL, 3,563 **6** The Metropolitan, Lincoln Center, NY; = Teatro San Carlo, Naples, Italy, 3,500 **8** = Teatro Massimo, Palermo, Italy; = The Hummingbird Center, Toronto, Canada, 3,200 **10** Halle aux Grains, Toulouse, France, 3,000

* For indoor venues, seating capacity given; numbers may be increased by standing capacity   # Open-air venue

Although there are many more venues where opera is regularly performed, this list is limited to those venues where the principal performances are opera.

Did You Know? After performing *Otello* at the Vienna Staatsoper on July 30, 1991, Placido Domingo received 101 curtain calls and was applauded for 1 hour 20 minutes.

Stage & Screen

MONEY FOR NOTHING

Much Ado About Nothing, *starring Emma Thompson and Kenneth Branagh (who also directed it), achieved both critical and commercial success.*

THE 10 ★
LATEST WINNERS OF TONY AWARDS FOR A PLAY

YEAR	PLAY
1999	Side Man
1998	Art
1997	The Last Night of Ballyhoo
1996	Master Class
1995	Love! Valour! Compassion!
1994	Angels in America Part II: Perestroika
1993	Angels in America Part I: Millennium Approaches
1992	Dancing at Lughnasa
1991	Lost in Yonkers
1990	The Grapes of Wrath

The Tony Awards, established by the American Theater Wing, honor outstanding Broadway plays and musicals, actors and actreseses, music, costume and other contributions. They are named after the actress and director Antoinette Perry (1988–46), who headed the American Theater Wing during World War II.

THE 10 ★
LATEST WINNERS OF TONY AWARDS FOR A MUSICAL

YEAR	PLAY
1999	Fosse
1998	The Lion King
1997	Titanic
1996	Rent
1995	Sunset Boulevard
1994	Passion
1993	Kiss of the Spider Woman
1992	Crazy for You
1991	The Will Rogers Follies
1990	City of Angels

TOP 10 🍁
SHAW FESTIVAL PRODUCTIONS*

	PRODUCTION
1	Cavalcade
2	Peter Pan
3	A Foggy Day
4	You Can't Take It with You
5	Hobson's Choice
6	Pygmalion
7	You Can Never Tell
8	Will Any Gentleman?
9	Doctor's Dilemma
10	Mrs. Warren's Profession

* Ranked in terms of paid attendance

TOP 10 ★
MOST PRODUCED PLAYS BY SHAKESPEARE, 1961–99

	PLAY	PRODUCTIONS
1	A Midsummer Night's Dream	30
2 =	Macbeth	26
2 =	Twelfth Night	26
4	Romeo and Juliet	25
5	The Taming of the Shrew	24
6 =	As You Like It	23
6 =	Richard III	23
8	King Lear	22
9 =	Hamlet	21
9 =	Much Ado About Nothing	21

TOP 10 MOST-FILMED PLAYS BY SHAKESPEARE

1 Hamlet **2** Romeo and Juliet **3** Macbeth **4** A Midsummer Night's Dream **5** Julius Caesar **6** Othello **7** Richard III **8** Henry V **9** The Merchant of Venice **10** Antony and Cleopatra

Counting modern versions, including those in foreign languages, but discounting made-for-TV films, parodies, and stories derived from the plays, it appears that *Hamlet* is the most-filmed of all Shakespeare's works, with some 70 releases to date, while *Romeo and Juliet* has been remade on at least 40 occasions.

TOP 10 🍁
OLDEST CANADIAN THEATRE COMPANIES*

THEATRE/LOCATION	YEAR FOUNDED
1 Théâtre du Rideau Vert, Montreal, Que.	1949
1 Red Barn Theatre, Jackson's Point, Ont.	1949
3 Théâtre du Nouveau Monde, Montreal, Que.	1951
4 Stratford Festival, Stratford, Ont.	1953
5 Manitoba Theatre Centre, Winnipeg, Man.	1958
6 Shaw Festival, Niagara-on-the-Lake, Ont.	1962
7 Neptune Theatre, Halifax, N.S.	1963
7 Vancouver Playhouse, Vancouver, B.C.	1963
9 Charlottetown Festival, Charlottetown. P.E.I.	1964
10 Citadel Theatre, Edmonton, Alta.	1965

* Oldest professional theatre companies still operating

Source: *Association for Canadian Theatre Research*

TOP 10 ★
LATEST PULITZER DRAMA AWARDS

YEAR*	AUTHOR/PLAY
2000	Jhumpa Lahiri, *Dinner with Friends*
1999	Margaret Edson, *Wit*
1998	Paula Vogel, *How I Learned to Drive*
1996	Jonathan Larson, *Rent*
1995	Horton Foote, *The Young Man from Atlanta*
1994	Edward Albee, *Three Tall Women*
1993	Tony Kushner, *Angels in America: Millennium Approaches*
1992	Robert Schenkkan, *The Kentucky Cycle*
1991	Neil Simon, *Lost in Yonkers*
1990	August Wilson, *The Piano Lesson*

* No award was made in 1997

The Pulitzer Drama Award is made for "an American play, preferably original and dealing with American life."

TOP 10 ★
LONGEST-RUNNING SHOWS ON BROADWAY

SHOW/YEARS	PERFORMANCES
1 *Cats*, 1982–2000	7,397
2 *A Chorus Line*, 1975–90	6,137
3 *Oh! Calcutta!*, 1976–89	5,962
4 *Les Misérables*, 1987–	5,378*
5 *The Phantom of the Opera*, 1988–	5,008*
6 *Miss Saigon*, 1991–	3,619*
7 *42nd Street*, 1980–89	3,486
8 *Grease*, 1972–80	3,388
9 *Fiddler on the Roof*, 1964–72	3,242
10 *Life with Father*, 1939–47	3,224

* Total as of January 1, 2000; still running

Source: *The League of American Theaters and Producers*

Cats became the longest-running Broadway show of all time on June 19, 1997, when it notched up its 6,138th performance. *Les Misérables* celebrated its 13th anniversary on March 12, 2000 with its 5,351st performance. By that date, it had been seen by 7.5 million people in New York and 42 million worldwide. *Life with Father*, the earliest show to be listed here, was a roaring success from the moment it opened. Its popularity had not been predicted, and after the lead parts were refused by major actors and actresses, the author, Howard Lindsay, and his wife, Dorothy Stickney, decided to play the roles themselves. They continued to do so, to rave reviews, for the following five years.

TOP 10 ★
LONGEST-RUNNING MUSICALS ON BROADWAY

MUSICAL/YEARS	PERFORMANCES
1 *Cats*, 1982–2000	7,397
2 *A Chorus Line*, 1975–90	6,137
3 *Les Misérables*, 1987–	5,278*
4 *The Phantom of the Opera*, 1988–	5,008*
5 *Miss Saigon*, 1901–	3,619*
6 *42nd Street*, 1980–89	3,486
7 *Grease*, 1972–80	3,388
8 *Fiddler on the Roof*, 1964–72	3,242
9 *Hello Dolly!*, 1964–71	2,844
10 *My Fair Lady*, 1956–62	2,717

* Total as of January 1, 2000; still running

Source: *The League of American Theaters and Producers*

OUT OF THEIR MISERY

Les Misérables has achieved the dual feat of being one of the longest-running musicals both in London and on Broadway.

Box-Office Winners

TOP 10 HIGHEST-GROSSING MOVIES OF ALL TIME

	MOVIE	YEAR	GROSS INCOME (US$) US	GROSS INCOME (US$) WORLD
1	*Titanic*	1997	600,800,000	1,835,100,000
2	*Star Wars: Episode I – The Phantom Menace*	1999	431,100,000	922,600,000
3	*Jurassic Park*	1993	357,100,000	920,100,000
4	*Independence Day*	1996	306,200,000	811,200,000
5	*Star Wars*	1977/97	461,000,000	798,000,000
6	*The Lion King*	1994	312,900,000	767,900,000
7	*E.T.: The Extra-Terrestrial*	1982	399,800,000	704,800,000
8	*Forrest Gump*	1994	329,700,000	679,700,000
9	*The Lost World: Jurassic Park*	1997	229,100,000	614,400,000
10	*Men in Black*	1997	250,100,000	586,100,000

TOP 10 ★ MOVIE OPENINGS OF ALL TIME IN THE US

	MOVIE/RELEASE DATE	OPENING WEEKEND GROSS (US$)
1	*The Lost World: Jurassic Park*, May 23, 1997	72,132,785
2	*Star Wars: Episode I – The Phantom Menace*, May 21, 1999	64,820,970
3	*Toy Story 2*, Nov 24, 1999	57,388,839
4	*Austin Powers: The Spy Who Shagged Me*, Jun 11, 1999	54,917,604
5	*Batman Forever*, Jun 16, 1995	52,784,433
6	*Men in Black*, Jul 2, 1997	51,068,455
7	*Independence Day*, Jul 3, 1996	50,228,264
8	*Jurassic Park*, Jun 11, 1993	47,059,560
9	*Batman Returns*, Jun 19, 1992	45,687,711
10	*Mission: Impossible*, May 22, 1996	45,436,830

MONSTER MOVIE
Jurassic Park set new standards for animatronic action and reigned as the world's highest-earning movie for five years, before being toppled by Titanic.

Did You Know? On May 19, 1999, *Star Wars: Episode I – The Phantom Menace* became the highest-earning movie in a single day, taking a total of US$28,540,000 at 2,970 box offices across the US.

TOP 10 🍁
HIGHEST-GROSSING CANADIAN MOVIES OF ALL TIME*

	MOVIE	YEAR
1	Porky's	1981
2	Les Boys	1998
3	Les Boys 2	1999
4	Meatballs	1979
5	The Red Violin	1999
6	Air Bud	1997
7	Black Robe	1992
8	Crash	1996
9	The Sweet Hereafter	1997
10	The Changeling	1979

* Worldwide box office

Source: Take One

THE 10 🍁
LAST WINNERS OF THE GOLDEN REEL AWARD*

YEAR	MOVIE	DOMESTIC BOX OFFICE ($)
1999	Les Boys 2	5,500,000
1998	Les Boys	6,800,000
1997	Air Bud	over 1,600,000
1996	Crash	over 1,230,000
1995	Johnny Mnemonic	over 3,000,000
1994	Louis 19, le roi des ondes	1,800,000
1993	La Florida	1,640,000
1992	Black Robe	2,850,000
1991	Ding et dong, le film	2,350,000
1990	Jésus de Montréal	2,530,000

* Given by the Academy of Canadian Cinema & Television to the Canadian movie which has earned the most revenue at the box office

Source: Academy of Canadian Cinema & Television

BEST OF BRITISH

The highest-earning British-made movie, The Full Monty, was successful both in the UK and worldwide, grossing in excess of US$250 million.

BACK FROM THE FUTURE

In the second of the two Terminator movies, Arnold Schwarzenegger is a caring cyborg who protects a boy and his mother from a near-indestructible rival.

TOP 10 ⭐
MOVIE SEQUELS THAT EARNED MORE THAN THE ORIGINAL*

	ORIGINAL	OUTEARNED BY
1	The Terminator	Terminator 2: Judgment Day
2	First Blood	Rambo: First Blood Part II / Rambo III
3	Lethal Weapon	Lethal Weapon 2 / Lethal Weapon 3 / Lethal Weapon 4
4	Austin Powers: International Man of Mystery	Austin Powers: The Spy Who Shagged Me
5	Die Hard	Die Hard 2 / Die Hard With a Vengeance
6	Rocky	Rocky III / Rocky IV
7	Raiders of the Lost Ark	Indiana Jones and the Last Crusade
8	Ace Ventura: Pet Detective	Ace Ventura: When Nature Calls
9	48 HRS	Another 48 HRS
10	Patriot Games	Clear and Present Danger

* Ranked by greatest differential between original and highest-earning sequel

Movie Hits

MOST EXPENSIVE MOVIES EVER MADE

	MOVIE	YEAR	BUDGET (US$)
1	Titanic	1997	200,000,000
2 =	Waterworld	1995	175,000,000
2 =	Wild Wild West	1999	175,000,000
4 =	Speed 2: Cruise Control	1997	150,000,000
4 =	Armageddon	1998	150,000,000
6	Lethal Weapon 4	1998	140,000,000
7 =	Batman and Robin	1997	125,000,000
7 =	Godzilla	1998	125,000,000
9 =	Dante's Peak	1997	115,000,000
9 =	Star Wars: Episode I – The Phantom Menace	1999	115,000,000
9 =	The 13th Warrior	1999	115,000,000

It is coincidental that several of the most expensive movies ever made, including the first two in this Top 10, along with *Speed 2: Cruise Control*, are water-based. Large casts and large-scale special effects, such as those featured in *Titanic*, are major factors in escalating budgets.

HIGH WATER

Produced by and starring Kevin Costner, Waterworld *was one of the most expensive movies ever made, being topped only by* Titanic.

BEST-ATTENDED MOVIES

	MOVIE	YEAR	ATTENDANCE
1	Gone with the Wind	1939	208,100,000
2	Star Wars	1977	198,600,000
3	The Sound of Music	1965	170,600,000
4	E.T.: The Extraterrestrial	1982	151,600,000
5	The Ten Commandments	1956	132,800,000
6	The Jungle Book	1967	126,300,000
7	Titanic	1997	124,300,000
8	Jaws	1975	123,300,000
9	Doctor Zhivago	1965	122,700,000
10	101 Dalmatians	1961	119,600,000

This list is based on the actual number of people purchasing tickets at the US box office. Because it takes account of the relatively greater numbers of tickets sold to children and other discounted sales (such as matinees for certain movies), it differs both from lists that present total box-office receipts (which, as ticket prices increase, tend to feature more recent movies) and from those that are adjusted for inflation. However, it is interesting to observe that if inflation were factored in, *Gone with the Wind* would also top the all-time list, outearning even mega-blockbuster *Titanic* – the only movie from the 1990s to feature in this list. The 1960s stand out from other decades, contributing four movies to this list.

MOVIE SERIES OF ALL TIME

	FILM SERIES	DATES
1	Star Wars / The Empire Strikes Back / Return of the Jedi / Star Wars Episode I: The Phantom Menace	1977–99
2	Jurassic Park / The Lost World: Jurassic Park	1993–97
3	Batman / Batman Returns / Batman Forever / Batman & Robin	1989–97
4	Raiders of the Lost Ark / Indiana Jones and the Temple of Doom / Indiana Jones and the Last Crusade	1981–89
5	Star Trek: The Motion Picture / II: The Wrath of Khan / III: The Search for Spock / IV: The Voyage Home / V: The Final Frontier / VI: The Undiscovered Country / Generations / First Contact / Insurrection	1979–98
6	Back to the Future / II / III	1985–90
7	Lethal Weapon / II / III / IV	1987–98
8	Home Alone / Home Alone 2: Lost in New York	1990–92
9	Jaws / 2 / 3D / The Revenge	1975–87
10	Die Hard / 2 / Die Hard with a Vengeance	1988–95

Based on total earnings of the original movie and all its sequels up to 1998, George Lucas's *Star Wars* series just beats Steven Spielberg's *Jurassic Park* and its sequel *The Lost World*, which have grossed US$2,806,400,000 and US$1,534,500,000 respectively around the world. Each of the other movie series in the Top 10 have achieved cumulative global earnings of more than US$700 million.

"BLOCKBUSTER"

During World War II, "blockbuster" was air force slang for a bomb heavy enough to flatten an entire city block. Once the word had become widely used in military reports, it was adopted by journalists to describe a book or film that had a great impact. "Blockbuster" has since acquired the meaning of a film that has made more than US$100 million on its North American release. This was once a rare phenomenon, but now some 200 films have gained this sobriquet.

WHY DO WE SAY?

TOP 10 MOVIES OF 1999

	MOVIE	GROSS INCOME (US$) US	WORLD TOTAL
1	Star Wars: Episode I – The Phantom Menace	430,500,000	977,900,000
2	The Sixth Sense	276,400,000	470,400,000
3	The Matrix	171,400,000	456,400,000
4	The Mummy	155,200,000	401,700,000
5	Tarzan	170,800,000	391,800,000
6	Notting Hill	116,000,000	354,800,000
7	Austin Powers: The Spy Who Shagged Me	205,400,000	308,400,000
8	Runaway Bride	152,100,000	281,600,000
9	The World Is Not Enough	118,600,000	265,200,000
10	Toy Story 2	211,200,000	234,700,000

TOP 10 ★ MOVIES OF 1999 IN THE US

	MOVIE	US GROSS (US$)
1	Star Wars: Episode I – The Phantom Menace	430,443,350
2	The Sixth Sense	276,386,495
3	Toy Story 2	208,851,257
4	Austin Powers: The Spy Who Shagged Me	205,887,913
5	The Matrix	171,383,253
6	Tarzan	170,904,824
7	Big Daddy	163,479,795
8	The Mummy	155,247,825
9	Runaway Bride	152,054,428
10	The Blair Witch Project	140,530,114

This list features only movies released in the US during 1999. Certain films released late in 1998, such as Patch Adams and Shakespeare in Love, continued to earn at the box office well into 1999, giving both these a place in the latter year's Top 20.

NEO CLASSIC
Keanu Reeves as Neo/Thomas A. Anderson shoots to thrill in The Matrix, one of the sci-fi movies that led the world's box office in 1999.

According to the Consumer Price Index, what increased the most in cost between 1999 and 2000?
see p.206 for the answer
A Tuition fees
B Oranges
C Fuel oil

Movies of the Decades

TOP 10 ★
MOVIES OF THE 1930s

1	Gone with the Wind*	1939
2	Snow White and the Seven Dwarfs	1937
3	The Wizard of Oz	1939
4	The Woman in Red	1935
5	King Kong	1933
6	San Francisco	1936
7 =	Hell's Angels	1930
7 =	Lost Horizon	1937
7 =	Mr. Smith Goes to Washington	1939
10	Maytime	1937

Winner of "Best Picture" Academy Award

Gone with the Wind and Snow White and the Seven Dwarfs have generated more income than any other prewar movie. However, if the income of Gone with the Wind is adjusted to allow for inflation in the period since its release, it could be regarded as the most successful movie ever, earning some US$885 million in the US alone.

TOP 10 ★
MOVIES OF THE 1940s

1	Bambi	1942
2	Pinocchio	1940
3	Fantasia	1940
4	Cinderella	1949
5	Song of the South	1946
6	The Best Years of Our Lives*	1946
7	The Bells of St. Mary's	1945
8	Duel in the Sun	1946
9	Mom and Dad	1948
10	Samson and Delilah	1949

Winner of "Best Picture" Academy Award

With the top four movies of the decade classic Disney cartoons, the 1940s may be regarded as the "golden age" of the animated movie.

TALL STORY

In one of movie history's most famous scenes, King Kong fights off his attackers atop the newly opened Empire State Building. The movie was one of the 1930s' highest earners.

TOP 10 ★
MOVIES OF THE 1950s

1	Lady and the Tramp	1955
2	Peter Pan	1953
3	Ben-Hur*	1959
4	The Ten Commandments	1956
5	Sleeping Beauty	1959
6	Around the World in 80 Days*	1956
7 =	The Robe	1953
7 =	The Greatest Show on Earth*	1952
9	The Bridge on the River Kwai*	1957
10	Peyton Place	1957

Winner of "Best Picture" Academy Award

While the popularity of animated movies continued, the 1950s was outstanding as the decade of the "big" picture (in cast and scale).

TOP 10 MOVIES OF THE 1960s

1 One Hundred and One Dalmatians, 1961 **2** The Jungle Book, 1967 **3** The Sound of Music*, 1965 **4** Thunderball, 1965 **5** Goldfinger, 1964 **6** Doctor Zhivago, 1965 **7** You Only Live Twice, 1967 **8** The Graduate, 1968 **9** Mary Poppins, 1964 **10** Butch Cassidy and the Sundance Kid, 1969

Winner of "Best Picture" Academy Award

TOP 10 ⭐

MOVIES OF THE 1990s

1	Titanic*	1997
2	Star Wars: Episode I – The Phantom Menace	1999
3	Jurassic Park	1993
4	Independence Day	1996
5	The Lion King	1994
6	Forrest Gump*	1994
7	The Lost World: Jurassic Park	1997
8	Men in Black	1997
9	The Sixth Sense	1999
10	Armageddon	1998

* Winner of "Best Picture" Academy Award

Each of the Top 10 movies of the 1990s has earned more than US$550 million around the world.

BRINGING THE HOUSE DOWN

The White House sustains a direct hit from the invading spacecraft in a scene from Independence Day, *one of the top movies of the 1990s.*

TOP 10 ⭐

MOVIES OF THE 1970s

1	Star Wars	1977/97
2	Jaws	1975
3	Close Encounters of the Third Kind	1977/80
4	The Exorcist	1973/98
5	Moonraker	1979
6	The Spy Who Loved Me	1977
7	The Sting*	1973
8	Grease	1978
9	The Godfather*	1972
10	Saturday Night Fever	1977

* Winner of "Best Picture" Academy Award

In the 1970s, the arrival of Steven Spielberg and George Lucas set the scene for the high-adventure blockbusters whose domination has continued ever since. Lucas wrote and directed *Star Wars*, formerly the highest-earning movie of all time.

JAWS OF DEATH

Although it once held the record as the world's highest-earning movie, Jaws *was eventually beaten by* Star Wars, *directed by George Lucas.*

TOP 10 MOVIES OF THE 1980s

❶ *E.T.: The Extra-Terrestrial*, 1982 ❷ *Indiana Jones and the Last Crusade*, 1989 ❸ *Batman*, 1989 ❹ *Rain Man*, 1988 ❺ *Return of the Jedi*, 1983 ❻ *Raiders of the Lost Ark*, 1981 ❼ *The Empire Strikes Back*, 1980 ❽ *Who Framed Roger Rabbit*, 1988 ❾ *Back to the Future*, 1985 ❿ *Top Gun*, 1986

Who was the last winner of the CPGA Women's championships?
see p.264 for the answer

A Lanie Cahill
B Nancy Harvey
C Lorie Kane

Movie Genres

TOP 10 ★
HORROR MOVIES

1	*Jurassic Park*	1993
2	*The Lost World: Jurassic Park*	1997
3	*The Sixth Sense*	1999
4	*Jaws*	1975
5	*The Mummy*	1999
6	*Godzilla*	1998
7	*The Exorcist*	1973
8	*The Blair Witch Project*	1999
9	*Interview with the Vampire*	1994
10	*Jaws II*	1978

TOP 10 ★
VAMPIRE MOVIES

1	*Interview with the Vampire*	1994
2	*Bram Stoker's Dracula*	1992
3	*From Dusk Till Dawn*	1996
4	*Love at First Bite*	1979
5	*The Lost Boys*	1987
6	*Vampires*	1998
7	*Dracula*	1979
8	*Fright Night*	1985
9	*Vampire in Brooklyn*	1995
10	*Buffy the Vampire Slayer*	1992

TOP 10 ★
WESTERNS

1	*Dances with Wolves*	1990
2	*Wild Wild West*	1999
3	*Maverick*	1994
4	*Unforgiven*	1992
5	*Butch Cassidy and the Sundance Kid*	1969
6	*Jeremiah Johnson*	1972
7	*How the West Was Won*	1962
8	*Young Guns*	1988
9	*Young Guns II*	1990
10	*Pale Rider*	1985

TOP 10 ★
GHOST MOVIES

1	*The Sixth Sense*	1999
2	*Ghost*	1990
3	*Ghostbusters*	1984
4	*Casper*	1995
5	*Ghostbusters II*	1989
6	*The Haunting*	1999
7	*Sleepy Hollow*	1999
8	*Beetlejuice*	1988
9	*Scrooged*	1988
10	*The House on Haunted Hill*	1999

TOP 10 ★
SCIENCE-FICTION MOVIES

1	*Star Wars: Episode I – The Phantom Menace*	1999
2	*Jurassic Park*	1993
3	*Independence Day*	1996
4	*Star Wars*	1977/97
5	*E.T.: The Extra-Terrestrial*	1982
6	*The Lost World: Jurassic Park*	1997
7	*Men in Black*	1997
8	*Return of the Jedi*	1983/97
9	*Armageddon*	1998
10	*Terminator 2: Judgment Day*	1991

TOP 10 ★
WAR MOVIES

1	*Saving Private Ryan*	1998
2	*Platoon*	1986
3	*Good Morning, Vietnam*	1987
4	*Apocalypse Now*	1979
5	*The Thin Red Line*	1998
6	*M*A*S*H*	1970
7	*Patton*	1970
8	*The Deer Hunter*	1978
9	*Full Metal Jacket*	1987
10	*Midway*	1976

This list excludes successful movies that are not technically "war" films but that have military themes, such as *A Few Good Men* (1992), *The Hunt for Red October* (1990), *Crimson Tide* (1995), and *An Officer and a Gentleman* (1982), which would otherwise be placed in the top five, and *Top Gun* (1986), which would feature prominently in the list.

WHO YOU GONNA CALL?
Ghostbusters starred Bill Murray alongside Dan Aykroyd and Harold Ramis, both of whom also co-wrote the first movie and its sequel.

FUTURE PERFECT

Schoolkid Marty McFly (Michael J. Fox) and scientist Dr. Emmett "Doc" L. Brown (Christopher Lloyd) are dazzled as the Doc's DeLorean zips back to 1955. The first Back to the Future film earned US$350 million.

TOP 10 ★ TIME TRAVEL MOVIES

1	Terminator 2: Judgment Day	1991
2	Back to the Future	1985
3	Back to the Future Part III	1990
4	Back to the Future Part II	1989
5	Timecop	1994
6	The Terminator	1984
7	Pleasantville	1998
8	Time Bandits	1981
9	Bill and Ted's Excellent Adventure	1989
10	Highlander III: The Sorcerer	1994

TOP 10 ★ COP MOVIES

1	Die Hard with a Vengeance	1995
2	The Fugitive	1993
3	Basic Instinct	1992
4	Se7en	1995
5	Lethal Weapon 3	1992
6	Beverly Hills Cop	1984
7	Beverly Hills Cop II	1987
8	Lethal Weapon 4	1998
9	Speed	1994
10	Lethal Weapon 2	1989

Although movies in which one of the central characters is a police officer have never been among the most successful movies of all time, many have earned respectable amounts at the box office. They are divided between those with a comic slant, such as all three *Beverly Hills Cop* movies, and darker police thrillers, such as *Basic Instinct*. Movies featuring FBI and CIA agents have been excluded here, thus eliminating blockbusters such as *Mission: Impossible* and *The Silence of the Lambs*.

TOP 10 COMEDY MOVIES

1 *Forrest Gump*, 1994 **2** *Home Alone*, 1990 **3** *Ghost*, 1990 **4** *Pretty Woman*, 1990 **5** *Mrs. Doubtfire*, 1993 **6** *The Flintstones*, 1994 **7** *Notting Hill*, 1999 **8** *Who Framed Roger Rabbit*, 1988 **9** *There's Something About Mary*, 1998 **10** *The Mask*, 1994

TOP 10 ★ DISASTER MOVIES

1	Titanic	1997
2	Armageddon	1998
3	Twister	1996
4	Die Hard With a Vengeance	1995
5	Deep Imapct	1998
6	Apollo 13	1995
7	Outbreak	1995
8	Dante's Peak	1997
9	Daylight	1996
10	Die Hard	1988

TOP 10 ★ MOVIES STARRING ANIMALS

	MOVIE/YEAR	ANIMAL
1	Jaws, 1975	Shark
2	101 Dalmatians, 1996	Dogs
3	Babe, 1995	Pig
4	Jaws II, 1978	Shark
5	Free Willy, 1993	Orca whale
6	Turner & Hooch, 1989	Dog
7	Jaws 3-D, 1983	Shark
8	Babe: Pig in the City, 1998	Pig
9	Beethoven, 1992	Dog
10	Homeward Bound II: Lost in San Francisco, 1996	Dogs

This list is of films where real animals are acknowledged as central rather than secondary characters. Man-eating sharks, dogs, and pigs stand out as the most popular subjects!

"LIFE IS LIKE A BOX OF CHOCOLATES ..."

As Forrest Gump, Tom Hanks plays a man whose simple homespun philosophy enables him to succeed against all odds.

Did You Know? The 1980 British movie *Raise the Titanic!* itself became a disaster movie, losing over US$30 million of its budget US$40 million, and it sank without trace at the box office.

Oscar-Winning Movies

TOP 10 ★

HIGHEST-EARNING "BEST PICTURE" OSCAR WINNERS

	MOVIE	YEAR
1	Titanic	1997
2	Forrest Gump	1994
3	Dances with Wolves	1990
4	Rain Man	1988
5	Schindler's List	1993
6	Shakespeare in Love	1999
7	The English Patient	1996
8	American Beauty	1999
9	Braveheart	1995
10	Gone with the Wind	1939

THE 10 "BEST PICTURE" OSCAR WINNERS OF THE 1950s

(Year/movie)

1 1950 *All About Eve* **2** 1951 *An American in Paris* **3** 1952 *The Greatest Show on Earth* **4** 1953 *From Here to Eternity* **5** 1954 *On the Waterfront* **6** 1955 *Marty* **7** 1956 *Around the World in 80 Days* **8** 1957 *The Bridge on the River Kwai* **9** 1958 *Gigi* **10** 1959 *Ben-Hur*

The first winning film of the 1950s, *All About Eve*, received the most Oscar nominations (14), while the last, *Ben-Hur*, won the most (11).

THE 10 "BEST PICTURE" OSCAR WINNERS OF THE 1960s

(Year/movie)

1 1960 *The Apartment* **2** 1961 *West Side Story* **3** 1962 *Lawrence of Arabia* **4** 1963 *Tom Jones* **5** 1964 *My Fair Lady* **6** 1965 *The Sound of Music* **7** 1966 *A Man for All Seasons* **8** 1967 *In the Heat of the Night* **9** 1968 *Oliver!* **10** 1969 *Midnight Cowboy*

The 1960 winner, *The Apartment*, was the last black-and-white winner until *Schindler's List* in 1993.

HEALTHY PATIENT
Nominated for 12 and winner of nine Oscars, The English Patient is also among the highest-earning of all "Best Picture" winners.

TOP 10 MOVIES NOMINATED FOR THE MOST OSCARS*

(Movie/year/awards/nominations)

1 = *All About Eve*, 1950, 6, 14; = *Titanic*, 1997, 11, 14 **3** = *Gone with the Wind*, 1939 ,8#, 13; = *From Here to Eternity*, 1953, 8, 13; = *Mary Poppins*, 1964, 5, 13; = *Who's Afraid of Virginia Woolf?*, 1966, 5, 13; = *Forrest Gump*, 1994, 6, 13; = *Shakespeare in Love*, 1998, 7, 13 **9** = *Mrs. Miniver*, 1942, 6, 12; = *The Song of Bernadette*, 1943, 4, 12; = *Johnny Belinda*, 1948, 1, 12; = *A Streetcar Named Desire*, 1951, 4, 12; = *On the Waterfront*, 1954, 8, 12; = *Ben-Hur*, 1959, 11, 12; = *Becket*, 1964, 1, 12; = *My Fair Lady*, 1964, 8, 12; = *Reds*, 1981, 3, 12; = *Dances With Wolves*, 1990, 7, 12; = *Schindler's List*, 1993, 7, 12; = *The English Patient*, 1996 , 9, 12

* Oscar® is a Registered Trademark
 # Plus two special awards

THE 10 ★

"BEST PICTURE" OSCAR WINNERS OF THE 1970s

YEAR	MOVIE
1970	Patton
1971	The French Connection
1972	The Godfather
1973	The Sting
1974	The Godfather Part II
1975	One Flew Over the Cuckoo's Nest
1976	Rocky
1977	Annie Hall
1978	The Deer Hunter
1979	Kramer vs. Kramer

THE 10 ★

"BEST PICTURE" OSCAR WINNERS OF THE 1980s

YEAR	MOVIE
1980	Ordinary People
1981	Chariots of Fire
1982	Gandhi
1983	Terms of Endearment
1984	Amadeus
1985	Out of Africa
1986	Platoon
1987	The Last Emperor
1988	Rain Man
1989	Driving Miss Daisy

Did You Know? *Who's Afraid of Virginia Woolf?* (1966) was the first film in which the entire cast was nominated for Oscars, with wins for both Elizabeth Taylor and Sandy Dennis.

DRAMATIC ENTRANCE

Career woman (Annette Benning) confronts drop-out husband (Kevin Spacey) in the suburban satire American Beauty, winner of the 1999 "Best Picture" Oscar.

THE 10 ★
LATEST "BEST PICTURE" OSCAR WINNERS

YEAR	MOVIE
1999	American Beauty
1998	Shakespeare in Love
1997	Titanic
1996	The English Patient
1995	Braveheart
1994	Forrest Gump
1993	Schindler's List
1992	Unforgiven
1991	The Silence of the Lambs
1990	Dances with Wolves

TOP 10 ★
MOVIES TO WIN THE MOST OSCARS

MOVIE	YEAR	NOMINATIONS	AWARDS
1 =Ben-Hur	1959	12	11
1 =Titanic	1997	14	11
3 West Side Story	1961	11	10
4 =Gigi	1958	9	9
4 =The Last Emperor	1987	9	9
4 =The English Patient	1996	12	9
7 =Gone with the Wind	1939	13	8*
7 =From Here to Eternity	1953	13	8
7 =On the Waterfront	1954	12	8
7 =My Fair Lady	1964	12	8
7 =Cabaret	1972	10	8
7 =Gandhi	1982	11	8
7 =Amadeus	1984	11	8

* Plus two special awards

TOP 10 STUDIOS WITH THE MOST "BEST PICTURE" OSCARS
(Studio/awards)

1. United Artists, 13 2. Columbia, 12
3. Paramount, 11 4. MGM, 9
5. Twentieth Century Fox, 7 6. Warner Bros, 6
7. Universal, 5 8. Orion, 4 9. = Miramax; = RKO, 2

HEART'S CONTENT

In addition to its financial success, Mel Gibson's 1995 film Braveheart won five Oscars, including "Best Director" and "Best Actor."

ACTING HIS AGE

The late septuagenarian actor John Gielgud secured a "Best Supporting Actor" Oscar for his role as Hobson, the acerbic valet in Arthur.

"OSCAR"

Founded on May 4, 1927, the Hollywood-based Academy of Motion Picture Arts and Sciences proposed improving the image of the movie industry by issuing "awards for merit or distinction" in various categories. The award itself, a statuette designed by Cedric Gibbons, was modeled by a young artist, George Stanley. The gold-plated naked male figure holds a sword and stands on a reel of film. It was simply called "the statuette" until 1931, when Academy librarian Margaret Herrick commented, "It looks like my Uncle Oscar!" – and the name stuck. **WHY DO WE SAY?**

THE 10 "BEST ACTRESS" OSCAR WINNERS OF THE 1950s

(Year/actress/movie)

1. 1950 Judy Holiday, *Born Yesterday*
2. 1951 Vivien Leigh, *A Streetcar Named Desire*
3. 1952 Shirley Booth, *Come Back, Little Sheba*
4. 1953 Audrey Hepburn, *Roman Holiday*
5. 1954 Grace Kelly, *The Country Girl*
6. 1955 Anna Magnani, *The Rose Tattoo*
7. 1956 Ingrid Bergman, *Anastasia*
8. 1957 Joanne Woodward, *The Three Faces of Eve*
9. 1958 Susan Hayward, *I Want to Live*
10. 1959 Simone Signoret, *Room at the Top*

THE 10 ★ "BEST ACTOR" OSCAR WINNERS OF THE 1950s

YEAR	ACTOR/MOVIE
1950	Jose Ferrer, *Cyrano de Bergerac*
1951	Humphrey Bogart, *The African Queen*
1952	Gary Cooper, *High Noon*
1953	William Holden, *Stalag 17*
1954	Marlon Brando, *On the Waterfront**
1955	Ernest Borgnine, *Marty**
1956	Yul Brynner, *The King and I*
1957	Alec Guinness, *The Bridge on the River Kwai**
1958	David Niven, *Separate Tables*
1959	Charlton Heston, *Ben-Hur**

* Winner of "Best Picture" Oscar

THE 10 ★ "BEST ACTRESS" OSCAR WINNERS OF THE 1960s

YEAR	ACTRESS/MOVIE
1960	Elizabeth Taylor, *Butterfield 8*
1961	Sophia Loren, *Two Women*
1962	Anne Bancroft, *The Miracle Worker*
1963	Patricia Neal, *Hud*
1964	Julie Andrews, *Mary Poppins*
1965	Julie Christie, *Darling*
1966	Elizabeth Taylor, *Who's Afraid of Virginia Woolf?*
1967	Katharine Hepburn, *Guess Who's Coming to Dinner*
1968 =	Katharine Hepburn,* *The Lion in Winter*
1968 =	Barbra Streisand,* *Funny Girl*
1969	Maggie Smith, *The Prime of Miss Jean Brodie*

* The only tie for "Best Actress"

TOP 10 ★ OLDEST OSCAR-WINNING ACTORS AND ACTRESSES

	ACTOR OR ACTRESS	AWARD/MOVIE	YEAR	AGE*
1	Jessica Tandy	"Best Actress" (*Driving Miss Daisy*)	1989	80
2	George Burns	"Best Supporting Actor" (*The Sunshine Boys*)	1975	80
3	Melvyn Douglas	"Best Supporting Actor" (*Being There*)	1979	79
4	John Gielgud	"Best Supporting Actor" (*Arthur*)	1981	77
5	Don Ameche	"Best Supporting Actor" (*Cocoon*)	1985	77
6	Peggy Ashcroft	"Best Supporting Actress" (*A Passage to India*)	1984	77
7	Henry Fonda	"Best Actor" (*On Golden Pond*)	1981	76
8	Katharine Hepburn	"Best Actress" (*On Golden Pond*)	1981	74
9	Edmund Gwenn	"Best Supporting Actor" (*Miracle on 34th Street*)	1947	72
10	Ruth Gordon	"Best Supporting Actress" (*Rosemary's Baby*)	1968	72

* At the time of the Award ceremony; those of apparently identical age have been ranked according to their precise age in days at the time of the ceremony

THE 10 ★ "BEST ACTOR" OSCAR WINNERS OF THE 1960s

YEAR	ACTOR/MOVIE
1960	Burt Lancaster, *Elmer Gantry*
1961	Maximilian Schell, *Judgment at Nuremberg*
1962	Gregory Peck, *To Kill a Mockingbird*
1963	Sidney Poitier, *Lilies of the Field*
1964	Rex Harrison, *My Fair Lady* *
1965	Lee Marvin, *Cat Ballou*
1966	Paul Scofield, *A Man for All Seasons* *
1967	Rod Steiger, *In the Heat of the Night* *
1968	Cliff Robertson, *Charly*
1969	John Wayne, *True Grit*

* *Winner of "Best Picture" Oscar*

THE 10 ★ "BEST ACTOR" OSCAR WINNERS OF THE 1970s

YEAR	ACTOR/MOVIE
1970	George C. Scott, *Patton* *
1971	Gene Hackman, *The French Connection* *
1972	Marlon Brando, *The Godfather* *
1973	Jack Lemmon, *Save the Tiger*
1974	Art Carney, *Harry and Tonto*
1975	Jack Nicholson, *One Flew Over the Cuckoo's Nest* *#
1976	Peter Finch, *Network*
1977	Richard Dreyfuss, *The Goodbye Girl*
1978	Jon Voight, *Coming Home*
1979	Dustin Hoffman, *Kramer vs. Kramer* *

* *Winner of "Best Picture" Oscar*

\# *Winner of "Best Director," "Best Actress," and "Best Screenplay" Oscars*

CABARET STAR

Liza Minnelli won "Best Actress" Oscar for her role as Sally Bowles in Cabaret. The movie itself received 10 nominations and eight wins, but lost "Best Picture" to The Godfather.

THE 10 "BEST ACTRESS" OSCAR WINNERS OF THE 1970s

(Year/actress/movie)

1 1970 Glenda Jackson, *Women in Love* **2** 1971 Jane Fonda, *Klute* **3** 1972 Liza Minnelli, *Cabaret* **4** 1973 Glenda Jackson, *A Touch of Class* **5** 1974 Ellen Burstyn, *Alice Doesn't Live Here Any More* *# **6** 1975 Louise Fletcher, *One Flew Over the Cuckoo's Nest* *# **7** 1976 Faye Dunaway, *Network* **8** 1977 Diane Keaton, *Annie Hall* * **9** 1978 Jane Fonda, *Coming Home* **10** 1979 Sally Field, *Norma Rae*

* *Winner of "Best Picture" Oscar*
\# *Winner of "Best Director," "Best Actor," and "Best Screenplay" Oscars*

What is the oldest Canadian magazine still publishing?
see p.107 for the answer

A *Saturday Night*
B *The Canadian Entomologist*
C *The United Church Observer*

THE 10 ★
"BEST ACTRESS" OSCAR WINNERS OF THE 1980s

YEAR	ACTRESS/MOVIE
1980	Sissy Spacek, *Coal Miner's Daughter*
1981	Katharine Hepburn, *On Golden Pond**
1982	Meryl Streep, *Sophie's Choice*
1983	Shirley MacLaine, *Terms of Endearment*#
1984	Sally Field, *Places in the Heart*
1985	Geraldine Page, *The Trip to Bountiful*
1986	Marlee Matlin, *Children of a Lesser God*
1987	Cher, *Moonstruck*
1988	Jodie Foster, *The Accused*
1989	Jessica Tandy, *Driving Miss Daisy*#

* *Winner of "Best Actor" Oscar*

Winner of "Best Picture" Oscar

THE 10 ★
"BEST ACTOR" OSCAR WINNERS OF THE 1980s

YEAR	ACTOR/MOVIE
1980	Robert De Niro, *Raging Bull*
1981	Henry Fonda, *On Golden Pond**
1982	Ben Kingsley, *Gandhi*#
1983	Robert Duvall, *Tender Mercies*
1984	F. Murray Abraham, *Amadeus*#
1985	William Hurt, *Kiss of the Spider Woman*
1986	Paul Newman, *The Color of Money*
1987	Michael Douglas, *Wall Street*
1988	Dustin Hoffman, *Rain Man*#
1989	Daniel Day-Lewis, *My Left Foot*

* *Winner of "Best Actress" Oscar*

Winner of "Best Picture" Oscar

GETTING IN ON THE ACT

Jack Nicholson, winner of "Best Actor" Oscar for As Good as It Gets, *confronts Jill, a Brussels Griffon performing the part of Verdell.*

THE 10 ★
LATEST "BEST ACTOR" OSCAR WINNERS

YEAR	ACTOR/MOVIE
1999	Kevin Spacey, *American Beauty**
1998	Roberto Benigni, *La Vita è Bella (Life Is Beautiful)*
1997	Jack Nicholson, *As Good as It Gets*#
1996	Geoffrey Rush, *Shine*
1995	Nicolas Cage, *Leaving Las Vegas*
1994	Tom Hanks, *Forrest Gump**
1993	Tom Hanks, *Philadelphia*
1992	Al Pacino, *Scent of a Woman*
1991	Anthony Hopkins, *The Silence of the Lambs**#
1990	Jeremy Irons, *Reversal of Fortune*

* *Winner of "Best Picture" Oscar*

Winner of "Best Actress" Oscar

Tom Hanks shares the honor of two consecutive wins with Spencer Tracy (1937: *Captains Courageous* and 1938: *Boys Town*). Only four other actors have won twice: Marlon Brando (1954; 1972), Gary Cooper (1941; 1952), Dustin Hoffman (1977; 1988), and Jack Nicholson (1975; 1997),

GOLDEN DOUBLE

Katharine Hepburn and Henry Fonda won "Best Actress" and "Best Actor" Academy Awards for On Golden Pond. *It was Hepburn's fourth but Fonda's only Oscar, awarded just four months before his death.*

ROLE REVERSAL

Former television actress Hilary Swank (right) won the 1999 "Best Actress" Oscar for her demanding role as a girl who adopts the persona of a boy.

THE 10 ★
LATEST "BEST ACTRESS" OSCAR WINNERS

YEAR	ACTRESS/MOVIE
1999	Hilary Swank, *Boys Don't Cry*
1998	Gwyneth Paltrow, *Shakespeare in Love*
1997	Helen Hunt, *As Good as It Gets*
1996	Frances McDormand, *Fargo*
1995	Susan Sarandon, *Dead Man Walking*
1994	Jessica Lange, *Blue Sky*
1993	Holly Hunter, *The Piano*
1992	Emma Thompson, *Howard's End*
1991	Jodie Foster, *The Silence of the Lambs**
1990	Kathy Bates, *Misery*

* *Winner of "Best Picture" and "Best Actor" Oscars*

TOP 10 ★
YOUNGEST OSCAR-WINNING ACTORS AND ACTRESSES

	ACTOR OR ACTRESS	AWARD/MOVIE (WHERE SPECIFIED)	YEAR	AGE*
1	Shirley Temple	Special Award – outstanding contribution during 1934	1934	6
2	Margaret O'Brien	Special Award (*Meet Me in St Louis*)	1944	8
3	Vincent Winter	Special Award (*The Little Kidnappers*)	1954	8
4	Ivan Jandl	Special Award (*The Search*)	1948	9
5	Jon Whiteley	Special Award (*The Little Kidnappers*)	1954	10
6	Tatum O'Neal	"Best Supporting Actress" (*Paper Moon*)	1973	10
7	Anna Paquin	"Best Supporting Actress" (*The Piano*)	1993	11
8	Claude Jarman, Jr.	Special Award (*The Yearling*)	1946	12
9	Bobby Driscoll	Special Award (*The Window*)	1949	13
10	Hayley Mills	Special Award (*Pollyanna*)	1960	13

* *At the time of the Award ceremony; those of apparently identical age have been ranked according to their precise age in days at the time of the ceremony*

The Academy Awards ceremony usually takes place at the end of March in the year following that in which the film was released in the US, so the winners are generally at least a year older when they receive their Oscars than when they acted in their award-winning movies.

Who was the last winner of Much Music's video of the Year award?
see p.192 for the answer

A Len's *Steal My Sunshine*
B Sarah McLachlan's *Sweet Surrender*
C The Tragically Hip's *Ahead By a Century*

THE 10 ★

LATEST WINNERS OF THE CANNES PALME D'OR FOR "BEST FILM"

YEAR	MOVIE/COUNTRY
1999	*Rosetta*, France
1998	*Eternity and a Day*, Greece
1997	*The Eel*, Japan/ *The Taste of Cherries*, Iran
1996	*Secrets and Lies*, UK
1995	*Underground*, Yugoslavia
1994	*Pulp Fiction*, US
1993	*Farewell My Concubine*, China/ *The Piano*, Australia
1992	*Best Intentions*, Denmark
1991	*Barton Fink*, US
1990	*Wild at Heart*, US

THE 10 ★

LATEST GOLDEN GLOBE AWARDS FOR "BEST PERFORMANCE BY AN ACTOR IN A MOTION PICTURE – MUSICAL OR COMEDY"

YEAR	ACTOR/MOVIE
2000	Jim Carrey, *Man on the Moon*
1999	Michael Caine, *Little Voice*
1998	Jack Nicholson, *As Good As It Gets*
1997	Tom Cruise, *Jerry Maguire*
1996	John Travolta, *Get Shorty*
1995	Hugh Grant, *Four Weddings and a Funeral*
1994	Robin Williams, *Mrs. Doubtfire*
1993	Tim Robbins, *The Player*
1992	Robin Williams, *The Fisher King*
1991	Gerard Depardieu, *Green Card*

During the past 10 years, more than half the Golden Globe awards in this category went to the stars of movies that earned in excess of US$100 million apiece. *Four Weddings and a Funeral* was the all-time highest-earning British film until overtaken in 1998 by *The Full Monty*.

THE 10 ★

LATEST GOLDEN GLOBE AWARDS FOR "BEST PERFORMANCE BY AN ACTRESS IN A MOTION PICTURE – MUSICAL OR COMEDY"

YEAR	ACTRESS/MOVIE
2000	Janet McTeer, *Tumbleweeds*
1999	Gwyneth Paltrow, *Shakespeare in Love*
1998	Helen Hunt, *As Good As It Gets*
1997	Madonna, *Evita*
1996	Nicole Kidman, *To Die For*
1995	Jamie Lee Curtis, *True Lies*
1994	Angela Bassett, *What's Love Got to Do With It*
1993	Miranda Richardson, *Enchanted April*
1992	Bette Midler, *For the Boys*
1991	Julia Roberts, *Pretty Woman*

Although romantic comedies feature predominantly among the winners, a number of the successful actresses in this category received their awards for roles in movies that are either traditional musicals, or have a high musical content.

RISE OF *SHINE*

Geoffrey Rush received a Golden Globe, as well as the 1997 "Best Actor" Oscar, for his role in Shine, the story of the turbulent life of pianist David Helfgott.

THE 10 🍁

LATEST GENIE AWARDS FOR "BEST MOTION PICTURE" IN CANADA

YEAR	MOVIE
1999	*Sunshine*
1998	*The Red Violin*
1997	*The Sweet Hereafter*
1996	*Lilies*
1995	*Le Confessional*
1994	*Exotica*
1993	*Thirty-Two Short Films About Glenn Gould*
1992	*Naked Lunch*
1991	*Black Robe*
1990	*Jésus de Montréal*

Director Atom Egoyan snared two Genies for *Exotica* and *The Sweet Hereafter*, while Québécois director François Girard took home the statuette twice, for *Thirty-Two Short Films About Glenn Gould* and *The Red Violin*.

TRUE TO FORM

Jim Carrey gained a Golden Globe for his part in The Truman Show, *a satire in which every detail of his life is secretly filmed for public broadcast.*

THE 10 ★
LATEST GOLDEN GLOBE AWARDS FOR "BEST PERFORMANCE BY AN ACTRESS IN A MOTION PICTURE – DRAMA"

YEAR	ACTRESS/MOVIE
2000	Hilary Swank, *Boys Don't Cry*
1999	Cate Blanchett, *Elizabeth*
1998	Judi Dench, *Mrs. Brown*
1997	Brenda Blethyn, *Secrets and Lies*
1996	Sharon Stone, *Casino*
1995	Jessica Lange, *Blue Sky*
1994	Holly Hunter, *The Piano*
1993	Emma Thompson, *Howard's End*
1992	Jodie Foster, *The Silence of the Lambs*
1991	Kathy Bates, *Misery*

THE 10 ★
LATEST GOLDEN GLOBE AWARDS FOR "BEST PERFORMANCE BY AN ACTOR IN A MOTION PICTURE – DRAMA"

YEAR	ACTOR/MOVIE
2000	Denzel Washington, *The Hurricane*
1999	Jim Carrey, *The Truman Show*
1998	Peter Fonda, *Ulee's Gold*
1997	Geoffrey Rush, *Shine*
1996	Nicolas Cage, *Leaving Las Vegas*
1995	Tom Hanks, *Forrest Gump*
1994	Tom Hanks, *Philadelphia*
1993	Al Pacino, *Scent of a Woman*
1992	Nick Nolte, *The Prince of Tides*
1991	Jeremy Irons, *Reversal of Fortune*

No fewer than six of the 10 most recent Golden Globe Awards won by leading actors – those in 1990, and 1992–96 – were subsequently mirrored by the same actors' Oscar wins.

TOP 10 🍁
LAST OSCARS* WON BY CANADIANS

YEAR	RECIPIENT	BIRTHPLACE	AWARD
1998	Norman Jewison	Toronto, Ontario	Irving G. Thalberg Award
1997	James Cameron	Kapuskasing, Ontario	Best Director
1995	Mary Pickford	Toronto, Ontario	Honorary
1948	Walter Huston	Toronto, Ontario	Best Supporting Actor
1946	Harold Russell	Sydney, Nova Scotia	Best Supporting Actor
1946	Harold Russell	Sydney, Nova Scotia	Honorary
1938	Deanna Durbin	Winnipeg, Manitoba	Special Award (Juvenile)
1937	Mack Sennett	Danville, Quebec	Honorary
1930/31	Marie Dressler	Cobourg, Ontario	Best Actress
1929/30	Norma Shearer	Montreal, Quebec	Best Actress

* For honorary, acting, and directing categories

Source: *Academy of Motion Picture Arts & Sciences*

James Cameron, the intensely driven director of blockbuster films such as *Terminator*, *Aliens*, and *True Lies*, finally got the nod from the Academy for his expensive and spectacular re-creation of the sinking of the *Titanic*. Walter Huston was the father of the great director John Huston, and won his Oscar playing opposite Humphrey Bogart in *Treasure of the Sierra Madre*.

What is the top participation sport, game or physical activity in Canada?
see p.278 for the answer
A Ice hockey
B Swimming
C Golf

Leading Men

LEONARDO DiCAPRIO MOVIES

1	Titanic	1997
2	The Man in the Iron Mask	1998
3	Romeo + Juliet	1996
4	The Beach	2000
5	The Quick and the Dead	1995
6	Marvin's Room	1996
7	What's Eating Gilbert Grape	1993
8	Celebrity	1998
9	This Boy's Life	1993
10	The Basketball Diaries	1995

NICOLAS CAGE MOVIES

1	The Rock	1996
2	Face/Off	1997
3	Con Air	1997
4	City of Angels	1998
5	Snake Eyes	1998
6	8MM	1999
7	Moonstruck	1987
8	Leaving Las Vegas	1995
9	Peggy Sue Got Married	1986
10	It Could Happen to You	1994

RATTLING THE CAGE

Nicolas Cage stars as FBI biochemist Dr. Stanley Godspeed in the 1996 movie The Rock, *which is his highest-earning movie to date.*

PIERCE BROSNAN MOVIES

1	Mrs. Doubtfire	1993
2	GoldenEye	1995
3	Tomorrow Never Dies	1997
4	The World Is Not Enough	1999
5	Dante's Peak	1997
6	The Thomas Crown Affair	1999
7	Mars Attacks!	1996
8	The Mirror Has Two Faces	1996
9	The Lawnmower Man	1992
10	Love Affair	1994

Pierce Brosnan, now best known as James Bond, provided the voice of King Arthur in *Quest for Camelot* (1998). If included, it would be ranked ninth. *The World Is Not Enough*, and six other movies in which Brosnan starred, have each earned well over $100 million apiece. His Top 10 total now approaches $2 billion.

PIERCING LOOK

Irish-born Pierce Brosnan took over the role of James Bond with GoldenEye. *This, along with* Tomorrow Never Dies *and* The World Is Not Enough, *are the highest earning of all the Bond series.*

ARNOLD SCHWARZENEGGER MOVIES

1	Terminator 2: Judgment Day	1991
2	True Lies	1994
3	Total Recall	1990
4	Eraser	1996
5	Twins	1988
6	Kindergarten Cop	1990
7	End of Days	1999
8	Jingle All the Way	1996
9	Last Action Hero	1993
10	Junior	1994

TOM CRUISE MOVIES

1	Mission: Impossible	1996
2	Rain Man	1988
3	Top Gun	1986
4	Jerry Maguire	1996
5	The Firm	1993
6	A Few Good Men	1992
7	Interview with the Vampire	1994
8	Days of Thunder	1990
9	Eyes Wide Shut	1999
10	Cocktail	1988

TOP 10 ★
MEL GIBSON MOVIES

1	Lethal Weapon 4	1998
2	Lethal Weapon 2	1989
3	Lethal Weapon 3	1992
4	Braveheart*	1995
5	Ransom	1996
6	Payback	1999
7	Conspiracy Theory	1997
8	Forever Young	1992
9	Maverick	1994
10	Bird on a Wire	1990

* Academy Award for "Best Director"

Mel Gibson also provided the voice of John Smith in *Pocahontas* (1995) and appeared uncredited as himself in *Casper* (1995). If included, these would enter in first and third positions respectively. Nine out of Gibson's Top 10 movies have earned more than US$100 million each worldwide.

TOP 10 ★
BRAD PITT MOVIES

1	Se7en	1995
2	Interview with the Vampire	1994
3	Sleepers	1996
4	Legends of the Fall	1994
5	Twelve Monkeys	1995
6	The Devil's Own	1997
7	Seven Years in Tibet	1997
8	Meet Joe Black	1998
9	Fight Club	1999
10	Thelma & Louise	1991

PITT STOPPER

Brad (William Bradley) Pitt plays Detective David Mills in Se7en, his most successful movie to date. Pitt appeared in more than 20 films during the 1990s.

TOP 10 ★
JACK NICHOLSON MOVIES

1	Batman	1989
2	A Few Good Men	1992
3	As Good As It Gets*	1997
4	Terms of Endearment#	1983
5	Wolf	1994
6	One Flew Over the Cuckoo's Nest*	1975
7	Mars Attacks!	1996
8	The Witches of Eastwick	1987
9	The Shining	1980
10	Broadcast News	1987

* Academy Award for "Best Actor"

\# Academy Award for "Best Supporting Actor"

TOP 10 ★
TOM HANKS MOVIES

1	Forrest Gump*	1994
2	Saving Private Ryan	1998
3	Apollo 13	1995
4	Sleepless in Seattle	1993
5	Philadelphia*	1993
6	You've Got Mail	1998
7	The Green Mile	1999
8	Big	1988
9	A League of Their Own	1992
10	Turner & Hooch	1989

* Academy Award for "Best Actor"

Tom Hanks also appeared in a voice-only part as Woody in *Toy Story* (1995) and *Toy Story 2* (1999). If included, these would be ranked third and fourth.

TOP 10 ★
JOHN TRAVOLTA MOVIES

1	Look Who's Talking	1989
2	Face/Off	1997
3	Pulp Fiction	1994
4	Grease	1978
5	The General's Daughter	1999
6	Phenomenon	1996
7	Saturday Night Fever*	1977
8	The Thin Red Line	1998
9	Get Shorty	1995
10	Broken Arrow	1996

* Nominated for Academy Award for "Best Actor"

TOP 10 DENZEL WASHINGTON MOVIES

❶ *Philadelphia*, 1993 ❷ *The Pelican Brief*, 1993 ❸ *Crimson Tide*, 1995 ❹ *The Siege*, 1998 ❺ *Courage Under Fire*, 1996 ❻ *The Bone Collector*, 1999 ❼ *The Preacher's Wife*, 1996 ❽ *Malcolm X*, 1992 ❾ *The Hurricane*, 1999 ❿ *Virtuosity*, 1995

TOP 10 JOHNNY DEPP MOVIES

❶ *Platoon*, 1986 ❷ *Donnie Brasco*, 1997 ❸ *Sleepy Hollow*, 1999 ❹ *Edward Scissorhands*, 1990 ❺ *Don Juan DeMarco*, 1995 ❻ *Freddy's Dead: The Final Nightmare*,* 1991 ❼ *A Nightmare on Elm Street*, 1984 ❽ *The Astronaut's Wife*, 1999 ❾ *Fear and Loathing in Las Vegas*, 1998 ❿ *What's Eating Gilbert Grape*, 1993

* Uncredited appearance

What sport has Canada won the most gold medals in at the Olympics?
see p.242 for the answer

A Swimming
B Athletics
C Hockey

RYAN'S DAUGHTER

Born Margaret Mary Emily Anne Hyra, Meg Ryan took her mother's maiden name before her movie debut in 1981. She has gone on to enjoy huge success in a range of romantic comedies.

TOP 10 ★
MICHELLE PFEIFFER MOVIES

1	Batman Returns	1992
2	Dangerous Minds	1995
3	Wolf	1994
4	Up Close & Personal	1996
5	One Fine Day	1996
6	The Witches of Eastwick	1987
7	Tequila Sunrise	1988
8	Scarface	1983
9	Dangerous Liaisons	1988
10	The Age of Innocence	1993

Michelle Pfeiffer also provided the voice of Tzipporah in the animated movie *The Prince of Egypt* (1998). If this was included in her Top 10, it would feature in second place.

CATWOMAN

Batman Returns is Michelle Pfeiffer's most successful movie to date, but half the movies in her Top 10 have earned a healthy US$100 million-plus.

TOP 10 ★
MEG RYAN MOVIES

1	Top Gun	1986
2	You've Got Mail	1998
4	Sleepless in Seattle	1993
5	City of Angels	1998
5	French Kiss	1995
6	Courage Under Fire	1996
7	When Harry Met Sally	1989
8	Addicted to Love	1997
9	When a Man Loves a Woman	1994
10	Joe Versus the Volcano	1990

Meg Ryan provided the voice of Anastasia in the 1997 movie of that title. If included, it would appear in ninth place.

TOP 10 ★
RENE RUSSO MOVIES

1	Lethal Weapon 3	1992
2	Ransom	1996
3	Lethal Weapon 4	1998
4	Outbreak	1995
5	In the Line of Fire	1993
6	The Thomas Crown Affair	1999
7	Get Shorty	1995
8	Tin Cup	1996
9	Major League II	1994
10	Major League	1989

TOP 10 NICOLE KIDMAN MOVIES

1 *Batman Forever*, 1995 **2** *Days of Thunder*, 1990 **3** *Eyes Wide Shut*, 1999 **4** *The Peacemaker*, 1997 **5** *Practical Magic*, 1998 **6** *Far and Away*, 1992 **7** *Malice*, 1993 **8** *To Die For*, 1995 **9** *My Life*, 1993 **10** *Portrait of a Lady*, 1996

TOP 10 ★
SHARON STONE MOVIES

1	Basic Instinct	1992
2	Total Recall	1990
3	The Specialist	1995
4	Last Action Hero	1993
5	Sliver	1993
6	Sphere	1998
7	Casino*	1995
8	Diabolique	1996
9	Police Academy 4: Citizens on Patrol	1987
10	Intersection	1994

* *Academy Award nomination for "Best Actress"*

Sharon Stone's part in *Last Action Hero* amounted to no more than a brief cameo. If it was discounted, *Action Jackson* (1988) would occupy 10th place.

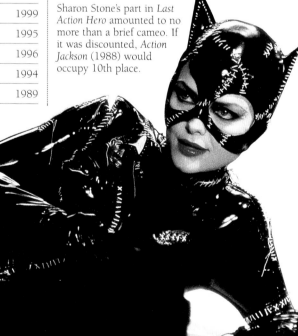

PRETTY WOMAN

Former model Julia Roberts, shown here in My Best Friend's Wedding, became the first Hollywood actress to be paid US$10 million. She now commands almost US$20 million.

TOP 10 ★
WINONA RYDER MOVIES

1	Bram Stoker's Dracula	1992
2	Alien: Resurrection	1997
3	Edward Scissorhands	1990
4	Beetlejuice	1988
5	Little Women	1994
6	Mermaids	1990
7	The Age of Innocence	1993
8	How to Make an American Quilt	1995
9	Reality Bites	1994
10	The Crucible	1996

TOP 10 GWYNETH PALTROW MOVIES

1 *Se7en*, 1995 **2** *Hook*, 1991
3 *Shakespeare in Love,** 1998
4 *A Perfect Murder*, 1998
5 *The Talented Mr. Ripley*, 1999
6 *Sliding Doors*, 1998 **7** *Great Expectations*, 1998 **8** *Malice*, 1993
9 *Emma*, 1996 **10** *Hush*, 1998

* Academy Award for "Best Actress"

TOP 10 ★
DEMI MOORE MOVIES

1	Ghost	1990
2	Indecent Proposal	1993
3	A Few Good Men	1992
4	Disclosure	1995
5	Striptease	1996
6	G.I. Jane	1997
7	The Juror	1996
8	About Last Night...	1986
9	St. Elmo's Fire	1985
10	Young Doctors in Love	1982

Demi Moore provided the voice of Esmeralda in *The Hunchback of Notre Dame* (1996). If included in her Top 10, it would be in second place.

TOP 10 ★
JULIA ROBERTS MOVIES

1	Pretty Woman*	1990
2	Notting Hill	1999
3	Hook	1991
4	My Best Friend's Wedding	1997
5	Runaway Bride	1999
6	The Pelican Brief	1993
7	Sleeping with the Enemy	1991
8	Stepmom	1998
9	Conspiracy Theory	1997
10	Steel Magnolias#	1989

* Academy Award nomination for "Best Actress"

 # Academy Award nomination for "Best Supporting Actress"

Julia Roberts also appeared in a cameo role as herself in *The Player* (1992), which just failed to make her personal Top 10.

TOP 10 ★
DREW BARRYMORE MOVIES

1	E.T.: The Extra-Terrestrial	1982
2	Batman Forever	1995
3	Scream	1996
4	The Wedding Singer	1998
5	Never Been Kissed	1999
6	Ever After	1998
7	Wayne's World 2	1993
8	Everyone Says I Love You	1996
9	Boys on the Side	1995
10	Mad Love	1995

TOP 10 ★
GEENA DAVIS MOVIES

1	Tootsie	1982
2	Stuart Little	1999
3	A League of Their Own	1992
4	The Long Kiss Goodnight	1996
5	Beetlejuice	1988
6	Hero	1992
7	Fletch	1985
8	Thelma & Louise	1991
9	The Fly	1986
10	The Accidental Tourist	1988

TOP 10 ★
UMA THURMAN MOVIES

1	Batman & Robin	1997
2	Pulp Fiction	1994
3	The Truth About Cats & Dogs	1996
4	The Avengers	1998
5	Dangerous Liaisons	1988
6	Final Analysis	1992
7	Beautiful Girls	1996
8	Les Misérables	1988
9	Johnny Be Good	1997
10	Gattaca	1998

What is Canada's most profitable food export?
see p.216 for the answer

A *Dairy products, eggs and honey*
B *Beverages, spirits and vinegar*
C *Grains, bulk or cereals*

177

Character Actors

KEVIN SPACEY MOVIES

1	Se7en	1995
2	Outbreak	1995
3	A Time to Kill	1996
4	American Beauty*	1999
5	L.A. Confidential	1997
6	The Negotiator	1998
7	The Usual Suspects#	1995
8	See No Evil, Hear No Evil	1989
9	Heartburn	1986
10	Midnight in the Garden of Good and Evil	1997

* Academy Award for "Best Actor"
\# Academy Award for "Best Supporting Actor"

An actor with roots in the theater, Kevin Spacey made his mark with critically acclaimed roles in *Glengarry Glen Ross* (1992) and *Se7en* (1995) before his Oscar-winning performance in *American Beauty* (1999). Spacey drew rave reviews for his performance in *The Iceman Cometh* on the London and New York stages in 1999. He also directed the thriller *Albino Alligator* in 1996.

TOP 10 MORGAN FREEMAN MOVIES

1 *Robin Hood: Prince of Thieves*, 1991
2 *Deep Impact*, 1998 3 *Se7en*, 1995
4 *Outbreak*, 1995 5 *Unforgiven*, 1992
6 *Driving Miss Daisy*, 1989 7 *Kiss the Girls*, 1997 8 *Amistad*, 1997
9 *The Shawshank Redemption*, 1994
10 *Chain Reaction*, 1996

KEVIN BACON MOVIES

1	Apollo 13	1995
2	A Few Good Men	1992
3	JFK	1991
4	Sleepers	1996
5	Animal House	1978
6	The River Wild	1994
7	Footloose	1984
8	Wild Things	1998
9	Flatliners	1990
10	Planes, Trains & Automobiles	1987

STRANGE STEVE

Steve Buscemi has carved out a movie career playing quirky roles, such as that of Carl Showalter in the Coen Brothers' Fargo.

TOP 10 STEVE BUSCEMI MOVIES

1 *Armageddon*, 1998 2 *Big Daddy*, 1999
3 *Con Air*, 1997 4 *Pulp Fiction*, 1994
5 *The Wedding Singer*,* 1998
6 *Rising Sun*, 1993 7 *Desperado*, 1995
8 *Fargo*, 1996 9 *Escape from L.A.*, 1996
10 *The Big Lebowski*, 1998

* Uncredited

SAMUEL L. JACKSON MOVIES

1	Star Wars: Episode I – The Phantom Menace	1999
2	Jurassic Park	1993
3	Die Hard with a Vengeance	1995
4	Coming to America	1988
5	Pulp Fiction	1994
6	Patriot Games	1992
7	Deep Blue Sea	1999
8	A Time to Kill	1996
9	Sea of Love	1989
10	Jackie Brown	1997

ACTION JACKSON

Samuel Jackson received a Silver Bear award at the Berlin Film Festival for his role in Jackie Brown, one of a series of bad-guy roles.

TOP 10
TIM ROTH MOVIES

1 *Pulp Fiction*, 1994 **2** *Rob Roy*, 1995
3 *Everyone Says I Love You*, 1996
4 *Hoodlum*, 1997 **5** *Reservoir Dogs*,
1992 **5** *The Cook, the Thief, His Wife &
Her Lover*, 1989 **6** *Gridlock'd*, 1997
7 *Four Rooms*, 1995 **8** *A World Apart*,
1988 **10** *Vincent & Theo*, 1990

"LET'S GO TO WORK ..."
*British actor Tim Roth (second from right) appeared
as Mr. Orange in writer–director Quentin Tarantino's
cult debut, the violent gangster movie Reservoir Dogs.*

TOP 10 ⭐
JOHN MALKOVICH
MOVIES

1	In the Line of Fire	1993
2	The Man in the Iron Mask	1998
3	The Messenger: The Story of Joan of Arc	1999
4	Dangerous Liaisons	1988
5	Places in the Heart	1984
6	The Killing Fields	1984
7	Rounders	1998
8	Being John Malkovich	1999
9	Con Air	1997
10	Empire of the Sun	1987

Although uncredited, John Malkovich was the
narrator of the movie *Alive* (1993). If included, this
would be in fourth place. *Being John Malkovich*
(1999), in which a puppeteer enters the mind of
the actor, is a newcomer to his personal Top 10.

TOP 10 HARVEY KEITEL MOVIES

1 *Sister Act*, 1992 **2** *Pulp Fiction*, 1994 **3** *Get Shorty*,* 1995 **4** *Cop Land*, 1997
5 *Rising Sun*, 1993 **6** *From Dusk Till Dawn*, 1996 **7** *Bugsy*, 1991
8 *Thelma & Louise*, 1991 **9** *The Piano*, 1993 **10** *Point of No Return*, 1993

* Uncredited cameo

TOP 10 ⭐
JOE PESCI MOVIES

1	Home Alone	1990
2	Lethal Weapon 3	1992
3	Lethal Weapon 4	1998
4	Home Alone 2: Lost in New York	1992
5	Lethal Weapon 2	1989
6	JFK	1991
7	Casino	1995
8	My Cousin Vinny	1992
9	GoodFellas	1990
10	Raging Bull	1980

TOP 10 ⭐
GARY BUSEY MOVIES

1	The Firm	1993
2	Under Siege	1992
3	Lethal Weapon	1987
4	Rookie of the Year	1993
5	Point Break	1991
6	Black Sheep	1996
7	Predator 2	1990
8	Drop Zone	1994
9	The Player	1992
10	Soldier	1998

Did You Know? *Reservoir Dogs* (1992) is not the first movie in which the
gangsters use colors as names: *The Taking of Pelham 123*
(1974) has characters called Blue, Green, Gray, and Brown.

Character Actresses

FAMILY JEWEL

A member of the Fonda movie family (daughter of Peter, granddaughter of Henry, niece of Jane) Bridget Fonda – shown here in Jackie Brown – has built a successful movie career since her 1982 debut.

TOP 10 ★
BRIDGET FONDA MOVIES

1	The Godfather Part III	1990
2	Jackie Brown	1997
3	The Road to Wellville	1994
4	Doc Hollywood	1991
5	Single White Female	1992
6	It Could Happen to You	1994
7	City Hall	1996
8	Lake Placid	1999
9	Point of No Return	1993
10	Singles	1992

TOP 10 ★
ALFRE WOODARD MOVIES

1	Star Trek: First Contact	1996
2	Primal Fear	1996
3	Scrooged	1988
4	Grand Canyon	1991
5	How to Make an American Quilt	1995
6	Blue Chips	1994
7	Heart and Souls	1993
8	Crooklyn	1994
9	Extremities	1986
10	Down in the Delta	1998

TOP 10 ★
CATHERINE KEENER MOVIES

1	8MM	1999
2	Out of Sight	1998
3	About Last Night...	1986
4	Being John Malkovich	1999
5	Switch	1991
6	Your Friends & Neighbors	1998
7	The Gun in Betty Lou's Handbag	1992
8	Walking and Talking	1996
9	Living in Oblivion	1995
10	Box of Moonlight	1996

TOP 10 ★
FRANCES McDORMAND MOVIES

1	Primal Fear	1996
2	Fargo*	1996
3	Madeline	1998
4	Mississippi Burning	1988
5	Darkman	1990
6	Raising Arizona	1987
7	Lone Star	1996
8	Beyond Rangoon	1995
9	The Butcher's Wife	1991
10	Short Cuts	1993

* Academy Award for "Best Actress"

TOP 10 JENNIFER JASON LEIGH MOVIES

1 *Backdraft*, 1991 **2** *Single White Female*, 1992 **3** *Dolores Claiborne*, 1995 **4** *Miami Blues*, 1990 **5** *A Thousand Acres*, 1997 **6** *Rush*, 1991 **7** *Short Cuts*, 1993 **8** *Georgia*, 1995 **9** *The Hudsucker Proxy*, 1994 **10** *eXistenZ*, 1999

TOP 10 ★ JULIE KAVNER MOVIES

1	*Forget Paris*	1995
2	*Awakenings*	1990
3	*Hannah and Her Sisters*	1986
4	*Radio Days*	1987
5	*Deconstructing Harry*	1997
6	*New York Stories*	1989
7	*I'll Do Anything*	1994
8	*Alice*	1990
9	*Surrender*	1987
10	*This Is My Life*	1992

Although an actress with a number of movies to her credit, Julie Kavner is best known for providing the voice of Marge Simpson and other characters in the TV series *The Simpsons*. She was also the voice of a pigeon in *Doctor Dolittle* (1998).

TOP 10 ★ EMMA THOMPSON MOVIES

1	*Sense and Sensibility*	1995
2	*Junior*	1994
3	*Primary Colors*	1998
4	*Dead Again*	1991
5	*Howards End**	1992
6	*In the Name of the Father* #	1993
7	*The Remains of the Day* #	1993
8	*Much Ado About Nothing*	1993
9	*Henry V*	1989
10=	*Impromptu*	1991
10=	*Peter's Friends*	1992

* *Academy Award for "Best Actress"*
# *Academy Award nomination*

TOP 10 ★ HOLLY HUNTER MOVIES

1	*The Firm**	1993
2	*Copycat*	1995
3	*Always*	1989
4	*Broadcast News*	1987
5	*The Piano* #	1993
6	*Raising Arizona*	1987
7	*Crash*	1996
8	*Home for the Holidays*	1995
9	*Once Around*	1991
10	*Living Out Loud*	1998

* *Academy Award nomination*
# *Academy Award for "Best Actress"*

TOP 10 MARY-LOUISE PARKER MOVIES

1 *The Client*, 1994 **2** *Fried Green Tomatoes*, 1991 **3** *Boys on the Side*, 1995 **4** *Grand Canyon*, 1991 **5** *Portrait of a Lady*, 1996 **6** *Bullets Over Broadway*, 1994 **7** *Longtime Companion*, 1990 **8** *Mr. Wonderful*, 1993 **9** *Goodbye Lover*, 1999 **10** *Naked in New York*, 1994

DRIVEN MAD

Kathy Bates has appeared in diverse roles, from the psychotic Annie Wilkes in Stephen King's Misery to "Unsinkable" Molly Brown in Titanic – her most successful movie.

TOP 10 ★ KATHY BATES MOVIES

1	*Titanic*	1997
2	*The Waterboy*	1998
3	*Dick Tracy*	1990
4	*Fried Green Tomatoes*	1991
5	*A Civil Action**	1998
6	*Misery*	1990
7	*Diabolique*	1996
8	*Dolores Claiborne*	1995
9	*Primary Colors*	1998
10	*The Morning After*	1986

* *Uncredited*

What was the top-selling Canadian album of the 1980s?
see p.131 for the answer

A Shania Twain's *Come on Over*
B Alanis Morissette's *Jagged Little Pill*
C Celine Dion's *The Colour of My Love*

The Directors

TOP 10 ★
MOVIES DIRECTED BY ACTORS

MOVIE/YEAR	DIRECTOR
1 *Pretty Woman*, 1990	Garry Marshall
2 *Dances with Wolves*, 1990	Kevin Costner
3 *The Bodyguard*, 1992	Kevin Costner
4 *Apollo 13*, 1995	Ron Howard
5 *Ransom*, 1996	Ron Howard
6 *Rocky IV*, 1985	Sylvester Stallone
7 *Doctor Dolittle*, 1998	Betty Thomas
8 *Runaway Bride*, 1999	Garry Marshall
9 *Waterworld*, 1995	Kevin Costner
10 *A Few Good Men*, 1992	Rob Reiner

The role of actor–director has a long cinema tradition, numbering such luminaries as Charlie Chaplin, Buster Keaton, Orson Welles, and John Huston among its ranks. Heading this list, *Pretty Woman* director Garry Marshall is the brother of actress–director Penny Marshall.

WOMAN'S WORLD

The rock 'n' roll comedy Wayne's World was directed by Penelope Spheeris, who also directed The Beverly Hillbillies (1993) and The Little Rascals (1994).

TOP 10 ★
MOVIES DIRECTED BY WOMEN

MOVIE/YEAR	DIRECTOR
1 *Look Who's Talking*, 1989	Amy Heckerling
2 *Doctor Dolittle*, 1998	Betty Thomas
3 *Sleepless in Seattle*, 1993	Nora Ephron
4 *The Birdcage*, 1996	Elaine May
5 *You've Got Mail*, 1998	Nora Ephron
6 *Wayne's World*, 1992	Penelope Spheeris
7 *Big*, 1988	Penny Marshall
8 *Michael*, 1996	Nora Ephron
9 *A League of Their Own*, 1992	Penny Marshall
10 *Father of the Bride*, 1991	Nancy Meyers

TOP 10 ★
MOVIES DIRECTED BY MARTIN SCORSESE

1	*Cape Fear*	1991
2	*Casino*	1995
3	*The Color of Money*	1986
4	*GoodFellas*	1990
5	*The Age of Innocence*	1993
6	*Taxi Driver*	1976
7	*Raging Bull*	1980
8	*Bringing Out the Dead*	1999
9	*Alice Doesn't Live Here Anymore*	1975
10	*New York, New York*	1977

RUNAWAY SUCCESS

Actor–director Garry Marshall has achieved outstanding directorial triumphs with box-office smash hits such as Runaway Bride, in which he appears in an uncredited role.

TOP 10 ★
MOVIES DIRECTED BY STEVEN SPIELBERG

1	*Jurassic Park*	1993
2	*E.T.: The Extra-Terrestrial*	1982
3	*The Lost World: Jurassic Park*	1997
4	*Indiana Jones and the Last Crusade*	1989
5	*Saving Private Ryan*	1998
6	*Jaws*	1975
7	*Raiders of the Lost Ark*	1981
8	*Indiana Jones and the Temple of Doom*	1984
9	*Schindler's List*	1993
10	*Hook*	1991

Steven Spielberg has directed some of the most successful movies of all time: the top five in this list appear among the top 20 movies of all time, while the cumulative world box-office gross of his Top 10 amounts to over US$5 billion. If his credits as producer are included, further blockbusters, such as *Deep Impact*, *The Mask of Zorro*, *Men in Black*, *The Flintstones*, *Casper*, *Twister*, the *Back to the Future* trilogy, *Gremlins*, *Poltergeist* (which he also wrote), the animated movie *An American Tail*, and the part-animated *Who Framed Roger Rabbit*, would all score highly.

Did You Know? Hollywood director D. W. Griffith (1875–1948) is considered the most prolific director of all time, with a remarkable 545 movies credited to him in the period 1908–36, spanning both the silent and talkie eras.

TOP 10
MOVIES DIRECTED BY NORMAN JEWISON

1	Moonstruck	1987*
2	Fiddler on the Roof	1971*
3	The Hurricane	1999
4	Best Friends	1982
5	Other People's Money	1991
6	...And Justice for All	1979
7	Jesus Christ Superstar	1973
8	Agnes of God	1985
9	A Soldier's Story	1984
10	In the Heat of the Night	1967*

* Academy Award nomination for "Best Director"

TOP 10
MOVIES DIRECTED BY STANLEY KUBRICK

1	Eyes Wide Shut	1999
2	The Shining	1980
3	2001: A Space Odyssey	1968
4	Full Metal Jacket	1987
5	A Clockwork Orange	1971
6	Spartacus	1960
7	Barry Lyndon	1975
8	Dr. Strangelove or: How I Learned to Stop Worrying and Love the Bomb	1964
9	Lolita	1962
10	Paths of Glory	1957

TOP 10
MOVIES DIRECTED OR PRODUCED BY GEORGE LUCAS

1	Star Wars: Episode I – The Phantom Menace (D/P)	1999
2	Star Wars (D)	1977/97
3	Return of the Jedi (P)	1983/97
4	The Empire Strikes Back (P)	1980/97
5	Indiana Jones and the Last Crusade (P)	1989
6	Raiders of the Lost Ark (P)	1981
7	Indiana Jones and the Temple of Doom (P)	1984
8	American Graffiti (D)	1973
9	Willow (P)	1988
10	The Land Before Time (P)	1988

D = Director; P = Producer

George Lucas made the move from directing to producing after the phenomenal success of *Star Wars*. The first five movies on this list rank among the 20 highest-earning movies of all time.

TOP 10 MOVIES DIRECTED BY IVAN REITMAN

1 *Ghostbusters*, 1984 **2** *Twins*, 1988 **3** *Ghostbusters II*, 1989 **4** *Kindergarten Cop*, 1990 **5** *Six Days Seven Nights*, 1998 **6** *Junior*, 1994 **7** *Stripes*, 1981 **8** *Dave*, 1993 **9** *Legal Eagles*, 1986 **10** *Fathers' Day*, 1997

TOP 10
MOVIES DIRECTED BY JOHN CARPENTER

1	Halloween	1978
2	Escape from L.A.	1996
3	Starman	1984
4	Escape from New York	1981
5	Vampires	1998
6	The Fog	1980
7	Christine	1983
8	Memoirs of an Invisible Man	1992
9	Prince of Darkness	1987
10	They Live	1988

GREAT ESCAPES

Kurt Russell stars in Escape from L.A., *the futuristic sequel to* Escape from New York, *both movies directed by John Carpenter.*

Movie Outtakes

MOVIES WITH THE MOST EXTRAS

MOVIE/COUNTRY/YEAR	EXTRAS	MOVIE/COUNTRY/YEAR	EXTRAS
1 *Gandhi*, UK, 1982	300,000	6 *Tonko*, Japan, 1988	100,000
2 *Kolberg*, Germany, 1945	187,000	7 *The War of Independence*, Romania, 1912	80,000
3 *Monster Wang-magwi*, South Korea, 1967	157,000	8 *Around the World in 80 Days*, US, 1956	68,894
4 *War and Peace*, USSR, 1967	120,000	9 =*Intolerance*, US, 1916	60,000
5 *Ilya Muromets*, USSR, 1956	106,000	9 =*Dny Zrady*, Czechoslovakia, 1972	60,000

A CAST OF THOUSANDS

Some 300,000 Delhi residents were drafted as extras on Gandhi for a sequence that occupied just 125 seconds of screen time.

TOP 10 COUNTRIES WITH THE MOST MOVIE THEATERS

(Country/movie theaters)

❶ China, 65,000 ❷ US, 34,186
❸ India, 12,900 ❹ France, 4,762
❺ Germany, 4,244 ❻ Spain, 2,968
❼ UK, 2,638 ❽ Italy, 2,500
❾ Canada, 2,486 ❿ Indonesia, 2,100

Source: Screen Digest

MOVIE COUNTRIES

COUNTRY	NO. OF MOVIE SCREENS PER MILLION INHABITANTS
1 Iceland	165.2
2 Sweden	131.3
3 US	128.3
4 Norway	89.2
5 Australia	86.1
6 Azerbaijan	85.8
7 France	81.1
8 Canada	81.0
9 New Zealand	78.1
10 Switzerland	75.8

Source: Screen Digest

MOST PROLIFIC MOVIE-PRODUCING COUNTRIES

COUNTRY	AVERAGE NO. OF FILMS PRODUCED PER ANNUM, 1989–98
1 India	787
2 US	591
3 Japan	255
4 Philippines	160
5 France	148
6 China	127
7 Russia	124
8 =South Korea	73
8 =Thailand	73
10 UK	67

Source: Screen Digest

CHINESE MOVIE-GOERS

Although in relation to its vast population it remains a minor player, China is steadily joining the ranks of the world's foremost makers and watchers of movies.

TOP 10 MOVIE-GOING COUNTRIES

(Country/total annual attendance)

❶ India, 2,860,000,000 **❷** US, 1,480,700,000 **❸** Indonesia, 222,200,000 **❹** France, 170,110,000 **❺** Japan, 153,100,000 **❻** Germany, 148,880,000 **❼** Brazil, 137,160,000 **❽** UK, 136,500,000 **❾** China, 121,000,000 **❿** Italy, 117,900,000

Source: Screen Digest

TOP 10 COUNTRIES SPENDING THE MOST ON MOVIE PRODUCTION

(Country/average investment per movie in US$)

❶ US, 14,000,000 **❷** UK, 8,250,000 **❸** France, 5,260,000 **❹** Ireland, 5,140,000 **❺** Australia, 4,370,000 **❻** Italy, 3,930,000 **❼** Argentina, 3,800,000 **❽** Japan, 3,570,000 **❾** Spain, 3,180,000 **❿** Canada, 3,160,000

Source: Screen Digest

TOP 10 COUNTRIES WITH THE BIGGEST INCREASE IN MOVIE PRODUCTION

(Country/percentage increase in production, 1989–98)

❶ Ireland, 400.0 **❷** Luxembourg, 200.0 **❸** UK, 117.5 **❹** Iceland, 100.0 **❺** New Zealand, 75.0 **❻** Australia, 72.7 **❼** Norway, 55.6 **❽** Venezuela, 42.9 **❾** France, 33.6 **❿** = Austria; = Brazil, 33.3

Source: Screen Digest

TOP 10 ★

MOST EXPENSIVE ITEMS OF MOVIE MEMORABILIA EVER SOLD AT AUCTION

ITEM/SALE	PRICE (US$)
1 Clark Gable's Oscar for *It Happened One Night*, Christie's, Los Angeles, Dec 15, 1996	607,500
2 Vivien Leigh's Oscar for *Gone with the Wind*, Sotheby's, New York, Dec 15, 1993	562,500
3 Poster for *The Mummy*, 1932, Sotheby's, New York, Mar 1, 1997	453,500
4 James Bond's Aston Martin DB5 from *Goldfinger*, Sotheby's, New York, Jun 28, 1986	275,000
5 Clark Gable's personal script for *Gone with the Wind*, Christie's, Los Angeles, Dec 15, 1996	244,500
6 "Rosebud" sled from *Citizen Kane*, Christie's, Los Angeles, Dec 15, 1996	233,500
7 Herman J. Mankiewicz's scripts for *Citizen Kane* and *The American*, Christie's, New York, Jun 21, 1989	231,000
8 Judy Garland's ruby slippers from *The Wizard of Oz*, Christie's, New York, Jun 21, 1988	165,000
9 Piano from the Paris scene in *Casablanca*, Sotheby's, New York, Dec 16, 1988	154,000
10 Charlie Chaplin's hat and cane, Christie's, London, Dec 11, 1987	130,350*

* £ to US$ conversion at rate then prevailing

TOP 10 ★

LONGEST MOVIES EVER SCREENED

MOVIE/COUNTRY	YEAR	DURATION HRS	MINS
1 *The Longest and Most Meaningless Movie in the World*, UK	1970	48	0
2 *The Burning of the Red Lotus Temple*, China	1928–31	27	0
3 ****, US	1967	25	0
4 *Heimat*, West Germany	1984	15	40
5 *Berlin Alexanderplatz*, West Germany/Italy	1980	15	21
6 *The Journey*, Sweden	1987	14	33
7 *The Old Testament*, Italy	1922	13	0
8 *Comment Yukong déplace les montagnes*, France	1976	12	43
9 *Out 1: Noli me Tangere*, France	1971	12	40
10 *Ningen No Joken* (*The Human Condition*), Japan	1958–60	9	29

The list includes commercially screened movies, but not "stunt" movies created solely to break endurance records (particularly those of their audiences), among which is the 85-hour *The Cure for Insomnia*.

What is the fastest-declining crime in Canada?
see p.71 for the answer
A Failure to stop or remain (traffic violation)
B Attempted murder
C Motor vehicle theft

Toon Town

THE 10 ★ FIRST FULL-LENGTH SIMPSONS EPISODES

	EPISODE	FIRST SCREENED
1	Simpsons Roasting on an Open Fire*	Dec 17, 1989
2	Bart the Genius	Jan 14, 1990
3	Homer's Odyssey	Jan 21, 1990
4	There's No Disgrace Like Homer	Jan 28, 1990
5	Bart the General	Feb 4, 1990
6	Moaning Lisa	Feb 11, 1990
7	The Call of the Simpsons	Feb 18, 1990
8	The Telltale Head	Feb 25, 1990
9	Life on the Fast Lane#	Mar 18, 1990
10	Homer's Night Out	Mar 25, 1990

* aka The Simpsons Christmas Special
\# aka Jacques to Be Wild

ON THE COUCH

The infinitely changing couch gag has been an enduring feature of the opening sequence of The Simpsons – one of the most popular cartoons currently being screened on television.

TOP 10 ★ ANIMATED MOVIES

1	The Lion King	1994
2	Aladdin	1992
3	Tarzan	1999
4	A Bug's Life	1998
5	Toy Story	1995
6	Beauty and the Beast	1991
7	Who Framed Roger Rabbit*	1988
8	Pocahontas	1995
9	The Hunchback of Notre Dame	1996
10	Mulan	1998

* Part animated, part live action

The 1990s provided nine of the 10 most successful animated movies of all time, which, in turn, ejected a number of their high-earning predecessors from this Top 10. Animated movies stand out among the leading money-makers of each decade: in the 1930s, Snow White was the second highest-earning movie after Gone with the Wind.

THE 10 ★ LATEST OSCAR-WINNING ANIMATED MOVIES*

YEAR	FILM	DIRECTOR/COUNTRY
1999	The Old Man and the Sea	Aleksandr Petrov, USA
1998	Bunny	Chris Wedge, US
1997	Geri's Game	Jan Pinkava, US
1996	Quest	Tyron Montgomery, UK
1995	A Close Shave	Nick Park, UK
1994	Bob's Birthday	David Fine and Alison Snowden, UK
1993	The Wrong Trousers	Nick Park, UK
1992	Mona Lisa Descending a Staircase	Joan C. Gratz, US
1991	Manipulation	Daniel Greaves, UK
1990	Creature Comforts	Nick Park, UK

* In the category "Short Subjects (Animated Films)"

THE 10 ★ FIRST OSCAR-WINNING ANIMATED MOVIES*

YEAR	FILM	DIRECTOR#
1932	Flowers and Trees	Walt Disney
1934	The Three Little Pigs	Walt Disney
1935	The Tortoise and the Hare	Walt Disney
1936	Three Orphan Kittens	Walt Disney
1937	The Country Cousin	Walt Disney
1938	The Old Mill	Walt Disney
1939	Ferdinand the Bull	Walt Disney
1940	The Ugly Duckling	Walt Disney
1941	The Milky Way	Rudolf Ising
1942	Lend a Paw	Walt Disney

* In the category "Short Subjects (Cartoons)"
\# All from the US

Oscars were awarded in the category "Short Subjects (Cartoons)" until 1971, when it was altered to "Short Subjects (Animated Films)."

Did You Know? Walt Disney (1901–66) won an unequaled individual total of 26 Oscars and six special Academy Awards for his animated movies.

THE 10 ★
FIRST DISNEY ANIMATED FEATURES

1	Snow White and the Seven Dwarfs	1937
2	Pinocchio	1940
3	Fantasia	1940
4	Dumbo	1941
5	Bambi	1942
6	Victory Through Air Power	1943
7	The Three Caballeros	1945
8	Make Mine Music	1946
9	Fun and Fancy Free	1947
10	Melody Time	1948

Excluding part-animated movies such as *Song of the South* and *Mary Poppins*, and movies made specially for television serialization, Disney has made a total of 40 full-length animated feature movies up to the end of 1999, when *Fantasia 2000* was released.

TOP 10 ★
PART ANIMATION/PART LIVE-ACTION MOVIES

1	Who Framed Roger Rabbit	1988
2	Casper	1995
3	Space Jam	1996
4	9 to 5	1980
5	Mary Poppins	1964
6	Small Soldiers	1999
7	Song of the South	1946
8	James and the Giant Peach	1976
9	Pete's Dragon	1977
10	Fletch Lives	1989

With the increasing use of computer animation, the distinction between animation and live action is becoming blurred: even long-dead actors and actresses are now capable of being resurrected on film through sophisticated computer techniques.

THE 10 ★
FIRST BUGS BUNNY CARTOONS

	TITLE	RELEASED
1	Porky's Hare Hunt	Apr 30, 1938
2	Hare-um Scare-um	Aug 12, 1939
3	Elmer's Candid Camera	Mar 2, 1940
4	A Wild Hare	Jul 27, 1940
5	Elmer's Pet Rabbit	Jan 4, 1941
6	Tortoise Beats Hare	Mar 15, 1941
7	Hiawatha's Rabbit Hunt	Jun 7, 1941
8	The Heckling Hare	Jul 5, 1941
9	All This and Rabbit Stew	Sep 13, 1941
10	Wabbit Twouble	Dec 20, 1941

Bugs Bunny's debut was as a co-star alongside Porky Pig in *Porky's Hare Hunt*. *A Wild Hare* was the first film in which he said the line that became his trademark: "Eh, what's up, Doc?"

TOP 10 ★
NON-DISNEY ANIMATED FEATURE MOVIES

1	The Prince of Egypt	1998
2	Antz	1998
3	Pokémon the First Movie: Mewtwo Strikes Back	1999
4	The Rugrats Movie	1998
5	South Park: Bigger, Longer and Uncut	1999
6	Pocket Monsters: Revelation Lugia	1999
7	The Land Before Time	1988
8	An American Tail	1986
9	The Lord of the Rings	1978
10	All Dogs Go to Heaven	1989

Such was the success of *Pocket Monsters: Revelation Lugia* in Japan that it earned a place in this list before being released elsewhere.

CAT AND MOUSE

Tom and Jerry, and their occasional accomplices, have been battling on celluloid for over 60 years. Despite current concern by the politically correct about the level of violence, the cartoons remain firm favorites with children of all ages.

TOP 10 ★
FIRST TOM AND JERRY CARTOONS

	CARTOON	RELEASE DATE		CARTOON	RELEASE DATE
1	Puss Gets the Boot*	Feb 20, 1940	6	Puss 'N' Toots	May 30, 1942
2	The Midnight Snack	Jul 19, 1941	7	The Bowling Alley-Cat	Jul 18, 1942
3	The Night Before Christmas*	Dec 6, 1941	8	Fine Feathered Friend	Oct 10, 1942
4	Fraidy Cat	Jan 17, 1942	9	Sufferin' Cats!	Jan 16, 1943
5	Dog Trouble	Apr 18, 1942	10	The Lonesome Mouse	May 22, 1943

* Academy Award nomination

TOP 10 ★
RADIO FORMATS IN CANADA

	FORMAT	PERCENTAGE SHARE*
1	Adult contemporary	24.8
2	Gold/Oldies/Rock	12.6
3	Talk	11.5
4	Contemporary	10.2
5	CBC	9.5
6	Other	6.5
7	Album-oriented rock	4.1
8	U.S. Stations	3.4
9	Middle-of-the-road	2.5
10	Easy listening	1.9

* Average share of radio listening, persons aged 12 and over, fall 1998

Source: Statistics Canada

TOP 10 ★
RADIO-OWNING COUNTRIES

	COUNTRY	RADIO SETS PER 1,000 POPULATION
1	US	2,093
2	UK	1,433
3	Australia	1,304
4	Canada	1,053
5	Denmark	1,034
6	South Korea	1,024
7	Monaco	1,019
8	Finland	1,008
9	New Zealand	997
10	Germany	944

Source: UNESCO

In addition to the countries on this list, many small island communities have very high numbers of radios to enable people to maintain regular contact with the outside world.

TOP 10 ★
MOST LISTENED-TO RADIO STATIONS IN CANADA

	STATION	CITY	FORMAT	WEEKLY CIRCULATION*
1	CKOI-FM	Montreal	Grands Succès Contemporains	1,192,900
2	CHUM-FM	Toronto	Adult Contemporary	1,175,000
3	CKFM-FM	Toronto	Adult Rock	1,127,800
4	CHFI-FM	Toronto	Adult Contemporary	1,090,300
5	CFRB	Toronto	News Talk	942,300
6	CILQ-FM	Toronto	Rock/Talk	921,200
7	CKAC	Montreal	Info-Commentaire-Sports	864,000
8	CFTR	Toronto	All News	813,200
9	CBLA-FM	Toronto	News Talk	797,100
10	CITE-FM	Montreal	Adulte Contemporain	724,300

* Total number of listeners aged 12+ tuning to a station during an average week

Source: RadioWorks Inc. of Hennessy & Bray Communications; Spring 1999 BBM survey

THE 10 ★
CANADIAN FIRSTS IN RADIO BROADCASTING

	RADIO BROADCAST	DATE
1	Broadcast of the first licensed radio station in North America, XWA Montreal	1919
2	Scheduled programs begin to air on XWA Montreal	1920
3	CKCK Regina broadcasts first hockey play-by-play	1923
4	Broadcast of the first Dominion Observatory time signals	1924
5	Livestock market reports begin	1924
6	First broadcast of the Stanley Cup	1924
7	Buckingham Palace's first Christmas day broadcast	1932
8	First daily news bulletins by Canadian Press	1933
9	Live telephone coverage of trapped miners in Nova Scotia carried by 58 stations across the country	1936
10	Regular broadcasts begin on CBC National News Service	1941

Source: The Canadian Global Almanac

Background image: EKCO RADIO MODEL AD 65, 1932–34

TOP 10

MOST POPULAR
CBC RADIO ONE SHOWS

SHOW	NUMBER OF LISTENERS*
1 **World Report** (Mon–Fri 8 am)	658,700
2 **World Report** (Mon–Fri 6 am)	647,700
3 **Local Weekdays** (Mon–Fri 6–9 am)	534,100
4 **World Report** (Sat 9 am)	476,000
5 **World Report** (Sat 8 am)	459,500
6 **The House**	413,700
7 **World Report** (Sun 8 am)	412,600
8 **World Report** (Sun 9 am)	407,000
9 **Basic Black**	395,200
10 **Quirks and Quarks**	320,100

* Ranked by average ¼ hour for all persons 12+ for the fall of 1999

Source: *Canadian Broadcasting Corporation*

TOP 10

MOST POPULAR
CBC RADIO TWO SHOWS

SHOW	NUMBER OF LISTENERS*
1 **World Report** (Mon–Fri 8 am)	133,900
2 **Canada at Five**	132,700
3 **World Report** (Sat 9 am)	129,500
4 **Vinyl Café**	128,800
5 **Disc Drive**	124,500
6 **Pearls of Wisdom**	122,400
7 **Take Five**	116,600
8 **Sound Advice**	115,200
9 **World Report** (Sat 8 am)	108,000
10 **Music and Company** (Mon–Fri)	105,900

* Ranked by average ¼ hour for all persons 12+ for the fall of 1999

Source: *Canadian Broadcasting Corporation*

SNAP SHOTS

RADIO FOR ALL

London inventor Trevor Bayliss, a former international swimmer and swimming-pool salesman, was inspired to develop his clockwork radio after seeing a television program about communication problems in Africa. After the necessary financial backing had been secured, his Freeplay® wind-up radio went into production in Cape Town, South Africa, in 1994, and is now available worldwide. Its simple operating mechanism – a coil spring that drives a dynamo, providing 40 minutes of play time, with optional solar cells – is a perfect solution for radio communication in communities without electricity and where batteries are expensive.

Top TV

TOP 10 ✳
MOST-WATCHED TV SERIES IN CANADA 1998–99

PROGRAM	VIEWERS
1 Ally McBeal	1,684,000
2 ER	1,649,000
3 L.A. Doctors	1,299,000
4 Royal Canadian Air Farce	1,234,000
5 Law and Order	1,224,000
6 Jeopardy	1,169,000
7 Wheel of Fortune	1,143,000
8 CTV Evening News	1,141,000
9 Hockey Night in Canada	1,108,000
10 CTV Sunday Movie	1,085,000

© Copyright 2000 Nielsen Media Research

✳ TOP 10 SPECIALTY CABLE CHANNELS IN CANADA
(Channel/residential subscribers*)

❶ CBC Newsworld, 8,295,194 ❷ Youth Television (YTV), 7,676,427 ❸ The Sports Network (TSN), 7,554,631 ❹ Le Réseau de l'Information (RDI), 7,392,224 ❺ Country Music Television (Canada), 7,040,365 ❻ The Weather Network, 6,661,150 ❼ Vision TV, 6,598,216 ❽ CTV Sports Net, 6,516,960 ❾ The Learning Channel (TLC), 6,479,202 ❿ MuchMusic, 6,099,973

*For January 2000
Source: MediaSTATS

TOP 10 CABLE TELEVISION COUNTRIES
(Country/subscribers)

❶ US, 67,011,180 ❷ Germany, 18,740,260 ❸ Netherlands, 6,227,472 ❹ Russia, 5,784,432 ❺ Belgium, 3,945,342 ❻ Poland, 3,830,788 ❼ Romania, 3,000,000 ❽ UK, 2,666,783 ❾ France, 2,478,630 ❿ Switzerland, 2,156,120

Source: The Phillips Group

TOP 10 ★
SYNDICATED PROGRAMS ON US TV, 1998–99

PROGRAM	VIEWERS
1 WCW Wrestling	6,828,000
2 Judge Judy	6,675,000
3 Friends	6,328,000
4 Jerry Springer	6,185,000
5 Seinfeld	6,017,000
6 Entertainment Tonight	5,656,000
7 Frasier	4,932,000
8 =X-Files	4,860,000
8 =Home Improvement	4,860,000
10 ER	4,065,000

© Copyright 2000 Nielsen Media Research

TOP 10 ★
TELEVISION-WATCHING COUNTRIES

COUNTRY	AVERAGE DAILY VIEWING TIME HOURS	MINS
1 US	3	58
2 Greece	3	39
3 =Italy	3	36
3 =UK	3	36
5 Spain	3	31
6 =Canada	3	14
6 =Ireland	3	14
8 Germany	3	8
9 France	3	7
10 Belgium	2	57

Source: Screen Digest

A survey of television-viewing habits in Western Europe and North America showed that the number of channels, including new digital channels, is proliferating at a much faster rate than the time spent actually watching them, thus creating, in the jargon of the industry, "audience fragmentation." North American viewers watch, on average, 23 percent more than those in Europe, but this is decreasing by about half a percent per annum.

TOP 10 ★
PROGRAMS OF ALL TIME ON PBS TV*

PROGRAM/BROADCAST	AVERAGE AUDIENCE
1 The Civil War, Sep 1990	8,800,000
2 Life on Earth, Jan 1982	7,900,000
3 The Living Planet: A Portrait of the Earth, Feb 1985	7,800,000
4 The American Experience: The Kennedys, Sep 1992	7,000,000
5 Nature: Kingdom of the Ice Bear, Feb 1986	6,900,000
6 Cosmos, Sep 1980	6,500,000
7 =Planet Earth, Jan 1986	6,300,000
7 =Lewis & Clark: The Journey of the Corps of Discovery, Nov 1997	6,300,000
9 The Scarlet Letter, Sep 1979	5,700,000
10 Baseball, Sep 1994	5,000,000

* As of January 2000
Source: PBS

THE 10 ★
LATEST WINNERS OF THE DAYTIME EMMY AWARD FOR A CHILDREN'S PROGRAM

YEAR	PROGRAM
1998/99	The Island on Bird Street
1997/98	In His Father's Shoes
1996/97	Elmo Saves Christmas
1995/96	Stand Up
1994/95	A Child Betrayed: The Calvin Mire Story
1993/94	Dead Drunk: The Kevin Tunnel Story
1992/93	ABC Afterschool Special: Shades of a Single Protein
1991/92	Vincent and Me
1990/91	Lost in the Barrens
1989/90	CBS Schoolbreak Special: A Matter of Conscience

Did You Know? The funeral of Diana, Princess of Wales, on September 6, 1997, attracted the biggest television audience of all time, with an estimated 2.5 billion viewers worldwide.

TOP 10 ★
TV AUDIENCES OF ALL TIME
IN THE US

	PROGRAM	DATE	HOUSEHOLDS VIEWING TOTAL	%
1	M*A*S*H Farewell Special	Feb 28, 1983	50,150,000	60.2
2	Dallas	Nov 21, 1980	41,470,000	53.3
3	Roots Part 8	Jan 30, 1977	36,380,000	51.1
4	Super Bowl XVI	Jan 24, 1982	40,020,000	49.1
5	Super Bowl XVII	Jan 30, 1983	40,480,000	48.6
6	XVII Winter Olympics	Feb 23, 1994	45,690,000	48.5
7	Super Bowl XX	Jan 26, 1986	41,490,000	48.3
8	Gone with the Wind Pt. 1	Nov 7, 1976	33,960,000	47.7
9	Gone with the Wind Pt. 2	Nov 8, 1976	33,750,000	47.4
10	Super Bowl XII	Jan 15, 1978	34,410,000	47.2

© Copyright 2000 Nielsen Media Research

TOP 10 ★
MOVIES OF ALL TIME
ON PRIMETIME NETWORK TV

	MOVIE/YEAR RELEASED	BROADCAST	RATING (%)*
1	Gone with the Wind Pt. 1, 1939	Nov 7, 1976	47.7
2	Gone with the Wind Pt. 2, 1939	Nov 8, 1976	47.4
3 =	Love Story, 1970	Oct, 1 1972	42.3
3 =	Airport, 1970	Nov 11, 1973	42.3
5	The Godfather, Part II, 1974	Nov 18, 1974	39.4
6	Jaws, 1975	Nov 4, 1979	39.1
7	The Poseidon Adventure, 1972	Oct 27, 1974	39.0
8 =	True Grit, 1969	Nov 12, 1972	38.9
8 =	The Birds, 1963	Jan 6, 1968	38.9
10	Patton, 1970	Nov 19, 1972	38.5

* Of households viewing

© Copyright 2000 Nielsen Media Research

All the movies listed are dramas made for theatrical release, but if made-for-TV productions were included, then the controversial 1983 post-nuclear war movie, *The Day After* (screened on Nov 20, 1983), would rank in third place with a rating of 46.0 percent. It is significant that all the most watched movies on TV were broadcast before the dawn of the video era.

RAT RACE

After attracting a huge following as a television series, Rugrats was developed into a film – The Rugrats Movie – by Nickelodeon Pictures; it became a box-office smash.

Music on TV

THE 10 ★
LATEST RECIPIENTS OF MUCH MUSIC'S VIDEO OF THE YEAR AWARD

YEAR	ARTIST OR GROUP/TITLE
1999	Len, *Steal My Sunshine*
1998	Sarah McLachlan, *Sweet Surrender*
1997	Moist, *Tangerine*
1996	The Tragically Hip, *Ahead By a Century*
1995	Jann Arden, *Insensitive*
1994	Blue Rodeo, *Hasn't Hit Me Yet*
1993	The Tragically Hip, *Locked In the Trunk of a Car*
1992	54:40, *She-la*
1991	Crash Test Dummies, *Superman's Song*
1990	Cowboy Junkies, *Sun Comes Up, It's Tuesday Morning*

THE 10 ★
LATEST RECIPIENTS OF THE MTV "BEST VIDEO" AWARD

YEAR	ARTIST OR GROUP/TITLE
1999	Lauryn Hill, *Doo Wop (That Thing)*
1998	Madonna, *Ray of Light*
1997	Jamiroquai, *Virtual Insanity*
1996	The Smashing Pumpkins, *Tonight, Tonight*
1995	TLC, *Waterfalls*
1994	Aerosmith, *Cryin'*
1993	Pearl Jam, *Jeremy*
1992	Van Halen, *Right Now*
1991	R.E.M., *Losing My Religion*
1990	Sinead O'Connor, *Nothing Compares 2 U*

THE 10 ★
LATEST RECIPIENTS OF THE MTV "BEST GROUP VIDEO" AWARD

YEAR	ARTIST OR GROUP/TITLE
1999	TLC, *No Scrubs*
1998	Backstreet Boys, *Everybody (Backstreet's Back)*
1997	No Doubt, *Don't Speak*
1996	Foo Fighters, *Big Me*
1995	TLC, *Waterfalls*
1994	Aerosmith, *Cryin'*
1993	Pearl Jam, *Jeremy*
1992	U2, *Even Better Than the Real Thing*
1991	R.E.M., *Losing My Religion*
1990	The B-52s, *Love Shack*

TOP 10 MUSIC VIDEOS OF THE 20TH CENTURY ON MTV
(Artist or group/title)

1 Michael Jackson, *Thriller* **2** Madonna, *Vogue* **3** Nirvana, *Smells Like Teen Spirit* **4** Peter Gabriel, *Sledgehammer* **5** Run DMC with Aerosmith, *Walk This Way* **6** Guns N' Roses, *Sweet Child O' Mine* **7** Beastie Boys, *Sabotage* **8** Robert Palmer, *Addicted to Love* **9** 2Pac and Dr. Dre, *California Love* **10** Madonna, *Express Yourself*

PRODIGIOUS SUCCESS

Prodigy, featuring lead singer Keith Flint, won MTV US's "Viewer's Choice" award as well as three MTV Europe Music awards in 1997 for their single Breathe.

THE 10 ★
LATEST RECIPIENTS OF THE MTV "BEST FEMALE VIDEO" AWARD

YEAR	ARTIST/TITLE
1999	Lauryn Hill, *Doo Wop (That Thing)*
1998	Madonna, *Ray of Light*
1997	Jewel, *You Were Meant for Me*
1996	Alanis Morissette, *Ironic*
1995	Madonna, *Take a Bow*
1994	Janet Jackson, *If*
1993	k.d. lang, *Constant Craving*
1992	Annie Lennox, *Why*
1991	Janet Jackson, *Love Will Never Do Without You*
1990	Sinead O'Connor, *Nothing Compares 2 U*

THE 10 ⭐
LATEST RECIPIENTS OF THE MTV "BEST RAP VIDEO" AWARD

YEAR	ARTIST/TITLE
1999	Jay-Z featuring Ja Rule/Amil-lion, *Can I Get a...*
1998	Will Smith, *Gettin' Jiggy Wit It*
1997	The Notorious B.I.G., *Hypnotize*
1996	Coolio featuring LV, *Gangsta's Paradise*
1995	Dr. Dre, *Keep Their Heads Ringin'*
1994	Snoop Doggy Dogg, *Doggy Dogg World*
1993	Arrested Development, *People Everyday*
1992	Arrested Development, *Tennessee*
1991	L. L. Cool J, *Mama Said Knock You Out*
1990	MC Hammer, *U Can't Touch This*

Launched in 1981, MTV introduced its video awards three years later. The "Best Rap Video" category was added in 1989, when the winner was DJ Jazzy Jeff and the Fresh Prince for *Parents Just Don't Understand*.

THE 10 FIRST ARTISTS TO APPEAR IN PEPSI-COLA COMMERCIALS

1. Michael Jackson
2. Lionel Richie
3. Glenn Frey
4. Robert Palmer
5. Linda Ronstadt
6. Tina Turner
7. David Bowie
8. Gloria Estefan
9. MC Hammer
10. Ray Charles

THE 10 ⭐
FIRST ARTISTS TO FEATURE IN A COCA-COLA TELEVISION COMMERCIAL

	ACT/JINGLE	YEAR
1	McGuire Sisters, *Pause for a Coke*	1958
2=	Brothers Four,* *Refreshing New Feeling*	1960
2=	Anita Bryant, *Refreshing New Feeling*	1960
2=	Connie Francis, *Refreshing New Feeling*	1960
5=	Fortunes, *Things Go Better with Coke*	1963
5=	Limeliters,* *Things Go Better with Coke*	1963
7	Ray Charles, *Things Go Better with Coke*	1969
8=	Bobby Goldsboro, *It's the Real Thing*	1971
8=	New Seekers,* *It's the Real Thing*	1971
10	Dottie West,* *It's the Real Thing (Country Sunshine)*	1972

* *Artist(s) provided only the audio soundtrack for the commercial*

ALL IN THE FAMILY
David Cassidy and real-life stepmother Shirley Jones starred in the popular TV series The Partridge Family, *screened from 1970 to 1974.*

TOP 10 ⭐
HIGHEST-RATED NETWORKED MUSIC TELEVISION SERIES IN THE US, 1950–99

	PROGRAMME	YEAR	PERCENT OF TV AUDIENCE*
1	*Stop the Music*	1951	34.0
2	*Your Hit Parade*	1958	33.6
3	*The Perry Como Show*	1956	32.6
4	*Name That Tune*	1958	26.7
5	*The Dean Martin Show*	1966	24.8
6	*The Sonny & Cher Hour*	1973	23.3
7	*The Partridge Family*	1972	22.6
8	*The Glen Campbell Goodtime Hour*	1968	22.5
9	*The Johnny Cash Show*	1969	21.8
10	*Cher*	1975	21.3

* *Percentage of American households with TV sets watching the broadcast: the total number of households rose from 3.8 million in 1950 to 99.4 million in 1999.*

© 2000, Nielsen Media Research

What was the most rented DVD in Canada in 1999?
see p.194 for the answer

A *The Matrix*
B *American Pie*
C *Austin Powers: The Spy Who Shagged Me*

Top Videos

DVD RENTALS IN CANADA, 1999

DVD/LABEL

1 *The Matrix*, Warner
2 *The Mummy*, Universal
3 *Ronin*, Warner
4 *American Pie*, Universal
5 *Deep Blue Sea*, Warner
6 *Arlington Road*, Columbia TriStar
7 *Austin Powers: The Spy Who Shagged Me*, Universal
8 *The Siege*, Buena Vista
8 *Entrapment*, Fox
10 *Titanic*, Paramount

Source: *Jumbo Video*

DVD was launched in North America in March 1997. In that year, total sales of DVD players was 315,136. This increased in 1998 to 1,089,261, and in 1999 to 4,019,389, as traditional videotape recordings, which had been the industry standard for almost 25 years, became progressively eclipsed by DVD. It is predicted that worldwide shipments of DVD discs will rise from 77 million units in 1999 to over 2 billion by 2005, by which time 144 million players will be installed globally.

MOVIE RENTALS ON VIDEO IN CANADA, 1999

MOVIE/LABEL

1 *There's Something About Mary*, Fox
2 *Big Daddy*, Columbia/TriStar
3 *Saving Private Ryan*, Universal
4 *Enemy of the State*, Buena Vista
5 *American Pie*, Universal
6 *The Waterboy*, Buena Vista
7 *The Matrix*, Warner
8 *The Mummy*, Universal
9 *Austin Powers: The Spy Who Shagged Me*, Universal
10 *Analyse This*, Warner

Source: *Jumbo Video*

VIDEO-RENTING COUNTRIES

COUNTRY	AVERAGE NO. OF RENTALS PER VHS HOUSEHOLD, 1998
1 South Korea	88.6
2 Taiwan	57.4
3 USA	39.1
4 South Africa	37.7
5 India	37.3
6 Philippines	33.9
7 Australia	31.2
8 Canada	29.3
9 Japan	22.0
10 Pakistan	18.8

This list is at odds with the list of European countries because here only those homes that have a VHS video player are included in the statistics.

Source: Screen Digest

COUNTRIES WITH THE MOST VCRs

COUNTRY	VIDEO HOUSEHOLDS
1 US	91,602,000
2 Japan	38,982,000
3 Germany	31,425,000
4 China	23,956,000
5 Brazil	21,330,000
6 UK	21,306,000
7 France	18,903,000
8 Russia	14,555,000
9 Italy	12,706,000
10 South Korea	11,616,000

Source: Screen Digest

The 1980s has rightly been described as the "video decade": according to estimates published by *Screen Digest*, the period from 1980 to 1990 saw an increase of more than 17 times in the number of video recorders in use in the world, from 7,687,000 to 210,159,000. Since 1992, more than one-third of all world homes with television have also had video.

BESTSELLING MUSIC VIDEOS OF 1999 IN THE US

VIDEO/ARTIST

1 *'N the Mix with 'N Sync*, 'N Sync
2 *Night Out with the Backstreet Boys*, Backstreet Boys
3 *All Access Video*, Backstreet Boys
4 *Homecoming - Live in Orlando*, Backstreet Boys
5 *Cunning Stunts*, Metallica
6 *Family Values Tour '98*, Various Artists
7 *Second Coming*, Kiss
8 *Kennedy Center Homecoming*, Bill & Gloria Gaither
8 *Live*, Shania Twain
10 *Live at Wembley*, Spice Girls

Source: *VideoScan*

BESTSELLING VIDEOS OF THE 1990s IN THE US*

YEAR	VIDEO/LABEL
1999	*Austin Powers: International Man of Mystery*, New Line/Warner
1998	*Titanic*, Paramount/20th Century Fox
1997	*Men in Black*, Columbia
1996	*Babe*, Universal
1995	*The Lion King*, Buena Vista
1994	*Aladdin*, Walt Disney
1993	*Beauty and the Beast*, Walt Disney
1992	*Fantasia*, Walt Disney
1991	*Pretty Woman*, Touchstone
1990	*Bambi*, Walt Disney

* By year

TOP 10 ★
MOVIE SALES ON VIDEO IN THE US, 1999

MOVIE/LABEL

1 *Austin Powers: International Man of Mystery*, New Line/Warner

2 *Armageddon*, Touchstone/Buena Vista

3 *A Bug's Life*, Walt Disney/Buena Vista

4 *Blade*, New Line/Warner

5 *Mulan*, Walt Disney/Buena Vista

6 *The Wedding Singer*, New Line/Warner

7 *You've Got M@il*, Warner

8 *The Lion King II: Simba's Pride*, Walt Disney/Buena Vista

9 *There's Something About Mary*, Fox

10 *Ever After: A Cinderella Story*, Fox

Source: *VideoScan*

MARY, MARY
Blockbuster comedy There's Something About Mary, *starring Cameron Diaz in the title role, became the US's No. 2 video of 1999.*

TOP 10 ★
BESTSELLING VIDEOS IN THE US*

VIDEO/RELEASE	LABEL	SALES (US$)
1 *Titanic*, Sep 9, 1998	Paramount	30,000,000
2 *The Lion King*, Mar 3, 1995	Buena Vista/ Disney	27,500,000
3 *Snow White*, Oct 28, 1994	Buena Vista/ Disney	27,000,000
4 *Aladdin*, Oct 1, 1993	Buena Vista/ Disney	25,000,000
5 *Independence Day*, Nov 19, 1996	Fox Video	21,955,000
6 *Jurassic Park*, Oct 4, 1994	MCA/Universal	21,500,000
7 *Toy Story*, Oct 29, 1996	Buena Vista/ Disney	21,000,000
8 *Beauty and the Beast*, Oct 30, 1992	Buena Vista/ Disney	20,000,000
9 *Pocahontas*, Feb 26, 1996	Buena Vista/ Disney	18,000,000
10 *Men in Black*, Nov 25, 1997	Columbia TriStar	18,000,000

* *Since 1992*

Source: Video Store *magazine*

TOP 10 ★
BESTSELLING CHILDREN'S VIDEOS OF 1999 IN THE US

VIDEO/LABEL

1 *The Lion King II – Simba's Pride*, Walt Disney/Buena Vista

2 *Mulan*, Walt Disney/Buena Vista

3 *The Lady and the Tramp*, Walt Disney/Buena Vista

4 *Mary-Kate & Ashley: Billboard Dad*, Dualstar/Warner

5 *Pokémon: I Choose You, Pikachu*, VIZ/Pioneer Entertainment

6 *The Rugrats Movie*, Nickelodeon/Paramount

7 *Teletubbies: Dance with the Teletubbies*, PBS/Warner

8 *101 Dalmatians*, Walt Disney/Buena Vista

9 *The Little Mermaid: The Special Edition*, Walt Disney/Buena Vista

10 *Teletubbies: Here Come the Teletubbies*, PBS/Warner

Source: *VideoScan*

TOP 10 ★
BESTSELLING SPORT VIDEOS OF 1999 IN THE US

VIDEO

1 *WWF: Austin 3:16 Uncensored*

2 *WWF: 'Cause Stone Cold Said So*

3 *WWF: The Rock – Know Your Role*

4 *WWF: Hell Yeah – Stone Cold's Saga Continues*

5 *WWF: Best of Survivor Series – 1987-1997*

6 *WWF: Best of Raw Vol. 1*

7 *WWF: Best of Wrestlemania I–XIV*

8 *WWF: Sable Unleashed*

9 *WWF: Undertaker the Phenom*

10 *WWF: Wrestlemania 14*

All the bestselling sport videos were of wrestling matches. The highest placed non-wrestling video in 1999 was *Michael Jordan: His Airness* at No.12.

Source: *VideoScan*

Did You Know? A massive 60 million copies of the video of *Titanic* were shipped worldwide, making it the bestselling videocassette of all time.

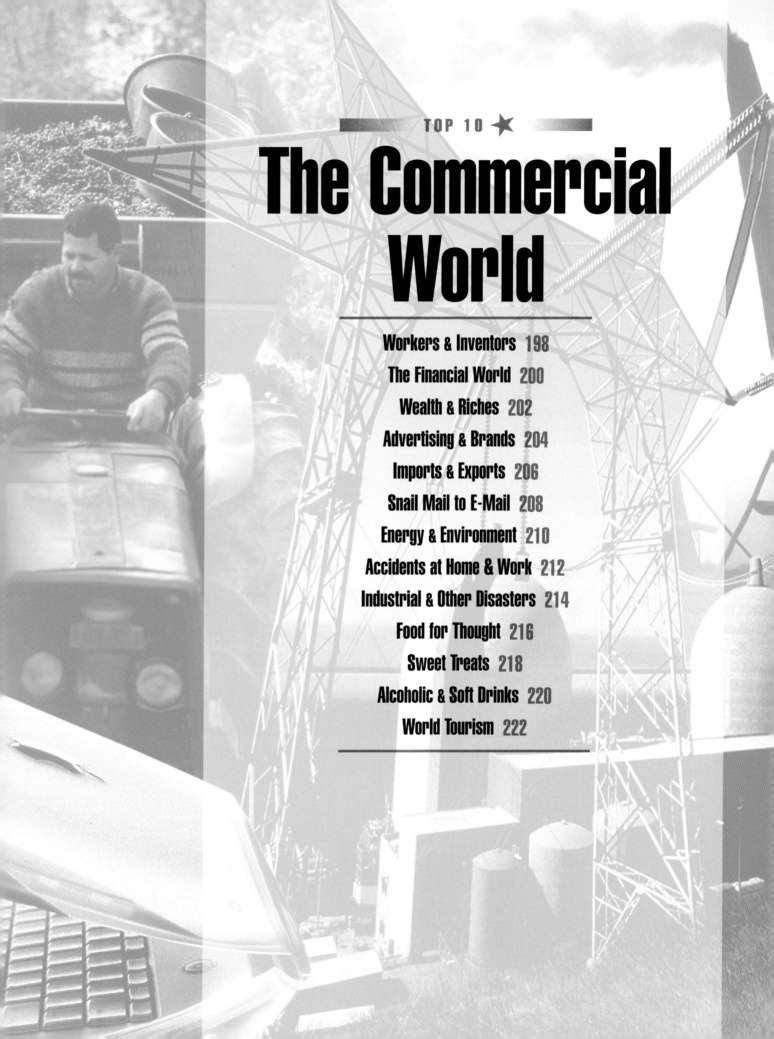

TOP 10 ★

The Commercial World

Workers & Inventors

COUNTRIES WITH THE MOST WORKERS

	COUNTRY	WORKERS*
1	China	736,000,000
2	India	423,000,000
3	US	136,000,000
4	Indonesia	94,000,000
5	Russia	78,000,000
6	Brazil	75,000,000
7	Japan	68,000,000
8	Bangladesh	63,000,000
9	Pakistan	48,000,000
10	Nigeria	47,000,000

* Based on people aged 15–64 who are currently employed; unpaid groups are not included.

Source: World Bank

COUNTRIES WITH THE HIGHEST PROPORTION OF FEMALE WORKERS*

	COUNTRY	LABOR FORCE PERCENTAGE
1	Latvia	50
2 =	Belarus	49
2 =	Burundi	49
2 =	Estonia	49
2 =	Malawi	49
2 =	Moldova	49
2 =	Russia	49
2 =	Rwanda	49
2 =	Tanzania	49
2 =	Ukraine	49
2 =	Vietnam	49

* Based on people aged 15–64 who are currently employed; unpaid groups are not included

COUNTRIES WITH THE HIGHEST PROPORTION OF FARMERS

	COUNTRY	PERCENTAGE IN AGRICULTURE
1	Bhutan	93.9
2	Nepal	93.3
3	Burkina Faso	92.4
4	Rwanda	91.2
5	Burundi	90.7
6 =	Niger	89.2
6 =	Mali	89.2
8	Ethiopia	85.3
9	Guinea Bissau	84.1
10	Uganda	83.1

Source: Food and Agriculture Organization of the United Nations

EMPLOYERS IN CANADA

	COMPANY	EMPLOYEES
1	George Weston Ltd.	119,000
2	Onex Corp.	83,000
3	Nortel Networks Corp.	77,000
4	Laidlaw Inc.	71,300
5	Hudson's Bay Co.	65,000
6	Quebecor Inc.	60,000
7	Magna International Inc.	58,000
8	Bombardier Inc.	56,000
9	BCE Inc.	55,000
10	Royal Bank of Canada	51,891

Source: Business 500

HARD LABOR

India's huge work force relies on traditional manual labor, but the country is increasingly becoming a major center for computer technology.

THE 10 🍁
FASTEST-GROWING OCCUPATIONS IN CANADA

	OCCUPATION	ANTICIPATED AVERAGE ANNUAL GROWTH RATE (%) 1999–2004
1	Plumbers and pipefitters	5.0
2	Management, advertising, and marketing consultants	4.2
3	Computer systems analysts and programmers	4.0
4	Pharmacists, dieticians, and nutritionists	3.5
5	Medical technologists and technicians	3.3
6 =	Heavy equipment operators	3.0
6 =	Supervisors – sales and service, trades, logging, forestry, oil and gas mining, processing and assembly and fabrication	3.0
8	Management occupations	2.6
9	Engineers	2.4
10	Lawyers	2.3

Source: *Statistics Canada Labour Force Survey, 1998*

THE 10 🍁
FIRST PATENTS IN CANADA

	PATENTEE	PATENT	DATE
1	Noah Cushing	Washing and fulling machine	Jun 8, 1824
2	Isaac Jones Barnard	Improved machine for cutting nails	Jul 21, 1824
3	James George	Improvement in the construction of wooden railroads	Dec 13, 1824
4	Robert Dalkin	Improvement in the manufacture of ropes, cables, etc.	Nov 30, 1825
5 =	Justin Jacob	A lever engine	Oct 31, 1826
5 =	Charles Laurier	Instrument for ascertaining the number of revolutions of carriage wheels, millstones, etc.	Oct 31, 1826
5 =	Noah Cushing	Threshing and winnowing machine	Oct 31, 1826
8	Robert Hoyle	Improved machine for dressing flax or hemp	Oct 3, 1829
9	William John Spence	Machine for distributing ink over printing types	Dec 19, 1829
10	Philip Schoolcraft	Machine for cutting timber into sidings, clapboards, shingles, etc.	May 15, 1830

A patent is an exclusive license to manufacture and exploit a unique product or process for a fixed period. The world's first patent, by which the architect Filippo Brunelleschi was granted the exclusive license to make a barge crane to transport marble, was issued in Florence in 1421.

FACTORY-MADE

Despite the growth of the service sector, manufacturing remains a vital component of most developed economies, providing employment for countless workers.

THE 10 🍁
FIRST TRADEMARKS ISSUED IN CANADA

	ISSUED TO	PRODUCT	DATE
1	D. Crawford & Co.	Soap	Jul 29, 1865
2	J.D. King & Co.	Cigars	Jun 12, 1866
3	Northrup & Russell	Washing machines	Jul 17, 1868
4 =	W. H. Bilton	Soda and ginger ale	Jul 18, 1868
4 =	Alfred Savage & Son	Soap	Jul 18, 1868
4 =	Damon & Baker	Unknown	Jul 18, 1868
4 =	T. Graham & Son	Cure-all "medicine"	Jul 18, 1868
8	C.P. Reid & Co.	Cigars	Jul 20, 1868
9 =	Buchanan, Leckie & Co.	Brandy put up in bottles	Jul 30, 1868
9 =	Buchanan, Leckie & Co.	Brandy put up in casks	Jul 30, 1868

Source: *Canadian Intellectual Property Office*

🍁 TOP 10 CANADIAN INVENTIONS OF ALL TIME
(Inventors/invention or discovery/date)

1 Dr. Abraham Gesner, Kerosene, 1846

2 Henry Woodward and Matthew Evans, The light bulb, 1873

3 Unknown, Organized hockey in Montreal, 1875

4 Alexander Graham Bell, Telephone, 1876 **5** Sir Sandford Fleming, Standard time, 1879 **6** James Naismith, Basketball, 1891 **7** Reginald Fessenden, Radio, 1908

8 Sir Charles Saunders, Marquis wheat, 1908

9 = Dr. Frederick G. Banting and Charles Herbert Best, Insulin; = Armand Bombardier, Snowmobile, 1922

Source: *Canadian Industrial Innovation Centre/Waterloo*

Did You Know? Thomas Alva Edison (1847–1931) is the world's most prolific inventor, with 1,093 patents issued to him solely or jointly between June 1, 1869 and May 16, 1933.

The Financial World

TOP 10
BANKS IN CANADA

	BANK	1999 REVENUE ($000s)
1	Canadian Imperial Bank of Commerce	20,133,000
2	Royal Bank of Canada	19,683,000
3	Bank of Montreal	16,685,000
4	The Bank of Nova Scotia	16,654,000
5	The Toronto-Dominion Bank	15,683,000
6	National Bank of Canada	4,756,641
7	HSBC Bank Canada	1,877,000
8	Deutsche Bank Canada	1,193,436
9	Laurentian Bank of Canada	987,553
10	Alberta Treasury Branches	704,704

Source: Business 500

TOP 10
COMPANIES IN CANADA

	COMPANY	1999 REVENUE ($000s)
1	General Motors of Canada Ltd., Oshawa	39,677,811
2	Nortel Networks Corp., Brampton	32,992,245
3	Ford Motor Co. of Canada, Ltd., Oakville	29,976,737
4	DaimlerChrysler Canada Inc., Windsor	22,445,000
5	George Weston Ltd., Toronto	20,851,000
6	Canadian Imperial Bank of Commerce, Toronto	20,133,000
7	Royal Bank of Canada, Montreal	19,683,000
8	The Seagram Co. Ltd., Montreal	18,591,120
9	Bank of Montreal, Toronto	16,685,000
10	The Bank of Nova Scotia, Toronto	16,654,000

Source: Business 500

TOP 10
CORPORATIONS IN THE US

	CORPORATION	1998 REVENUE (US$)
1	General Motors	161,315,000,000
2	Ford Motor Company	144,416,000,000
3	Wal-Mart Stores	139,208,000,000
4	Exxon Corp.	100,697,000,000
5	General Electric	100,469,000,000
6	IBM	81,667,000,000
7	Citigroup	76,431,000,000
8	Philip Morris	57,813,000,000
9	Boeing	56,154,000,000
10	AT&T	53,588,000,000

Source: Fortune 500

TOP 10
RICHEST COUNTRIES IN THE WORLD

	COUNTRY	GDP PER CAPITA 1998 (US$)
1	Liechtenstein	50,000*
2	Luxembourg	43,570
3	Switzerland	40,080
4	Norway	34,330
5	Denmark	33,260
6	Japan	32,380
7	Singapore	30,060
8	US	29,340
9	Iceland	28,010
10	Austria	26,850
	World	4,890
	Canada	20,020

* World Bank estimate for the purpose of ranking

Source: World Bank, World Development Indicators

EASTERN STAR

Despite recent economic setbacks, the wealth of cities such as Tokyo has helped Japan to maintain its prominent place among the world's richest countries.

TOP 10
US COMPANIES MAKING THE GREATEST PROFIT PER SECOND

	COMPANY	PROFIT PER SEC (US$)
1	Ford Motor Company	699
2	General Electric	294
3	AT&T	202
4	Exxon Corporation	201
5	IBM	200
6	Intel Corporation	192
7	Citigroup	184
8	Philip Morris Companies, Inc.	170
9	Merck	166
10	BankAmerica Corporation	163

THE 10 ★
COUNTRIES MOST IN DEBT

COUNTRY	TOTAL EXTERNAL DEBT (US$)
1 Brazil	193,663,000,000
2 Mexico	149,690,000,000
3 China	146,697,000,000
4 South Korea	143,373,000,000
5 Indonesia	136,174,000,000
6 Russia	125,645,000,000
7 Argentina	123,221,000,000
8 India	94,404,000,000
9 Thailand	93,416,000,000
10 Turkey	91,205,000,000

Source: *World Bank*

The World Bank's annual debt calculations estimated the total indebtedness of low- and middle-income countries at US$2.177 trillion in 1996.

THE 10 ★
POOREST COUNTRIES

COUNTRY	GDP PER CAPITA 1998 (US$)
1 Ethiopia	100
2 Dem. Rep. of Congo	110
3 =Sierra Leone	140
3 =Burundi	140
5 Guinea-Bissau	160
6 Niger	190
7 =Eritrea	200
7 =Malawi	200
9 =Mozambique	210
9 =Nepal	210
9 =Tanzania	210

Source: *World Bank*

It is hard to imagine living on as little as US$36 per year, but US$1 in Sudan, for example, purchases far more than in North America.

DROUGHT-STRICKEN LAND

Factors including civil war and severe droughts affecting their rural economy mean that several sub-Saharan African countries are among the world's poorest.

TOP 10 🍁
COMPANIES THAT GAINED THE MOST ON THE TSE IN 1999

COMPANY	INCREASE IN SHARE PRICE ($)	FINAL SHARE PRICE IN 1999
1 JDS Uniphase	172.05	234.00
2 Nortel Networks	107.60	145.85
3 JDS Fitel	83.05	121.05
4 Biovail Corporation	77.00	135.00
5 BCE Inc.	73.30	131.15
6 B Split	71.25	104.00
7 Certicom Corporation	71.15	86.00
8 QLT Phototherapeutics	67.37	85.00
9 BCE Emergis	63.65	77.50
10 C-Mac Industries	57.25	82.50

Source: *Toronto Stock Exchange*

A listing by percentage increase would not be as meaningful as a straight dollar increase, as some companies that experience the greatest percentage increase in their share prices are penny stocks.

TOP 10 ★
INTERNATIONAL INDUSTRIAL COMPANIES

COMPANY/ LOCATION/SECTOR	ANNUAL SALES ($)
1 General Motors Corp., US, Transport	161,315,000,000
2 DaimlerChrysler, Germany, Transport	154,615,000,000
3 Ford Motor Co., US, Transport	144,416,000,000
4 Wal-Mart Stores, Inc., US, Retailing	139,208,000,000
5 Mitsui and Co. Ltd., Japan, Trading	109,372,000,000
6 Itochu Corp., Japan, Trading	108,749,100,000
7 Mitsubishi Corp., Japan, Trading	107,184,000,000
8 Exxon Corp., US, Oil, gas, fuel	100,697,000,000
9 General Electric, US, Electronics, electrical equipment	100,469,000,000
10 Toyota Motor, Japan, Transport	99,740,100,000

Source: Fortune Global 500

Which province has the highest graduation rate in Canada?
see p.98 for the answer

A Quebec
B New Brunswick
C Nova Scotia

Wealth & Riches

TAKING A BACK SEAT

Jerry Seinfeld formerly headed the richest entertainers' list with earnings of US$225 million, but dropped out of the Top 10 with the end of his TV series.

TOP 10 ★
HIGHEST-EARNING ENTERTAINERS IN THE WORLD

ENTERTAINER	PROFESSION	1999 INCOME (US$)
1 George Lucas	Film producer/director	400,000,000
2 Oprah Winfrey	TV host/producer	150,000,000
3 David Kelley	TV writer/producer (*Ally McBeal*, etc.)	118,000,000
4 Tom Hanks	Movie actor	71,500,000
5= Backstreet Boys	Pop band	60,000,000
5= Steven Spielberg	Movie producer/director	60,000,000
7 Bruce Willis	Movie actor	54,500,000
8= David Copperfield	Illusionist	50,000,000
8= Julia Roberts	Movie actress	50,000,000
8= The Rolling Stones	Rock band	50,000,000

Source: Forbes *magazine*

TOP 10 ★
RICHEST RULERS

RULER/COUNTRY/YEAR CAME TO POWER	ESTIMATED WEALTH (US$)
1 Sultan Hassanal Bolkiah, Brunei, 1967	30,000,000,000
2 King Fahd bin Abdulaziz Al Saud, Saudi Arabia, 1982	28,000,000,000
3 Sheikh Zayed bin Sultan al-Nahyan, UAE (Abu Dhabi), 1966	20,000,000,000
4 Amir Jaber al-Ahmed al Jaber Al-Sabah, Kuwait, 1977	17,000,000,000
5 Sheikh Maktoum bin Rashid Al Maktoum, UAE (Dubai), 1990	12,000,000,000
6 President Saddam Hussein, Iraq, 1979	6,000,000,000
7 Queen Beatrix, Netherlands, 1980	5,200,000,000
8 Amir Hamad bin Khalifa Al Thani, Qatar, 1995	5,000,000,000
9 President Hafez Al-Assad, Syria, 1971	2,000,000,000
10 Queen Elizabeth II, UK, 1952	450,000,000

Based on data published in Forbes *magazine*

TOP 10 ★
RICHEST PEOPLE IN THE US

NAME/PROFESSION OR SOURCE	ASSETS (US$)
1 William Henry Gates III, Computer software	58,400,000,000
2 Warren Edward Buffett, Textiles, etc.	29,400,000,000
3 Paul Gardner Allen, Computer software	21,000,000,000
4 Michael Dell, Computers	13,000,000,000
5 Steven Ballmer, Computer software	12,000,000,000
6= Helen R. Walton, Retailing	11,000,000,000
6= John T. Walton, Retailing	11,000,000,000
6= Alice L. Walton, Retailing	11,000,000,000
6= S. Robson Walton, Retailing	11,000,000,000
6= Jim C. Walton, Retailing	11,000,000,000

Used by permission of Forbes *magazine*

TOP 10 🍁
RICHEST CANADIANS

NAME/INDUSTRY SECTOR	NET WORTH (BILLIONS)
1 Kenneth Roy Thompson, Information services	20.06
2 Irving Family,* Oil and shipping	6.30
3 J. R. Shaw, Media	5.90
4 Charles Rosner Bronfman, Liquor/media	5.30
5 Williard Gordon Galen Weston, Retail	4.50
6 Jeff Skoll, Internet	4.30
7 Laurent Beaudoin & Family, Transportation	3.40
8 Edward S. (Ted) Rogers, Jr., Media	2.80
9 James A. (Jimmy) Pattison, Diversified investments	2.30
10 Phillip Mannix and Ronald Neil Mannix, Diversified investments	2.20

* Brothers James, Arthur, and John

Source: *National Post Business*

Did You Know? The weight of diamonds is measured in carats (the word derives from the carob bean, which was once used as a measure). There are approximately 142 carats to the ounce.

MOST EXPENSIVE SINGLE DIAMONDS SOLD AT AUCTION

	DIAMOND/SALE	PRICE (US$)
1	*Star of the Season*, pear-shaped 100.10-carat "D" flawless diamond, Sotheby's, Geneva, May 17, 1995	16,548,750 (SF19,858,500)
2	*The Mouawad Splendor*, pear-shaped 11-sided 101.84-carat diamond, Sotheby's, Geneva, November 14, 1990	12,760,000 (SF15,950,000)
3	*Star of Happiness*, rectangular-cut 100.36-carat diamond, Sotheby's, Geneva, November 17, 1993	11,882,333 (SF17,823,500)
4	Fancy blue emerald-cut 20.17-carat diamond ring, Sotheby's, New York, October 18, 1994	9,902,500
5	*Eternal Light*, pear-shaped 85.91-carat pendant, Sotheby's, New York, April 19, 1988	9,130,000
6	Rectangular-cut fancy deep blue 13.49-carat diamond ring, Christie's, New York, April 13, 1995	7,482,500
7	Rectangular-cut 52.59-carat diamond ring, Christie's, New York, April 20, 1988	7,480,000
8	Fancy pink rectangular-cut 19.66-carat diamond, Christie's, Geneva, November 17, 1994	7,421,318 (SF9,573,500)
9	*The Jeddah Bride*, rectangular-cut 80.02-carat diamond, Sotheby's, New York, October 24, 1991	7,150,000
10	*The Agra Diamond*, fancy light pink cushion-shaped 32.24-carat diamond, Christie's, London, June 20, 1990	6,959,700 (£4,070,000)

COUNTRIES WITH THE MOST DOLLAR BILLIONAIRES*

	COUNTRY	BILLIONAIRES
1	US	50
2	Germany	43
3	Japan	30
4	France	15
5 =	China (Hong Kong)	13
5 =	Switzerland	13
7	UK	12
8	Mexico	10
9 =	Brazil	8
9 =	Canada	8

* Individuals and families with a net worth of US$1 billion or more

Based on data published in Forbes *magazine*

GOLD-PRODUCING COUNTRIES

	COUNTRY	1998 PRODUCTION IN TONNES
1	South Africa	473.8
2	US	364.4
3	Australia	313.0
4	Canada	164.0
5	China	161.0
6	Indonesia	139.3
7	Russia	127.3
8	Peru	89.2
9	Uzbekistan	80.6
10	Ghana	73.3

As reported by Gold Fields Mineral Services Ltd., world-dominating gold producer South Africa saw its output fall yet again for the sixth consecutive year, although it has still held on to the top slot as the world's largest gold producer.

LARGEST ROUGH DIAMONDS

	DIAMOND/DESCRIPTION	CARATS
1	*Cullinan*	3,106.00

Measuring roughly 10 x 6.5 x 5 cm (4 x 2½ x 2 in), and weighing 621 g (1 lb 6 oz), the Cullinan was unearthed in 1905, and bought by the Transvaal government for £150,000. It was presented to King Edward VII, who had it cut; the most important of the separate gems are among the British Crown Jewels.

2	*Excelsior*	995.20

Found at the Jagersfontein Mine on June 30, 1893, it was cut by the celebrated Amsterdam firm of Asscher in 1903, producing 21 superb stones.

3	*Star of Sierra Leone*	968.80

Found in Sierra Leone on St. Valentine's Day, 1972, the rough diamond weighed 225 g (8 oz) and measured 63.5 x 38.1 mm (2½ x 1½ in).

4	*Incomparable*	890.00

Discovered in 1980 at Mbuji-Mayi, Dem. Rep. of Congo (then Zaïre).

5	*Great Mogul*	787.50

When found in 1650 in the Gani Mine, India, it was presented to Shah Jehan, the builder of the Taj Mahal.

6	*Millennium Star*	777.00

Recently discovered near the village of Mbuji-Mayi in the Dem. Rep. of Congo, the polished stone cut from it is 203.04 carats and measures 50.06 x 36.56 x 18.5 mm (2 x 1½ x ¾ in).

7	*Woyie River*	770.00

Found in 1945 beside the Woyie River in Sierra Leone, it was cut into 30 stones. The largest of these, known as Victory and weighing 31.35 carats, was auctioned at Christie's, New York in 1984 for US$880,000.

8	*Golden Jubilee*	755.50

Found in 1986 in the Premier Mine (the home of the Cullinan), the polished diamond cut from it is, at 545.67 carats, the largest in the world.

9	*Presidente Vargas*	726.60

Discovered in the Antonio River, Brazil, in 1938, it was named after the then President, Getulio Vargas.

10	*Jonker*	726.00

In 1934 Jacobus Jonker found this massive diamond. Acquired by Harry Winston, it was exhibited in the American Museum of Natural History.

WORTH ITS WEIGHT IN GOLD

International trade in gold is customarily carried out with either 1-kg (32.15-troy ounce) or 12.5-kg (400-troy ounce) gold bars.

Advertising & Brands

TOP 10 ★
NETWORK TV ADVERTISERS IN THE US

ADVERTISER	MEASURED NETWORK TV ADVERTISING (US$)
1 General Motors Corp.	778,200,000
2 Procter & Gamble Co.	670,400,000
3 Johnson & Johnson	420,500,000
4 Philip Morris Cos.	412,300,000
5 Ford Motor Co.	340,800,000
6 DaimlerChrysler	310,700,000
7 Unilever	294,000,000
8 Diageo	290,200,000
9 Walt Disney Co.	290,100,000
10 McDonald's Corp.	274,600,000

Source: Advertising Age

TOP 10 ★
CORPORATE ADVERTISERS IN THE US

CORPORATION	TOTAL ADVERTISING EXPENDITURE (US$)
1 General Motors Corp.	2,940,400,000
2 Procter & Gamble Co.	2,650,300,000
3 Philip Morris Cos.	2,049,300,000
4 DaimlerChrysler	1,646,700,000
5 Sears, Roebuck & Co.	1,578,300,000
6 Ford Motor Co.	1,520,700,000
7 AT&T Corp.	1,428,000,000
8 Walt Disney Co.	1,358,700,000
9 PepsiCo	1,263,400,000
10 Diageo	1,205,700,000

Source: Advertising Age

TOP 10 ★
ADVERTISING CAMPAIGNS OF THE 20TH CENTURY*

CAMPAIGN	COMPANY OR PRODUCT	FIRST YEAR
1 "Think small"	Volkswagen	1959
2 "The pause that refreshes"	Coca-Cola	1929
3 The Marlboro Man	Marlboro	1955
4 "Just do it"	Nike	1988
5 "You deserve a break today"	McDonald's	1971
6 "A diamond is forever"	DeBeers	1948
7 The Absolut bottle	Absolut vodka	1981
8 "Tastes great, less filling"	Miller Lite beer	1974
9 "Does she...or doesn't she?"	Clairol	1957
10 "We try harder"	Avis	1963

* Based on industry research
Source: Advertising Age

TOP 10 MOST VALUABLE FOOD AND DRINK BRANDS
(Brand name/industry/brand value in US$)*

1 Coca-Cola, Beverages, 83,845,000,000 **2 McDonald's**, Food, 26,231,000,000 **3 Nescafe**, Switzerland, Beverages, 17,595,000,000 **4 Heinz**, Food, 11,806,000,000 **5 Budweiser**, Alcohol, 8,510,000,000 **6 Kelloggs**, Food, 7,052,000,000 **7 Pepsi-Cola**, Beverages, 5,932,000,000 **8 Wrigley's**, Food, 4,404,000,000 **9 Burger King**, Food, 2,806,000,000 **10 Moët & Chandon**, France, Alcohol, 2,804,000,000

* US is country of origin unless otherwise stated
Source: Interbrand

BIG MAC
Global fast-food company McDonald's is ranked second only to Coca-Cola as one of the world's most valuable food and drink brands.

"SHOPPING MALL"
In 16th-century London, a croquet-like game called pall-mall (from the Italian *pallamaglio*, "ball to mallet") was played in long alleys in two parallel streets called Pall Mall and The Mall, where fashionable London society promenaded. By the 18th century, the game had fallen out of favor and Pall Mall had become renowned for its expensive shops. Later, "mall" became synonymous with any strolling and shopping area – especially the shopping malls of the United States.

WHY DO WE SAY?

Crowd cheers! Coke nears!
Game goes better refreshed.
Coca-Cola, never too sweet,
gives that special zing...refreshes best.

TOP 10 ★
COSMETIC AND TOILETRY BRANDS

	BRAND	MANUFACTURER	% OF WORLD MARKET BY VALUE
1	Nivea	Beiersdorf	2.20
2	Colgate	Colgate-Palmolive	2.01
3	Gillette	Gillette	1.87
4 =	Johnson's	Johnson & Johnson	1.25
4 =	Pantene Pro-V	Procter & Gamble	1.25
6	Clinique	Estée Lauder	0.86
7	Lux	Unilever	0.84
8	Oil of Olay	Procter & Gamble	0.82
9 =	Lancôme	L'Oréal	0.72
9 =	Revlon	Revlon	0.72

Source: *Euromonitor*

Many of the leading cosmetic brands are also among the oldest-established. Colgate was founded in the US in 1806 by William Colgate (1783–1857), who had emigrated from England. King Camp Gillette (1855–1932) made his first safety razors in 1895, while Johnson & Johnson's partnership dates back to 1885, Estée Lauder to 1946, Lux to 1900, and Revlon to 1932.

THE REAL THING

Bestselling, most advertised, and most valuable are only three of the many superlatives applied to Coca-Cola's world-beating status.

TOP 10 ★
MOST VALUABLE GLOBAL BRANDS

	BRAND NAME	INDUSTRY	BRAND VALUE (US$)
1	Coca-Cola	Beverages	83,845,000,000
2	Microsoft	Software	56,654,000,000
3	IBM	Computers	43,781,000,000
4	General Electric	Diversified	33,502,000,000
5	Ford	Automobiles	33,197,000,000
6	Disney	Entertainment	32,275,000,000
7	Intel	Computers	30,021,000,000
8	McDonald's	Food	26,231,000,000
9	AT&T	Telecommunications	24,181,000,000
10	Marlboro	Tobacco	21,048,000,000

Source: *Interbrand*

Brand consultants Interbrand use a method of estimating value that takes account of the profitability of individual brands within a business (rather than the companies that own them), as well as such factors as their potential for growth.

♣ TOP 10 LEADING ADVERTISERS IN CANADA

(Advertiser/ad spending in US$ millions, 1997)

1 General Motors, 93.0   **2** BCE, 65.4
3 Procter & Gamble, 62.4   **4** Hudson's Bay Company, 53.2
5 Rogers Communications, 52.2   **6** Eatons of Canada, 50.4
7 Sears Roebuck & Company, 49.0   **8** Government of Canada, 45.2   **9** Interbrew, 44.3   **10** Molson, 41.1

Source: *Marketing Information Net Directory, ACNielsen, Advertising Age Magazine*

♣ TOP 10 ADVERTISERS BY CATEGORY IN CANADA

(Category/ad spending in $ millions, 1998)

1 Retail, 953.5   **2** Automotive,* 753.8
3 Business equipment and services, 521.6   **4** Food, 395.6
5 Financial services and insurance services, 388.0
6 Entertainment, 314.8   **7** Local automotive dealers, 266.6
8 Travel & transportation, 249.3   **9** Restaurants,# 199.3
10 Media,+ 165.5

* *Includes cars, minivans, trucks, vans, dealer associations*
\# *Includes catering services and nightclubs*   + *Includes TV and radio*
Source: Marketing *Magazine*

Imports & Exports

GOODS EXPORTED FROM CANADA

	TYPE OF GOODS	DOMESTIC EXPORT VALUE ($)
1	Motor vehicles and parts	86,001,250,000
2	Mineral fuels and oils	30,165,780,000
3	Machinery	28,601,080,000
4	Wood and articles of wood	21,006,150,000
5	Electrical machinery	19,761,310,000
6	Paper and paperboard	15,611,950,000
7	Plastics	9,262,386,000
8	Wood pulp	7,570,237,000
9	Furniture	7,480,341,000
10	Aircraft and parts	7,210,396,000

Source: *Statistics Canada, International Trade Division*

GOODS IMPORTED TO CANADA

	TYPE OF GOODS	DOMESTIC EXPORT VALUE ($)
1	Machinery	62,452,450,000
2	Motor vehicles and parts	59,817,210,000
3	Electrical machinery	41,743,990,000
4	Optical and photographic equipment	11,113,060,000
5	Mineral fuels and oils	10,644,960,000
6	Plastics	10,581,410,000
7	Articles of iron or steel	6,482,623,000
8	Aircrafts and parts	6,087,781,000
9	Paper and paperboard	5,565,436,000
10	Furniture	5,191,653,000

Source: *Statistics Canada, International Trade Division*

CHANGES IN CONSUMER PRICE INDEX

	ITEM	% CHANGE FROM 1999–2000
1	Fuel oil and other fuel	+59.8
2	Gasoline	+38.0
3	Oranges	−29.1
4	Lettuce	−28.3
5	Natural gas	+8.4
6	Ham and bacon	+8.3
7	Traveler accommodation	+8.0
8	Parking fees	+6.8
9	Tuition fees	+6.7
10	Travel tours	+6.6

Source: *Statistics Canada*

EXPORT MARKETS FOR GOODS FROM THE US

	COUNTRY	TOTAL VALUE OF 1998 EXPORTS ($)
1	Canada	156,307,600,000
2	Mexico	79,010,100,000
3	Japan	57,887,900,000
4	UK	39,070,200,000
5	Germany	26,641,900,000
6	Netherlands	19,003,800,000
7	Taiwan	18,157,100,000
8	France	17,728,000,000
9	South Korea	16,538,300,000
10	Singapore	15,673,500,000

Source: *US Census Bureau,* Statistical Abstract of the United States: 1999

In 1901, the US exported merchandise valued at $1,488,000,000, of which $106,000,000 went to Canada and £631,000,000 to the UK, its then leading trading partner. By 1946, the situation had reversed, Canada receiving $1,442,000,000-worth of goods compared with the UK's $855,000,000 out of a US total of $9,738,000,000. Canada has remained the USA's principal export market since that year.

EXPORT MARKETS FOR GOODS FROM CANADA IN 1999

	COUNTRY	EXPORT VALUE ($)
1	United States	308,320,200,000
2	Japan	8,353,759,000
3	United Kingdom	4,723,204,000
4	China	2,624,215,000
5	Germany	2,408,498,000
6	South Korea	1,974,155,000
7	France	1,878,108,000
8	Mexico	1,626,269,000
9	Netherlands	1,553,466,000
10	Italy	1,431,884,000

Source: *Statistics Canada, International Trade Division*

COUNTRIES FOR DUTY-FREE SHOPPING

	COUNTRY	ANNUAL SALES (US$)
1	UK	2,480,000,000
2	US	1,775,000,000
3	Finland	1,046,000,000
4	Germany	885,000,000
5	France	724,000,000
6	South Korea	704,000,000
7	Denmark	652,000,000
8	Sweden	620,000,000
8	US Virgin Islands	601,000,000
10	Japan	491,000,000

Source: *Generation AB*

Duty-free sales began in 1951 with the opening of a small kiosk at Shannon Airport in Ireland, where transatlantic flights stopped for refueling on the final leg of their journey to New York. This has grown into a huge international business of which Europe takes almost half (49.8 percent) of global sales, Asia and Oceania 20.9 percent, the Americas 28.4 percent, and the whole of Africa just 1 percent.

CALL OF DUTY

Worldwide, duty-free sales have virtually doubled during the past decade, and now exceed US$20 billion. The top 10 countries account for almost half the total.

TOP 10 ★
DUTY-FREE AIRPORTS

AIRPORT/LOCATION	ANNUAL SALES (US$)
1 London Heathrow, UK	433,200,000
2 Amsterdam Schiphol, Netherlands	361,800,000
3 Paris Charles De Gaulle, France	320,700,000
4 Frankfurt, Germany	260,500,000
5 Singapore Changi, Singapore	250,000,000
6 Honolulu, Hawaii	242,500,000
7 London Gatwick, UK	208,300,000
8 = Copenhagen, Denmark	200,000,000
8 = Tel Aviv Ben Gurion, Israel	200,000,000
10 São Paulo, Brazil	*

* *Precise figure confidential*

Source: *Generation AB*

SCENT OF MONEY

Women's fragrances were once the foremost duty- and tax-free item, but since 1990 they have been overtaken by cigarettes.

TOP 10 DUTY-FREE SHOPS
(Shop/location)

1 London Heathrow Airport, UK
2 Silja Ferries, Finland **3** P & O Stena Line, UK **4** Amsterdam Schiphol Airport, Netherlands **5** Viking Line Ferries, Finland **6** Paris Charles de Gaulle Airport, France **7** London Gatwick Airport, UK **8** Frankfurt Airport, Germany **9** Eurotunnel, UK/France **10** Stena Line, Sweden

Source: *Generation AB*

In 1998, total global duty- and tax-free sales were worth US$20.5 billion, down 2.2 percent on 1997 sales. Under recently introduced EC laws, duty-free sales in member countries have been axed since July 1999.

TOP 10 ★
DUTY-FREE PRODUCTS

PRODUCT	SALES (US$)
1 Cigarettes	2,477,000,000
2 Women's fragrances	2,157,000,000
3 Scotch whisky	1,423,000,000
4 Jewelry	1,331,000,000
5 Women's cosmetics	1,267,000,000
6 Confectionery	1,096,000,000
7 Men's fragrances and toiletries	995,000,000
8 Accessories	984,000,000
9 Leather goods (handbags, belts, etc)	890,000,000
10 Cognac	807,000,000

Source: *Generation AB*

Did You Know? Bestselling perfume Chanel No. 5 was invented in 1921 by Ernest Beaux. It was so called because it was the fifth sample he submitted to Coco Chanel.

Snail Mail to E-Mail

THEY'VE GOT MAIL

India's high population and tradition of bureaucracy combine to make it the world leader in number of post offices. The country's postal service employs some 600,000 people.

TOP 10 ★
COUNTRIES WITH THE MOST POST OFFICES

	COUNTRY	POST OFFICES*
1	India	153,021
2	China	112,204
3	Russia	43,900
4	US	38,159
5	Japan	24,678
6	Indonesia	20,139
7	UK	18,760
8	France	17,038
9	Turkey	16,984
10	Ukraine	15,227

* *1998 or latest year available*

Source: *Universal Postal Union*

TOP 10 ★
COUNTRIES MAKING THE MOST INTERNATIONAL PHONE CALLS*

	COUNTRY	MINUTES PER HEAD	TOTAL MINUTES OUTGOING CALLS PER ANNUM
1	US	90.3	24,593,000,000
2	UK	98.7	5,820,000,000
3	Canada	158.8	4,805,000,000
4	Germany	57.4	4,711,000,000
5	France	56.9	3,400,000,000
6	Italy	47.1	2,705,000,000
7	Switzerland	266.8	1,901,000,000
8	Japan	14.9	1,895,000,000
9	Netherlands	114.6	1,805,000,000
10	Spain	45.7	1,803,000,000

Source: *International Telecommunication Union*

TOP 10 ★
COUNTRIES WITH THE HIGHEST RATIO OF CELLULAR MOBILE PHONE USERS

	COUNTRY	SUBSCRIBERS*	MOBILE PHONES PER 1,000 INHABITANTS*
1	Finland	2,966,000	577.0
2	Sweden	4,527,000	511.5
3	Norway	2,081,000	471.9
4	Italy	20,300,000	352.9
5	Denmark	1,854,000	351.1
6	Australia	6,000,000	323.8
7	Japan	39,786,000	315.7
8	Portugal	3,075,000	311.9
9	South Korea	13,988,000	304.2
10	Austria	2,270,000	281.3
	Canada	*5,300,000*	*175.0*

* *Figures partly Siemens estimates*

Source: *Siemens AG*

TOP 10 ★
LETTER-SENDING COUNTRIES

	COUNTRY	AVERAGE NO. OF LETTER POST ITEMS SENT PER INHABITANT*
1	Vatican City	6,700.0
2	US	728.9
3	Norway	554.9
4	Sweden	502.8
5	France	435.9
6	Austria	371.6
7	Belgium	345.7
8	Luxembourg	339.7
9	Denmark	334.7
10	UK	324.9

* *In 1998 or latest year for which data available*

TOP 10 ★
COUNTRIES WITH THE MOST TELEPHONES

	COUNTRY	TELEPHONE LINES PER 100 INHABITANTS*
1	Luxembourg	71.00
2	Sweden	69.64
3	US	67.66
4	Switzerland	67.41
5	Norway	65.42
6	Denmark	65.38
7	Iceland	62.86
8	Canada	61.51
9	Netherlands	58.45
10	Hong Kong	58.36

* *Figures partly Siemens estimates*

Source: *Siemens AG*

The world average "teledensity" is 14.36 phone lines per 100 inhabitants. On a continental basis, Oceania (Australia, New Zealand, and their neighbors) has the highest ratio of telephone lines per 100 people – an average of 41.19 – followed by Europe with 36.74. The Americas as a whole have an average of 32.70, because even the high US figure fails to compensate for the much lower numbers in Central and South America.

Did You Know? In 1876 Elisha Gray attempted to patent the telephone, only to discover that Alexander Graham Bell had beaten him to it by a matter of hours. Undaunted, he invented the telautograph, a pen-driven precursor of the fax machine.

VATICAN POST

The list of the countries sending the most letters per person is headed by the Vatican City, with an average of over 27 per person daily, or almost 10,000 annually. The Vatican's population (which is variable, but seldom exceeds 750) is small, and this statistical anomaly results in part from the large numbers of official missives dispatched via the Holy See's post office and its 32 mailboxes, but mainly because Rome's inhabitants have discovered that mail posted there and bearing Vatican stamps is treated as priority and so is delivered more promptly.

SNAP SHOTS

TOP 10
CANADIAN WEBSITES*

	DOMAIN	UNIQUE VISITORS (000s)
1	sympatico.ca	2,107
2	msn.ca	1,894
3	yahoo.ca	1,512
4	canoe.ca	1,214
5	chapters.ca	574
6	hrdc-drhc.gc.ca#	547
7	tdbank.ca	500
8	futureshop.ca	455
9	airmiles.ca	430
10	altavista.ca	336

* *Canadian Internet sites ending with the .ca domain. Excludes .com sites*
\# *Human Resources Development Canada*

"CYBERSPACE"

The English word cybernetics – the communication and control of living things or machines – was coined in 1948 by American mathematician Norbert Wiener (1894–1964). He may have derived it from the French word *cybernétique* – the art of governing – created in 1834 by André Marie Ampère. The term "cyberspace" was invented by Vancouver-based science-fiction writer William Gibson in his 1982 short story *Burning Chrome*, and developed in his 1984 novel *Neuromancer*. The term now refers to the ethereal electronic space that the Internet is thought to occupy.

WHY DO WE SAY?

TOP 10
BUSIEST INTERNET SITES

	SITE	HITS*
1	Yahoo	32,263,000
2	AOL.com	30,545,000
3	msn.com	25,579,000
4	geocities.com	23,270,000
5	lycos.com	18,099,000
6	passport.com	17,793,000
7	microsoft.com	16,182,000
8	netscape.com	15,524,000
9	bluemountain.com	14,755,000
10	tripod.com	14,661,000

* *Number of accesses during December 1999*
Source: *PC Data Online*

One of the principal aims of the Internet is the dissemination of information, but information about its own users is rather patchy and erratic.

TOP 10
COUNTRIES WITH THE MOST INTERNET USERS

	COUNTRY	PERCENTAGE OF POPULATION	INTERNET USERS*
1	US	41	110,825,000
2	Japan	14	18,156,000
3	UK	23	13,975,000
4	Canada	44	13,277,000
5	Germany	15	12,285,000
6	Australia	36	6,837,000
7	Brazil	4	6,790,000
8	China	0.5	6,308,000
9	France	10	5,696,000
10	South Korea	12	5,688,000
	World total	4.2	25?

* *Estimates for weekly usage as at end of ?*
Source: *Computer Industry Almanac, Inc.*

LAPTOP OF LUXURY

Ever-increasing power, reducing costs, and the growth of the Internet have resulted in the global explosion of the computer industry.

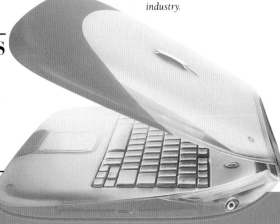

TOP 10 COUNTRIES WITH THE MOST COMPUTERS
(Country/computers)

1 US, 164,100,000   **2** Japan, 49,900,000   **3** Germany, 30,600,000
4 UK, 26,000,000   **5** France, 21,800,000   **6** Italy, 17,500,000   **7** Canada, 16,000,000
8 China, 15,900,000   **9** = Australia; = South Korea, 10,600,000

Source: *Computer Industry Almanac, Inc.*
Computer industry estimates put the number of computers in the world at 98 million in 1990, 222 million in 1995, and 579 million in 2000 – a sixfold increase over the decade.

POWER TO THE PEOPLE

In the 20th century, the creation of national grids for the transmission of electricity brought power to even the remotest communities.

TOP 10 ★
ELECTRICITY-CONSUMING COUNTRIES

	COUNTRY	CONSUMPTION KW/HR
1	US	3,278,500,000,000
2	China	955,980,000,000
3	Japan	904,600,000,000
4	Russia	712,400,000,000
5	Germany	477,270,000,000
6	Canada	475,120,000,000
7	India	397,280,000,000
8	France	375,550,000,000
9	Brazil	322,650,000,000
10	UK	309,590,000,000

Source: *Energy Information Administration*

TOP 10 🍁
WORST POLLUTING INDUSTRIES IN CANADA

	INDUSTRY	POLLUTANTS RELEASED 1997 (TONNES)*
1	Chemical and chemical products industries	39,094.8
2	Paper and allied products industries	19,904.2
3	Primary metals industries	19,783.5
4	Other utility industries	18,304.5
5	Crude petroleum and natural gas industries	11,546.3
6	Refined petroleum and coal products industries	10,246.2
7	Transportation equipment industries	8,326.0
8	Plastic products industries	5,242.3
9	Industrial and heavy (engineering) construction industries	4,932.7
10	Mining industries	4,394.6

* *Of 176 substances in Canada meeting NPRI (National Pollutant Release Inventory) reporting thresholds*

Source: *Environment Canada*

Facilities that do not meet the reporting thresholds because of their size (either the number of employees or the quantity of substances used), such as dry cleaners and gas stations, do not report to the NPRI. Collectively however, releases from these sources may account for the majority of releases of some pollutants.

🍁 TOP 10 POLLUTANTS RELEASED INTO THE ENVIRONMENT IN CANADA

(Pollutant/thousands of tonnes released, 1997)

❶ **Ammonia**, 34,737.8 ❷ **Methanol**, 19,967.3 ❸ **Sulphuric acid**, 10,814.2 ❹ **Hydrochloric acid**, 10,771.4 ❺ **Xylene** (mixed isomers), 7,371.9 ❻ **Toluene**, 6,994.0 ❼ **Zinc** (and its compounds), 6,739.2 ❽ **Methyl ethyl ketone**, 5,164.3 ❾ **Ethylene glycol**, 4,887.2 ❿ **Nitrate ion***, 4,679.2

* *In solution at pH$ 6.0*

THE 10 ★
COUNTRIES EMITTING THE MOST CARBON DIOXIDE

	COUNTRY	ANNUAL CO_2 EMISSIONS PER HEAD (TONNES)
1	Qatar	52.18
2	United Arab Emirates	36.20
3	Kuwait	25.24
4	Luxembourg	20.12
5	USA	19.68
6	Singapore	19.45
7	Bahrain	18.53
8	Trinidad and Tobago	17.14
9	Australia	16.96
10	Brunei	16.89

Source: *Carbon Dioxide Information Analysis Center*

CO_2 emissions derive from three principal sources – fossil fuel burning, cement manufacturing, and gas flaring.

TOP 10 ★
COAL-CONSUMING COUNTRIES

	COUNTRY	1998 CONSUMPTION IN TONNES OF OIL EQUIVALENT
1	China	615,400,000
2	USA	533,700,000
3	India	153,600,000
4	Russia	102,800,000
5	Japan	88,400,000
6	South Africa	87,900,000
7	Germany	84,700,000
8	Poland	60,900,000
9	Australia	45,800,000
10	UK	40,700,000

Source: *BP Statistical Review of World Energy 1999*

POWER PLANT

Opened in 1985–86, Pacific Gas and Electric's Diablo Canyon Nuclear Power Station, California, is one of the US's 104 reactors.

TOP 10 COUNTRIES WITH THE MOST NUCLEAR REACTORS

(Country/reactors)

1 US, 104 **2** France, 58 **3** Japan, 53 **4** UK, 35 **5** Russia, 29 **6** Germany, 20 **7** Ukraine, 16 **8** South Korea, 15 **9** Canada, 14 **10** Sweden, 12

Source: *International Atomic Energy Agency*
There are some 434 nuclear power stations in operation in a total of 32 countries around the world, with a further 36 under construction. Lithuania has the greatest reliance on nuclear power, obtaining 77.2 percent of its electricity from nuclear sources.

TOP 10 ★
ENERGY-CONSUMING COUNTRIES

	COUNTRY	OIL	GAS	1998 ENERGY CONSUMPTION* COAL	NUCLEAR	HEP#	TOTAL
1	US	852.4	551.2	533.7	183.0	26.7	2,146.9
2	China	190.3	17.4	615.4	3.9	17.1	844.0
3	Russia	122.3	328.3	102.8	26.9	13.6	593.8
4	Japan	255.0	62.5	88.4	84.0	9.3	499.2
5	Germany	136.6	71.6	84.7	41.7	1.8	336.3
6	India	86.1	20.9	153.6	2.8	7.2	270.6
7	France	94.5	33.7	15.1	100.0	5.7	249.1
8	UK	80.5	79.9	40.7	25.8	0.6	227.5
9	Canada	83.2	63.3	25.9	18.5	28.6	219.3
10	South Korea	93.3	14.1	36.1	23.1	0.5	167.1
	World	3,389.0	2,016.4	2,219.4	626.6	226.4	8,477.4

* Millions of tonnes of oil equivalent   # Hydroelectric power

Source: BP Statistical Review of World Energy 1999

THE 10 MOST DEFORESTING COUNTRIES

(Country/average annual forest loss 1990–95 in sq km/sq miles)

1 Brazil, 25,544/9,862 **2** Indonesia, 10,844/4,186 **3** Dem. Rep. of Congo, 7,400/2,857 **4** Bolivia, 5,814/2,244 **5** Mexico, 5,080/1,961 **6** Venezuela, 5,034/1,943 **7** Malaysia, 4,002/1,545 **8** Myanmar, 3,874/1,495 **9** Sudan, 3,526/1,361 **10** Thailand, 3,294/1,271

Source: *Food and Agriculture Organization of the United Nations*

TOP 10 ★
NATURAL GAS-CONSUMING COUNTRIES

	COUNTRY	1998 CONSUMPTION BILLION CU M	BILLION CU FT
1	USA	612.4	24,005.4
2	Russia	364.7	14,297.9
3	UK	88.8	3,479.7
4	Germany	79.6	3,118.3
5	Canada	70.3	2,756.8
6	Japan	69.4	2,722.0
7	Ukraine	68.8	2,695.8
8	Italy	57.2	2,242.9
9	Iran	51.7	2,025.1
10	Saudi Arabia	46.0	1,803.0
	World total	2,240.2	87,816.6

Source: BP Statistical Review of World Energy 1999

TOP 10 ★
OIL-CONSUMING COUNTRIES

	COUNTRY	1998 CONSUMPTION TONNES
1	USA	852,400,000
2	Japan	255,000,000
3	China	190,300,000
4	Germany	136,600,000
5	Russia	122,300,000
6	Italy	94,700,000
7	France	94,500,000
8	South Korea	93,300,000
9=	Brazil	83,200,000
9=	Canada	83,200,000

Source: BP Statistical Review of World Energy 1999

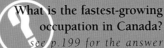

What is the fastest-growing occupation in Canada?
see p.199 for the answer

A Computer systems analysts and programmers
B Plumbers and pipefitters
C Management, advertising, and marketing consultants

Accidents at Home & Work

TOP 10 ⚜
MOST DANGEROUS INDUSTRIES IN CANADA

INDUSTRY	NUMBER OF FATALITIES, 1998
1 Construction	166
2 Manufacturing	164
3 Transportation and storage	94
4 Mining, quarrying, and oil wells	85
5 Government services	35
6 Communications and other utilities	28
7 Retail trade	26
8 Logging and forestry	25
9 Wholesale trade	22
10 Business services	18

Source: *Association of Workers' Compensation Boards of Canada*

THE 10 MOST DANGEROUS JOBS IN THE US
(Job sector/fatalities per year)

❶ Agriculture, forestry, fishing, 830 ❷ Special trade contractors, 648 ❸ Trucking and warehousing, 569 ❹ Heavy construction, other than building, 252 ❺ Wholesale trade, 241 ❻ Lumber and wood products, 199 ❼ General building contractors, 194 ❽ Food stores, 189 ❾ Business services, 181 ❿ Mining, 158   Source: *US Bureau of Labor Statistics*

TOP 10 ⚜
CAUSES OF INJURY AT WORK IN CANADA

EVENT	NUMBER OF TIME-LOSS INJURIES, 1998
1 Overexertion	91,652
2 Bodily reaction	56,170
3 Struck by	52,057
4 Fall on same level	30,443
5 Struck against	23,554
6 Fall from elevation	23,471
7 Caught in, under or below	20,398
8 Rubbed or abraded	12,355
9 Contact with radiation, caustics, toxic and noxious substances	7,480
10 Contact with temperature extremes	6,877

Source: *Association of Workers' Compensation Boards of Canada*

THE 10 ★
MOST COMMON PRODUCTS INVOLVED IN ACCIDENTS IN US HOMES

PRODUCT GROUP	ACCIDENTS
1 Sports activities and equipment	3,431,390
2 Home structures	2,499,588
3 Home furnishings and fixtures	1,933,937
4 Household containers	274,690
5 Personal use items	260,862
6 Home workshop tools	257,806
7 Heating and air conditioning	256,323
8 Yard and garden equipment	206,717
9 Household appliances	142,471
10 Toys	136,399

A survey of injuries caused by some 15,000 products, based on a sample of 101 US hospitals during 1997, showed that their ERs were kept busy with patients suffering from injuries caused by these broad product groups and several others.

Source: *US Consumer Product Safety Commission/NEISs (National Electronic Injury Surveillance System)*

THE 10 MOST ACCIDENT-PRONE COUNTRIES
(Country/accidental death rate per 100,000)*

❶ South Korea, 120.2 ❷ Moldova, 114.0 ❸ Russia, 112.3 ❹ South Africa, 99.4 ❺ Lithuania, 95.0 ❻ Estonia, 94.5 ❼ Latvia, 94.1 ❽ Ukraine, 89.0 ❾ Belarus, 82.0 ❿ Slovenia, 56.5 US, 35.5

* *Traffic accidents, accidental falls, and other accidents*
Source: *UN Demographic Yearbook*

DANGER ON DECK

Exposure to extreme weather conditions and other hazards places fishing among the world's most dangerous industries.

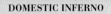

DOMESTIC INFERNO

A combination of deliberate and accidental fires, many of which result from avoidable causes, contributes to losses of life and property.

THE 10 ★
ARTICLES MOST FREQUENTLY INVOLVED IN ACCIDENTS IN THE HOME

	ARTICLE	ACCIDENTS PER ANNUM*
1	Construction feature	775,000
2	Furniture	329,000
3	Person	230,000
4	Outdoor surface	194,000
5	Clothing/footwear	191,000
6	Building/raw materials	159,000
7	Furnishings	145,000
8	Cooking/kitchen equipment	134,000
9	Animal/insect	113,000
10	Food/drink	109,000
	Total	2,502,000

* National estimates based on actual Home Accident Surveillance System figures for sample population

TOP 10 🍁
CAUSES OF FIRE IN CANADA

	SOURCE OF IGNITION	NUMBER OF FIRES 1997
1	Cooking equipment	5,829
2	Electrical distribution equipment	4,648
3	Heating equipment	3,858
4	Smoker's material or "open flame," unclassified	3,743
5	Smoker's material	3,448
6	Other electrical equipment	3,420
7	Exposure	2,813
8	Match, light (not used with smoking), lamp, candle, taper	2,659
9	Non-igniting object (e.g. lightning)	1,157
10	Cutting torch, welding equipment, varied torches	778

Source: *Canadian Council of Fire Marshals and Fire Commissioners*

🍁 TOP 10 CAUSES OF POISONING IN BRITISH COLUMBIA

① Suspected food poisoning
② Alcoholic beverage
③ Household bleach ④ Extra-Strength Tylenol ⑤ Silica gel ⑥ Dimetapp Elixir
⑦ Gasoline* ⑧ Advil ⑨ Insect stings
⑩ Tylenol with codeine

* Through siphoning
Source: *BC Poison Control Centre*

There are no comprehensive national poisoning statistics currently available for Canada.

"HAZARD"

Before it came to mean a risk, hazard was a dice game, popular in Europe since the 14th century. It comes from the Arabic word *al* (the) and *zahr* (dice). The uncertainty of casting the dice led to adoption of *al-zahr* in Spanish as *azahr*, an unexpected accident. In French this became *hasard*, and in English *hazard*.

WHY DO WE SAY ?

★ **Did You Know?** In the US, in a single year, a total of 162 people aged 65 and over were treated for skateboarding injuries.

213

Industrial & Other Disasters

WORST DISASTERS AT SPORTS VENUES IN THE 20TH CENTURY

LOCATION/DATE/TYPE	NO. KILLED
1 Hong Kong Jockey Club, Feb 26, 1918, Stand collapse and fire	604
2 Lenin Stadium, Moscow, Oct 20, 1982, Crush in soccer stadium	340
3 Lima, Peru, May 24, 1964, Riot in soccer stadium	320
4 Sinceljo, Colombia, Jan 20, 1980, Bullring stand collapse	222
5 Hillsborough, Sheffield, UK, Apr 15, 1989, Crush in soccer stadium	96
6 Guatemala City, Guatemala, Oct 16, 1996, Stampede in Mateo Flores National Stadium during World Cup soccer qualifying match, Guatemala vs. Costa Rica, with 127 injured	83
7 Le Mans, France, Jun 11, 1955, Racing car crash	82
8 Katmandu, Nepal, Mar 12, 1988, Stampede in soccer stadium	80
9 Buenos Aires, Argentina, May 23, 1968, Riot in soccer stadium	74
10 Ibrox Park, Glasgow, Scotland, Jan 2, 1971, Barrier collapse in soccer stadium	66

Before the Ibrox Park disaster, the worst accident at a British stadium was caused by the collapse of a stand at Burnden Park, Bolton, on March 9, 1946, in an FA Cup Tie against Stoke City, which left 33 dead and 400 injured. If stunt-flying is included as a "sport," the worst airshow disaster of all time occurred at the Ramstein Air Force base, Germany, on August 28, 1988, when three fighters in an Italian aerobatic team collided, one of them crashing into the crowd, leaving 70 dead and 150 injured. Such tragedies are not an exclusively modern phenomenon: during the reign of Roman Emperor Antoninus Pius (AD 138–161), a stand at the Circus Maximus collapsed during a gladiatorial spectacle and 1,162 spectators were killed.

WORST MINING DISASTERS

LOCATION/DATE	NO. KILLED
1 Hinkeiko, China, Apr 26, 1942	1,549
2 Courrières, France, Mar 10, 1906	1,060
3 Omuta, Japan, Nov 9, 1963	447
4 Senghenydd, UK, Oct 14, 1913	439
5 Coalbrook, South Africa, Jan 21, 1960	437
6 Wankie, Rhodesia, Jun 6, 1972	427
7 Dhanbad, India, May 28, 1965	375
8 Chasnala, India, Dec 27, 1975	372
9 Monongah, US, Dec 6, 1907	362
10 Barnsley, UK, Dec 12, 1866	361*

* Including 27 killed the following day while searching for survivors

A mine disaster at the Fushun mines, Manchuria, in February 1931 may have resulted in up to 3,000 deaths, but information was suppressed by the Chinese government. Soviet security was also responsible for obscuring details of an explosion at the East German Johanngeorgendstadt uranium mine on November 29, 1949, when as many as 3,700 may have died. Among the most tragic disasters of this century was a mine disaster at Aberfan, Wales, on October 20, 1966. Waste from the local mine had been building up for many years to become a heap some 244 m (800 ft) in height. Weakened by the presence of a spring, a huge volume of slurry suddenly flowed down and engulfed the local school, killing 116 children.

WORST FIRES AT THEATER AND ENTERTAINMENT VENUES*

LOCATION/DATE/TYPE	NO. KILLED
1 Canton, China, May 25, 1845, Theater	1,670
2 Shanghai, China, Jun 1871, Theater	900
3 Vienna, Austria, Dec 8, 1881, Ring Theater	640–850
4 St. Petersburg, Russia, Feb 14, 1836, Lehmann Circus	800
5 Antoung, China, Feb 13, 1937, Movie theater	658
6 Chicago, Illinois, Dec 30, 1903, Iroquois Theater	591
7 Boston, Mass., Nov 28, 1942, Cocoanut Grove Night Club	491
8 Abadan, Iran, Aug 20, 1978, Theater	422
9 Niteroi, Brazil, Dec 17, 1961, Circus	323
10 Brooklyn Theater, New York, Dec 5, 1876	295

* 19th and 20th centuries, excluding sports stadiums and race tracks

All the worst theater disasters have been caused by fire. The figure given for the first entry in this list is a conservative estimate, some sources putting the figure as high as 2,500, but, even in recent times, reports of disasters in China are often unreliable.

WORST FIRES OF THE 20TH CENTURY*

LOCATION/DATE/TYPE	NO. KILLED
1 Kwanto, Japan, Sep 1, 1923, Following earthquake	60,000
2 Chungking, China, Sep 2, 1949, Docks	1,700
3 Hakodate, Japan, Mar 22, 1934, City	1,500
4 San Francisco, US, Apr 18, 1906, Following earthquake	600–700
5 Cloquet, Minnesota, US, Oct 12, 1918, Forest	559
6 = Lagunillas, Venezuela, Nov 14, 1939, Oil refinery and city	over 500
6 = Mandi Dabwali, India, Dec 23, 1995, School tent	over 500
8 Hoboken, New Jersey, US, Jun 30, 1900, Docks	326
9 Brussels, Belgium, May 22, 1967, Department store	322
10 Columbus, Ohio, US, Apr 21, 1930, State Penitentiary	320

* Excluding sports and entertainment venues, mining disasters, and the results of military action

Did You Know? One of the worst fires in history was that which engulfed the wooden London Bridge on July 11, 1212, with some 3,000 victims burned, crushed, or drowned in the ensuing panic.

THE 10 ★

WORST COMMERCIAL AND INDUSTRIAL DISASTERS*

	LOCATION/DATE	TYPE	NO. KILLED
1	**Bhopal**, India, Dec 3, 1984	Methyl isocyanate gas escape at Union Carbide plant	up to 3,000
2	**Oppau**, Germany, Sep 21, 1921	Chemical plant explosion	561
3	**Mexico City**, Mexico Nov 20, 1984	Explosion at a PEMEX liquefied petroleum gas plant	540
4	**Seoul**, Korea, Jun 29, 1995	Collapse of Sampoong department store	501
5	**Brussels**, Belgium May 22, 1967	Fire in l'Innovation department store	322
6	**Novosibirsk**, USSR Apr 1979#	Anthrax infection following accident at biological and chemical warfare plant	up to 300
7	**Guadalajara**, Mexico Apr 22, 1992	Explosions caused by gas leak into sewers	230
8	**Sâo Paulo**, Brazil Feb 1, 1974	Fire in Joelma bank and office building	227
9	**Oakdale**, US, May 18, 1918	Chemical plant explosion	193
10	**Bangkok**, Thailand, May 10, 1993	Fire engulfed a four-story doll factory	187

* Including industrial sites, factories, offices, and stores; excluding military, mining, marine, and other transport disasters   # Precise date unknown

THE 10 ★

WORST EXPLOSIONS*

	LOCATION/DATE	TYPE	NO. KILLED
1	**Rhodes**, Greece, 1856#	Lightning strike of gunpowder store	4,000
2	**Brescia**, Italy, 1769#	Arsenal	over 3,000
3	**Salang Tunnel**, Afghanistan, Nov 3, 1982	Gasoline tanker collision	over 2,000
4	**Lanchow**, China, Oct 26, 1935	Arsenal	2,000
5	**Halifax**, Nova Scotia, Dec 6, 1917	Ammunition ship *Mont Blanc*	1,963
6	**Memphis**, Tenn., Apr 27, 1865	*Sultana* boiler explosion	1,547
7	**Bombay**, India, Apr 14, 1944	Ammunition ship *Fort Stikine*	1,376
8	**Cali**, Colombia, Aug 7, 1956	Ammunition trucks	up to 1,200
9	**Chelyabinsk**, USSR, Jun 3, 1989	Liquid gas beside railroad	up to 800
10	**Texas City**, Texas, Apr 16, 1947	Ammonium nitrate on cargo ships	576

* Excluding mining disasters, terrorist and military bombs, and natural explosions such as volcanoes   # Precise date unknown

TROUBLE IN STORE

Some 1,500 people were inside the Sampoong Department Store, Seoul, when it collapsed, leaving over a third of them dead and as many as 900 injured.

THE 10 FIRST HEINZ'S "57 VARIETIES"

(Product/year introduced)

1 Horseradish, 1869 **2** = Sour gherkins; = Sour mixed pickles; = Chow chow pickle; = Sour onions; = Prepared mustard; = Sauerkraut in crocks, 1870 **8** = Heinz and Noble catsup: = Vinegar, 1873 **10** Tomato ketchup, 1876

LABOR SAVER

When Heinz was restructured in 1876, its first product was tomato ketchup. Although a staple product in every American household, until then making it involved stirring a huge cauldron over an open fire for a day.

TOP 10

HOTTEST CHILIES

	EXAMPLES OF CHILES	SCOVILLE UNITS
1	Datil, Habañero, Scotch Bonnet	100,000–350,000
2	Chiltepin, Santaka, Thai	50,000–100,000
3	Aji, Cayenne, Piquin, Tabasco	30,000–50,000
4	de Arbol	15,000–30,000
5	Serrano, Yellow Wax	5,000–15,000
6	Chipotle, Jalapeño, Mirasol	2,500–5,000
7	Cascabel, Sandia, Rocotillo	1,500–2,500
8	Ancho, Española, Pasilla, Poblano	1,000–1,500
9	Anaheim, New Mexico	500–1,000
10	Cherry, Peperoncini	100–500

Hot peppers contain substances called capsaicinoids, which determine how "hot" they are. In 1912 pharmacist Wilbur Scoville pioneered a test, based on which chilies are ranked by Scoville Units. According to this scale, one part of capsaicin (the principal capsaicinoid) per million equals 15,000 Scoville Units.

TOP 10

CANADIAN FOOD EXPORTS FOR 1999

	FOOD PRODUCT	VALUE OF EXPORT ($)
1	Grains, bulk or cereals	21,670,975,243
2	Meat products	4,129,423,633
3	Beverages, spirits, and vinegar	1,457,240,001
4	Edible vegetables and certain roots and tubers, pulses	1,428,838,196
5	Preparations of grains, pasta	1,246,030,985
6	Preparations of vegetables, fruits, and nuts	845,208,121
7	Animal/vegetable fats and oils, margarine	759,244,756
8	Cocoa and cocoa preparations	528,943,952
9	Sugars and sugar confectionary	480,780,716
10	Dairy products, eggs, and honey	403,709,130

Source: *Statistics Canada*

If included, a category called "miscellaneous edible preparations" would occupy 7th place in this Top 10, with $733,371,175 in exports.

TOP 10 — BEEF-CONSUMING COUNTRIES

	COUNTRY	ANNUAL CONSUMPTION PER CAPITA		
		KG	LB	OZ
1	Uruguay	58.8	129	10
2	Argentina	50.5	111	5
3	US	43.3	95	7
4	Paraguay	39.8	87	11
5	Australia	37.5	82	10
6	New Zealand	36.7	80	14
7	Mongolia	35.8	78	14
8	Canada	32.5	71	10
9	Bahamas	32.1	70	12
10	French Polynesia	30.9	68	1

Source: *Meat and Livestock Commission*

TOP 10 — POULTRY-CONSUMING COUNTRIES

	COUNTRY	ANNUAL CONSUMPTION PER CAPITA		
		KG	LB	OZ
1	Antigua & Barbuda	69.6	142	6
2	Saint Lucia	54.6	120	5
3	Bahamas	51.5	113	5
4	Brunei	50.6	111	8
5	St. Kitts & Nevis	50.3	110	14
6	US	45.3	99	13
7 =	Israel	44.0	97	0
7 =	Saint Vincent	44.0	97	0
9	Barbados	43.2	95	3
10	Dominica	40.5	89	4

Source: *Meat and Livestock Commission*

TOP 10 — PORK-CONSUMING COUNTRIES

	COUNTRY	ANNUAL CONSUMPTION PER CAPITA		
		KG	LB	OZ
1	Austria	63.9	140	14
2	Yugoslavia	60.1	132	7
3	Denmark	57.4	126	8
4	Spain	56.2	123	4
5	Hungary	52.8	116	6
6	Cyprus	52.3	115	4
7	Germany	51.9	114	6
8	Slovakia	48.2	106	4
9	Netherlands	47.7	105	2
10	Czech Republic	44.6	98	5

Source: *Meat and Livestock Commission*

TOP 10 — FISH-CONSUMING COUNTRIES

	COUNTRY	ANNUAL CONSUMPTION PER CAPITA*		
		KG	LB	OZ
1	Maldives	153.4	338	3
2	Iceland	95.7	211	0
3	Kiribati	78.6	173	4
4	Japan	76.1	167	12
5	Seychelles	60.5	133	6
6	Portugal	58.7	129	7
7	Norway	54.6	120	6
8	Malaysia	54.1	119	4
9	French Polynesia	51.8	114	3
10	South Korea	51.6	113	12

* Combines sea and freshwater fish totals

Source: *Food and Agriculture Organization of the UN*

✤ CANADIAN FOOD FIRSTS

(Name/discovered, developed or introduced)

1 McIntosh apple, 1811 **2** Montreal smoked meat, early 1900s **3** Canada Dry, 1907 **4** Marquis wheat, 1909 **5** Chocolate bar (Ganong), 1910 **6** Pablum, late 1920s **7** Frozen food, 1929 **8** Instant food, 1962 **9** Bloody Caesar, 1969 **10** Poutine, 1970s

John J. McLaughlin, a Toronto chemist and pharmacist, introduced "Pale Dry Ginger Ale" in 1904, then patented his creation as "Canada Dry Ginger Ale" in 1907. Arthur D. Ganong and factory supervisor George F. Ensor, of Ganong Brothers Limited, St. Stephen, N.B., invented and introduced the first five-cent chocolate nut bar. Dr. Archibald G. Huntsman, a marine scientist, developed "ice fillets" and introduced the first frozen food to the Toronto market. Dr. Edward Asselbergs and his group at the Food Research Institute in Ottawa discovered the potato was a key ingredient for a range of dried instant foods. Poutine (a Quebec favorite made from french fries topped with cheese curds and gravy) claims many originators and its exact date of origin is difficult to determine.

FISH DISH

The national popularity of sushi (raw fish and rice) and other recipes help to make Japan one of the worlds leading fish consumers.

Sweet Treats

A MARS A DAY ...
Mars's first product, the Milky Way bar, was renamed Mars bar when launched in the UK in 1932. The name did not appear in the US until 1940, when a new bar was introduced.

THE 10 ★
FIRST MARS PRODUCTS

	PRODUCT	YEAR INTRODUCED
1=	Milky Way bar	1923
1=	Snickers bar (non-chocolate)	1923
3	Snickers bar (chocolate)	1930
4	3 Musketeers bar	1932
5	Maltesers	1937
6	Kitekat (catfood; now Whiskas)	1939
7	Mars almond bar	1940
8	M&M's plain chocolate candies	1941
9	Uncle Ben's Converted brand rice	1942
10=	M&M's peanut chocolate candies	1954
10=	Pal (dogfood)	1954

American candy manufacturer Franklin C. Mars set up his first business in Tacoma, Washington, in 1911, and formed the Mar-O-Bar company in Minneapolis in 1922, with the first of its products, the Milky Way bar. The founder's son, Forrest E. Mars, set up in the UK in 1932, merging the firm with its American counterpart in 1964. Strangely, outside the US the Milky Way bar is known as a Mars bar, while in the UK a Milky Way is a rather different product, introduced in 1935. In the UK, the Snickers bar began life as a Marathon, but was renamed to bring it in line with the US.

TOP 10 ★
SUGAR-CONSUMING COUNTRIES

	COUNTRY	ANNUAL CONSUMPTION PER CAPITA KG	LB	OZ
1	Israel	100.2	220	14
2	Belize	70.8	156	1
3	Trinidad and Tobago	61.1	134	11
4	Cuba	58.7	129	7
5	Barbados	58.0	127	14
6	Brazil	56.5	124	9
7	Swaziland	54.2	119	8
8=	Costa Rica	53.6	118	3
8=	Malta	53.6	118	3
10	Iceland	53.3	117	8
	World average	20.2	44	8

Source: *Food and Agriculture Organization of the United Nations*

TOP 10 🍁
CANDY-CONSUMING PROVINCES

	PROVINCE	AMOUNT SPENT PER PERSON IN 1996 ON SUGAR PREPARATIONS, INCLUDING CONFECTIONERY ($)
1	British Columbia	48
2	Manitoba	45
3=	Alberta	41
3=	Saskatchewan	41
5	Quebec	40
6	Nova Scotia	39
7=	Prince Edward Island	38
7=	Newfoundland	38
9	New Brunswick	35
10	Ontario	34

Source: *Statistics Canada*, Food Consumption in Canada 1996

TOP 10 ★
CANDY MANUFACTURERS IN THE US*

	MANUFACTURER	MARKET SHARE %*
1	Hershey Chocolate	26.2
2	Mars	19.9
3	Nestlé	5.7
4	William Wrigley Jr. Co.	4.8
5	Warner-Lambert	3.8
6	RJR Nabisco	3.7
7	Russell Stover Candies	3.5
8	Favorite Brands	2.8
9	Brach & Brock Confections	1.9
10	Tootsie Roll Industries	1.6

* Based on US$ sales volume

Source: *Euromonitor*

Background image: CHOCOLATE SELECTION

TOP 10 ★
CHOCOLATE-CONSUMING NATIONS

COUNTRY	TOTAL COCOA CONSUMPTION TONNES
1 US	653,947
2 Germany	289,061
3 UK	191,921
4 France	177,228
5 Japan	124,259
6 Brazil	120,359
7 Russia	119,271
8 Italy	91,154
9 Canada	78,002
10 Spain	69,658
World	2,720,637

Europe has the highest intake of the continents, with a cocoa consumption of 1,351,430 tonnes; the Americas are next with 1,050,306; then Asia and Oceania with 295,682; and lastly Africa, where only 58,955 tonnes are consumed across the entire continent.

TOP 10 ★
ICE CREAM-CONSUMING COUNTRIES

COUNTRY	PRODUCTION PER CAPITA LITERS	PINTS
1 New Zealand	26.48	55.98
2 US	22.04	46.59
3 Canada	18.78	39.70
4 Australia	17.90	37.83
5 Belgium	14.71	31.09
6 Sweden	14.03	29.66
7 Finland	13.92	29.42
8 Norway	13.34	28.20
9 Denmark	10.24	21.64
10 Israel	7.23	15.93

Source: *International Dairy Foods Association*

Global statistics for ice cream consumption are hard to come by, but this list presents recent and reliable estimates for per capita production of ice cream and related products.

TOP 10 ★
SUGAR PRODUCERS, 1999

COUNTRY	TONNES*
1 Brazil	20,995,000
2 India	16,826,000
3 China	8,958,000
4 US	7,556,000
5 Australia	5,778,000
6 Mexico	4,985,000
7 France	4,891,000
8 Thailand	4,314,000
9 Germany	4,054,000
10 Pakistan	3,817,000
World	133,089,042

* Raw centrifugal sugar

Source: *Food and Agriculture Organization of the United Nations*

TOP 10 CONSUMERS OF KELLOGG'S CORNFLAKES*

1 Ireland **2** UK **3** Australia
4 Denmark **5** Sweden **6** Norway
7 Canada **8** US **9** Mexico
10 Venezuela

* Based on per capita consumption
In 1894, the brothers Will Keith Kellogg and Dr. John Harvey Kellogg discovered, by accident, that boiled and rolled wheat dough turned into flakes if left overnight; once baked, they became a tasty cereal. In 1898, they replaced wheat with corn, thereby creating the Cornflakes we know today. Will Keith Kellogg went into business manufacturing Cornflakes, with his distinctive signature on the packet. Today, Cornflakes remain Kellogg's bestselling product.

CEREAL SUCCESS

One of the world's most popular breakfast foods, Kellogg's Cornflakes have a history spanning more than a century.

Alcoholic & Soft Drinks

TOP 10 ★
SOFT DRINK-CONSUMING COUNTRIES*

| COUNTRY | ANNUAL CONSUMPTION PER CAPITA | |
	LITERS	PINTS
1 US	212	447.6
2 =Iceland	138	290.4
2 =Mexico	138	290.4
4 Malta	127	267.6
5 Norway	121	254.4
6 Canada	117	246.0
7 Australia	115	242.4
8 Israel	110	232.8
9 Chile	106	223.2
10 Ireland	103	222.0

* Carbonated only

Source: Zenith International

As one might expect, affluent Western countries feature prominently in this list and, despite the spread of the so-called "Coca-Cola culture," former Eastern Bloc and Third World countries rank very low.

TOP 10 🍁
CANADIAN MICROBREWERIES*

MICROBREWERY	EST. HECTOLITERS SHIPPED 1998
1 Brasal-Brasserie Allemande, QC	17,000
2 Bear Brewing Co., BC	14,000
3 Bayou Brewing Co., BC	10,182
4 =Tree Brewing Company Ltd., BC	7,000
4 =Whistler Brewing Co., BC	7,000
6 Hart Breweries Ltd., ON	6,000
7 Hogtown Brewery, ON	5,000
8 =Nelson Brewing Co. Ltd., BC	4,000
8 =Fort Garry Brewing Co. Ltd., MB	4,000
10 Tin Whistle Brewing Co., AB	2,700

* A brewery producing less than 17,600 hectoliters of beer per year. Some of Canada's popular "microbrews" such as Big Rock, Brick, and McAuslan are actually regional breweries, as they produce between 17,600 and 2,346,800 hectoliters annually.

Source: Institute for Brewing Studies

THE 10 FIRST COCA-COLA PRODUCTS IN THE US
(Product/date introduced)

1 Coca-Cola, May 1886　2 Fanta, Jun 1960　3 Sprite, Feb 1961　4 TAB, May 1963　5 Fresca, Feb 1966　6 Mr. PiBB*, Jun 1972　7 Hi-C Soft Drinks, Aug 1977　8 Mello Yello, Mar 1979　9 Ramblin' Root Beer, Jun 1979　10 Diet Coke, Jul 1982

* Mr. PiBB without Sugar launched Sep 1974; changed name to Sugar-free Mr. PiBB, 1975

TOP 10 ★
ALCOHOL-CONSUMING COUNTRIES

| COUNTRY | ANNUAL CONSUMPTION PER CAPITA (100 PERCENT ALCOHOL) | |
	LITERS	PINTS
1 Luxembourg	13.3	28.1
2 Portugal	11.2	23.6
3 =France	10.8	22.8
3 =Ireland	10.8	22.8
5 Germany	10.6	22.3
6 Czech Republic	10.2	21.5
7 Spain	10.1	21.2
8 =Denmark	9.5	20.0
8 =Romania	9.5	20.0
10 Hungary	9.4	19.8
Canada	5.2	10.9

Source: Productschap voor Gedistilleerde Dranken

🍁 TOP 10 PROVINCES & TERRITORIES WITH THE HIGHEST BEER CONSUMPTION
(Province/territory/liters per person)

1 Yukon, 110.26　2 Quebec, 75.41　3 Newfoundland, 68.13　4 Alberta, 67.56　5 Ontario, 64.44　6 British Columbia, 63.82　7 Nova Scotia, 63.25　8 New Brunswick, 62.89　9 Prince Edward Island, 60.14　10 Manitoba, 59.91

Canada, 66.85

Source: Brewers Association of Canada

GRAPE HARVEST

Although Italy's wine production has led the world, it has recently been overtaken by that of France, which produced almost 6 million tons in 1999.

TOP 10 ★
WINE-DRINKING COUNTRIES

| COUNTRY | ANNUAL CONSUMPTION PER CAPITA | |
	LITERS	PINTS
1 Luxembourg	70.0	147.4
2 France	58.1	122.6
3 Portugal	53.2	112.3
4 Italy	52.0	109.8
5 Switzerland	43.2	91.2
6 Argentina	38.8	81.8
7 Greece	35.9	75.7
8 Spain	35.6	75.1
9 Austria	30.1	63.5
10 Denmark	29.0	61.2
Canada	7.3	15.4

Source: Productschap voor Gedistilleerde Dranken

The US still does not make it into the Top 10 or even Top 30 wine-drinking countries in the world.

TOP 10 ★
BEER-DRINKING COUNTRIES

	COUNTRY	ANNUAL CONSUMPTION PER CAPITA	
		LITERS	PINTS
1	Czech Republic	161.8	341.6
2	Ireland	150.5	317.7
3	Germany	127.4	268.9
4	Luxembourg	110.9	234.1
5	Austria	108.6	229.3
6	Denmark	105.0	221.6
7	UK	99.4	209.9
8	Belgium	98.0	206.9
9	Australia	94.5	199.4
10	Slovak Republic	91.8	193.8
	Canada	56.6	119.4

Source: *Productschap voor Gedistilleerde Dranken*

Despite its position as the world's leading producer of beer, the US misses being placed in the Top 10 – it is ranked in 13th position.

HERE FOR THE BEER

During the 1990s, beer consumption in Ireland rose by 20 percent, elevating the country from eighth to second place among the world's beer consumers.

TOP 10 ★
MILK-DRINKING COUNTRIES*

	COUNTRY	ANNUAL CONSUMPTION PER CAPITA	
		LITERS	PINTS
1	Iceland	149.1	314.8
2 =	Finland	139.3	294.1
2 =	Ireland	139.3	294.1
4	Norway	115.8	244.5
5	UK	114.4	241.7
6	Sweden	113.0	138.6
7	New Zealand	99.4	209.9
8	US	96.0	202.7
9	Spain	91.5	193.3
10	Switzerland	91.2	192.6

* *Those reporting to the International Dairy Federation*

Source: *National Dairy Council*

TOP 10 ★
CHAMPAGNE-IMPORTING COUNTRIES

	COUNTRY	BOTTLES IMPORTED (1999)
1	UK	32,261,232
2	US	23,700,839
3	Germany	17,496,865
4	Belgium	10,753,197
5	Italy	9,431,994
6	Switzerland	8,658,165
7	Japan	3,946,155
8	Canada	2,462,938
9	Spain	1,731,055
10	Australia	1,686,231

In 1998 France consumed 179,004,405 bottles of champagne and exported 113,453,686. In that year Canada increased its imports by a record 45 percent, entering the Top 10 for the first time.

TOP 10 ★
COFFEE-DRINKING COUNTRIES

	COUNTRY	ANNUAL CONSUMPTION PER CAPITA			
		KG	LB	OZ	CUPS*
1	Finland	11.71	25	13	1,756
2	Denmark	9.57	21	14	1,435
3	Norway	9.52	20	15	1,428
4	Sweden	8.47	18	10	1,270
5	Austria	8.04	17	11	1,206
6	Netherlands	7.82	17	3	1,173
7	Germany	7.07	15	9	1,060
8	Switzerland	6.85	15	1	1,027
9	France	5.39	11	14	808
10	Italy	5.13	11	5	772

* *Based on 150 cups per 1 kg (2 lb 3 oz)*

Source: *International Coffee Organization*

Did You Know? Until the invention of pasteurization, milk-drinkers risked contracting the disease scrofula. It was known as "King's Evil," because it was believed the only cure was to be touched by a king.

World Tourism

TOP 10 ★
TOURIST DESTINATIONS

	COUNTRY	TOTAL VISITORS, 1999
1	France	71,400,000
2	Spain	51,958,000
3	US	46,983,000
4	China	37,480,000*
5	Italy	35,839,000
6	UK	25,740,000
7	Mexico	20,216,000
8	Canada	19,556,000
9	Poland	17,940,000
10	Austria	17,630,000

Includes 10,433,000 visitors to Hong Kong

Source: *World Tourism Organization*

TOP 10 ★
TOURIST EARNING COUNTRIES

	COUNTRY	TOTAL RECEIPTS (US$), 1999
1	US	73,000,000,000
2	Italy	31,000,000,000
3	Spain	25,179,000,000*
4	France	24,657,000,000*
5	UK	20,972,000,000
6	China	14,099,000,000
7	Austria	11,259,000,000
8	Canada	10,282,000,000
9	Germany	9,570,000,000#
10	Mexico	7,850,000,000

Estimates based on first nine months

 # Estimates based on first seven months

Source: *World Tourism Organization*

❋ TOP 10 DESTINATIONS OF CANADIAN TOURISTS*

(Destinations/trips in 1998)

① New York, 2,209,000 **②** Florida, 1,720,000
③ Washington State, 1,541,000 **④** Michigan, 1,205,000 **⑤** California, 973,000
⑥ United Kingdom, 816,000 **⑦** Nevada, 694,000 **⑧** France, 597,000
⑨ Maine, 595,000 **⑩** Pennsylvania, 561,000

Destinations most visited by Canadians for an overnight stay

Source: *Tourism Industries/International Trade Administration, Department of Commerce*

"FERRIS WHEEL"

Pennsylvania bridge engineer George W. Ferris gave his name to the Ferris wheels that are popular attractions at many of the world's amusement parks. He invented the first one for the Chicago Columbian Exposition of 1893. It had a diameter of 76 m (250 ft), its 36 wooden cars carried up to 60 people, and its 14-m (45-ft) axle was the largest steel object ever forged. Modern versions, such as the BA London Eye, opened in 2000, have improved on Ferris's original.

WHY DO WE SAY ?

TOP 10 ★
OLDEST ROLLER COASTERS*

	ROLLER COASTER/LOCATION	YEAR FOUNDED
1	**Leap-the-Dips**, Lakemont Park, Altoona, PA	1902
2	**Scenic Railway**, Luna Park, Melbourne, Australia	1912
3	**Rutschbanen**, Tivoli, Copenhagen, Denmark	1914
4	**Jack Rabbit**, Clementon Amusement Park, Clementon, NJ	1919
5=	**Jack Rabbit**, Sea Breeze Park, Rochester, NY	1920
5=	**Scenic Railway**, Dreamland, Margate, UK	1920
7=	**Jack Rabbit**, Kennywood, West Mifflin, PA	1921
7=	**Roller Coaster**, Lagoon, Farmington, UT	1921
9=	**Big Dipper**, Blackpool Pleasure Beach, Blackpool, UK	1923
9=	**Thunderhawk**, Dorney Park, Allentown, PA	1923
9=	**Zippin Pippin**, Libertyland, Memphis, TN	1923

In operation at same location since founded

Leap-the-Dips at Lakemont Park, Altoona, Pennsylvania, was out of operation from 1985 but was restored and reopened in 1999.

IT JUST KEEPS ROLLING ALONG

In operation since 1914, the Rutschbanen in Copenhagen's Tivoli Gardens is Europe's oldest working roller coaster. The oldest American one predates this by twelve years.

TOP 10
BUSIEST CANADA/US BORDER CROSSINGS

LAND BORDER	# OF INBOUND TRAVELERS*
1 Ambassador Bridge, Windsor, Ont.	10,460,640
2 Detroit and Canada Tunnel, Windsor, Ont.	8,547,631
3 Peace Bridge, Fort Erie, Ont.	6,673,942
4 Rainbow Bridge, Niagara Falls, Ont.	5,597,456
5 Blue Water Bridge, Point Edward, Ont.	4,922,567
6 Queenston-Lewiston Bridge, Queenston, Ont.	4,428,033
7 Douglas, B.C.	4,421,353
8 Sault Ste. Marie, Ont.	4,102,885
9 Pacific Highway, B.C.	3,537,191
10 Cornwall, Ont.	1,969,440

* From April 1, 1998–March 31, 1999

Source: *Canada Customs and Revenue Agency*

TOP 10
OLDEST AMUSEMENT PARKS

PARK/LOCATION	YEAR FOUNDED
1 **Bakken**, Klampenborg, Denmark	1583
2 **The Prater**, Vienna, Austria	1766
3 **Blackgang Chine Cliff Top Theme Park**, Ventnor, Isle of Wight, UK	1842
4 **Tivoli**, Copenhagen, Denmark	1843
5 **Lake Compounce Amusement Park**, Bristol, CT	1846
6 **Hanayashiki**, Tokyo, Japan	1853
7 **Grand Pier**, Teignmouth, UK	1865
8 **Blackpool Central Pier**, Blackpool, UK	1868
9 **Cedar Point**, Sandusky, OH	1870
10 **Clacton Pier**, Clacton, UK	1871

TOP 10 MOST VISITED TOURISM REGIONS IN CANADA*

REGION	TOTAL PERSON-VISITS, 1997
1 Lakelands, Ont.	3,494,000
2 Ontario East	2,600,000
3 Festival Country, Ont.	2,538,000
4 Metro Toronto	2,360,000
5 Getaway Country, Ont.	2,262,000
6 Southwestern British Columbia	1,921,000
7 Vancouver Island	1,786,000
8 Quebec City	1,676,000
9 Southwestern Ontario	1,641,000
10 Alberta's Heartland	1,516,000

Source: *Statistics Canada*

The Lakelands region of Ontario includes Georgian Bay Islands National Park, the Bruce Peninsula, and Fathom Five National Marine Park.

TOP 10
COUNTRIES OF ORIGIN OF VISITORS TO THE US

COUNTRY	VISITORS TO THE US, 1998
1 **Canada**	13,421,832
2 **Mexico**	9,276,000
3 **Japan**	4,885,369
4 **UK**	3,974,976
5 **Germany**	1,901,938
6 **France**	1,013,222
7 **Brazil**	909,477
8 **Venezuela**	540,685
9 **Italy**	610,796
10 **South Korea**	364,061

Source: *Tourism Industries/International Trade Administration, Department of Commerce*

The number of inbound Canadian tourists in 1998 actually represented an 11.3 percent drop on the 15,127,000 of the previous year, while those from South Korea plummeted by 51.2 percent, from 746,550.

TOP 10
OVERSEAS COUNTRIES VISITED BY CANADIANS

COUNTRY	NUMBER OF OVERNIGHT VISITS (1998)
1 **United Kingdom**	816,000
2 **Mexico**	597,000
3 **France**	452,000
4 **Germany**	252,000
5 **Italy**	194,000
6 **Cuba**	181,000
7 **Netherlands**	174,000
8 **Switzerland**	142,000
9 **Dominican Republic**	140,000
10 **Hong Kong**	119,000

Source: *Statistics Canada*

Despite the fact the Canadian dollar lost value with most European currencies between 1997 and 1998, Canadian travelers took more trips to Europe than in previous years. France, Germany, Switzerland, and the Netherlands all saw double-digit percentage increases in Canadian visitation. The biggest jump in visits was seen in the Bahamas (No. 14), with a 31 percent increase in visits by Canadians.

Background image: FRANCE

Did You Know? The first roller coaster, invented by Lemarcus Adna Thompson in 1884, was installed at Coney Island, Brooklyn, New York.

TOP 10 ★

Transportation

Speed Records

FIRST AMERICAN HOLDERS OF THE LAND SPEED RECORD

	DRIVER*/CAR/LOCATION	DATE	KM/H	MPH
1	**William Vanderbilt**, *Mors*, Albis, France	Aug 5, 1902	121.72	76.08
2	**Henry Ford**, *Ford Arrow*, Lake St. Clair, Michigan	Jan 12, 1904	146.19	91.37
3	**Fred Marriott**, *Stanley Rocket*, Daytona Beach, Florida	Jan 23, 1906	195.65	121.57
4	**Barney Oldfield**, *Benz*, Daytona Beach, Florida	Mar 16, 1910	210.03	131.27
5	**Bob Burman**, *Benz*, Daytona Beach, Florida	Apr 23, 1911	226.19	141.37
6	**Ralph de Palma**, *Packard*, Daytona Beach, Florida	Feb 17, 1919	239.79	149.87
7	**Tommy Milton**, *Duesenberg*, Daytona Beach, Florida	Apr 27, 1920	249.64	156.03
8	**Ray Keech**, *White Triplex*, Daytona Beach, Florida	Apr 22, 1928	332.08	207.55
9	**Craig Breedlove**, *Spirit of America*, Bonneville Salt Flats, Utah	Aug 5, 1963	651.92	407.45
10	**Tom Green**, *Wingfoot Express*, Bonneville Salt Flats, Utah	Oct 2, 1964	661.12	413.20

* Excluding those who subsequently broke their own records

ICE RACER

In 1904 Henry Ford set the land speed record – although it was actually achieved on ice – on the frozen Lake St. Clair. A former employee of Thomas Edison, Ford (standing) had established the Ford Motor Company the previous year.

FASTEST PRODUCTION MOTORCYCLES

	MAKE/MODEL	KM/H	MPH
1	Suzuki GSX1300R Hayabusa	309	192
2=	Honda CBR1100XX Blackbird	291	181
2=	Honda RC45(m)	291	181
4=	Harris Yamaha YZR500	289	180
4=	Kawasaki ZZR1100 D7	289	180
6	Bimota YB10 Biposto	283	176
7	Suzuki GSX-R1100WP(d)	280	174
8	Suzuki GSX-R750-WV	279	173
9=	Bimota Furano	278	173
9=	Kawasaki ZZR1100 C1	278	173

Since Honda (1940s), Suzuki and Yamaha (1950s), and Kawasaki (1960s) were established as motorcycle manufacturers, their machines have dominated the world's superbike league.

LATEST HOLDERS OF THE MOTORCYCLE SPEED RECORD

	RIDER/MOTORCYCLE	YEAR	KM/H	MPH
1	**Dave Campos**, Twin 1,491 cc Ruxton Harley-Davidson Easyrider	1990	518.45	322.15
2	**Donald A. Vesco**, Twin 1,016 cc Kawasaki Lightning Bolt	1978	512.73	318.60
3	**Donald A. Vesco**, 1,496 cc Yamaha Silver Bird	1975	487.50	302.93
4	**Calvin Rayborn**, 1,480 cc Harley-Davidson	1970	426.40	264.96
5	**Calvin Rayborn**, 1,480 cc Harley-Davidson	1970	410.37	254.99
6	**Donald A. Vesco**, 700 cc Yamaha	1970	405.25	251.82
7	**Robert Leppan**, 1,298 cc Triumph	1966	395.27	245.62
8	**William A. Johnson**, 667 cc Triumph	1962	361.40	224.57
9	**Wilhelm Herz**, 499 cc NSU	1956	338.08	210.08
10	**Russell Wright**, 998 cc Vincent HRD	1955	297.64	184.95

All the records listed here were achieved at the Bonneville Salt Flats, Utah, with the exception of No. 10, which was attained at Christchurch, New Zealand. To break a Fédération Internationale Motocycliste record, the motorcycle has to cover a measured distance, making two runs within one hour and taking the average of the two. American Motorcycling Association records require a turnaround within two hours. Although all those listed were specially adapted for their record attempts, the two most recent had two engines and were stretched to 6.4 m (21 ft) and 7 m (23 ft) respectively.

Did You Know? The last steam vehicle to hold the land speed record was the Stanley Rocket, in which Fred Marriott achieved 195.65 km/h (121.57 mph) in Daytona Beach, Florida, on Jan 23, 1906.

THE 10 ⭐
FIRST HOLDERS
OF THE LAND SPEED RECORD

DRIVER/CAR/LOCATION	DATE	KM/H	MPH
1 Gaston de Chasseloup-Laubat, *Jeantaud*, Achères, France	Dec 18, 1898	62.78	39.24
2 Camile Jenatzy, *Jenatzy*, Achères, France	Jan 17, 1899	66.27	41.42
3 Gaston de Chasseloup-Laubat, *Jeantaud*, Achères, France	Jan 17, 1899	69.90	43.69
4 Camile Jenatzy, *Jenatzy*, Achères, France	Jan 27, 1899	79.37	49.92
5 Gaston de Chasseloup-Laubat, *Jeantaud*, Achères, France	Mar 4, 1899	92.16	57.60
6 Camile Jenatzy, *Jenatzy*, Achères, France	Apr 29, 1899	105.26	65.79
7 Leon Serpollet, *Serpollet*, Nice, France	Apr 13, 1902	120.09	75.06
8 William Vanderbilt, *Mors*, Albis, France	Aug 5, 1902	121.72	76.08
9 Henri Fournier, *Mors*, Dourdan, France	Nov 5, 1902	122.56	76.60
10 M. Augières, *Mors*, Dourdan, France	Nov 17, 1902	123.40	77.13

The first official land speed records were all broken within three years, the first six of them by rival French racers Comte Gaston de Chasseloup-Laubat and Camile Jenatzy. Both the *Jeantaud* and the *Jenatzy* were electrically powered.

THE 10 ⭐
LATEST HOLDERS
OF THE LAND SPEED RECORD

DRIVER/CAR	DATE	KM/H	MPH
1 Andy Green, *Thrust SSC**	Oct 15, 1997	1,227.99	763.04
2 Richard Noble, *Thrust 2**	Oct 4, 1983	1,013.47	633.47
3 Gary Gabelich, *The Blue Flame*	Oct 23, 1970	995.85	622.41
4 Craig Breedlove, *Spirit of America – Sonic 1*	Nov 15, 1965	960.96	600.60
5 Art Arfons, *Green Monster*	Nov 7, 1965	922.48	576.55
6 Craig Breedlove, *Spirit of America – Sonic 1*	Nov 2, 1965	888.76	555.48
7 Art Arfons, *Green Monster*	Oct 27, 1964	858.73	536.71
8 Craig Breedlove, *Spirit of America*	Oct 15, 1964	842.04	526.28
9 Craig Breedlove, *Spirit of America*	Oct 13, 1964	749.95	468.72
10 Art Arfons, *Green Monster*	Oct 5, 1964	694.43	434.02

* Location, Black Rock Desert, Nevada. All other speeds were achieved at Bonneville Salt Flats, Utah.

TOP 10 FASTEST PRODUCTION CARS

(Model/country of manufacture/top speed in km/h#/mph#)*

1 McLaren F1, UK, 386/240   **2** Lister Storm, UK, 323/201
3 Lamborghini Diablo GT, Italy, 341/200
4 Ferrari 550 Maranello, Italy, 320/199
5 Renault Espace F1, France, 312/194
6 = Ascari Ecosse, Italy; = Pagani Zonda, Italy, >305/190
8 = Callaway C12, US; = Porsche 911 Turbo, Germany, 305/190
10 Aston Martin DB7 Vantage, UK, 297/185

* Fastest of each manufacturer
# May vary according to specification modifications to meet national legal requirements
Source: *Auto Express*

TOP 10 PRODUCTION CARS WITH
THE FASTEST 0–60 MPH TIMES

(Model/country of manufacture/seconds taken#)*

1 Renault Espace F1, France, 2.8   **2** McLaren F1, UK, 3.2
3 Caterham Superlight R500, UK, 3.5   **4** Porsche 911 Turbo, Germany, 3.6   **5** Lamborghini Diablo GT, Italy 3.8
6 Westfield FW400, UK, 4.0   **7** = Ascari Ecosse, Italy; = Marcos Mantis, UK, 4.1   **9** = AC Cobra Superblower, UK; = Callaway C12, US; = TVR Tuscan Speed Six, UK, 4.2

* Fastest of each manufacturer
# May vary according to specification modifications to meet national legal requirements
Source: *Auto Express*

RED HOT

One of the fastest cars ever built (with a top speed of 320 km/h/199 mph), the Ferrari 550M (Maranello) has been acclaimed as the best-handling car in the world.

Cars & Road Transportation

THE 10 ★
FIRST COUNTRIES TO MAKE SEAT BELTS COMPULSORY

	COUNTRY	INTRODUCED
1	Czechoslovakia	Jan 1969
2	Ivory Coast	Jan 1970
3	Japan	Dec 1971
4	Australia	Jan 1972
5 =	Brazil	Jun 1972
5 =	New Zealand	Jun 1972
7	Puerto Rico	Jan 1974
8	Spain	Oct 1974
9	Sweden	Jan 1975
10 =	Netherlands	Jun 1975
10 =	Belgium	Jun 1975
10 =	Luxembourg	Jun 1975

Seat belts, long in use on airplanes, were not designed for use in private cars until the 1950s. Ford was the first manufacturer in Europe to use anchor points, and belts were first installed as standard equipment in Swedish Volvos from 1959.

TOP 10 🍁
MOST STOLEN MOTOR VEHICLES IN CANADA

	MOTOR VEHICLE*	RELATIVE THEFT CLAIM FREQUENCY#
1	Acura Integra	483
2	Hyundai Tiburon FX	329
3 =	Jeep TJ (4WD)	301
3 =	Chevrolet Cavalier Z24	301
5	Volkswagen Golf (2-door)	268
6	Toyota 4Runner (4WD)	248
7	Mazda MPV (4WD)	236
8	Hyundai Accent (2-door)	232
9	Dodge Dakota (4WD)	208
10	Honda Civic (2-door)	203

* 1997–98 models
\# The number of theft claims reported as a percentage of cars insured with comprehensive coverage
Source: *Vehicle Information Centre of Canada*
Theft of automobiles and their components costs consumers almost $600 million per year in insurance premiums. Quebec continues to have the highest loss cost per vehicle for vehicle theft.

TOP 10 🍁
BEST-SELLING SPORT UTILITY VEHICLES IN CANADA 1999

	VEHICLE	NUMBER SOLD
1	Ford Explorer	24,928
2	Chevy/GMC Blazer/Jimmy	23,758
3	Jeep Grand Cherokee	19,003
4	Honda CRV	14,511
5	Nissan Pathfinder	10,013
6	Chevy/GMC Tahoe/Yukon	9,327
7	Dodge Durango	8,025
8	Toyota 4Runner	7,537
9	Ford Expedition	7,267
10	Jeep Cherokee	6,203

Source: *Canadian Auto World*

TOP 10 ★
MOTOR VEHICLE-OWNING COUNTRIES

	COUNTRY	CARS	COMMERCIAL VEHICLES	TOTAL
1	US	134,981,000	65,465,000	200,446,000
2	Japan	44,680,000	22,173,463	66,853,463
3	Germany	40,499,442	3,061,874	43,561,316
4	Italy	30,000,000	2,806,500	32,806,500
5	France	25,100,000	5,195,000	30,295,000
6	UK	24,306,781	3,635,176	27,941,957
7	Russia	13,638,600	9,856,000	23,494,600
8	Spain	14,212,259	3,071,621	17,283,880
9	Canada	13,182,996	3,484,616	16,667,612
10	Brazil	12,000,000	3,160,689	15,160,689
	World total	477,010,289	169,748,819	646,759,108

FRENCH JAM
France has one of the world's highest ratios of cars to people and can claim a record traffic jam of 176 km (110 miles), which occurred between Paris and Lyons.

TOP 10 ⭐
COUNTRIES PRODUCING THE MOST MOTOR VEHICLES

	COUNTRY	CARS	COMMERCIAL VEHICLES	TOTAL
1	US	6,083,227	5,715,678	11,798,905
2	Japan	7,863,763	2,482,023	10,345,786
3	Germany	4,539,583	303,326	4,842,909
4	France	3,147,622	442,965	3,590,587
5	South Korea	2,264,709	548,005	2,812,714
6	Spain	2,213,102	199,207	2,412,309
7	Canada	1,279,312	1,117,731	2,397,043
8	UK	1,686,134	238,263	1,924,397
9	Brazil	1,466,900	345,700	1,812,600
10	Italy	1,317,995	227,370	1,545,365
	World total	37,318,281	14,194,882	51,513,163

Source: *American Automobile Manufacturers Association*

A CAR IS BORN

Japan's car production, which places increasing reliance on advanced robotic technology, closely rivals that of world leader the US.

TOP 10 BESTSELLING CARS OF ALL TIME

	MANUFACTURER/MODEL	FIRST YEAR PRODUCED	ESTIMATED NO. MADE
1	Toyota Corolla	1966	23,000,000
2	Volkswagen Beetle	1937*	21,376,331
3	Lada Riva	1972	19,000,000
4	Volkswagen Golf	1974	18,453,646
5	Ford Model T	1908	16,536,075
6	Nissan Sunny/Pulsar	1966	13,571,100
7 =	Ford Escort/Orion	1967	12,000,000
7 =	Honda Civic	1972	12,000,000
9	Mazda 323	1977	9,500,000
10	Renault 4	1961	8,100,000

* Original model still produced in Mexico and Brazil

Estimates of manufacturers' output of their bestselling models vary from the vague to the unusually precise: 16,536,075 of the Model T Ford, with 15,007,033 produced in the US and the rest in Canada and the UK in 1908–27.

TOP 10 🍁
MOST POPULAR VEHICLES IN CANADA

	VEHICLE	NUMBER SOLD (1999)
1	Ford F-Series	79,785
2	Chevrolet Silverado/ GMC Sierra	78,776
3	Dodge Caravan	73,930
4	Honda Civic	58,122
5	Ford Windstar	55,528
6	Chevrolet Cavalier	50,711
7	GM FWD Minivans	50,469
8	Pontiac Sunfire	46,526
9	Toyota Corolla	41,630
10	Dodge Ram Pickups	30,064

Source: *Canadian Auto World*

THE CAR IN FRONT ...

The Toyota Motor Company was started in 1937, in Koromo, Japan, by Kiichiro Toyoda. Its Corolla model became the world's bestselling car.

Road Accidents & Disasters

THE 10 ★
COUNTRIES WITH THE HIGHEST NUMBER OF ROAD DEATHS

	COUNTRY	TOTAL DEATHS*
1	US	41,967
2	Thailand	15,176
3	South Korea	13,343
4	Japan	11,254
5	Germany	8,549
6	France	8,444
7	Poland	7,310
8	Brazil	6,759
9	Turkey	6,735
10	Italy	6,724

* In latest year for which figures are available

Based on the ratio of fatalities to distance traveled, road deaths in the US have declined markedly from 24.1 deaths per 100 million vehicle miles traveled in 1921, to under 1.6 today.

THE 10 SAFEST CAR COLORS
(Color/light reflection percentage)

1 White, 84.0 **2** Cream, 68.8 **3** Ivory, 66.7 **4** Light pink, 66.5 **5** Yellow, 57.0 **6** Pink, 51.6 **7** = Buff; = Light gray, 51.5 **9** Light green, 45.2 **10** Aluminum gray, 41.0

Source: *Mansell Color Company Inc., published by the National Safety Council*

DRIVEN TO DESTRUCTION
In 1998, a total of 150,919 collisions were reported on Canada's highways. That year also saw 217,614 injuries and 2,927 fatalities reported.

THE 10 ★
COUNTRIES WITH THE MOST DEATHS BY MOTOR ACCIDENTS

	COUNTRY	DEATH RATE PER 100,000 POPULATION
1	South Africa	99.4
2	Latvia	35.3
3	South Korea	33.1
4	Estonia	26.7
5	Russia	23.6
6	Portugal	22.8
7	Lithuania	22.1
8	Greece	21.3
9	Venezuela	20.7
10=	El Salvador	20.3
10=	Kuwait	20.3

Source: *United Nations*

✦ THE 10 PROVINCES AND TERRITORIES WITH THE HIGHEST TRAFFIC FATALITY RATES
(Province/territory/fatalities)*

1 Northwest Territories, 5.7 **2** Saskatchewan, 2.3 **3** = New Brunswick; = Prince Edward Island, 2.2 **5** Alberta, 2.1 **6** Quebec, 2.0 **7** Manitoba, 1.8 **8** British Columbia, 1.7 **9** Nova Scotia, 1.6 **10** Ontario, 1.4

* Per 10,000 motor vehicles registered, 1997

DANGEROUS COLORS
Black cars are reputed to be the least safe because they are less visible at night, but types of vehicle and age and experience of drivers are equally salient factors.

The 1995 underground gas explosion at Taegu, South Korea, destroyed scores of vehicles, leaving 110 dead and 250 injured.

THE 10 ★
WORST MOTOR VEHICLE AND ROAD DISASTERS

LOCATION/DATE/INCIDENT	NO. KILLED

1 Afghanistan, Nov 3, 1982 — over 2,000
Following a collision with a Soviet army truck, a gasoline tanker exploded in the 2.7-km (1.7-mile) Salang Tunnel. Some authorities have put the death toll from the explosion, fire, and fumes as high as 3,000.

2 Colombia, Aug 7, 1956 — 1,200
Seven army ammunition trucks exploded at night in the center of Cali, destroying eight city blocks, including a barracks where 500 soldiers were sleeping.

3 Thailand, Feb 15, 1990 — over 150
A dynamite truck exploded.

4 Nepal, Nov 23, 1974 — 148
Hindu pilgrims were killed when a suspension bridge over the Mahahali River collapsed.

5 Egypt, Aug 9, 1973 — 127
A bus drove into an irrigation canal.

6 Togo, Dec 6, 1965 — over 125
Two trucks collided with dancers during a festival at Sotouboua.

7 Spain, Jul 11, 1978 — over 120
A liquid gas tanker exploded in a campsite at San Carlos de la Rapita.

8 South Korea, Apr 28, 1995 — 110
An undergound explosion destroyed vehicles and caused about 100 cars and buses to plunge into the pit it created.

9 =The Gambia, Nov 12, 1992 — c.100
After brake failure, a bus carrying passengers to a dock plunged into a river.

9 =Kenya, early Dec 1992 — c.100
A bus carrying 112 people skidded, hit a bridge, and plunged into a river.

The worst motor racing accident occurred on June 13, 1955, at Le Mans, France, when Pierre Levegh's Mercedes-Benz 300 SLR went out of control, hit a wall, and exploded in mid-air, showering wreckage into the crowd and killing 82. The worst accident involving a single car was on Dec 17, 1956: 12 people were killed when their car was hit by a train near Phoenix, Arizona.

❦ THE 10 WORST HOURS OF THE DAY FOR MOTOR VEHICLE ACCIDENTS IN CANADA
(Time of day/no. casualties, 1997)

1 4:00–4:59 p.m., 18,534 **2** 3:00–3:59 p.m., 18,047 **3** 5:00–5:59 p.m., 17,872
4 2:00–2:59 p.m., 14,820 **5** 6:00–6:59 p.m., 14,060 **6** 1:00–1:59 p.m., 13,496
7 Noon–12:59 p.m., 13,136 **8** 11:00–11:59 a.m., 11,362 **9** 7:00–7:59 p.m., 11,319
10 9:00–9:59 a.m., 8,083

TOP 10 🍁
WORST HOURS OF THE DAY FOR SCHOOL BUS COLLISIONS IN CANADA*

	TIME OF DAY	FATALITIES[#]	INJURIES[#]	TOTAL
1	8:00–8:59 am	9	1,142	1,151
2	3:00–3:59 pm	13	859	872
3	4:00–4:59 pm	8	430	438
4	7:00–7:59 am	6	258	264
5	12:00–12:59 pm	3	196	199
6	9:00–9:59 am	1	184	185
7	11:00–11:59 am	3	158	161
8	2:00–2:59 pm	1	133	134
9	5:00–5:59 pm	1	104	105
10	1:00–1:59 pm	0	50	50

* 1988–97

[#] *Includes school bus occupants and pedestrians*

Source: *Transport Canada*

Rail Transportation

LONGEST RAIL NETWORKS

	LOCATION	TOTAL RAIL LENGTH KM	MILES
1	US	240,000	149,129
2	Russia	150,000	93,205
3	Canada	67,773	42,112
4	China	64,900	40,327
5	India	62,915	39,093
6	Germany	46,300	28,769
7	Australia	38,563	23,962
8	Argentina	37,830	23,506
9	France	32,027	19,901
10	Mexico	31,048	19,292

RAILROAD

Although the US still has the longest rail network in the world, US rail mileage has declined considerably since its 1916 peak of 408,773 km (254,000 miles).

TOP 10 🍁

BUSIEST STATIONS ON THE TORONTO SUBWAY

	STATION	RIDERSHIP (AVERAGE DAY)
1	Yonge*	157,625
2	Bloor#	152,676
3	St. George#	92,035
4	St. George*	91,352
5	Finch	78,667
6	Union#	74,014
7	Kennedy*	67,181
8	Eglinton#	66,447
9	King#	54,776
10	Dundas#	54,193

* Bloor–Danforth line
 # Yonge–University–Spadina line

Source: *Toronto Transit Commission*

Although it has one name, St. George station has two separate platforms serving the Bloor–Danforth line and the Yonge–University–Spadina line.

TOP 10 🍁

BUSIEST STATIONS ON THE MONTREAL METRO

	STATION	RIDERSHIP (AVERAGE DAY)
1	McGill	40,000
2	Berri–UQAM	38,000
3	Henri-Bourassa	29,000
4	Longueuil	25,000
5	Guy–Concordia	24,500
6	Atwater	23,000
7	Bonaventure	22,500
8	Place-des-Arts	22,000
9	Peel	21,500
10	Côte-Vertu	21,000

Source: *MUCTC*

The Montreal Metro's busiest day ever was Sep 11, 1984, the day the Pope appeared at Jarry Park during his visit to Montreal. Two million passengers rode the Metro that day. The only time the Metro operated for a full 24 hours was on March 3, 1971, during the "snowstorm of the century."

TOP 10 🍁

BUSIEST STATIONS ON VANCOUVER'S SKYTRAIN

	STATION	RIDERSHIP AVERAGE DAY	RIDERSHIP AVERAGE WEEKDAY
1	Metrotown*	13,956	16,105
2	Granville	12,319	14,215
3	Broadway	11,455	13,218
4	Burrard	9,891	11,414
5	Main Street	7,407	8,548
6	Joyce	6,873	7,931
7	Surrey Central*	5,695	6,572
8	Stadium	5,657	6,528
9	King George*	5,045	5,822
10	Scott Road*	5,041	5,818

* Located in neighboring municipalities outside Vancouver

Source: *SkyTrain*

Did You Know? The world's first passenger rail fatality occurred on the Stockton and Darlington Railway on March 19, 1828, when a boiler explosion killed the driver, John Gillespie.

TOP 10 ★
FASTEST RAIL JOURNEYS*

JOURNEY/COUNTRY/TRAIN	DISTANCE		SPEED	
	KM	MILES	KM/H	MPH
1 Hiroshima–Kokura, Japan, Nozomi 500	192.0	119.3	261.8	162.7
2 Massy–St. Pierre des Corps, France, 7 TGV	206.9	128.5	253.3	157.4
3 Brussels–Paris, Belgium/France, Thalys 9342	313.4	194.7	226.5	140.7
4 Madrid–Seville, Spain, 5 AVE	470.5	292.4	209.1	129.9
5 Karlsruhe–Mannheim, Germany, 2 trains	71.0	44.1	193.8	120.4
6 London–York, UK, 1 IC225	303.4	188.5	180.2	112.0
7 Skövde–Södertälje, Sweden, 3 X2000	277.0	172.1	171.3	106.4
8 Piacenza–Parma, Italy, ES 9325	57.0	35.4	171.0	106.2
9 North Philadelphia–Newark Penn, US, 1 NE Direct	122.4	76.0	153.0	95.0
10 Salo–Karjaa, Finland, S220 132	53.1	33.0	151.7	94.3

* Fastest journey for each country; all those in the Top 10 have other similarly or equally fast services   Source: Railway Gazette International

THE 10 FIRST CITIES IN NORTH AMERICA TO HAVE SUBWAY SYSTEMS
(City/year opened)

1 New York, 1867 **2** Chicago, 1892
3 Boston, 1901 **4** Philadelphia, 1908 **5** Toronto, 1954
6 Cleveland, 1955 **7** Montreal, 1966 **8** San Francisco, 1972
9 Washington, D.C., 1976
10 Atlanta, 1979

TOP 10 ★
BUSIEST UNDERGROUND RAILROAD NETWORKS

CITY	YEAR OPENED	TRACK LENGTH		STATIONS	PASSENGERS PER ANNUM
		KM	MILES		
1 Moscow	1935	243.6	153	150	3,183,900,000
2 Tokyo	1927	169.1	106	154	2,112,700,000
3 Mexico City	1969	177.7	112	154	1,422,600,000
4 Seoul	1974	133.0	84	112	1,354,000,000
5 Paris	1900	201.4	127	372	1,170,000,000
6 New York	1867	398.0	249	469	1,100,000,000
7 Osaka	1933	105.8	66	99	988,600,000
8 St. Petersburg	1955	91.7	58	50	850,000,000
9 Hong Kong	1979	43.2	27	38	804,000,000
10 London	1863	392.0	247	245	784,000,000

THE 10 ★
WORST RAIL DISASTERS

LOCATION/DATE/INCIDENT	NO. KILLED

1 Bagmati River, India, Jun 6, 1981 — *c.*800
The carriages of a train traveling from Samastipur to Banmukhi in Bihar plunged off a bridge over the Bagmati River, near Mansi, when the driver braked, apparently to avoid hitting a sacred cow. Although the official death toll was said to have been 268, many authorities have claimed that the train was so massively overcrowded that the actual figure was in excess of 800, making it probably the worst rail disaster of all time.

2 Chelyabinsk, Russia, Jun 3, 1989 — up to 800
Two passenger trains, laden with vacationers heading to and from Black Sea resorts, were destroyed when liquid gas from a nearby pipeline exploded.

3 Guadalajara, Mexico, Jan 18, 1915 — over 600
A train derailed on a steep incline, but political strife in the country meant that full details of the disaster were suppressed.

4 Modane, France, Dec 12, 1917 — 573
A troop-carrying train ran out of control and was derailed. It has been claimed that the train was overloaded and that as many as 1,000 may have died.

5 Balvano, Italy, Mar 2, 1944 — 521
A heavily laden train stalled in the Armi Tunnel, and many passengers were asphyxiated. Like the disaster at Torre (No. 6), wartime secrecy prevented full details from being published.

6 Torre, Spain, Jan 3, 1944 — over 500
A double collision and fire in a tunnel resulted in many deaths – some have put the total as high as 800.

7 Awash, Ethiopia, Jan 13, 1985 — 428
A derailment hurled a train laden with some 1,000 passengers into a ravine.

8 Cireau, Romania, Jan 7, 1917 — 374
An overcrowded passenger train crashed into a military train and was derailed.

9 Quipungo, Angola, May 31, 1993 — 355
A train was derailed by UNITA guerrilla action.

10 Sangi, Pakistan, Jan 4, 1990 — 306
A train was diverted on to the wrong line, resulting in a fatal collision.

PARIS METRO
Now 100 years old, the Paris Metro – with its distinctive Art Deco entrances – is among the world's longest and most used underground railroad systems.

Water Transportation

BUSIEST PORTS

	PORT/LOCATION	GOODS HANDLED PER ANNUM (TONNES)
1	Rotterdam, Netherlands	350,000,000
2	Singapore	290,000,000
3	Chiba, Japan	173,700,000
4	Kobe, Japan	171,000,000
5	Hong Kong	147,200,000
6	Houston, US	142,000,000
7	Shanghai, China	139,600,000
8	Nagoya, Japan	137,300,000
9	Yokohama, Japan	128,300,000
10	Antwerp, Belgium	109,500,000

LARGEST CRUISE SHIPS

	SHIP/YEAR BUILT/ COUNTRY	PASSENGER CAPACITY	GROSS TONNAGE
1 =	*Explorer of the Seas*, 2000, Finland	3,840	142,000
1 =	*Voyager of the Seas*, 1999, Finland	3,840	142,000
3	*Grand Princess*, 1998, Italy	3,300	108,806
4	*Carnival Triumph*, 1999, Italy	3,473	101,672
5	*Carnival Destiny*, 1996, Italy	3,336	101,353
6	*Disney Magic*, 1998, Italy	2,500	83,338
7	*Disney Wonder*, 1999, Italy	6,000	83,308
8	*Rhapsody of the Seas*, 1997, France	2,416	78,491
9	*Vision of the Seas*, 1995, Italy	2,416	78,340
10	*Sun Princess*, 1995, Italy	2,272	77,441

Source: *Lloyd's Register of Shipping, MIPG/PPMS*

PORT OF CALL

Singapore's substantial and well-protected harbor has contributed to the city-state's status as the most important commercial center in Southeast Asia.

"WOMEN AND CHILDREN FIRST"

The movie *Titanic* brought home to many the significance of a ship built with insufficient lifeboats, requiring choices to be made as to who would have a seat to safety and who would have to take their chances in the sea. The first such incident involved the sinking of the *Birkenhead* off South Africa in 1852. The 20 women and children on board were placed in the only three lifeboats that were serviceable, while the British soldiers remained on deck, 445 of them drowning in the incident. This subsequently became a naval tradition known to all as the "Birkenhead Drill."

WHY DO WE SAY ?

FLOATING GIANT

One of the world's largest cruise ships, the 1997 French-built Rhapsody of the Seas *is also one of the longest afloat, at 915 ft 2 in (278.94 m).*

BUSIEST PORTS IN CANADA

	PORT	1997 TONNAGE*
1	Vancouver	71,798
2	Sept-Îles/Pte-Noire	24,471
3	Port-Cartier	20,902
4	Saint John	20,610
5	Montreal/Contrecoeur	20,609
6	Port Hawkesbury	15,943
7	Quebec/Lévis	14,953
8	Halifax	14,813
9	Thunder Bay	12,849
10	Prince Rupert	12,538

* *Tonnage of cargo loaded and unloaded, both domestic and international, thousands of tonnes*

Source: *Statistics Canada*

If only domestic shipping were considered, Thunder Bay would be No. 1 in this Top 10, with a total tonnage of 8,342,000 tonnes for 1997.

THE 10 ★
WORST MARINE DISASTERS
OF THE 20TH CENTURY

LOCATION/DATE/INCIDENT	APPROX. NO. KILLED
1 Off Gdansk, Poland, Jan 30, 1945	up to 7,800

The German liner Wilhelm Gustloff, *crowded with refugees, was torpedoed by a Soviet submarine, S-13. The precise death toll remains uncertain, but is in the range of 5,348 to 7,800.*

2 Off Cape Rixhöft (Rozeewie), Poland, Apr 16, 1945	6,800

The German ship Goya, *carrying evacuees from Gdansk, was torpedoed in the Baltic.*

3 Off Yingkow, China, Nov 1947	over 6,000

The boilers of an unidentified Chinese troop ship, carrying Nationalist soldiers from Manchuria, exploded, detonating ammunition.

4 Lübeck, Germany, May 3, 1945	5,000

The German ship Cap Arcona, *carrying concentration camp survivors, was bombed and sunk by British aircraft.*

5 Off St. Nazaire, France, Jun 17, 1940	3,050

The British troop ship Lancastria *sank.*

6 Off Stolpmünde (Ustka), Poland, Feb 9, 1945	3,000

German war-wounded and refugees were lost when the Steuben *was torpedoed by the same Russian submarine that had sunk the* Wilhelm Gustloff.

LOCATION/DATE/INCIDENT	APPROX. NO. KILLED
7 Tabias Strait, Philippines, Dec 20, 1987	up to 3,000

The ferry Dona Paz *was struck by oil tanker* MV Victor.

8 Woosung, China, Dec 3, 1948	over 2,750

The overloaded steamship Kiangya, *carrying refugees, struck a Japanese mine.*

9 Lübeck, Germany, May 3, 1945	2,750

The refugee ship Thielbeck *sank during the British bombardment of Lübeck harbor in the closing weeks of World War II.*

10 South Atlantic, Sep 12, 1942	2,279

The British passenger vessel Laconia, *carrying Italian prisoners-of-war, was sunk by German U-boat U-156.*

Other disasters occurring during wartime and resulting in losses of more than 1,000 include the explosion of *Mont Blanc*, a French ammunition ship, following its collision with the Belgian steamer *Imo* in Halifax harbor on December 6, 1917, with 1,635 lost; the sinking of the British cruiser HMS *Hood* by the German battleship *Bismarck* on May 24, 1941, with 1,418 killed; and the torpedoing by German submarine *U-20* of the *Lusitania*, a British passenger liner, on May 7, 1915, with the loss of 1,198 civilians.

THE 10 ★
WORST OIL TANKER
SPILLS

TANKER(S)/LOCATION/DATE	APPROX. SPILLAGE TONNES
1 *Atlantic Empress* and *Aegean Captain*, Trinidad, Jul 19, 1979	300,000
2 *Castillio de Bellver*, Cape Town, South Africa, Aug 6, 1983	255,000
3 *Olympic Bravery*, Ushant, France, Jan 24, 1976	250,000
4 *Showa-Maru*, Malacca, Malaya, Jun 7, 1975	237,000
5 *Amoco Cadiz*, Finistère, France, Mar 16, 1978	223,000
6 *Odyssey*, Atlantic, off Canada, Nov 10, 1988	140,000
7 *Torrey Canyon*, Isles of Scilly, UK, Mar 18, 1967	120,000
8 *Sea Star*, Gulf of Oman, Dec 19, 1972	115,000
9 *Irenes Serenada*, Pilos, Greece, Feb 23, 1980	102,000
10 *Urquiola*, Corunna, Spain, May 12, 1976	101,000

ENVIRONMENTAL DISASTER
The 1979 collision of the Atlantic Empress and the Aegean Captain off Trinidad resulted in the worst oil spill of all time.

THE 10 ★
FIRST TRANSATLANTIC FLIGHTS

AIRCRAFT/CREW/COUNTRY	CROSSING	DATE*
1 **US Navy/Curtiss flying boat** *NC-4*, Lt.-Cdr. Albert Cushing Read and crew of five, US	Trepassy Harbor, Newfoundland, to Lisbon, Portugal	May 16–27, 1919
2 **Twin Rolls-Royce-engined converted Vickers Vimy bomber**#, Capt. John Alcock and Lt. Arthur Whitten Brown, UK	St. John's, Newfoundland, to Galway, Ireland	Jun 14–15, 1919
3 **British R-34 airship**+, Maj. George Herbert Scott and crew of 30, UK	East Fortune, Scotland, to Roosevelt Field, New York	Jul 2–6, 1919
4 **Fairey IIID seaplane** *Santa Cruz*, Adm. Gago Coutinho and Cdr. Sacadura Cabral, Portugal	Lisbon, Portugal, to Recife, Brazil	Mar 30–Jun 5, 1922
5 **Two Douglas seaplanes,** ***Chicago* and *New Orleans*,** Lt. Lowell H. Smith and Leslie P. Arnold/ Erik Nelson and John Harding, US	Orkneys, Scotland, to Labrador, Canada	Aug 2–31, 1924
6 *Los Angeles*, **a renamed German-built** *ZR 3* **airship**, Dr. Hugo Eckener, with 31 passengers and crew, Germany	Friedrichshafen, Germany, to Lakehurst, New Jersey	Oct 12–15, 1924
7 *Plus Ultra*, **a Dornier Wal twin-engined flying boat**, Capt. Julio Ruiz and crew, Spain	Huelva, Spain, to Recife, Brazil	Jan 22–Feb 10, 1926
8 *Santa Maria*, **a Savoia-Marchetti S.55 flying boat**, Francesco Marquis de Pinedo, Capt. Carlo del Prete, and Lt. Vitale Zacchetti, Italy	Cagliari, Sardinia, to Recife, Brazil	Feb 8–24, 1927
9 **Dornier Wal flying boat**, Sarmento de Beires and Jorge de Castilho, Portugal	Lisbon, Portugal, to Natal, Brazil	Mar 16–17, 1927
10 **Savoia-Marchetti flying boat**, João De Barros and crew, Brazil	Genoa, Italy, to Natal, Brazil	Apr 28–May 14, 1927

* *All dates refer to the actual Atlantic legs of the journeys; some started earlier and ended beyond their first transatlantic landfalls* # *First nonstop flight* + *First east–west flight*

THE 10 ★
FIRST PEOPLE TO FLY IN HEAVIER-THAN-AIR AIRCRAFT

PILOT/COUNTRY/AIRCRAFT	DATE
1 **Orville Wright**, US, *Wright Flyer I*	Dec 17, 1903
2 **Wilbur Wright**, US, *Wright Flyer I*	Dec 17, 1903
3 **Alberto Santos-Dumont**, Brazil, *No. 14-bis*	Oct 23, 1906
4 **Charles Voisin**, France, *Voisin-Delagrange I*	Mar 30, 1907
5 **Henri Farman**, UK, later France, *Voisin-Farman I-bis*	Oct 7, 1907
6 **Léon Delagrange**, France, *Voisin-Delagrange I*	Nov 5, 1907
7 **Robert Esnault-Pelterie**, France, *REP No. 1*	Nov 16, 1907
8 **Charles W. Furnas***, US, *Wright Flyer III*	May 14, 1908
9 **Louis Blériot**, France, *Blériot VIII*	Jun 29, 1908
10 **Glenn Hammond Curtiss**, US, *AEA June Bug*	Jul 4, 1908

* *As a passenger in a plane piloted by Wilbur Wright, Furnas was the first airplane passenger in the US.*

"MACH NUMBER"

A Mach number is a unit of speed, related to the speed of sound, that varies according to such factors as altitude and the moisture content of the air. In dry air at sea level, Mach 1 is 1,229 km/h (763.67 mph). The land speed record set in 1997 was undertaken early in the morning, when high humidity and a cool temperature lower the speed of sound. The word Mach derives from the name of Ernst Mach (1838–1916), an Austrian physicist and philosopher.

WHY DO WE SAY?

COAST TO COAST

A previous transatlantic crossing had been made as a series of "hops," but Alcock and Brown's Vickers Vimy flight of 1919 was the first nonstop crossing.

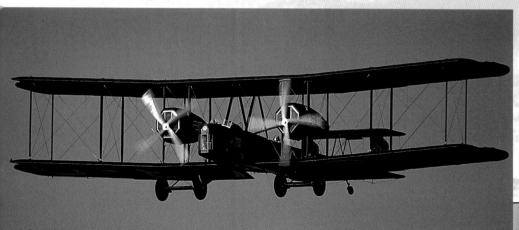

TOP 10 ★
FASTEST X-15 FLIGHTS

	PILOT/DATE	MACH*	SPEED KM/H	MPH
1	William J. Knight, Oct 3, 1967	6.70	7,274	4,520
2	William J. Knight, Nov 18, 1966	6.33	6,857	4,261
3	Joseph A. Walker, Jun 27, 1962	5.92	6,606	4,105
4	Robert M. White, Nov 9, 1961	6.04	6,589	4,094
5	Robert A. Rushworth, Dec 5, 1963	6.06	6,466	4,018
6	Neil A. Armstrong, Jun 26, 1962	5.74	6,420	3,989
7	John B. McKay, Jun 22, 1965	5.64	6,388	3,938
8	Robert A. Rushworth, Jul 18, 1963	5.63	6,317	3,925
9	Joseph A. Walker, Jun 25, 1963	5.51	6,294	3,911
10	William H. Dana, Oct 4, 1967	5.53	6,293	3,910

* Mach no. varies with altitude – the list ranked is on actual speed

THE 10 ★
FIRST ROCKET AND JET AIRCRAFT

	AIRCRAFT/COUNTRY	FIRST FLIGHT
1	Heinkel He 176*, Germany	Jun 20, 1939
2	Heinkel He 178, Germany	Aug 27, 1939
3	DFS 194*, Germany	Aug 1940#
4	Caproni-Campini N-1, Italy	Aug 28, 1940
5	Heinkel He 280V-1, Germany	Apr 2, 1941
6	Gloster E.28/39, UK	May 15, 1941
7	Messerschmitt Me 163 Komet*, Germany	Aug 13, 1941
8	Messerschmitt Me 262V-3, Germany	Jul 18, 1942
9	Bell XP-59A Airacomet, US	Oct 1, 1942
10	Gloster Meteor F Mk 1, UK	Mar 5, 1943

* Rocket-powered   # Precise date unknown

FASTEST AIRCRAFT

The speeds attained by the rocket-powered X-15 and X-15A-2 aircraft remain the greatest by piloted vehicles in the Earth's atmosphere. They were air-launched by being released from B-52 bombers, and so do not qualify for the official air speed record, for which aircraft must take off and land under their own power. An X-15 also set an unofficial altitude record when, on August 22, 1963, Joseph A. Walker piloted one to 107,960 m (354,200 ft) – some 108 km (67 miles) high. The pioneering work of the pilots of the X-15s laid the foundations of US spaceflight.

THE 10 ★
FIRST FLIGHTS OF MORE THAN ONE HOUR

	PILOT	DURATION	DATE		PILOT	DURATION	DATE
1	Orville Wright	1:2:15	Sep 9, 1908	7	Wilbur Wright*	1:4:26	Oct 6, 1908
2	Orville Wright	1:5:52	Sep 10, 1908	8	Wilbur Wright	1:9:45	Oct 10, 1908
3	Orville Wright	1:10:0	Sep 11, 1908	9	Wilbur Wright	1:54:53	Dec 18, 1908
4	Orville Wright	1:15:20	Sep 12, 1908	10	Wilbur Wright	2:20:23	Dec 31, 1908
5	Wilbur Wright	1:31:25	Sep 21, 1908				
6	Wilbur Wright	1:7:24	Sep 28, 1908				

* First ever flight of more than one hour with a passenger (M. A. Fordyce)

TOP 10 ★
BIGGEST AIRSHIPS EVER BUILT

	AIRSHIP	COUNTRY	YEAR	VOLUME CU M	VOLUME CU FT	LENGTH M	LENGTH FT
1 =	Hindenburg	Germany	1936	200,000	7,062,934	245	804
1 =	Graf Zeppelin II	Germany	1938	200,000	7,062,934	245	804
3 =	Akron	US	1931	184,060	6,500,000	239	785
3 =	Macon	US	1933	184,060	6,500,000	239	785
5	R101	UK	1930	155,744	5,500,000	237	777
6	Graf Zeppelin	Germany	1928	105,000	3,708,040	237	776
7	L72	Germany	1920	68,500	2,419,055	226	743
8	R100	UK	1929	155,743	5,500,000	216	709
9	R38	UK*	1921	77,136	2,724,000	213	699
10 =	L70	Germany	1918	62,200	2,418,700	212	694
10 =	L71	Germany	1918	62,200	2,418,700	212	694

* UK-built, but sold to US Navy

The giant airships in this list ultimately suffered unfortunate fates: the *Hindenburg, Akron, Macon, R101, L72,* and *R38* crashed, the *L70* was shot down, and the remainder were broken up for scrap.

Which industry in Canada produces the most pollution?

see p.210 for the answer

A Chemical
B Pulp & Paper
C Petroleum & Gas

Air Transportation

WORST AIRSHIP DISASTERS

LOCATION/DATE/INCIDENT	NO. KILLED
1 Off the Atlantic coast, US, Apr 4, 1933	73
US Navy airship Akron crashed into the sea in a storm, leaving only three survivors in the world's worst airship tragedy.	
2 Over the Mediterranean, Dec 21, 1923	52
French airship Dixmude is assumed to have been struck by lightning and to have broken up and crashed into the sea. Wreckage, believed to be from the airship, was found off Sicily 10 years later.	
3 Near Beauvais, France, Oct 5, 1930	50
British airship R101 crashed into a hillside leaving 48 dead, with two dying later, and six survivors.	
4 Off the coast near Hull, UK, Aug 24, 1921	44
Airship R38, sold by the British government to the US and renamed USN ZR-2, broke in two on a training and test flight.	
5 Lakehurst, New Jersey, May 6, 1937	36
German Zeppelin Hindenburg caught fire when mooring.	
6 Hampton Roads, Virginia, Feb 21, 1922	34
Roma, an Italian airship bought by the US Army, crashed, killing all but 11 men on board.	
7 Berlin, Germany, Oct 17, 1913	28
German airship LZ18 crashed after engine failure during a test flight at Berlin-Johannisthal.	
8 Baltic Sea, Mar 30, 1917	23
German airship SL9 was struck by lightning on a flight from Seerappen to Seddin and crashed into the sea.	
9 Mouth of the Elbe River, Germany, Sep 3, 1915	19
German airship L10 was struck by lightning and plunged into the sea.	
10= Off Heligoland, Sep 9, 1913	14
German Navy airship L1 crashed into the sea, leaving six survivors.	
10= Caldwell, Ohio, Sep 3, 1925	14
US dirigible Shenandoah, the first airship built in the US and the first to use safe helium instead of inflammable hydrogen, broke up in a storm, scattering sections over a large area of the Ohio countryside.	

WORST AIR DISASTERS IN NORTH AMERICA

LOCATION/DATE/INCIDENT	NO. KILLED
1 Chicago, Illinois, May 25, 1979	273
(See Worst Air Disasters, No. 9)	
2 Gander, Newfoundland, Dec 12, 1985	256
A chartered DC-8 stalled and crashed shortly after takeoff, killing 256 passengers.	
3 Off Long Island, New York, Jul 17, 1996	230
Soon after takeoff from JFK, a TWA Boeing 747-100 en route for Paris exploded in midair and crashed into the Atlantic Ocean, killing all on board.	
4 Off Peggy's Cove, Nova Scotia, Sep 3, 1998	229
A fire in the cockpit forced Swissair Flight 111 to attempt an emergency landing at Halifax International Airport. The plane crashed into the sea, killing 215 passengers and 14 crew members.	
5 Romulus, Michigan, Aug 16, 1987	156
A Northwest Airlines McDonnell Douglas DC-9 crashed onto a road following an engine fire after takeoff from Detroit. Only one passenger survived.	
6 Kenner, Louisiana, Jul 9, 1982	153
A Pan Am Boeing 747 crashed after takeoff from New Orleans for Las Vegas, killing all on board.	
7 San Diego, California, Sep 25, 1978	144
A Pacific Southwest Airline Boeing 727 collided in the air with a Cessna 172 light aircraft, killing 135 in the plane, two in the Cessna, and seven on the ground.	
8 Dallas-Ft. Worth Airport, Texas, Aug 2, 1985	137
A Delta Airlines Tristar crashed when a severe down-draft affected it during landing, killing 136 on board and the driver of a truck on the ground.	
9 New York, Dec 16, 1960	134
A United Airlines DC-8 with 77 passengers and crew of seven and a TWA Super Constellation with 39 passengers and five crew collided in a snowstorm. The DC-8 crashed in Brooklyn, killing six on the ground; the Super Constellation crashed into New York Harbor, killing all on board.	
10 Pittsburgh, Pennsylvania, Sep 8, 1994	132
A USAir Boeing 737-400 en route from Chicago to West Palm Beach crashed, killing all on board.	

"BLACK BOX"

During World War II, the British Royal Air Force slang term for the radar apparatus that aided navigators and bomb-aimers was "black box," the mystery and secrecy surrounding this invention emphasized by its color. The name was later applied to the flight data recorder on a modern airliner, the device that records all the aircraft's principal actions. In fact, to make them easier to find after a crash, black boxes are now customarily painted a luminous orange.

WHY DO WE SAY?

FIERY FINALE

Astonishingly, 61 of the 97 people on board the Hindenburg survived its explosion, but the awesome and terrible images of the catastrophe ended the airship era.

Background image: **CHARLES DE GAULLE AIRPORT, PARIS, FRANCE**

top10

SIFTING THROUGH THE WRECKAGE
Military personnel inspect the wreckage of the airliner and cargo aircraft that collided at Charkhi Dadri, India, in 1996, leaving no survivors.

TOP 10 ★
BUSIEST INTERNATIONAL AIRPORTS

	AIRPORT/LOCATION	PASSENGERS PER ANNUM
1	**London Heathrow**, London, UK	48,275,000
2	**Frankfurt**, Frankfurt, Germany	30,919,000
3	**Hong Kong**, Hong Kong, China	29,543,000
4	**Charles de Gaulle**, Paris, France	28,665,000
5	**Schiphol**, Amsterdam, Netherlands	27,085,000
6	**Singapore International**, Singapore	23,130,000
7	**New Tokyo International (Narita)**, Tokyo, Japan	22,666,000
8	**London Gatwick**, Gatwick, UK	22,029,000
9	**J.F. Kennedy International**, New York, US	17,453,000
10	**Bangkok**, Bangkok, Thailand	16,380,000

Source: *International Civil Aviation Organization*

In addition to New York's JFK, only five airports in the US handle more than 5 million international passengers a year: notably Miami, Los Angeles, Chicago O'Hare, Honolulu, and San Francisco.

THE 10 ★
WORST AIR DISASTERS

LOCATION/DATE/INCIDENT	NO. KILLED
1 **Tenerife**, Canary Islands, Mar 27, 1977	583

Two Boeing 747s (Pan Am and KLM, carrying 364 passengers and 16 crew and 230 passengers and 11 crew respectively) collided and caught fire on the runway of Los Rodeos airport after the pilots received incorrect control-tower instructions.

2 **Mt. Ogura**, Japan, Aug 12, 1985	520

A JAL Boeing 747 on an internal flight from Tokyo to Osaka crashed, killing all but four on board in the worst-ever disaster involving a single aircraft.

3 **Charkhi Dadri**, India, Nov 12, 1996	349

Soon after taking off from New Delhi's Indira Gandhi International Airport, a Saudi Airways Boeing 747 collided with a Kazakh Airlines Ilyushin IL76 cargo aircraft on its descent and exploded, killing all 312 on the Boeing and 37 on the Ilyushin in the world's worst midair crash.

4 **Paris**, France, Mar 3, 1974	346

A Turkish Airlines DC-10 crashed at Ermenonville, north of Paris, immediately after takeoff for London, with many English rugby supporters among the dead.

5 **Off the Irish coast**, Jun 23, 1985	329

An Air India Boeing 747 on a flight from Vancouver to Delhi exploded in midair, perhaps as a result of a terrorist bomb.

6 **Riyadh**, Saudi Arabia, Aug 19, 1980	301

A Saudia (Saudi Arabian) Airlines Lockheed Tristar caught fire during an emergency landing.

7 **Kinshasa, Zaïre**, Jan 8, 1996	298

A Zaïrean Antonov-32 cargo plane crashed shortly after takeoff, killing shoppers in a market.

8 **Off the Iranian coast**, Jul 3, 1988	290

An Iran Air A300 airbus was shot down in error by a missile fired by the USS Vincennes.

9 **Chicago**, US, May 25, 1979	273

An engine fell off an American Airlines DC-10 as it took off from Chicago O'Hare airport; the plane plunged out of control, killing all 271 on board and two on the ground, in the US's worst-ever air disaster.

10 **Lockerbie**, Scotland, Dec 21, 1988	270

Pan Am Flight 103 from London Heathrow to New York exploded in midair as a result of a terrorist bomb, killing 243 passengers, 16 crew, and 11 on the ground in the UK's worst-ever air disaster.

TOP 10 COUNTRIES WITH THE MOST AIRPORTS
(Country/airports)

❶ **US**, 14,459 ❷ **Brazil**, 3,265
❸ **Russia**, 2,517 ❹ **Mexico**, 1,805
❺ **Argentina**, 1,374 ❻ **Canada**, 1,395
❼ **Bolivia**, 1,130 ❽ **Colombia**, 1,120
❾ **Paraguay**, 941 ❿ **South Africa**, 749

Source: *Central Intelligence Agency*
Airports, as defined by the CIA, range in size from those with paved runways over 10,000 ft (3,048 m) in length to those with only short landing strips. Among European countries those with the most airports are Germany (618), France (474), and the UK (387).

♣ THE 10 BUSIEST DAYS OF THE YEAR AT PEARSON INTERNATIONAL AIRPORT*
(Day/total passengers)

❶ July 30, 98,600 ❷ July 29, 98,300 ❸ August 10, 96,400 ❹ August 16, 95,700
❺ August 12, 95,400 ❻ = July 23; = August 20; = August 23; = August 19, 95,300
❿ August 9, 94,700

* For 1999
Source: *Greater Toronto Airports Authority*

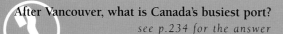
After Vancouver, what is Canada's busiest port?
see p.234 for the answer
A Saint John
B Montreal
C Sept-Îles/Pte-Noire

239

SYDNEY 2000

Indigenous Australian creatures welcome the world to the 27th Olympiad, held in Sydney from September 15 to October 1, 2000.

TM © SOCOG 1996

TOP 10 ★
LONGEST-STANDING CURRENT OLYMPIC TRACK AND FIELD RECORDS

	EVENT	WINNING DISTANCE, TIME, OR SCORE	COMPETITOR/ COUNTRY	DATE SET
1	Men's long jump	8.90 m	Bob Beamon, US	Oct 18, 1968
2	Women's shot put	22.41 m	Ilona Slupianek, East Germany	Jul 24, 1980
3	Women's 800 meters	1 min 53.43 sec	Nadezhda Olizarenko, USSR	Jul 27, 1980
4=	Women's 4 x 100 meters	41.60 sec	East Germany	Aug 1, 1980
4=	Men's 1500 meters	3 min 32.53 sec	Sebastian Coe, GB	Aug 1, 1980
6	Women's marathon	2 hr 24 min 52 sec	Joan Benoit, US	Aug 5, 1984
7	Decathlon	8,847 points	Daley Thompson, GB	Aug 9, 1984
8	Men's 5,000 meters	13 min 05.59 sec	Said Aouita, Morocco	Aug 11, 1984
9	Men's marathon	2 hr 9 min 21 sec	Carlos Lopes, Portugal	Aug 12, 1984
10=	Men's shot put	22.47 m	Ulf Timmermann, East Germany	Sep 23, 1988
10=	Men's 20-km walk	1 hr 19 min 57 sec	Jozef Pribilinec, Czechoslovakia	Sep 23, 1988

Bob Beamon's record-breaking jump in 1968 is regarded as one of the greatest achievements in athletics. He was aided by Mexico City's rarefied atmosphere, but to add a staggering 55.25 cm (21¾ in) to the old record, and win the competition by 72.39 cm (28½ in), was no mean feat. Beamon's jump of 8.90 m (29 ft 2½ in) was the first beyond both 8.53 and 8.84 m (28 and 29 ft). The next 8.53-m (28-ft) jump in the Olympics was not until 1980, 12 years after Beamon's leap.

THE 10 OLYMPIC DECATHLON EVENTS

❶ 100 meters ❷ Long jump ❸ Shot put ❹ High jump ❺ 400 meters
❻ 110 meter hurdles ❼ Discus
❽ Pole vault ❾ Javelin ❿ 1500 meters

TOP 10 🍁
OLYMPIC SPORTS IN WHICH CANADA HAS WON THE MOST MEDALS

	SPORT	GOLD	SILVER	BRONZE	TOTAL
1	Athletics	13	14	23	50
2	Swimming	7	13	18	38
3	Rowing	8	12	11	31
4	Speed Skating	6	10	11	27
5	Figure Skating	2	7	9	18
6	Boxing	3	7	7	17
7	Canoeing	3	7	4	14
8	Hockey	6	5	2	13
9=	Alpine skiing	4	1	5	10
9=	Wrestling	0	5	5	10

Source: *Canadian Olympic Association,* The Canadian Global Almanac

TOP 10 ★
OLYMPIC SPORTS IN WHICH THE US HAS WON THE MOST MEDALS

	SPORT	MEDALS			
		GOLD	SILVER	BRONZE	TOTAL
1	Track and field	299	216	177	692
2	Swimming	230	176	137	543
3	Diving	46	40	41	127
4	Wrestling	46	38	25	109
5	Boxing	47	21	34	102
6	Shooting	45	26	21	92
7	Gymnastics	26	23	28	77
8	Rowing	29	28	19	76
9	Yachting	16	19	16	51
10	Speed skating	22	16	10	48

Background image: **THE OLYMPIC STADIUM IN SYDNEY**

TOP 10 ★
COUNTRIES WITH THE MOST SUMMER OLYMPICS MEDALS, 1896–1996

COUNTRY	GOLD	MEDALS SILVER	BRONZE	TOTAL
1 US	833	634	548	2,015
2 Soviet Union*	485	395	354	1,234
3 Great Britain	177	233	225	635
4 France	176	181	205	562
5 Germany #	151	181	184	516
6 Sweden	134	152	173	459
7 Italy	166	136	142	444
8 Hungary	142	128	155	425
9 East Germany	153	130	127	410
10 Australia	87	85	122	294

Includes Unified Team of 1992; does not include Russia since this date

Not including West/East Germany 1968–88

The medals table was led by the host nations at the first three Games: Greece in 1896, France in 1900, and the US in 1904. Germany led at the 1936 Games, after which the US and the Soviet Union vied for preeminence.

OLYMPICS"

What we call the Olympics is a modern revival of games that took place at Olympia in Greece from as early as 1370 BC, as part of a religious festival held every four years. Originally foot races were the only events, and the earliest record is that of Coroibis of Olis, winner of a 186-yd (170-m) race in 776 BC. New sports were progressively added, but the Games were banned in AD 393 by Emperor Theodosius I. The Olympics were reborn with the first modern games held in Athens in 1896. **WHY DO WE SAY?**

MEDAL WINNER
Russian gymnast Nikolay Andrianov's tally of 15 individual and team medals won in three Olympics makes him the most decorated male athlete of all time.

TOP 10 SUMMER OLYMPICS ATTENDED BY THE MOST COMPETITORS, 1896–1996
(City/year/competitors)

1 Atlanta, 1996, 10,310 **2** Barcelona, 1992, 9,364 **3** Seoul, 1988, 9,101
4 Munich, 1972, 7,156 **5** Los Angeles, 1984, 7,058 **6** Montreal, 1976, 6,085
7 Mexico City, 1968, 5,530 **8** Rome, 1960, 5,346 **9** Moscow, 1980, 5,326
10 Tokyo, 1964, 5,140

The first Games in 1896 were attended by just 311 competitors, all men, representing 13 countries. Women took part for the first time four years later at the Paris Games.

TOP 10 ★
MEDAL WINNERS IN A SUMMER OLYMPICS CAREER

MEDALLIST	COUNTRY	SPORT	YEARS	GOLD	MEDALS SILVER	BRONZE	TOTAL
1 Larissa Latynina	USSR	Gymnastics	1956–64	9	5	4	18
2 Nikolay Andrianov	USSR	Gymnastics	1972–80	7	5	3	15
3 = Edoardo Mangiarotti	Italy	Fencing	1936–60	6	5	2	13
3 = Takashi Ono	Japan	Gymnastics	1952–64	5	4	4	13
3 = Boris Shakhlin	USSR	Gymnastics	1956–64	7	4	2	13
6 = Sawao Kato	Japan	Gymnastics	1968–76	8	3	1	12
6 = Paavo Nurmi	Finland	Athletics	1920–28	9	3	0	12
8 = Viktor Chukarin	USSR	Gymnastics	1952–56	7	3	1	11
8 = Vera Cáslavská	Czechoslovakia	Gymnastics	1964–68	7	4	0	11
8 = Carl Osborn	US	Shooting	1912–24	5	4	2	11
8 = Mark Spitz	US	Swimming	1968–72	9	1	1	11
8 = Matt Biondi	US	Swimming	1984–92	8	2	1	11

Did You Know? Several unusual Olympic events have been discontinued, including underwater swimming, long jump and high jump on horseback, club-swinging, and stone-throwing.

243

Sports Heroes

MOST POINTS SCORED BY MICHAEL JORDAN IN A GAME

	TEAM	DATE	POINTS
1	Cleveland Cavaliers	Mar 28, 1990	69
2	Orlando Magic	Jan 16, 1993	64
3	Boston Celtics	Apr 20, 1986	63
4 =	Detroit Pistons	Mar 4, 1987	61
4 =	Atlanta Hawks	Apr 16, 1987	61
6	Detroit Pistons	Mar 3, 1988	59
7	New Jersey Nets	Feb 6, 1987	58
8	Washington Bullets	Dec 23, 1992	57
9 =	Philadelphia 76ers	Mar 24, 1987	56
9 =	Miami Heat	Apr 29, 1992	56

Source: *NBA*

SEASONS BY WAYNE GRETZKY

	SEASON	GOALS	ASSISTS	POINTS
1	1985–86	52	163	215
2	1981–82	92	120	212
3	1984–85	73	135	208
4	1983–84	87	118	205
5	1982–83	71	125	196
6	1986–87	62	121	183
7	1988–89	54	114	168
8	1980–81	55	109	164
9	1990–91	41	122	163
10	1987–88	40	109	149

Wayne Gretzky, who retired in 1999 after 20 seasons in the NHL, is considered to be the greatest ice-hockey player of all time. He gained more records than any player in history, including the most goals, assists, and points in a career.

ICE MAN

Wayne Gretzky (pictured here during his 1984–85 season with the Edmonton Oilers) holds more career records than any player in ice-hockey history.

THE 10 LATEST WINNERS OF THE *SPORTS ILLUSTRATED* "SPORTSMAN OF THE YEAR" AWARD

(Year/winner(s)/sport)

1 1999 United States Women's World Cup Squad, Soccer **2** 1998 = Mark McGwire; = Sammy Sosa, Baseball **4** 1997 Dean Smith, Basketball coach **5** 1996 Tiger Woods, Golf **6** 1995 Cal Ripken, Jr., Baseball **7** 1994 = Johan Olav Koss; = Bonnie Blair, Ice skating **9** 1993 Don Shula, Football coach **10** 1992 Arthur Ashe, Tennis

♦ THE 10 MOST RECENT INDUCTEES TO CANADA'S SPORTS HALL OF FAME

(Year/name/sport or activity)

1 1999 = Marcel Aubut, Hockey builder; = Johnny Bower, Hockey; = Bernie Faloney, Football; = Sylvie Frechette, Synchronized swimming; = John Hiller, Baseball **6** 1998 = Myriam Bédard, Biathlete; = Sandy Hawley, Jockey; = Silken Laumann, Rower; = Mario Lemieux, Hockey **10** 1997 = Larry Cain, Canoeing; = Marcel Dionne, Hockey; = Dr. Phil Edwards, Running; = Kathleen Heddle, Rowing; = Marnie McBean, Rowing; = Dr. Maury Van Vliet, Sports educator

Source: *Canada's Sports Hall of Fame*

ON THE BALL

In many seasons during his exceptional career, Michael Jordan achieved an average of over 30 points per game, with those listed above standing out as his highest-scoring ones.

THE 10 ★
LATEST EVANDER HOLYFIELD WINS BY KNOCKOUT

	OPPONENT	ROUND	DATE
1	Michael Moorer	8	Nov 8, 1997
2	Mike Tyson	11*	Nov 9, 1996
3	Bobby Czyz	5	May 10, 1996
4	Riddick Bowe	8*	Nov 4, 1995
5	Bert Cooper	7	Nov 23, 1991
6	Buster Douglas	3	Oct 25, 1990
7	Seamus McDonagh	4*	Jun 1, 1990
8	Alex Stewart	8*	Nov 4, 1989
9	Adilson Rodrigues	2	Jul 15, 1989
10	Michael Dokes	10*	Mar 11, 1989

* Technical knockout

Born October 19, 1962, boxer Evander Holyfield won his first undisputed heavyweight title in 1990 when he defeated Buster Douglas. His 1993 defeat of Riddick Bowe (when Holyfield won on points) and his 1996 victory over Mike Tyson established him as the only fighter, apart from Muhammad Ali, to win the heavyweight title on three occasions.

TOP 10 ★
FASTEST 100-METER RUNS BY LINFORD CHRISTIE

	STADIUM/LOCATION	DATE	TIME SECS
1	Stuttgart, Germany	Aug 15, 1993	9.87
2	Victoria, B.C.	Aug 23, 1994	9.91
3	Tokyo, Japan	Aug 25, 1991	9.92
4	Barcelona, Spain	Aug 1, 1992	9.96
5=	Seoul, Korea	Sep 24, 1988	9.97
5=	Stuttgart, Germany	Aug 15, 1993	9.97
5=	Johannesburg, SA	Sep 23, 1995	9.97
8	Victoria, B.C.	Aug 23, 1994	9.98
9	Tokyo, Japan	Aug 25, 1991	9.99
10=	Barcelona, Spain	Aug 1, 1992	10.00
10=	Stuttgart, Germany	Aug 14, 1993	10.00

Christie made his international debut for Great Britain in 1980, became the fastest runner outside the US in 1986, and won Olympic gold in 1992.

TOP 10 ★
LONGEST LONG JUMPS BY CARL LEWIS

	STADIUM/LOCATION	DATE	DISTANCE M
1	Tokyo, Japan	Aug 30, 1991	8.87
2=	Indianapolis	Jun 19, 1983	8.79
2=	New York*	Jan 27, 1984	8.79
4=	Indianapolis	Jul 24, 1982	8.76
4=	Indianapolis	Jul 18, 1988	8.76
6	Indianapolis	Aug 16, 1987	8.75
7	Seoul, Korea	Sep 26, 1988	8.72
8=	Westwood	May 13, 1984	8.71
8=	Los Angeles	Jun 19, 1984	8.71
10	Barcelona, Spain	Aug 5, 1992	8.68

* Indoor performance

All-round athlete Lewis won four gold medals at the 1984 Olympics, two in 1988, two in 1992, and his ninth in 1996.

THE 10 ★
LATEST WINNERS OF THE JESSE OWENS INTERNATIONAL TROPHY

YEAR	WINNER	SPORT
2000	Lance Armstrong	Track and field
1999	Marion Jones	Track and field
1998	Haile Gebrselassie	Track and field
1997	Michael Johnson	Track and field
1996	Michael Johnson	Track and field
1995	Johann Olav Koss	Speed skating
1994	Wang Junxia	Track and field
1993	Vitaly Scherbo	Gymnastics
1992	Mike Powell	Track and field
1991	Greg LeMond	Cycling

The Jesse Owens International Trophy, named in honor of American Olympic athlete Jesse (James Cleveland) Owens (1913–80), has been presented by the Amateur Athletic Association since 1981, when it was won by speed skater Eric Heiden. Michael Johnson is the only sportsperson to have won on two occasions, while Marion Jones, the 1999 winner, is only the fourth woman to receive the award.

POLES APART

Ukrainian pole-vaulter Sergei Bubka (b. 1963) has ruled his sport since winning the 1983 World Championship. He has set 35 world records, which is more than any other athlete in sports history.

TOP 10 ★
HIGHEST POLE VAULTS BY SERGEI BUBKA

	STADIUM/LOCATION	DATE	HEIGHT M
1	Donetsk, Ukraine*	Feb 21, 1993	6.15
2=	Lievin, France*	Feb 13, 1993	6.14
2=	Sestriere, Italy	July 31, 1994	6.14
4=	Berlin, Germany*	Feb 21, 1992	6.13
4=	Tokyo, Japan	Sep 19, 1992	6.13
6=	Grenoble, France*	Mar 23, 1991	6.12
6=	Padua, Italy	Aug 30, 1992	6.12
8=	Donetsk, Ukraine*	Mar 19, 1991	6.11
8=	Dijon, France	June 13, 1992	6.11
10=	San Sebastián, Spain*	Mar 15, 1991	6.10
10=	Malmö, Sweden	Aug 5, 1991	6.10

* Indoor performance

Did You Know? In little over a century, the world pole-vaulting record leaped from 3.62 m (achieved by Raymond Clapp of the US in 1898) to today's 6.14-m outdoor record.

Football Feats

LARGEST NFL STADIUMS

STADIUM/HOME TEAM	CAPACITY
1 Pontiac Silverdome, Detroit Lions	80,311
2 FedExField, Washington Redskins	80,116
3 Giants Stadium, New York Giants*	79,469
4 Arrowhead Stadium, Kansas City Chiefs	79,409
5 Mile High Stadium, Denver Broncos	76,082
6 Ralph Wilson Stadium, Buffalo Bills	75,339
7 Pro Player Stadium, Miami Dolphins	74,916
8 Sun Devil Stadium, Arizona Cardinals	73,273
9 Alltel Stadium, Jacksonville Jaguars	73,000
10 Ericsson Stadium, Carolina Panthers	72,250

* Seating reduced to 77,803 for New York Jets games

Source: National Football League

The roof of the octagonal Pontiac Silverdome is the world's largest air-supported structure.

BIGGEST WINNING MARGINS IN THE SUPER BOWL

GAME*	YEAR	MARGIN
1 San Francisco 49ers vs. Denver Broncos	1990	45
2 Chicago Bears vs. New England Patriots	1986	36
3 Dallas Cowboys vs. Buffalo Bills	1993	35
4 Washington Redskins vs. Denver Broncos	1988	32
5 Los Angeles Raiders vs. Washington Redskins	1984	29
6 Green Bay Packers vs. Kansas City Chiefs	1967	25
7 San Francisco 49ers vs. San Diego Chargers	1995	23
8 San Francisco 49ers vs. Miami Dolphins	1985	22
9 Dallas Cowboys vs. Miami Dolphins	1972	21
10= Green Bay Packers vs. Oakland Raiders	1968	19
10= New York Giants vs. Denver Broncos	1987	19

* Winners first

MOST SUCCESSFUL NFL TEAMS*

TEAM	WINS	LOSSES	PTS
1 Dallas Cowboys	5	3	13
2 San Francisco 49ers	5	0	10
3 Pittsburgh Steelers	4	1	10
4 Washington Redskins	3	2	8
5 Denver Broncos	2	4	8
6= Green Bay Packers	3	1	7
6= Oakland/L.A. Raiders	3	1	7
8 Miami Dolphins	2	3	7
9 New York Giants	2	0	4
10= Buffalo Bills	0	4	4
10= Minnesota Vikings	0	4	4

* Based on two points for a Super Bowl win and one for a loss; wins take precedence over losses in determining ranking

Source: National Football League

MOST SUCCESSFUL COACHES IN AN NFL CAREER

COACH	GAMES WON
1 Don Shula	347
2 George Halas	324
3 Tom Landry	270
4 Curly Lambeau	229
5 Chuck Noll	209
6 Chuck Knox	193
7 Dan Reeves*	175
8 Paul Brown	170
9 Bud Grant	168
10 Marv Levy	154

* Still active

Source: National Football League

ATOP COACH

Don Shula retired at the end of the 1995 season, having achieved an NFL record of coaching his team, the Miami Dolphins, to 347 wins.

Background image: PONTIAC SILVERDOME

PASSING GREAT

Jerry Rice, who joined the San Francisco 49ers in 1985, is one of the greatest-ever pass catchers and the player with the most career touchdowns in the NFL.

TOP 10 🍁
CFL PLAYERS WITH THE MOST CAREER POINTS

	PLAYER	POINTS
1	Lui Passaglia	3,811
2	Dave Ridgeway	2,374
3	Paul Osbaldiston	2,332
4	Mark McLoughlin	2,318
5	Dave Cutler	2,237
6	Trevor Kennerd	1,840
7	Bernie Ruoff	1,772
8	Terry Baker	1,540
9	Lance Chomyc	1,498
10	Gerry Organ	1,462

Source: *Canadian Football League*

TOP 10 ★
NFL PLAYERS WITH THE MOST CAREER POINTS

	PLAYER	POINTS
1	George Blanda	2,002
2	Gary Anderson*	1,948
3	Morten Andersen*	1,840
4	Norm Johnson*	1,736
5	Nick Lowery	1,711
6	Jan Stenerud	1,699
7	Eddie Murray*	1,549
8	Pat Leahy	1,470
9	Jim Turner	1,439
10	Matt Bahr	1,422

* Still active 1999 season

Source: *National Football League*

TOP 10 ★
PLAYERS WITH THE MOST PASSING YARDS IN AN NFL CAREER

	PLAYER	PASSING YARDS
1	Dan Marino*	61,243
2	John Elway	51,475
3	Warren Moon*	49,117
4	Fran Tarkenton	47,003
5	Dan Fouts	43,040
6	Joe Montana	40,551
7	Johnny Unitas	40,239
8	Dave Krieg	37,946
9	Boomer Esiason	37,920
10	Jim Kelly	35,467

* Still active 1999 season

Source: *National Football League*

TOP 10 🍁
LEADING CFL PASSERS

	PLAYER	TOTAL YARDS GAINED PASSING
1	Ron Lancaster	50,535
2	Damon Allen	45,949
3	Matt Dunnigan	43,857
4	Doug Flutie	41,355
5	Tracy Ham	40,534
6	Tom Clements	39,041
7	Kent Austin	36,030
8	Dieter Brock	34,830
9	Tom Burgess	30,308
10	Danny McManus	29,332

Source: *Canadian Football League*

TOP 10 🍁
BIGGEST WINNING MARGINS IN THE GREY CUP

	GAME*	YEAR	MARGIN
1	Queen's University vs. Regina Roughriders	1923	54
2	Hamilton Tigers vs. Toronto Parkdale	1913	42
3	Winnipeg Blue Bombers vs. Edmonton Eskimos	1990	39
4	Edmonton Eskimos vs. Hamilton Tiger-Cats	1980	38
5=	Montreal Alouettes vs. Edmonton Ekimos	1977	35
5=	Toronto Argonauts vs. Winnipeg Blue Bombers	1945	35
7=	Hamilton Tigers vs. Regina Roughriders	1928	30
7=	Winnipeg Blue Bombers vs. Hamilton Tiger-Cats	1984	30
9	Hamilton Tiger-Cats vs. Saskatchewan Roughriders	1957	25
10=	Toronto Argonauts vs. Edmonton Eksimos	1997	24
10=	Hamilton Tiger-Cats vs. Edmonton Eskimos	1986	24

* Winners first

Source: *Canadian Football League*

THE 10 LATEST ATTENDANCES OF NFL TEAMS*
(Year/attendance)

1 1999 16,206,640   **2** 1998 16,187,758   **3** 1997 15,769,193   **4** 1996 15,381,727
5 1995 15,834,468   **6** 1994 14,810,173   **7** 1993 14,781,450   **8** 1992 14,644,797
9 1991 14,654,706   **10** 1990 14,807,439

* Regular season only   Source: *NFL*

What was the top motive for murder in Canada in 1999?
see p.72 for the answer

A   Revenge
B   Anger
C   Financial gain

Athletic Achievements

FASTEST WINNING TIMES
IN THE NEW YORK CITY MARATHON

MEN

	RUNNER/COUNTRY	YEAR	TIME*
1	Juma Ikangaa, Tanzania	1989	2.08.01
2	John Kagwe, Kenya	1997	2.08.12
3	Alberto Salazar, US	1981	2.08.13
4	Steve Jones, UK	1988	2.08.20
5	John Kagwe, Kenya	1998	2.08.45
6	Rod Dixon, New Zealand	1983	2.08.59
7	Joseph Chebet, Kenya	1999	2.09.14
8	Salvador Garcia, Mexico	1991	2.09.28
9=	Alberto Salazar, US	1982	2.09.29
9=	Willie Mtolo, South Africa	1992	2.09.29

WOMEN

	RUNNER/COUNTRY	YEAR	TIME*
1	Lisa Ondieki, Australia	1992	2.24.40
2	Adriana Fernandez, Mexico	1999	2.25.06
3	Franca Fiacconi, Italy	1998	2.25.17
4	Allison Roe, New Zealand	1981*	2.25.29
5	Ingrid Kristiansen, Norway	1989	2.25.30
6	Grete Waitz, Norway	1980	2.25.41
7	Uta Pippig, Germany	1993	2.26.24
8	Grete Waitz, Norway	1983	2.27.00
9	Grete Waitz, Norway	1982	2.27.14
10	Liz McColgan, Scotland	1991	2.27.23

* In 1981–83 the circuit was 155 m (170 yd) shorter.

TOP 10 LONGEST LONG JUMPS*

(Athlete/country/year/distance in meters)

1 Mike Powell, US, 1991, 8.95 **2** Bob Beamon, US, 1968, 8.90
3 Carl Lewis, US, 1991, 8.87 **4** Robert Emmiyan, USSR, 1987, 8.86
5 = Larry Myricks, US, 1988; = Eric Walder, US, 1994, 8.74
7 Ivan Pedroso, Cuba, 1995, 8.71 **8** Kareem Streete-Thompson, US, 1994, 8.63
9 James Beckford, Jamaica, 1997, 8.62 **10** Yago Lamela,# Spain, 1999, 8.56

* Longest by each athlete only # Indoor

JUMPING AHEAD

US athlete Mike Powell's long-jump record of 8.95 m, set in Tokyo on August 30, 1991, broke Bob Beamon's record, which had stood for 23 years.

HIGHEST POLE VAULTS*

	ATHLETE/COUNTRY	YEAR	HEIGHT METERS
1	Sergey Bubka,# Ukraine	1993	6.15
2	Maxin Tarasov, Russia	1999	6.05
3	Okkert Brits, South Africa	1995	6.03
4=	Rodion Gataullin,# USSR	1989	6.02
4=	Jeff Hartwig, US	1999	6.02
6	Igor Trandenkov, Russia	1996	6.01
7=	Jeane Galfione, France	1999	6.00
7=	Tim Lobinger, Germany	1997	6.00
7=	Dmitri Markov, Belarus	1998	6.00
10	Lawrence Johnson, US	1996	5.98

* Highest by each athlete only
 # Indoor

FIRST ATHLETES TO RUN A MILE
IN UNDER FOUR MINUTES

	ATHLETE/COUNTRY	LOCATION	MIN:SEC	DATE
1	Roger Bannister, UK	Oxford	3:59.4	May 6, 1954
2	John Landy, Australia	Turku, Finland	3:57.9	Jun 21, 1954
3	Laszlo Tabori, Hungary	London	3:59.0	May 28, 1955
4=	Chris Chataway, UK	London	3:59.8	May 28, 1955
4=	Brian Hewson, UK	London	3:59.8	May 28, 1955
6	Jim Bailey, Australia	Los Angeles	3:58.6	May 5, 1956
7	Gunnar Nielsen, Denmark	Compton, US	3:59.1	Jun 1, 1956
8	Ron Delany, Ireland	Compton, US	3:59.4	Jun 1, 1956
9	Derek Ibbotson, UK	London	3:59.4	Aug 6, 1956
10	István Rózsavölgyi, Hungary	Budapest	3:59.0	Aug 26, 1956

Within a little over two years of Roger Bannister's capturing the imagination of the world by shattering the four-minute-mile barrier, the number of athletes to do so had risen to 10.

TOP 10 ★ FASTEST WOMEN*

ATHLETE/COUNTRY	YEAR	TIME
1 Florence Griffith-Joyner, US	1988	10.49
2 Marion Jones, US	1998	10.65
3 Christine Arron, France	1998	10.73
4 Merlene Ottey, Jamaica	1996	10.74
5 Evelyn Ashford, US	1984	10.76
6 Irina Privalova, Russia	1994	10.77
7 Dawn Sowell, US	1989	10.78
8 Inger Miller, US	1999	10.79
9 Marlies Göhr, East Germany	1983	10.81
10= Gail Devers, US	1992	10.82
10= Gwen Torrence, US	1994	10.82

* Based on fastest time for the 100 meters

TOP 10 ★ FASTEST MEN*

ATHLETE/COUNTRY	YEAR	TIME
1 Maurice Green, US	1999	9.79
2= Donovan Bailey, Canada	1996	9.84
2= Bruny Surin, Canada	1999	9.84
4 Leroy Burrell, US	1994	9.85
5= Ato Boldon, Trinidad	1998	9.86
5= Frank Fredericks, Namibia	1996	9.86
5= Carl Lewis, US	1991	9.86
8= Linford Christie, UK	1993	9.87
8= Obadele Thompson, Barbados	1998	9.87
10 Dennis Mitchell, US	1991	9.91

* Based on fastest time for the 100 meters

TOP 10 HIGHEST HIGH JUMPS*

(Athlete/country/year/height in meters)

1 Javier Sotomayor, Cuba, 1993, 2.45 **2** = Patrik Sjöberg, Sweden, 1987; = Carlo Thränhardt,# West Germany, 1988, 2.42 **4** Igor Paklin, USSR, 1985, 2.41 **5** = Rudolf Povarnitsyn, USSR, 1985; = Sorin Matei, Romania, 1990; = Charles Austin, US, 1991; = Hollis Conway,# US, 1991, 2.40 **9** = Zhu Jianhua, China, 1984; = Hollis Conway, US, 1989; = Dietmar Mögenburg,# West Germany, 1985; = Ralph Sonn,# Germany, 1991, 2.39

* Highest by each athlete only   # Indoor

THE 10 — LAST CANADIAN PRESS ATHLETES OF THE YEAR

MEN ATHLETE	SPORT	YEAR	WOMEN SPORT	ATHLETE
Larry Walker	Baseball	1998	Golf	Lorie Kane
Jacques Villeneuve	Auto racing	1997	Golf	Lorie Kane
Donovan Bailey	Track	1996	Cycling	Alison Sydor
Jacques Villeneuve	Auto racing	1995	Speed skating	Susan Auch
Elvis Stojko	Figure skating	1994	Biathlon	Myriam Bédard
Mario Lemieux	Hockey	1993	Skiing	Kate Pace
Mark Tewksbury	Swimming	1992	Rowing	Silken Laumann
Kurt Browning	Figure skating	1991	Rowing	Silken Laumann
Kurt Browning	Figure skating	1990	Tennis	Helen Kelesi
Wayne Gretzky	Hockey	1989	Tennis	Helen Kelesi

Source: *Canadian Press*
No "Athlete of the Year" awards were given by CP in 1999. Instead, Wayne Gretzky and Nancy Greene were each voted Athlete of the Century, and Team Canada '72 was voted Team of the Century.

FASTEST MAN ON EARTH
US sprinter Maurice Green broke the world 100-m record on June 16, 1999, trimming 5/100ths of a second off Donovan Bailey's record.

Did You Know? The marathon distance was established at the Olympics in London in 1908. It was to have been 26 miles, but 385 yards were added to ensure that the race started beneath the Royal Nursery at Windsor Castle.

Basketball Bests

TOP 10 ★
BIGGEST ARENAS IN THE NBA

ARENA/LOCATION	HOME TEAM	CAPACITY
1 The Alamodome, San Antonio, Texas	San Antonio Spurs	34,215
2 Charlotte Coliseum, Charlotte, North Carolina	Charlotte Hornets	23,799
3 The Palace of Auburn Hills, Auburn Hills, Michigan	Detroit Pistons	22,076
4 United Center, Chicago, Illinois	Chicago Bulls	21,711
5 MCI Center, Washington, DC	Washington Wizards	20,674
6 Gund Arena, Cleveland, Ohio	Cleveland Cavaliers	20,562
7 First Union Center, Philadelphia, Pennsylvania	Philadelphia 76ers	20,444
8 Continental Airlines Arena, East Rutherford, New Jersey	New Jersey Nets	20,049
9 The Rose Garden, Portland, Oregon	Portland Trailblazers	19,980
10 Delta Center, Salt Lake City, Utah	Utah Jazz	19,911

The smallest arena in the NBA is the 15,200 capacity Miami Arena, home of the Miami Heat. The largest ever NBA stadium was the Louisiana Superdome, used by The New Orleans Jazz (now the Utah Jazz) from 1975 to 1979, which was capable of holding crowds of 47,284.

Source: NBA

TOP 10 NCAA COACHES
(Coach/wins)

1 Dean Smith, 879   2 Adolph Rupp, 876   3 Jim Phelan,* 803   4 Henry Iba, 767
5 Bob Knight,* 762   6 Ed Diddle, 759   7 Phog Allen, 746   8 Norm Stewart, 731
9 Ray Meyer, 724   10 Don Haskins, 719

* Still active 1999–2000 season   Source: NCAA

TOP 10 ★
MOST SUCCESSFUL DIVISION 1 NCAA TEAMS

COLLEGE	DIVISION 1 WINS
1 Kentucky	1,765
2 North Carolina	1,753
3 Kansas	1,708
4 Duke	1,606
5 St. John's	1,602
6 Temple	1,542
7 Syracuse	1,522
8 Pennsylvania	1,495
9 Oregon State	1,481
10 Indiana	1,472

Source: NCAA

TOP 10 ★
POINT SCORERS IN AN NBA CAREER*

PLAYER	TOTAL POINTS
1 Kareem Abdul-Jabbar	38,387
2 Wilt Chamberlain	31,419
3 Karl Malone #	31,041
4 Michael Jordan	29,277
5 Moses Malone	27,409
6 Elvin Hayes	27,313
7 Oscar Robertson	26,710
8 Dominique Wilkins	26,534
9 John Havlicek	26,395
10 Hakeem Olajuwon #	25,822

* Regular season games only
# Still active at end of 1999–2000 season

Source: NBA

TOP 10 ★
NBA COACHES

COACH	GAMES WON*
1 Lenny Wilkens #	1,179
2 Pat Riley #	999
3 Bill Fitch	944
4 Red Auerbach	938
5 Dick Motta	935
6 Don Nelson #	926
7 Jack Ramsay	864
8 Cotton Fitzsimmons	832
9 Gene Shue	784
10 John MacLeod	707

* Regular season games only
# Still active 1999–2000 season
Source: NBA

TOP 10 ★
POINTS AVERAGES IN AN NBA SEASON

PLAYER/TEAM	SEASON	AVERAGE
1 Wilt Chamberlain, Philadelphia 76ers	1961–62	50.4
2 Wilt Chamberlain, San Francisco Warriors	1962–63	44.8
3 Wilt Chamberlain, Philadelphia 76ers	1960–61	38.4
4 Elgin Baylor, Los Angeles Lakers	1961–62	38.3
5 Wilt Chamberlain, Philadelphia 76ers	1959–60	37.6
6 Michael Jordan, Chicago Bulls	1986–87	37.1
7 Wilt Chamberlain, San Francisco Warriors	1963–64	36.9
8 Rick Barry, San Francisco Warriors	1966–67	35.6
9 Michael Jordan, Chicago Bulls	1987–88	35.0
10= Elgin Baylor, Los Angeles Lakers	1960–61	34.8
10= Kareem Abdul-Jabbar, Milwaukee Bucks	1971–72	34.8

Source: NBA

Did You Know? When basketball was invented by Canadian phys ed teacher James Naismith in 1891, peach baskets were used instead of hoops, and the balls had to be retrieved by ladder.

TOP 10 ATTENDANCES IN THE 1990s
(Years/total attendances for all games)

1 1995–6 20,513,218   **2** 1997–8 20,373,079
3 1996–7 20,304,629   **4** 1999–2000 20,058,536
5 1994–5 18,516,484   **6** 1993–4 17,984,014   **7** 1992–3
17,778,295   **8** 1989–90 17,368,659   **9** 1991–2 17,367,240
10 1990–1 16,876,125

Source: *NBA*

TOP 10 ★ POINTS SCORED IN THE WNBA

PLAYER/GAME	DATE	PTS
1 Cynthia Cooper, Houston *vs.* Sacramento	July 25, 1997	44
2 Cynthia Cooper, Houston *vs.* Charlotte	Aug 11, 1997	39
3 Jennifer Gillom, Phoenix *vs.* Cleveland	Aug 10, 1998	36
4 =Cynthia Cooper, Houston *vs.* Los Angeles	Aug 1, 1997	34
4 =Cynthia Cooper, Houston *vs.* Phoenix	Aug 7, 1997	34
4 =Ruthie Bolton-Holifield, Sacramento *vs.* Utah	Aug 8, 1997	34
4 =Ruthie Bolton-Holifield, Sacramento *vs.* Cleveland	Aug 12, 1997	34
4 =Cynthia Cooper, Houston *vs.* Sacramento	July 3, 1998	34
4 =Cynthia Cooper, Houston *vs.* Detroit	Aug 7, 1998	34
10 Linda Burgess, Sacramento *vs.* Utah	Aug 15, 1998	33

Source: *WNBA*

TOP 10 ★ FREE THROW PERCENTAGES

PLAYER	ATTEMPTS	BASKETS	%
1 Mark Price	2,362	2,135	90.4
2 Rick Barry	4,243	3,818	90.0
3 Calvin Murphy	3,864	3,445	89.2
4 Scott Skiles	1,741	1,548	88.9
5 Larry Bird	4,471	3,960	88.6
6 Bill Sharman	3,559	3,143	88.3
7 Reggie Miller*	5,690	5,015	88.1
8 Ricky Pierce	3,871	3,389	87.5
9 Kiki Vandeweghe	3,997	3,484	87.2
10 Jeff Malone	3,383	2,947	87.1

* Still active at end of 1999–2000 season
Source: *NBA*

TOP 10 PLAYERS WITH THE MOST CAREER ASSISTS
(Player/assists)

1 John Stockton,* 13,790   **2** Magic Johnson,
10,141   **3** Oscar Robertson, 9,887   **4** Isiah
Thomas, 9,061   **5** Mark Jackson,* 8,574
6 Maurice Cheeks, 7,392   **7** Lenny
Wilkens, 7,211   **8** Bob
Cousy, 6,995   **9** Guy
Rodgers, 6,917
10 Nate Archibald, 6,476

** Still active at end of
1999–2000 season*
Source: *NBA*

MAGIC TOUCH

*Magic (Earvin) Johnson
turned professional in
1979, becoming one of
the NBA's most
legendary players.*

TOP 10 ★ PLAYERS TO HAVE PLAYED MOST GAMES IN THE NBA AND ABA

PLAYER	GAMES PLAYED*
1 Robert Parish	1,611
2 Kareem Abdul-Jabbar	1,560
3 Moses Malone	1,455
4 Buck Williams	1,348
5 Artis Gilmore	1,329
6 Elvin Hayes	1,303
7 Caldwell Jones	1,299
8 John Havlicek	1,270
9 John Stockton #	1,258
10 Paul Silas	1,254

* Regular season only
# Still active at end of 1999–2000 season
Source: *NBA*

Combat Sports

TOP 10 OLYMPIC JUDO COUNTRIES
(Country/medals)

1 Japan, 40 **2** Soviet Union,* 27 . **3** France, 26 **4** South Korea, 25 **5** = Cuba; = Great Britain, 15 **7** Netherlands, 10 **8** = Germany #; = East Germany, 9 **10** = US; = Poland; = West Germany; = Hungary; = Brazil, 8

* Including United Team of 1992; excludes Russia since this date
 # Not including West Germany or East Germany 1968–88

FIGHTING FIT

Judo was first introduced as an Olympic sport for men at the 1964 Tokyo Games, and for women in 1992. Min Soo Kim, from South Korea, here wins bronze at the Olympic Games, Atlanta, 1996.

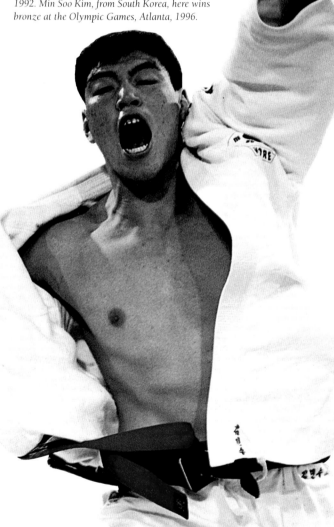

TOP 10 ★
OLYMPIC WRESTLING COUNTRIES/ GRECO-ROMAN

	COUNTRY	GOLD	SILVER	BRONZE	TOTAL
1	Soviet Union*	37	19	13	69
2	Finland	19	21	18	58
3	Sweden	19	16	19	54
4	Hungary	15	9	11	35
5	Bulgaria	8	14	7	29
6	Romania	6	8	13	27
7	Germany	4	13	8	25
8	Poland	5	8	6	19
9	Italy	5	4	9	18
10	Turkey	10	4	3	17

* Including United Team of 1992; excludes Russia since this date

TOP 10 ★
OLYMPIC WRESTLING COUNTRIES/FREESTYLE

	COUNTRY	GOLD	SILVER	BRONZE	TOTAL
1	US	44	33	22	99
2	Soviet Union*	31	17	15	63
3	Turkey	16	11	6	33
4	=Japan	16	9	7	32
4	=Bulgaria	7	16	9	32
6	Sweden	8	10	8	26
7	=Finland	8	7	10	25
7	=Iran	4	9	12	25
9	=Great Britain	3	4	10	17
9	=Hungary	4	7	6	17

* Including United Team of 1992; excludes Russia since this date

TOP 10 WRESTLING WEIGHT DIVISIONS
(Weight/limit kg/lb)

1 Heavyweight plus, over 100/over 220 **2** Heavyweight, 100/220 **3** Light-heavyweight, 90/198 **4** Middleweight, 82/181 **5** Welterweight, 74/163 **6** Lightweight, 68/150 **7** Featherweight, 62/137 **8** Bantamweight, 57/126 **9** Flyweight, 52/115 **10** Light-flyweight, 48/106

TOP 10 ★
HEAVIEST BOXING WEIGHT DIVISIONS

	WEIGHT	KG	LIMIT LB
1	Heavyweight	over 86	over 190
2	Cruiserweight	86	190
3	Light-heavyweight	79	175
4	Super-middleweight	76	168
5	Middleweight	73	160
6	Junior-middleweight/ Super-welterweight	70	154
7	Welterweight	67	147
8	Junior-welterweight/ Super-lightweight	65	140
9	Lightweight	61	135
10	Junior-lightweight/ Super-featherweight	59	130

TOP 10 ★
BOXERS WITH THE MOST KNOCKOUTS IN A CAREER

	BOXER*	CAREER	KOS
1	Archie Moore	1936–63	129
2	Young Stribling	1921–63	126
3	Billy Bird	1920–48	125
4	Sam Langford	1902–26	116
5	George Odwell	1930–45	114
6	Sugar Ray Robinson	1940–65	110
7	Sandy Saddler	1944–65	103
8	Henry Armstrong	1931–45	100
9	Jimmy Wilde	1911–23	99
10	Len Wickwar	1928–47	93

* All from the US except Jimmy Wilde, who was Welsh

TOP 10 ★
OLYMPIC FENCING COUNTRIES

	COUNTRY	MEDALS GOLD	SILVER	BRONZE	TOTAL
1	France	38	34	32	104
2	Italy	37	36	24	97
3	Hungary	32	20	26	78
4	Soviet Union*	19	17	18	54
5=	Poland	4	7	9	19
5=	US	2	6	11	19
7	Germany	6	6	6	18
8	West Germany#	7	8	1	16
9	Belgium	5	3	5	13
10	Romania	2	3	6	11

* Including United Team of 1992; excludes Russia since this date

\# Not including West Germany or East Germany 1968–88

THE 10 LATEST WORLD HEAVYWEIGHT BOXING CHAMPIONS*

(Years/boxer)

1 1999–2000, Lennox Lewis **2** 1997–99, Evander Holyfield **3** 1996–97, Mike Tyson
4 1995–96, Bruce Seldon **5** 1994–95, George Foreman **6** 1994, Michael Moorer
7 1993–94, Evander Holyfield **8** 1992–93, Riddick Bowe **9** 1990–92, Evander Holyfield
10 1990, James Douglas * WBA only

TOP 10 ★
FASTEST KNOCKOUTS IN WORLD TITLE FIGHTS

	FIGHT (WINNERS FIRST)	WEIGHT	DATE	SEC*
1	Gerald McClellan vs. Jay Bell	Middleweight	Aug 7, 1993	20
2	James Warring vs. James Pritchard	Cruiserweight	Sep 6, 1991	24
3	Lloyd Honeyghan vs. Gene Hatcher	Welterweight	Aug 30, 1987	45
4	Mark Breland vs. Lee Seung-soon	Welterweight	Feb 4, 1989	54
5	Emile Pladner vs. Frankie Genaro	Flyweight	Mar 2, 1929	58
6=	Jackie Paterson vs. Peter Kane	Flyweight	Jun 19, 1943	61
6=	Bobby Czyz vs. David Sears	Light-heavyweight	Dec 26, 1986	61
8	Michael Dokes vs. Mike Weaver	Heavyweight	Dec 10, 1982	63
9	Tony Canzoneri vs. Al Singer	Lightweight	Nov 14, 1930	66
10	Marvin Hagler vs. Caveman Lee	Middleweight	Mar 7, 1982	67

* Duration of fight

WORLD CHAMPION
After a much-disputed previous contest, Lennox Lewis finally defeated Evander Holyfield in Las Vegas on December 12, 1999, to take the World Heavyweight title.

Baseball Teams

TOP 10 ★
AVERAGE ATTENDANCES IN 1999

	TEAM	ATTENDANCE
1	Colorado Rockies	42,976
2	Baltimore Orioles	42,901
3	Cleveland Indians	42,820
4	St. Louis Cardinals	40,960
5	New York Yankees	40,662
6	Atlanta Braves	40,554
7	Los Angeles Dodgers	38,247
8	Arizona Diamondbacks	37,234
9	Chicago Cubs	36,075
10	Seattle Mariners	35,999

Source: *Major League Baseball*

TOP 10 ★
BIGGEST SINGLE GAME WINS IN THE WORLD SERIES

	TEAMS (WINNERS FIRST)/GAME	DATE	SCORE
1	New York Yankees vs. New York Giants (Game 2)	Oct 2, 1936	18–4
2	New York Yankees vs. Pittsburgh Pirates (Game 2)	Oct 6, 1960	16–3
3=	New York Yankees vs. New York Giants (Game 5)	Oct 9, 1951	13–1
3=	New York Yankees vs. Pittsburgh Pirates (Game 6)	Oct 12, 1960	12–0
3=	Detroit Tigers vs. St. Louis Cardinals (Game 6)	Oct 9, 1968	13–1
3=	New York Yankees vs. Milwaukee Brewers (Game 6)	Oct 19, 1982	13–1
7=	New York Yankees vs. Philadelphia Athletics (Game 6)	Oct 26, 1911	13–2
7=	Atlanta Braves vs. New York Yankees (Game 1)	Oct 20, 1996	12–1
7=	St. Louis Cardinals vs. Detroit Tigers (Game 7)	Oct 9, 1934	11–0
7=	Chicago White Sox vs. Los Angeles Dodgers (Game 1)	Oct 1, 1959	11–0
7=	Kansas City Royals vs. St. Louis Cardinals (Game 7)	Oct 27, 1985	11–0

Source: *Major League Baseball*

TOP 10 ★
TEAMS WITH THE MOST WORLD SERIES WINS

	TEAM*	WINS
1	New York Yankees	25
2=	St. Louis Cardinals	9
2=	Philadelphia/Kansas City/Oakland Athletics	9
4	Brooklyn/Los Angeles Dodgers	6
5=	New York/San Francisco Giants	5
5=	Boston Red Sox	5
5=	Cincinnati Reds	5
5=	Pittsburgh Pirates	5
9	Detroit Tigers	4
10=	Boston/Milwaukee/Atlanta Braves	3
10=	St. Louis/Baltimore Orioles	3
10=	Washington Senators/Minnesota Twins	3

* Teams separated by / indicate changes of franchise and are regarded as the same team for Major League record purposes

Source: *Major League Baseball*

Major League Baseball started in the United States with the forming of the National League in 1876. The rival American League was started in 1901, and two years later Pittsburgh, champion of the National League, invited American League champion Boston to take part in a best-of-nine games series to establish the "real" champion. Boston won 5–3. The following year the National League champion, New York, refused to play Boston and there was no World Series, but it was resumed in 1905.

TOP 10 ★
BASEBALL TEAM PAYROLLS, 1999

	TEAM	AVERAGE SALARY (US$)	TOTAL PAYROLL (US$)
1	New York Yankees	3,217,914	91,990,955
2	Texas Rangers	2,813,666	80,801,598
3	Atlanta Braves	2,491,388	79,256,599
4	Los Angeles Dodgers	2,413,389	76,607,247
5	Baltimore Orioles	2,495,937	75,443,363
6	Cleveland Indians	2,166,075	73,531,692
7	Boston Red Sox	2,218,787	72,330,656
8	New York Mets	2,199,903	71,510,523
9	Arizona Diamondbacks	2,267,995	70,046,818
10	Houston Astros	1,722,192	56,389,000

Source: *Major League Baseball Commissioner's Office*

THE 10 LAST YEARS OF MAJOR LEAGUE PLAYERS' SALARIES

(Year/average salary in US$)

❶ 1999, 1,720,050 ❷ 1998, 1,441,406 ❸ 1997, 1,383,578
❹ 1996, 1,176,967 ❺ 1995, 1,071,029 ❻ 1994, 1,188,679
❼ 1993, 1,120,254 ❽ 1992, 1,084,408 ❾ 1991, 891,188
❿ 1990, 578,930

Source: *Associated Press*

Did You Know? In 1869–70 the Cincinnati Red Stockings became the first baseball team to receive a regular salary. They received payments of US$800, rising to US$1,400 for the shortstop.

TOP 10 ★
OLDEST STADIUMS IN MAJOR LEAGUE BASEBALL

	STADIUM	HOME CLUB	FIRST GAME
1	Fenway Park	Boston Red Sox	Apr 20, 1912
2	Wrigley Field	Chicago Cubs	Apr 23, 1914
3	Yankee Stadium	New York Yankees	Apr 18, 1923
4	Dodger Stadium	Los Angeles Dodgers	Apr 10, 1962
5	Shea Stadium	New York Mets	Apr 17, 1964
6	Edison International Field of Anaheim*	Anaheim Angels	Apr 19, 1966
7	Busch Stadium	St. Louis Cardinals	May 12, 1966
8	Qualcomm Stadium#	San Diego Padres	Apr 5, 1968
9	Network Associates Coliseum+	Oakland Athletics	Apr 17, 1968
10	Cinergy Field	Cincinnati Reds	June 30, 1970

* Formerly known as Anaheim Stadium
# Formerly known as Jack Murphy Stadium
+ Formerly known as Oakland-Alameda County Coliseum
Source: Major League Baseball

TOP 10 ★
LAST WINNERS OF THE WORLD SERIES

YEAR*	WINNER/LEAGUE#	LOSER/LEAGUE#	SCORE
1999	New York, AL	Atlanta, NL	4–0
1998	New York, AL	San Diego, NL	4–0
1997	Florida, NL	Cleveland, AL	4–3
1996	New York, AL	Atlanta, NL	4–2
1995	Atlanta, NL	Cleveland, AL	4–2
1993	Toronto, AL	Philadelphia, NL	4–2
1992	Toronto, AL	Atlanta, NL	4–2
1991	Minnesota, AL	Atlanta, NL	4–2
1990	Cincinnati, NL	Oakland, AL	4–0
1989	Oakland, AL	San Francisco, NL	4–0

* The 1994 event was canceled due to a players' strike
# AL = American League
  NL = National League

TOP 10 ★
NEWEST MAJOR LEAGUE TEAMS

	TEAM	LEAGUE*	1ST SEASON
1=	Arizona Diamondbacks	NL	1998
1=	Tampa Bay Devil Rays	AL	1998
3=	Colorado Rockies	NL	1993
3=	Florida Marlins	NL	1993
5=	Seattle Mariners	AL	1977
5=	Toronto Blue Jays	AL	1977
7=	Kansas City Royals	AL	1969
7=	Montreal Expos	NL	1969
7=	Seattle Pilots/ Milwaukee Brewers	AL	1969
10=	Houston Astros	NL	1962
10=	New York Mets	NL	1962

* AL = American League
  NL = National League
Source: Major League Baseball

TOP 10 ★
LARGEST MAJOR LEAGUE BALLPARKS*

	STADIUM	HOME TEAM	CAPACITY
1	Veterans Stadium	Philadelphia Phillies	62,411
2	Qualcomm Stadium	San Diego Padres	59,960
3	Yankee Stadium	New York Yankees	57,746
4	Dodger Stadium	Los Angeles Dodgers	56,000
5	Shea Stadium	New York Mets	55,775
6	Cinergy Field	Cincinnati Reds	52,953
7	SkyDome	Toronto Blue Jays	50,516
8	Coors Field	Colorado Rockies	50,249
9	Turner Field	Atlanta Braves	50,062
10	Busch Stadium	St. Louis Cardinals	49,738

* By capacity
Source: Major League Baseball

Stadium capacities vary constantly, some being adjusted according to the event: Veterans Stadium, for example, holds fewer for baseball games than for football games.

Baseball Stars

PLAYERS WITH THE MOST CAREER STRIKEOUTS

PLAYER	STRIKEOUTS
1 Nolan Ryan	5,714
2 Steve Carlton	4,136
3 Bert Blyleven	3,701
4 Tom Seaver	3,640
5 Don Sutton	3,574
6 Gaylord Perry	3,534
7 Walter Johnson	3,508
8 Phil Niekro	3,342
9 Roger Clemens*	3,316
10 Ferguson Jenkins	3,192

* Still active in 1999 season

Source: *Major League Baseball*

Nolan Ryan was known as the "Babe Ruth of strikeout pitchers," pitching faster (a record 101 mph) and longer (27 seasons – 1966 and 1968–93) than any previous player.

PLAYERS WITH THE HIGHEST CAREER BATTING AVERAGES

PLAYER	AT BAT	HITS	AVERAGE*
1 Ty Cobb	11,434	4,189	.366
2 Rogers Hornsby	8,173	2,930	.358
3 Joe Jackson	4,981	1,772	.356
4 Ed Delahanty	7,505	2,597	.346
5 Tris Speaker	10,195	3,514	.345
6 = Billy Hamilton	6,268	2,158	.344
6 = Ted Williams	7,706	2,654	.344
8 = Dan Brouthers	6,711	2,296	.342
8 = Harry Heilmann	7,787	2,660	.342
8 = Babe Ruth	8,399	2,873	.342

* Calculated by dividing the number of hits by the number of times a batter was at bat

Source: *Major League Baseball*

Second only to the legendary Ty Cobb, Rogers Hornsby stands as the best second-hitting baseman of all time, with an average of over .400 in a five-year period.

PLAYERS WITH THE MOST RUNS IN A CAREER*

PLAYER	RUNS
1 Ty Cobb	2,245
2 = Babe Ruth	2,174
2 = Hank Aaron	2,174
4 Pete Rose	2,165
5 Rickey Henderson#	2,103
6 Willie Mays	2,062
7 Stan Musial	1,949
8 Lou Gehrig	1,888
9 Tris Speaker	1,882
10 Mel Ott	1,859

* Regular season only, excluding World Series
# Still active in 1999 season

Source: *Major League Baseball*

Ty Cobb is also the only player ever to collect six hits in six at bats and hit three home runs in the same game, which he achieved on May 5, 1925, helping the Detroit Tigers to a 14–8 win over the St. Louis Browns.

PLAYERS WITH THE MOST CONSECUTIVE GAMES PLAYED

PLAYER	GAMES
1 Cal Ripken, Jr.	2,600
2 Lou Gehrig	2,130
3 Everett Scott	1,307
4 Steve Garvey	1,207
5 Billy Williams	1,117
6 Joe Sewell	1,103
7 Stan Musial	895
8 Eddie Yost	829
9 Gus Suhr	822
10 Nellie Fox	798

Source: *Major League Baseball*

Cal Ripken took himself out of the starting lineup on September 21, 1998, in a game between the Orioles and the Yankees, having played in every game since May 30, 1982.

PLAYERS WHO PLAYED THE MOST GAMES IN A CAREER

PLAYER	GAMES
1 Pete Rose	3,562
2 Carl Yastrzemski	3,308
3 Hank Aaron	3,298
4 Ty Cobb	3,034
5 = Stan Musial	3,026
5 = Eddie Murray	3,026
7 Willie Mays	2,992
8 Dave Winfield	2,973
9 Rusty Staub	2,951
10 Brooks Robinson	2,896

Source: *Major League Baseball*

Pete Rose is the only player to appear in over 500 games in five different positions: he was at first base in 939 games, second in 628, third in 634, left field in 671, and right field in 595.

PITCHERS WITH THE MOST CAREER WINS

PLAYER	WINS
1 Cy Young	509
2 Walter Johnson	417
3 = Grover Alexander	373
3 = Christy Mathewson	373
5 Warren Spahn	363
6 = Kid Nichols	361
6 = Pud Galvin	361
8 Tim Keefe	344
9 Steve Carlton	329
10 = Eddie Plank	326
10 = John Clarkson	326

Source: *Major League Baseball*

In the 1925 season, Walter Johnson became the only pitcher to win 20 games and achieve a batting average for the season of 0.433 in 97 at bats – the highest of any pitcher in baseball history.

Did You Know? The first Major League baseball player killed in a game was Raymond Chapman of the Cleveland Indians, struck by a pitch thrown by New York Yankees' Carl Mays on August 16, 1920.

TOP 10 ★
HIGHEST PAID PLAYERS IN MAJOR LEAGUE BASEBALL, 1999

	PLAYER	TEAM	EARNINGS (US$)
1	Albert Belle	Baltimore Orioles	11,949,794
2	Pedro Martinez	Boston Red Sox	11,250,000
3	Kevin Brown	Los Angeles Dodgers	10,714,286
4	Greg Maddux	Atlanta Braves	10,600,000
5	Gary Sheffield	Los Angeles Dodgers	9,936,667
6	Bernie Williams	New York Yankees	9,857,143
7	Randy Johnson	Arizona Diamondbacks	9,650,000
8	David Cone	New York Yankees	9,500,000
9	Barry Bonds	San Francisco Giants	9,381,057
10	Mark McGwire	St. Louis Cardinals	9,308,667

The median salary for the 1999 season was US$495,000, up from US$427,500 in 1998.

Source: *Associated Press*

THE 10 ★
FIRST PITCHERS TO THROW PERFECT GAMES

	PLAYER	MATCH	DATE
1	Lee Richmond	Worcester vs. Cleveland	Jun 12, 1880
2	Monte Ward	Providence vs. Buffalo	Jun 17, 1880
3	Cy Young	Boston vs. Philadelphia	May 5, 1904
4	Addie Joss	Cleveland vs. Chicago	Oct 2, 1908
5	Charlie Robertson	Chicago vs. Detroit	Apr 30, 1922
6	Don Larsen*	New York vs. Brooklyn	Oct 8, 1956
7	Jim Bunning	Philadelphia vs. New York	Jun 21, 1964
8	Sandy Koufax	Los Angeles vs. Chicago	Sep 9, 1965
9	Catfish Hunter	Oakland vs. Minnesota	May 8, 1968
10	Len Barker	Cleveland vs. Toronto	May 15, 1981

* *Larsen's perfect game was, uniquely, in the World Series*

Fourteen pitchers have thrown perfect games; that is, they have pitched in all nine innings, dismissing 27 opposing batters, and without conceding a run. The last player to pitch a perfect nine innings was Kenny Rogers, for Texas against California, on July 28, 1994.

Source: *Major League Baseball*

TOP 10 ★
PLAYERS MOST AT BAT IN A CAREER

	PLAYER	AT BAT
1	Pete Rose	14,053
3	Hank Aaron	12.364
3	Carl Yastrzemski	11,988
4	Ty Cobb	11,434
5	Eddie Murray	11,336
6	Robin Yount	11,008
7	Dave Winfield	11,003
8	Stan Musial	10,906
9	Willie Mays	10,881
10	Paul Molitor	10,835

As well as his appearance in this roll of fame, Hank Aaron collected more bases than any other hitter in baseball history, overtaking Stan Musial's previous record of 6,134 in 1972, and going on to reach 6,856 in 1976.

TOP 10 ★
LOWEST EARNED RUN AVERAGES IN A CAREER

	PLAYER	EARNED RUN AVERAGES
1	Ed Walsh	1.82
2	Addie Joss	1.89
3	Three Finger Brown	2.06
4	John Ward	2.10
5	Christy Mathewson	2.13
6	Rube Waddell	2.16
7	Walter Johnson	2.17
8	Orval Overall	2.23
9	Tommy Bond	2.25
10	Ed Reulbach	2.28

Source: *Major League Baseball*

Although Addie Joss died in 1911 at the age of 31, he had gained his place in this list and also the distinction of being the only pitcher to achieve two non-hitters against the same team, playing for the Cleveland Indians against the Chicago White Sox on October 2, 1908, and April 20, 1910.

THE 10 ★
FIRST PLAYERS TO HIT FOUR HOME RUNS IN ONE GAME

	PLAYER	CLUB	DATE
1	Bobby Lowe	Boston	May 30, 1884
2	Ed Delahanty	Philadelphia	Jul 13, 1896
3	Lou Gehrig	New York	Jun 3, 1932
4	Chuck Klein	Philadelphia	Jul 10, 1936
5	Pat Seerey	Chicago	Jul 18, 1948
6	Gil Hodges	Brooklyn	Aug 31, 1950
7	Joe Adcock	Milwaukee	Jul 31, 1954
8	Rocky Colavito	Cleveland	Jun 10, 1959
9	Willie Mays	San Francisco	Apr 30, 1961
10	Mike Schmidt	Philadelphia	Apr 17, 1976

The only other players to score four homers in one game are Bob Horner, who did so for Atlanta on July 6, 1986, and Mark Whitten, for St. Louis on September 7, 1993.

BRAZIL'S 100th GOAL
Pelé celebrates not only the first goal of the 1970 World Cup Final against Italy, but also his country's 100th World Cup goal.

TOP 10 ★
HIGHEST-SCORING WORLD CUP FINALS

	YEAR	GAMES	GOALS	AVERAGE PER GAME
1	1954	26	140	5.38
2	1938	18	84	4.66
3	1934	17	70	4.11
4	1950	22	88	4.00
5	1930	18	70	3.88
6	1958	35	126	3.60
7	1970	32	95	2.96
8	1982	52	146	2.81
9=	1962	32	89	2.78
9=	1966	32	89	2.78

The lowest-scoring World Cup was Italia '90, which produced just 115 goals from 52 matches at an average of 2.21 per game. The 1994 final between Brazil and Italy was the first World Cup final to fail to produce a goal, with Brazil winning 3–2 on penalties.

TOP 10 COUNTRIES WITH THE MOST PLAYERS SENT OFF IN THE FINAL STAGES OF THE WORLD CUP
(Country/dismissals)

1 = Brazil; = Argentina, 8 **3** = Uruguay; = Cameroon, 6 **5** = Germany/West Germany; = Hungary, 5 **7** = Czechoslovakia; = Holland; = Italy; = Mexico, 4

A total of 97 players have received their marching orders in the final stages of the World Cup since 1930. The South American nations account for 27 of them. Brazil, Czechoslovakia, Denmark, Hungary, and South Africa have each had three players sent off in a single game – Brazil twice (1938 and 1954).

TOP 10 ★
WORLD CUP ATTENDANCES

	MATCH (WINNERS FIRST)	VENUE	YEAR	ATTENDANCE
1	Brazil vs. Uruguay	Rio de Janeiro*	1950	199,854
2	Brazil vs. Spain	Rio de Janeiro	1950	152,772
3	Brazil vs. Yugoslavia	Rio de Janeiro	1950	142,409
4	Brazil vs. Sweden	Rio de Janeiro	1950	138,886
5	Mexico vs. Paraguay	Mexico City	1986	114,600
6	Argentina vs. West Germany	Mexico City*	1986	114,590
7=	Mexico vs. Bulgaria	Mexico City	1986	114,580
7=	Argentina vs. England	Mexico City	1986	114,580
9	Argentina vs. Belgium	Mexico City	1986	110,420
10	Mexico vs. Belgium	Mexico City	1986	110,000

*Final tie

The biggest crowd outside Mexico or Brazil was that of 98,270 at Wembley Stadium in 1966 for England's game against France. The attendance for the Brazil–Uruguay final in 1950 is the world's highest for a soccer match.

TOP 10 ★
COUNTRIES IN THE WORLD CUP*

	COUNTRY	WIN	R/U	3RD	4TH	TOTAL
1	Brazil	4	2	2	1	27
2	Germany/West Germany	3	3	2	1	26
3	Italy	3	2	1	1	21
4	Argentina	2	2	–	–	14
5	Uruguay	2	–	–	2	10
6	France	1	–	2	1	9
7	Sweden	–	1	2	1	8
8	Holland	–	2	–	1	7
9=	Czechoslovakia	–	2	–	–	6
9=	Hungary	–	2	–	–	6

* Based on 4 points for winning the tournament, 3 points for runner-up, 2 points for 3rd place, and 1 point for 4th; up to and including the 1998 World Cup

Did You Know? When Daniel Xuereb of France played in the 1986 finals, it meant that every letter of the alphabet had been used in players' last names in the World Cup.

TOP 10 ★
EUROPEAN CUP WINNERS

COUNTRY	YEARS	WINS*
1 =England	1968–99	9
1 =Italy	1961–96	9
3 Spain	1956–98	8
4 Holland	1970–95	6
5 Germany	1974–97	5
6 Portugal	1961–87	3
7 =France	1993	1
7 =Romania	1986	1
7 =Scotland	1967	1
7 =Yugoslavia	1991	1

* Of first and last win

The European Cup, now known as the European Champions' League Cup, has been competed for annually since 1956. It was won in that year, and the next four, by Real Madrid (who also won it in 1966 and 1998) – a total of seven times. Italy's AC Milan is their only close competitor, with five wins, while Ajax and Liverpool have each won the Cup on four occasions.

INTERNATIONAL STAR
Lothar Matthäus, Germany's World Cup-winning captain and European Footballer of the Year in 1990, has played for his country on 143 occasions. As a still-active player, he may yet improve on this figure.

TOP 10 ★
RICHEST SOCCER TEAMS

CLUB/COUNTRY	INCOME (£ STERLING)
1 Manchester United, England	87,939,000
2 Barcelona, Spain	58,862,000
3 Real Madrid, Spain	55,659,000
4 Juventus, Italy	53,223,000
5 Bayern Munich, Germany	51,619,000
6 AC Milan, Italy	47,480,000
7 Borussia Dortmund, Germany	42,199,000
8 Newcastle United, England	41,134,000
9 Liverpool, England	39,153,000
10 Inter Milan, Italy	39,071,000

A survey conducted by accountants Deloitte & Touche and football magazine *FourFourTwo* compared incomes of the world's top soccer teams during the 1997/8 season. It revealed the extent to which soccer has become a major business enterprise, with many teams generating considerably more revenue from commercial activities such as the sale of merchandise and income from TV rights than they receive from admissions to matches.

TOP 10 ★
EUROPEAN TEAMS WITH THE MOST DOMESTIC LEAGUE TITLES

CLUB/COUNTRY	TITLES
1 Glasgow Rangers, Scotland	48
2 Linfield, Northern Ireland	42
3 Glasgow Celtic, Scotland	36
4 Rapid Vienna, Austria*	31
5 Benfica, Portugal	30
6 =CSKA Sofia, Bulgaria	28
6 =Olympiakos, Greece	28
8 =Ajax, Holland	27
8 =Real Madrid, Spain	27
10 =Ferencvaros, Hungary	26
10 =Jeunesse Esch, Luxembourg	26

* Rapid Vienna also won one German League title, in 1941

UNITED EFFORT
Manchester United confirmed their status as the world's richest team in 1999, and also captured the unique triple of League, Cup, and European Champions' League.

TOP 10 ★
MOST CAPPED INTERNATIONAL PLAYERS

PLAYER/COUNTRY	YEARS	CAPS
1 =Thomas Ravelli, Sweden	1981–97	143
1 =Lothar Matthäus,* West Germany/Germany	1980–99	143
3 Majed Abdullah, Saudi Arabia	1978–94	140
4 Claudio Suarez,* Mexico	1982–99	131
5 Marcelo Balboa,* US	1988–98	127
6 Andoni Zubizarreta, Spain	1985–98	126
7 Peter Shilton, England	1970–90	125
8 Masami Ihara,* Japan	1988–99	123
9 =Pat Jennings, Northern Ireland	1964–86	119
9 =Gheorghe Hagi,* Romania	1983–99	119
9 =Cobi Jones,* US	1982-99	119

* Still active in 1999

Cycling Champions

TOP 10 ★ FASTEST WORLD CHAMPIONSHIP RACES OF ALL TIME

	RIDER/COUNTRY	BIKE*	YEAR	AVERAGE SPEED KM/H	MPH
1	Barry Sheene, UK	Suzuki	1977	217.37	135.07
2	John Williams, UK	Suzuki	1976	214.83	133.49
3	Phil Read, UK	MV Agusta	1975	214.40	133.22
4	Wil Hartog, Holland	Suzuki	1978	213.88	132.90
5	Phil Read, UK	MV Agusta	1974	212.41	131.98
6	Giacomo Agostini, Italy	MV Agusta	1973	206.81	128.51
7	Walter Villa, Italy	Harley-Davidson	1977	204.43	127.03
8	Walter Villa, Italy	Harley-Davidson	1976	202.90	126.08
9	Giacomo Agostini, Italy	MV Agusta	1969	202.53	125.85
10	Kevin Schwartz, US	Suzuki	1991	201.72	125.34

500 cc except for Nos. 7 and 8, which were 250 cc

All races except for No. 10 were during the Belgian Grand Prix at the Spa-Francorchamps circuit. No. 10 was during the German Grand Prix at Hockenheim. The World Championships were first held in 1949, under the aegis of the Féderation Internationale Motocycliste, when R. Leslie Graham (UK) won the 500 cc class on an AJS.

TOP 10 ★ FASTEST WINNING SPEEDS OF THE DAYTONA 200

	RIDER/COUNTRY*	BIKE	YEAR	AVERAGE SPEED KM/H	MPH
1	Miguel Duhamel, Canada	Honda	1999	182.61	113.46
2	Kenny Roberts	Yamaha	1984	182.08	113.14
3	Kenny Roberts	Yamaha	1983	178.52	110.93
4	Graeme Crosby, New Zealand	Yamaha	1982	175.58	109.10
5	Steve Baker	Yamaha	1977	175.18	108.85
6	Johnny Cecotto, Venezuela	Yamaha	1976	175.05	108.77
7	Dale Singleton	Yamaha	1981	174.65	108.52
8	Kenny Roberts	Yamaha	1978	174.41	108.37
9	Kevin Schwartz	Suzuki	1988	173.49	107.80
10	Dale Singleton	Yamaha	1979	173.31	107.69

* From the US unless otherwise stated

The Daytona 200, which was first held in 1937, forms a round in the AMA (American Motorcyclist Association) Grand National Dirt Track series. It is raced over 57 laps of the 5.73-km (3.56-mile) Daytona International Speedway. The other non-US winners have been: Billy Matthews (Canada), Jaarno Saarinen (Finland), Giacomo Agostini (Italy), and Patrick Pons (France).

SUPERBIKE CHAMPION
British motorcycle legend Carl Fogarty (b. 1966) won his first Grand Prix in 1986. Up to the 2000 season, he had won a record 59 Superbike events.

THE 10 ★ LATEST WORLD CHAMPION SUPERBIKE RIDERS

YEAR	RIDER/COUNTRY	BIKE
1999	Carl Fogarty, UK	Ducati
1998	Carl Fogarty, UK	Ducati
1997	John Kocinski, US	Honda
1996	Troy Corser, Australia	Ducati
1995	Carl Fogarty, UK	Ducati
1994	Carl Fogarty, UK	Ducati
1993	Scott Russell, US	Kawasaki
1992	Doug Polen, US	Ducati
1991	Doug Polen, US	Ducati
1990	Raymond Roche, France	Ducati

TOP 10 ★ MOTORCYCLISTS WITH THE MOST WORLD TITLES

	RIDER/COUNTRY	YEARS	TITLES
1	Giacomo Agostini, Italy	1966–75	15
2	Angel Nieto, Spain	1969–84	13
3=	Carlo Ubbiali, Italy	1951–60	9
3=	Mike Hailwood, UK	1961–67	9
5=	John Surtees, UK	1956–60	7
5=	Phil Read, UK	1964–74	7
7	Geoff Duke, UK	1951–55	6
7=	Jim Redman, Southern Rhodesia	1962–65	6
7=	Klaus Enders, W. Germany	1967–74	6
10	Anton Mang, W. Germany	1980–87	5

TOP 10 ★ RIDERS WITH THE MOST GRAND PRIX RACE WINS

RIDER/COUNTRY	YEARS	RACE WINS
1 Giacomo Agostini, Italy	1965–76	122
2 Angel Nieto, Spain	1969–85	90
3 Mike Hailwood, UK	1959–67	76
4 Rolf Biland, Switzerland	1975–90	56
5 Mick Doohan, Australia	1990–98	54
6 Phil Read, UK	1961–75	52
7 Jim Redman, Southern Rhodesia	1961–66	45
8 Anton Mang, West Germany	1976–88	42
9 Carlo Ubbiali, Italy	1950–60	39
10 John Surtees, UK	1955–60	38

TOP 10 ★ OLYMPIC CYCLING COUNTRIES

COUNTRY	MEDALS			
	GOLD	SILVER	BRONZE	TOTAL
1 France	32	19	22	73
2 Italy	32	15	6	53
3 Great Britain	9	21	16	46
4 US	11	13	16	40
5 Netherlands	10	14	7	31
6 Germany*	8	9	9	26
7 Australia	6	11	8	25
8 Soviet Union #	11	4	9	24
9 Belgium	6	6	10	22
10 Denmark	6	6	10	21

* Not including West Germany or East Germany 1968–88

Including United Team of 1992, exludes Russia since

TOP 10 500 cc WORLD CHAMPIONSHIPS RIDERS, 1999

(Rider/country/points)

1 Alex Criville, Spain, 267 **2** Kenny Roberts, US, 220 **3** Tadayuki Okada, Japan, 211 **4** Max Biaggi, Italy, 194 **5** Sete Gibernau, Spain, 165 **6** Norick Abe, Japan, 136 **7** Carlos Checa, Spain, 125 **8** John Kocinski, US, 115 **9** Alex Barros, Brazil, 110 **10** Tetsuya Harada, Japan, 104

TOP 10 ★ TOUR DE FRANCE WINNERS

RIDER/COUNTRY	WINS
1= Jacques Anquetil, France	5
1= Eddy Merckx, Belgium	5
1= Bernard Hinault, France	5
1= Miguel Indurain, Spain	5
5= Philippe Thys, Belgium	3
5= Louison Bobet, France	3
5= Greg LeMond, US	3
8= Lucien Petit-Breton, France	2
8= Firmin Lambot, Belgium	2
8= Ottavio Bottecchia, Italy	2
8= Nicholas Frantz, Luxembourg	2
8= André Leducq, France	2
8= Antonin Magne, France	2
8= Gino Bartali, Italy	2
8= Sylvere Maës, Belgium	2
8= Fausto Coppi, Italy	2
8= Bernard Thevenet, France	2
8= Laurent Fignon, France	2

TOUR DE FORCE

The 1999 Tour de France approaches the Eiffel Tower. The world's foremost cycle event, the Tour de France was first contested in 1903.

Auto Racing

DRIVERS WITH THE MOST WINSTON CUP WINS

DRIVER*/YEARS		WINS
1	Richard Petty, 1958–92	200
2	David Pearson, 1960–86	105
3 =	Bobby Allison, 1975–88	84
3 =	Darrell Waltrip,# 1975–92	84
5	Cale Yarborough, 1957–88	83
6	Dale Earnhardt,# 1979–99	74
7	Lee Petty, 1949–64	54
8 =	Ned Jarrett, 1953–66	50
8 =	Junior Johnson, 1953–66	50
10 =	Rusty Wallace,# 1986–99	49
10 =	Jeff Gordon,# 1994–99	49

* All from the US
# Still driving at the end of the 1999 season
Source: NASCAR

The Winston Cup is a season-long series of races organized by the National Association of Stock Car Auto Racing, Inc. (NASCAR). Races, which take place over enclosed circuits such as Daytona speedway, are among the most popular motor races in the US. The series started in 1949 (when it was won by Red Byron) as the Grand National series, but changed its name to the Winston Cup in 1970, when it was sponsored by the R.J. Reynolds tobacco company, manufacturers of Winston cigarettes.

TOP 10 MONTE CARLO RALLY-WINNING CARS*

(Car/wins)

❶ Lancia, 12 ❷ = Hotchkiss; = Renault, 6 ❹ Ford, 5 ❺ Porsche, 4 ❻ = Mini-Cooper; = Subaru; = Toyota, 3 ❾ = Citroën; = Delahaye; = Fiat; = Mitsubishi; = Opel; = Saab, 2

* Up to and including 2000

The Monte Carlo Rally has been run since 1911 (with breaks in 1913–23, 1940–48, 1957, and 1974). The appearance of Hotchkiss in 2nd place is perhaps surprising, but it won the rally six times between 1932 and 1950.

NASCAR MONEYWINNERS OF ALL TIME*

	DRIVER	TOTAL PRIZES (US$)
1	Dale Earnhardt	36,526,665
2	Jeff Gordon	31,877,679
3	Mark Martin	22,269,442
4	Terry Labonte	21,258,305
5	Rusty Wallace	21,247,599
6	Dale Jarrett	21,113,115
7	Bill Elliott	21,107,134
8	Darrell Waltrip	18,170,338
9	Ricky Rudd	16,737,226
10	Geoffrey Bodine	14,013,963

* To January 1, 2000
Source: NASCAR

MONEYWINNERS AT THE INDIANAPOLIS 500, 1999

	DRIVER*	TOTAL PRIZES (US$)
1	Kenny Brack	1,465,190
2	Jeff Ward	583,150
3	Billy Boat	435,200
4	Arie Luyendyk	382,350
5	Buddy Lazier	285,100
6	John Hollansworth, Jr.	265,400
7	Robbie Buhl	257,500
8	Robby Gordon	253,270
9	Raul Boesel	248,600
10	Robby McGehee	247,750
	Total prize money for all drivers	9,047,150

* Chassis/engine for all drivers: Dallara/Oldsmobile Aurora
Source: Indianapolis Motor Speedway

Drivers are ranked here according to their winnings, which vary according to such designations as first using a brand of tire.

WINNERS OF THE INDIANAPOLIS 500 WITH THE HIGHEST STARTING POSITIONS*

	DRIVER/YEAR	STARTING POSITON
1 =	Ray Harroun, 1911	28
1 =	Louis Meyer, 1936	28
3	Fred Frame, 1932	27
4	Johnny Rutherford, 1974	25
5 =	Kelly Petillo, 1935	22
5 =	George Souders, 1927	22
7	L. L. Corum and Joe Boyer, 1924	21
8 =	Frank Lockart, 1926	20
8 =	Tommy Milton, 1921	20
8 =	Al Unser, Jr., 1987	20

* Winners who have started from furthest back in the starting lineup

ALL-TIME CHAMPIONSHIP CAR VICTORY LEADERS WITH THE MOST RACE WINS

	DRIVER/DATES	WINS
1	A. J. Foyt, Jr., 1960–81	67
2	Mario Andretti, 1965–93	52
3	Al Unser, 1965–87	39
4	Michael Andretti, 1986–97	38
5	Bobby Unser, 1966–81	35
6	Al Unser, Jr., 1984–95	31
7	Rick Mears, 1978–91	29
8	Johnny Rutherford, 1965–86	27
9	Rodger Ward, 1953–66	26
10	Gordon Johncock, 1965–83	25

Source: Championship Auto Racing Teams

Seventeen-year veteran Michael Andretti is the only leader on the list currently driving on the CART circuit. Colombian Juan Montoya seems likely to make the list in future.

TOP 10 ★
FASTEST WINNING SPEEDS OF THE DAYTONA 500

	DRIVER*	CAR/YEAR	SPEED KM/H	MPH
1	Buddy Baker	Oldsmobile, 1980	285.823	177.602
2	Bill Elliott	Ford, 1987	283.668	176.263
3	Dale Earnhardt	Chevrolet, 1998	277.953	172.712
4	Bill Elliott	Ford, 1985	277.234	172.265
5	Dale Earnhardt	Chevrolet, 1998	276.921	172.071
6	Richard Petty	Buick, 1981	273.027	169.651
7	Derrike Cope	Chevrolet, 1990	266.766	165.761
8	Jeff Gordon	Chevrolet, 1999	259.991	161.551
9	A. J. Foyt, Jr.	Mercury, 1972	259.990	161.550
10	Richard Petty	Plymouth, 1966	258.504	160.627#

* All winners from the US   # Race reduced to 797 km (495 miles)
Source: NASCAR

TOP 10 ★
FASTEST WINNING TIMES OF THE INDIANAPOLIS 500

	DRIVER*	CAR/YEAR	SPEED KM/H	MPH
1	Arie Luyendyk, Holland	Lola-Chevrolet, 1990	299.307	185.984
2	Rick Mears	Chevrolet-Lumina, 1991	283.980	176.457
3	Bobby Rahal	March-Cosworth, 1986	274.750	170.722
4	Emerson Fittipaldi, Brazil	Penske-Chevrolet, 1989	269.695	167.581
5	Rick Mears	March-Cosworth, 1984	263.308	163.612
6	Mark Donohue	McLaren-Offenhauser, 1972	262.619	162.962
7	Al Unser	March-Cosworth, 1987	260.995	162.175
8	Tom Sneva	March-Cosworth, 1983	260.902	162.117
9	Gordon Johncock	Wildcat-Cosworth, 1982	260.760	162.029
10	Al Unser	Lola-Cosworth, 1978	259.689	161.363

* All US drivers unless otherwise stated
Source: Indianapolis Motor Speedway

TOP 10 CARS IN THE LE MANS 24-HOUR RACE
(Car/wins)

❶ Porsche, 15 ❷ Ferrari, 9 ❸ Jaguar, 7 ❹ Bentley, 5
❺ = Alfa Romeo; = Ford, 4 ❼ Matra-Simca, 3 ❽ = Bugatti; = La Lorraine; = Mercedes-Benz; = Peugeot, 2

TOP 10 ★
DRIVERS IN THE LE MANS 24-HOUR RACE

	DRIVER/COUNTRY	YEARS	WINS
1	Jacky Ickx, Belgium	1969–82	6
2	Derek Bell, UK	1975–87	5
3=	Olivier Gendebien, Belgium	1958–62	4
3=	Henri Pescarolo, France	1972–84	4
5=	Woolf Barnato, UK	1928–30	3
5=	Luigi Chinetti, Italy/US	1932–49	3
5=	Phil Hill, US	1958–62	3
5=	Klaus Ludwig, West Germany	1979–85	3
5=	Al Holbert, US	1983–87	3
5=	Yannick Dalmas, France	1992–95	3

The Le Mans 24-Hour Race is one of the most demanding in autosport. The first race, held on May 26–27, 1923, was won by André Lagache and René Leonard in a Chenard et Walcker.

TOP 10 ★
FASTEST LE MANS 24-HOUR RACES

	DRIVERS/COUNTRY	CAR	YEAR	AVERAGE SPEED KM/H	MPH
1	Helmut Marko, Austria, Gijs van Lennep, Holland	Porsche	1971	222.304	138.133
2	Jan Lammers, Holland, Johnny Dumfries, Andy Wallace, UK	Jaguar	1988	221.665	137.737
3	Jochen Mass, Manuel Reuter, West Germany, Stanley Dickens, Sweden	Mercedes	1989	219.990	136.696
4	Dan Gurney, A. J. Foyt, Jr., US	Ford	1967	218.038	135.483
5	Geoff Brabham, Australia, Christophe Bouchot, Eric Hélary, France	Peugeot	1993	213.358	132.574
6	Klaus Ludwig, "John Winter" (Louis Krager), West Germany, Paulo Barilla, Italy	Porsche	1985	212.021	131.744
7	Chris Amon, Bruce McLaren New Zealand,	Ford	1966	210.795	130.983
8	Vern Schuppan, Austria, Hurley Haywood, Al Holbert, US	Porsche	1983	210.330	130.693
9	Jean-Pierre Jassaud, Didier Pironi, France	Renault Alpine	1978	210.189	130.606
10	Jacky Ickx, Belgium Jackie Oliver, UK	Ford	1969	208.250	129.401

What is the most common order of bugs in Canada?
see p.48 for the answer
A Coleoptera (beetles)
B Diptera (true flies)
C Lepidoptera (butterflies and moths)
263

Golfing Greats

TOP 10 PLAYERS TO WIN THE MOST MAJORS IN A CAREER

	PLAYER/COUNTRY*	BRITISH OPEN	US OPEN	MASTERS	PGA	TOTAL
1	Jack Nicklaus	3	4	6	5	18
2	Walter Hagen	4	2	0	5	11
3 =	Ben Hogan	1	4	2	2	9
3 =	Gary Player, South Africa	3	1	3	2	9
5	Tom Watson	5	1	2	0	8
6 =	Harry Vardon, England	6	1	0	0	7
6 =	Gene Sarazen	1	2	1	3	7
6 =	Bobby Jones	3	4	0	0	7
6 =	Sam Snead	1	0	3	3	7
6 =	Arnold Palmer	2	1	4	0	7

From the US unless otherwise stated

TOP 10 ★ LOWEST WINNING SCORES IN THE US MASTERS

	PLAYER/COUNTRY*	YEAR	SCORE
1	Tiger Woods	1997	270
2 =	Jack Nicklaus	1965	271
2 =	Raymond Floyd	1976	271
4 =	Ben Hogan	1953	274
4 =	Ben Crenshaw	1995	274
6 =	Severiano Ballesteros, Spain	1980	275
6 =	Fred Couples	1992	275
8 =	Arnold Palmer	1964	276
8 =	Jack Nicklaus	1975	276
8 =	Tom Watson	1977	276
8 =	Nick Faldo, England	1996	276

From the US unless otherwise stated

The US Masters is the only major played on the same course each year, in Augusta, Georgia. The course was built on the site of an old nursery, and the abundance of flowers, shrubs, and plants is a reminder of its former days, with each of the holes named after the plants growing adjacent to it.

TOP 10 ★ WINNERS OF WOMEN'S MAJORS

	PLAYER*	TITLES
1	Patty Berg	16
2 =	Mickey Wright	13
2 =	Louise Suggs	13
4	Babe Zaharias	12
5	Betsy Rawls	8
6	JoAnne Carner	7
7 =	Kathy Whitworth	6
7 =	Pat Bradley	6
7 =	Julie Inkster	6
7 =	Glenna Collett Vare	6

All from the US

Women's majors once numbered six, but today consist of the US Open (first staged 1946), LPGA Championship (1955), Du Maurier Classic (1973; major status since 1979), and Dinah Shore Tournament (1972).

IRON LADY

US golfer Kathy Whitworth (b. 1939) scored a total of 88 tour wins, achieving victories in six majors, and was voted player of the year on seven occasions.

♣ THE 10 LAST WINNERS OF THE CPGA MEN'S CHAMPIONSHIP

(Year/winner)

1. 1999, Scott Petersen
2. 1998, Tim Clark
3. 1997, Guy Hill
4. 1996, Ashley Chinner
5. 1995, Trevor Dodds
6. 1994, Stuart Hendley
7. 1993, Steve Stricker
8. 1992, Kip Byrne
9. 1991, Tom Harding
10. 1990, Rick Gibson

Source: *Canadian Professional Golf Association*

♣ THE 10 LAST WINNERS OF THE CPGA WOMEN'S CHAMPIONSHIP

(Year/winner)

1. 1999, Lorie Kane
2. 1998, Lorie Kane
3. 1997, Lorie Kane
4. 1996, Lorie Kane
5. 1995, Nancy Harvey
6. 1994, Nancy Harvey
7. 1993, Lanie Cahill
8. 1992, Terrie Brecher
9. 1991, Jackie Twamley
10. 1990, Cathy Sherk

Source: *Canadian Professional Golf Association*

Did You Know? Mary, Queen of Scots (1542–87), is regarded as the first female golfer. In 1567, she was criticized for playing within two weeks of her husband Darnley's murder.

TOP 10 ★
LOWEST WINNING TOTALS IN THE US OPEN

PLAYER/COUNTRY*/VENUE	YEAR	SCORE
1 =Jack Nicklaus, Baltusrol	1980	272
1 =Lee Janzen, Baltusrol	1993	272
3 David Graham, Australia, Merion	1981	273
4 =Jack Nicklaus, Baltusrol	1967	275
4 =Lee Trevino, Oak Hill	1968	275
6 =Ben Hogan, Riviera	1948	276
6 =Fuzzy Zoeller, Winged Foot	1984	276
6 =Ernie Els, South Africa, Congressional	1997	276
9 =Jerry Pate, Atlanta	1976	277
9 =Scott Simpson, Olympic Club	1987	277

* From the US unless otherwise stated

TOP 10 ★
MONEY-WINNING GOLFERS, 1999

	PLAYER/COUNTRY*	WINNINGS (US$)
1	Tiger Woods	6,981,836
2	David Duval	3,641,906
3	Davis Love III	2,475,328
4	Vijay Singh, Fiji	2,473,372
5	Colin Montgomerie, Scotland	2,281,884
6	Ernie Els, South Africa	2,151,574
7	Chris Perry	2,145,707
8	Hal Sutton	2,127,578
9	Payne Stewart	2,077,950
10	Justin Leonard	2,020,991

* From the US unless otherwise stated

This list is based on winnings of the world's five top tours: US PGA Tour, European PGA Tour, PGA Tour of Japan, Australasian PGA Tour, and FNB Tour of South Africa.

TOP 10 ★
GOLFERS TO PLAY MOST STROKES AT ONE HOLE*

	PLAYER/COUNTRY [#]/YEAR/EVENT	STROKES
1	Tommy Armour, 1927, Shawnee Open	23
2	Philippe Porquier, France, 1978, French Open	21
3	Ray Ainsley, 1938, US Open	19
4 =John Daly, 1998, Bay Hill Invitational		18
4 =Willie Chisolm, 1919, US Open		18
6 =Porky Oliver, 1953, Bing Crosby		16
6 =Ian Woosnam, Wales, 1986, French Open		16
8	Hermann Tissies, Germany, 1950, British Open	15
9 =Greg Norman, Australia, 1982, Martini International		14
9 =Orrin Vincent, 1992, Austrian Open		14

* In a leading professional tournament
[#] From the US unless otherwise stated

TOP 10 ★
PLAYERS WITH THE MOST CAREER WINS ON THE US TOUR

	PLAYER*	TOUR WINS
1	Sam Snead	81
2	Jack Nicklaus	71
3	Ben Hogan	63
4	Arnold Palmer	60
5	Byron Nelson	52
6	Billy Casper	51
7 =Walter Hagen		40
7 =Cary Midlecoff		40
9	Gene Sarazen	38
10	Lloyd Mangrum	36

* All from the US

For many years, Sam Snead's total of wins was held to be 84, but the PGA Tour amended his figure in 1990 after discrepancies had been found in their previous lists. They deducted 11 wins from his total, but added eight others that should have been included, giving a revised total of 81.

TOP 10 MONEY-WINNING GOLFERS OF ALL TIME
(Player/country/career winnings in US$[#])*

1 Greg Norman, Australia, 12,507,322 **2** Davis Love III, 12,487,463 **3** Payne Stewart, 11,737,008 **4** Nick Price, Zimbabwe, 11,386,236 **5** Tiger Woods, 11,315,128 **6** Fred Couples, 11,305,069 **7** Mark O'Meara, 11,162,269 **8** Tom Kite, 10,533,102 **9** Scott Hoch, 10,308,995 **10** David Duval, 10,047,947

* From the US unless otherwise stated   [#] As of December 6, 1999

DEATH OF A LEGEND

Payne Stewart (1957–99), one of the top professional golfers of the late 20th century, won 18 tournaments, including three major championships. In June 1999 he won his second US Open, by a single shot, with a 4.57 m (15-ft) putt. He was a leading money-winner and noted for his adherence to traditional golfing clothing of knickers and cap. On October 25, 1999, he was killed in a bizarre plane accident, when the Lear jet in which he was flying from Orlando, Florida, became depressurized and its pilots and passengers fell unconscious. The plane, shadowed by an F-16 fighter, flew on autopilot for some 2,250 km (1,400 miles) before crashing.

SNAP SHOTS

Background image: **THE CLUBHOUSE AT AUGUSTA, GEORGIA, US**

Horse Racing

THE 10
LAST JOCKEYS TO WIN THE QUEEN'S PLATE*

	JOCKEY	TIME	YEAR
1	Mickey Walls	2:03.13#	1999
2	Kent Desormeaux	2:02.2	1998
3	A. E. Smith	2:04	1997
4	Emile Ramsammy	2:03.8	1996
5	Todd Kabel	2:03.4	1995
6	Jack Laron	2:03.4	1994
7	Craig Perret	2:04.2	1993
8	Craig Perret	2:04.6	1992
9	Pat Day	2:03.2	1991
10	Don Seymour	2:01.4	1990

* Held at Toronto's Woodbine Race Track

\# Timing to one hundredth of a second was introduced to the race in 1999

TOP 10
JOCKEYS WITH THE MOST CANADIAN WINS IN 1999

	JOCKEY	STARTS	WINS
1	Patrick Husbands	953	175
2	David Clark	815	137
3	Ben Russell	632	130
4	Todd Kabel	556	126
5	Gerry Olgin	634	125
6	Quincy Welch	715	123
7	Real Simard	676	112
8	Martin Ramirez	626	106
9	Chris McGregor	563	100
10	Dave Wilson	556	95

Source: *Ontario Jockey Club*

TOP 10
JOCKEYS IN THE BREEDERS CUP

	JOCKEY	YEARS	WINS
1	Pat Day	1984–99	11
2 =	Mike Smith	1992–97	8
2 =	Jerry Bailey	1991–99	8
4 =	Eddie Delahoussaye	1984–93	7
4 =	Laffit Pincay Jr.	1985–93	7
4 =	Chris McCarron	1985–96	7
4 =	Gary Stevens	1990–99	7
8 =	Pat Valenzuela	1986–92	6
8 =	Jose Santos	1986–97	6
10	Corey Nakatani	1996–99	5

Source: *The Breeders Cup*

Held at a different venue each year, the Breeders Cup is an end-of-season gathering with seven races run during the day, and with the season's best thoroughbreds competing in each category. Staged in October or November, there is US$10 million prize money available, with US$3 million going to the winner of the day's senior race, the Classic.

TOP 10
MONEY-WINNING HORSES OF ALL TIME

	HORSE/STARTS/WINS	WINNINGS (US$)
1	Cigar, 33, 19	9,999,815
2	Skip Away, 38, 18	9,616,360
3	Silver Charm, 24, 12	6,944,369
4	Alysheba, 26, 11	6,679,242
5	John Henry, 83, 39	6,597,947
6	Singspiel, 20, 9	5,950,217
7	Best Pal, 47, 18	5,668,245
8	Taiki Blizzard, 22, 6	5,544,484
9	Sunday Silence, 14, 9	4,968,554
10	Easy Goer, 20, 14	4,873,770

Source: *National Thoroughbred Racing Association*

TOP 10
OLYMPIC EQUESTRIAN COUNTRIES

	COUNTRY	GOLD	SILVER	BRONZE	TOTAL
1	West Germany/Germany	31	17	20	68
2	Sweden	17	8	14	39
3	US	8	17	13	38
4	France	11	12	11	34
5	Italy	7	9	7	23
6	Great Britain	5	7	9	21
7	Switzerland	4	9	7	20
8 =	Holland	6	7	2	15
8 =	USSR	6	5	4	15
10	Belgium	4	2	5	11

TOP 10
FASTEST WINNING TIMES OF THE KENTUCKY DERBY

			TIME	
	HORSE	YEAR	MINS	SECS
1	Secretariat	1973	1	59.2
2	Northern Dancer	1964	2	00.0
3	Spend A Buck	1985	2	00.2
4	Decidedly	1962	2	00.4
5	Proud Clarion	1967	2	00.6
6	Grindstone	1996	2	01.0
7 =	Lucky Debonair	1965	2	01.2
7 =	Affirmed	1978	2	01.2
7 =	Thunder Gulch	1995	2	01.2
10	Whirlaway	1941	2	01.4

Source: *The Jockey Club*

The Kentucky Derby is held on the first Saturday in May at Churchill Downs, Louisville, Kentucky. The first leg of the Triple Crown, it was first raced in 1875 over a distance of 1 mile 4 furlongs, but after 1896 it was reduced to 1 mile 2 furlongs.

TOP 10 MONEY-WINNING HORSES, 1999
(Horse/winnings in US$)

1. Almutawakel, 3,290,000 2. Cat Thief, 3,020,500 3. Daylami, 2,190,000
4. Charismatic, 2,007,404 5. Budroyale, 1,735,640 6. Behrens, 1,735,000
7. Beautiful Pleasure, 1,716,404 8. Silverbulletday, 1,707,640 9. Menifee, 1,695,400
10. General Pleasure, 1,658,100

Source: *National Thoroughbred Racing Association*

THE 10 LAST TRIPLE CROWN-WINNING HORSES*

(Horse/year)

1 Affirmed, 1978 **2** Seattle Slew, 1977
3 Secretariat, 1973 **4** Citation, 1948
5 Assault, 1946 **6** Count Fleet, 1943
7 Whirlaway, 1941 **8** War Admiral, 1937 **9** Omaha, 1935
10 Gallant Fox, 1930

* Horses that have won the Kentucky Derby, the Preakness Stakes, and the Belmont Stakes in the same season

TOP 10 ★

STEEPLECHASE TRAINERS IN NORTH AMERICA

	TRAINER	WINNINGS (US$)	WINS
1	Jonathan Sheppard	866,389	26
2	Jack Fisher	509,695	19
3	Bruce Miller	539,946	14
4	Tom Voss	240,978	12
5	Sanna Neilson	306,220	11
6 =	Janet Elliot	382,720	10
6 =	Charlie Fenwick	225,453	10
8 =	Ricky Hendriks	117,990	9
8 =	Neil Morris	114,250	9
10	Toby Edwards	111,540	6

Source: Steeplechase Times/*National Steeplechase Association*

TOP 10 JOCKEYS IN THE PRIX DE L'ARC DE TRIOMPHE

(Jockey/wins)

1 = Jacko Doyasbère; = Pat Eddery; = Freddy Head; = Yves Saint-Martin, 4
5 = Enrico Camici; = Charlie Elliott; = Olivier Peslier; = Lester Piggot; = Roger Poincelet; = Charles Semblat, 3

TOP 10 ★

JOCKEYS IN THE TRIPLE CROWN RACES

	JOCKEY	KENTUCKY	PREAKNESS	BELMONT	TOTAL
1	Eddie Arcaro	5	6	6	17
2	Bill Shoemaker	4	2	5	11
3 =	Bill Hartack	5	3	1	9
3 =	Earle Sande	3	1	5	9
5 =	Pat Day	1	5	2	8
5 =	Jimmy McLaughlin	1	1	6	8
7 =	Angel Cordero, Jr.	3	2	1	6
7 =	Chas Kurtsinger	2	2	2	6
7 =	Ron Turcotte	2	2	2	6
7 =	Gary Stevens	3	1	2	6

The US Triple Crown consists of the Kentucky Derby, the Preakness Stakes, and the Belmont Stakes. Since 1875, only 11 horses have won all three races in one season. The only jockey to complete the Triple Crown twice is Eddie Arcaro, on Whirlaway in 1941 and Citation in 1948.

TOP 10 ★

MONEY-WINNING TROTTERS IN A HARNESS-RACING CAREER*

	HORSE	WINNINGS (US$)
1	Moni Maker	4,175,503
2	Peace Corps	4,137,737
3	Ourasi	4,010,105
4	Mack Lobell	3,917,594
5	Reve d'Udon	3,611,351
6	Zoogin	3,428,311
7	Sea Cove	3,138,986
8	Ina Scot	2,897,044
9	Ideal du Gazeau	2,744,777
10	Vrai Lutin	2,612,429

* A trotter is a horse whose diagonally opposite legs move forward together.

Harness racing is one of the oldest sports in the US; its origins go back to the Colonial period, when many races were held along the turnpikes of New York and the New England colonies. After growing in popularity in the nineteenth century, the exotically titled governing body, the National Association for the Promotion of the Interests of the Trotting Turf (now the National Trotting Association), was founded in 1870.

TOP 10 ★

MONEY-WINNING PACERS IN A HARNESS-RACING CAREER*

	HORSE	WINNINGS (US$)
1	Nihilator	3,225,653
2	Artsplace	3,085,083
3	Presidential Ball	3,021,363
4	Matt's Scooter	2,944,591
5	On the Road Again	2,819,102
6	Riyadh	2,793,527
7	Beach Towel	2,570,357
8	Western Hanover	2,541,647
9	Cam's Card Shark	2,498,204
10	Pacific Rocket	2,333,401

* A pacer's legs are extended laterally and with a "swinging motion"; pacers usually travel faster than trotters.

Unlike thoroughbred racehorses, standardbred harness-racing horses are trained to trot and pace, but do not gallop. While widespread in the United States, harness racing is also popular in Australia and New Zealand, and, increasingly, elsewhere in the globe.

What is the highest-grossing Canadian movie worldwide?
see p.159 for the answer
A *Porky's*
B *Les Boys*
C *The Red Violin*

Hockey Headlines

TOP 10 ★
GOAL SCORERS
IN AN NHL SEASON

PLAYER/TEAM		SEASON	GOALS
1 Wayne Gretzky, Edmonton Oilers		1981–82	92
2 Wayne Gretzky, Edmonton Oilers		1983–84	87
3 Brett Hull, St. Louis Blues		1990–91	86
4 Mario Lemieux, Pittsburgh Penguins		1988–89	85
5 =Phil Esposito, Boston Bruins		1970–71	76
5 =Alexander Mogilny, Buffalo Sabres		1992–93	76
5 =Teemu Selanne, Winnipeg Jets		1992–93	76
8 Wayne Gretzky, Edmonton Oilers		1984–85	73
9 Brett Hull, St. Louis Blues		1989–90	72
10 =Wayne Gretzky, Edmonton Oilers		1982–83	71
10 =Jari Kurri, Edmonton Oilers		1984–85	71

TOP 10 ★
BIGGEST NHL ARENAS

STADIUM/LOCATION	HOME TEAM	CAPACITY
1 Molson Center, Montreal	Montreal Canadiens	21,273
2 =United Center, Chicago	Chicago Blackhawks	20,500
2 =Raleigh Entertainment & Sports Arena, Raleigh	Carolina Hurricanes	20,500
4 =Canadian Airlines Saddledrome, Calgary	Calgary Flames	20,000
4 =Staples Center, Los Angeles	Los Angeles Kings	20,000
6 Joe Louis Arena, Detroit	Detroit Red Wings	19,983
7 MCI Center, Washington	Washington Capitals	19,740
8 First Union Center, Philadelphia	Philadelphia Flyers	19,511
9 Ice Palace, Tampa	Tampa Bay Lightning	19,500
10 Kiel Center, St. Louis	St. Louis Blues	19,260

TOP 10 TEAM SALARIES
IN THE NHL, 1999–2000
(Team/salary in US$)

1 New York Rangers, 64,509,011 **2** Philadelphia Flyers, 52,233,976 **3** Detroit Red Wings, 48,545,849 **4** Dallas Stars, 43,659,500 **5** Colorado Avalanche, 41,130,000 **6** Florida Panthers, 41,032,423 **7** Chicago Blackhawks, 39,999,500 **8** St. Louis Blues, 39,032,072 **9** San Jose Sharks, 38,276,806 **10** Los Angeles Kings, 36,958,000

Source: *National Hockey League Players Association*

TOP 10 GOAL SCORERS
IN 1998-99
(Player/team/goals)

1 Teemu Selanne, Mighty Ducks of Anaheim, 47 **2** = Jaromir Jagr, Pittsburgh Penguins; = Alexei Yashin, Ottawa Senators; = Tony Amonte, Chicago Blackhawks, 44 **5** John LeClair, Philadelphia Flyers, 43 **6** Joe Sakic, Colorado Avalanche, 41 **7** = Eric Lindros, Philadelphia Flyers; = Theoren Fleury, Colorado Avalanche; = Miroslav Satan, Buffalo Sabres, 40 **10** = Paul Kariya, Mighty Ducks of Anaheim; = Luc Robitaille, Los Angeles Kings, 39

Source: *National Hockey League*

TOP 10 ★
GOALTENDERS IN AN NHL CAREER*

PLAYER	SEASONS	GAMES WON
1 Terry Sawchuk	21	447
2 Jacques Plante	18	434
3 Tony Esposito	16	423
4 Patrick Roy #	14	412
5 Glenn Hall	18	407
6 Grant Fuhr #	18	398
7 Andy Moog	18	372
8 Rogie Vachon	16	355
9 Mike Vernon #	16	347
10 Tom Barrasso #	16	345

* Regular season only   # Still active at start of 1999–2000 season

TOP 10 ★
BEST-PAID PLAYERS IN THE NHL,
1999-2000

PLAYER	TEAM	SALARY (US$)
1 Jaromir Jagr	Pittsburgh Penguins	10,359,852
2 Paul Kariya	Anaheim Mighty Ducks	10,000,000
3 Peter Forsberg	Colorado Avalanche	9,000,000
4 =Theoren Fleury	New York Rangers	8,500,000
4 =Eric Lindros	Philadelphia Flyers	8,500,000
6 Pavel Bure	Florida Panthers	8,000,000
7 Patrick Roy	Colorado Avalanche	7,500,000
8 =Dominik Hasek	Buffalo Sabres	7,000,000
8 =Mats Sundin	Toronto Maple Leafs	7,000,000
10 Brian Leetch	New York Rangers	6,680,000

Source: *National Hockey League Players Association*

TOP 10 ★
WINNERS OF THE HART TROPHY

	PLAYER	YEARS	WINS
1	Wayne Gretzky	1980–89	9
2	Gordie Howe	1952–63	6
3	Eddie Shore	1933–38	4
4 =	Bobby Clarke	1973–76	3
4 =	Howie Morenz	1928–32	3
4 =	Bobby Orr	1970–72	3
4 =	Mario Lemieux	1988-96	3
8 =	Jean Beliveau	1956–64	2
8 =	Bill Cowley	1941–43	2
8 =	Phil Esposito	1969–74	2
8 =	Dominic Hasek	1997-98	2
8 =	Bobby Hull	1965–66	2
8 =	Guy Lafleur	1977–78	2
8 =	Mark Messier	1990–92	2
8 =	Stan Mikita	1967–68	2
8 =	Nels Stewart	1926–30	2

Source: *National Hockey League*

The Hart Trophy, named after Cecil Hart, former manager/coach of the Montreal Canadiens, has been awarded annually since 1924 to the player considered the most valuable to his team.

TOP 10 ★
TEAMS WITH THE MOST STANLEY CUP WINS

	TEAM	WINS
1	Montreal Canadiens	23
2	Toronto Maple Leafs	13
3	Detroit Red Wings	9
4 =	Boston Bruins	5
4 =	Edmonton Oilers	5
6 =	New York Islanders	4
6 =	New York Rangers	4
6 =	Ottawa Senators	4
9	Chicago Black Hawks	3
10 =	Philadelphia Flyers	2
10 =	Pittsburgh Penguins	2
10 =	Montreal Maroons	2

Source: *National Hockey League*

During his time as Governor General of Canada, from 1888 to 1893, Sir Frederick Arthur Stanley (Lord Stanley of Preston and 16th Earl of Derby) became interested in ice hockey, and in 1893 presented a trophy to be contested by the best amateur teams in Canada. The first trophy went to the Montreal Amateur Athletic Association, who won it without a challenge from any other team.

TOP 10 ★
POINT SCORERS IN STANLEY CUP PLAY-OFF MATCHES

	PLAYER	TOTAL POINTS
1	Wayne Gretzky	382
2	Mark Messier*	295
3	Jari Kurri	233
4	Glenn Anderson	214
5	Paul Coffey*	196
6	Bryan Trottier	184
7	Jean Beliveau	176
8	Denis Savard	175
9	Doug Gilmour*	171
10	Denis Potvin	164

* Still active at start of 1999–2000 season

In his 20 playing seasons, Wayne Gretzky, who heads virtually every ice hockey league table, achieved some 61 NHL records, leading Edmonton to four Stanley Cups (1984–85 and 1987–88). In addition to scoring the most points, he leads for most goals and most assists in Stanley Cup matches. The Stanley Cup itself is a silver bowl. Each winning team has its club name and year engraved on a silver ring that is fitted to the cup, and is obliged to return it in good condition.

TOP 10 ★
GOAL SCORERS IN AN NHL CAREER*

	PLAYER	SEASONS	GOALS
1	Wayne Gretzky	20	894
2	Gordie Howe	26	801
3	Marcel Dionne	18	731
4	Phil Esposito	18	717
5	Mike Gartner	19	708
6	Mario Lemieux	12	613
7 =	Bobby Hull	16	610
7 =	Mark Messier#	20	610
9	Dino Ciccarelli	19	608
10	Jari Kurri	17	601

* Regular season only

Still active at start of 1999–2000 season

TOP 10 ★
NHL GAMES TO PRODUCE THE MOST GOALS

GAME	SCORE	DATE	TOTAL GOALS
1 = Montreal Canadiens vs. Toronto St. Patricks	14—7	Jan 10, 1920	21
1 = Edmonton Oilers vs. Chicago Black Hawks	12—9	Dec 11, 1985	21
3 = Edmonton Oilers vs. Minnesota North Stars	12—8	Jan 4, 1984	20
3 = Toronto Maple Leafs vs. Edmonton Oilers	11—9	Jan 8, 1986	20
5 = Montreal Wanderers vs. Toronto Arenas	10—9	Dec 19, 1917	19
5 = Montreal Canadiens vs. Quebec Bulldogs	16—3	Mar 3, 1920	19
5 = Montreal Canadiens vs. Hamilton Tigers	13—3	Feb 26, 1921	19
5 = Boston Bruins vs. New York Rangers	10—9	Mar 4, 1944	19
5 = Boston Bruins vs. Detroit Red Wings	10—9	Mar 16, 1944	19
5 = Vancouver Canucks vs. Minnesota North Stars	10—9	Oct 7, 1983	19

What is the most-visited tourism region in Canada?
see p.223 for the answer

A   Lakelands, Ont.
B   Quebec City
C   Vancouver Island

Tennis Triumphs

MEN WITH THE MOST WIMBLEDON TITLES

	PLAYER/COUNTRY	YEARS	TITLES S	D	M	TOTAL
1	William Renshaw, UK	1880–89	7	7	0	14
2	Lawrence Doherty, UK	1897–1905	5	8	0	13
3	Reginald Doherty, UK	1897–1905	4	8	0	12
4	John Newcombe, Australia	1965–74	3	6	0	9
5 =Ernest Renshaw, UK		1880–89	1	7	0	8
5 =Tony Wilding, New Zealand		1907–14	4	4	0	8
7 =Wilfred Baddeley, UK		1891–96	3	4	0	7
7 =Bob Hewitt, Australia/S. Africa		1962–79	0	5	2	7
7 =Rod Laver, Australia		1959–69	4	1	2	7
7 =John McEnroe, US		1979–84	3	4	0	7

S – singles; D – doubles; M – mixed

TOP 10 TOURNAMENT WINNERS, MALE*

(Player/country/tournament wins)

1 Jimmy Connors, US, 109 **2** Ivan Lendl, Czechoslovakia, 94
3 John McEnroe, US, 77 **4** = Björn Borg, Sweden;
= Guillermo Vilas, Argentina, 62 **6** Ilie Nastase, Romania, 57
7 Pete Sampras, US, 56 **8** Boris Becker, Germany, 49
9 Rod Laver, Australia, 47 **10** Thomas Muster, Austria, 44

* *Tournament leaders since Open Tennis introduced in 1968. Totals include ATP tour, Grand Prix, and WCT tournaments.*

WINNERS OF MEN'S GRAND SLAM SINGLES TITLES

	PLAYER/COUNTRY	TITLES A	F	W	US	TOTAL
1	Roy Emerson, Australia	6	2	2	2	12
2 =Björn Borg, Sweden		0	6	5	0	11
2 =Rod Laver, Australia		3	2	4	2	11
2 =Pete Sampras, US		2	0	5	4	11
5	Bill Tilden, US	0	0	3	7	10
6 =Jimmy Connors, US		1	0	2	5	8
6 =Ivan Lendl, Czechoslovakia		2	3	0	3	8
6 =Fred Perry, UK		1	1	3	3	8
6 =Ken Rosewall, Australia		4	2	0	2	8
10=Henri Cochet, France		0	4	2	1	7
10=René Lacoste, France		0	3	2	2	7
10=William Larned, US		0	0	0	7	7
10=John McEnroe, US		0	0	3	4	7
10=John Newcombe, Australia		2	0	3	2	7
10=William Renshaw, UK		0	0	7	0	7
10=Richard Sears, US		0	0	0	7	7
10=Mats Wilander, Sweden		3	3	0	1	7

A – Australian Open; F – French Open; W – Wimbledon; US – US Open

THE 10 LAST WINNERS OF THE US OPEN MEN'S CHAMPIONSHIP

(Year/winner/country)

1 1999, Andre Agassi, US **2** 1998, Patrick Rafter, Australia **3** 1997, Patrick Rafter, Australia **4** 1996, Pete Sampras, US
5 1995, Pete Sampras, US
6 1994, Andre Agassi, US
7 1993, Pete Sampras, US
8 1992, Stefan Edberg, Sweden
9 1991, Stefan Edberg, Sweden
10 1990, Pete Sampras, US

TOP 10 MALE PLAYERS*

(Player/country/weeks at No. 1)

1 Pete Sampras, US, 276 **2** Ivan Lendl, Czechoslovakia, 270 **3** Jimmy Connors, US, 268 **4** John McEnroe, US, 170 **5** Björn Borg, Sweden, 109
6 Stefan Edberg, Sweden, 72
7 Jim Courier, US, 58 **8** Andre Agassi, US, 47 **9** Ilie Nastase, Romania, 40
10 Mats Wilander, Sweden, 20
* *Based on weeks at No. 1 in ATP rankings (1973 to 1999)*

WINNERS OF WOMEN'S GRAND SLAM SINGLES TITLES

PLAYER/COUNTRY	A	F	W	US	TOTAL
1 Margaret Court, Australia	11	5	3	5	24
2 Steffi Graf, Germany	4	5	7	5	21
3 Helen Wills-Moody, US	0	4	8	7	19
4 =Chris Evert, US	2	7	3	6	18
4 =Martina Navratilova, US	3	2	9	4	18
6 =Billie Jean King, US	1	1	6	4	12
6 =Suzanne Lenglen, France	0	6	6	0	12
8 =Maureen Connolly, US	1	2	3	3	9
8 =Monica Seles, US	4	3	0	2	9
10 Molla Mallory, US	0	0	0	8	8

(Header: TITLES spans A, F, W, US columns)

A – Australian Open; F – French Open; W – Wimbledon; US – US Open

TOURNAMENT WINNERS, FEMALE*

PLAYER/COUNTRY	TOURNAMENT WINS
1 Martina Navratilova, US	167
2 Chris Evert, US	154
3 Steffi Graf, Germany	106
4 Margaret Court, Australia	92
5 Billie Jean King, US	67
6 Evonne Goolagong Cawley, Australia	65
7 Virginia Wade, UK	55
8 Monica Seles, US	43
9 Conchita Martinez, Spain	30
10 Tracy Austin, US	29

* Tournament leaders since Open Tennis introduced in 1968

DAVIS CUP WINNING TEAMS

COUNTRY	WINS
1 United States	31
2 Australia	21
3 France	8
4 Sweden	7
5 Australasia	6
6 British Isles	5
7 Great Britain	4
8 West Germany	2
9 =Germany	1
9 =Czechoslovakia	1
9 =Italy	1
9 =South Africa	1

South Africa's sole win was gained when, for political reasons, India refused to meet them in the 1974 final.

BRILLIANT CAREER

In 1995, Andre Agassi was the 12th player to be ranked world No. 1. In 1999, he became only the fifth male player to complete a Grand Slam.

TOP 10 CAREER MONEY-WINNING WOMEN*

(Player/country/winnings in US$)

1 Steffi Graf, Germany, 20,646,410 **2** Martina Navratilova, US, 20,344,061 **3** Arantxa Sanchez-Vicario, Spain, 14,119,642 **4** Monica Seles, US, 10,928,640 **5** Jana Novotna, Czech Republic, 10,507,680 **6** Chris Evert, US, 8,896,195 **7** Gabriela Sabatini, Argentina, 8,785,850 **8** Martina Hingis, Switzerland, 8,331,496 **9** Conchita Martinez, Spain, 7,780,941 **10** Natasha Zvereva, Belarus, 7,036,143

* To end of 1999 season

GOLDEN GIRL

German-born Steffi Graf was one of the youngest players ever ranked, aged just 13 in 1982. As her career progressed, she was first ranked No. 1 in 1987, and held the No. 1 ranking for a record 374 weeks. Aged just 19 in 1988, she became the youngest-ever winner of the Grand Slam, and also won Olympic gold at Seoul. She continued to win at least one Grand Slam title a year for the next 10 years, until knee injuries prevented her from competing. In 1999, after winning her sixth French Open championship, and her 22nd Grand Slam title, Steffi Graf announced her decision to retire. In 2000, her romantic involvement with Andre Agassi made press headlines.

SNAP SHOTS

Team Games

WINNERS OF THE TABLE TENNIS WORLD CHAMPIONSHIP

	COUNTRY	MEN'S	WOMEN'S	TOTAL
1	China	13	13	26
2	Japan	7	8	15
3	Hungary	12	–	12
4	Czechoslovakia	6	3	9
5	Romania	–	5	5
6	Sweden	4	–	4
7 =England		1	2	3
7 =US		1	2	3
9	Germany	–	2	2
10=Austria		1	–	1
10=North Korea		–	1	1
10=South Korea		–	1	1
10=USSR		–	1	1

Originally a European event, it was later extended to a world championship.

TOP 10 POLO TEAMS WITH THE MOST BRITISH OPEN CHAMPIONSHIP WINS

(Team/wins)

1 = Stowell Park; = Tramontana, 5
3 = Ellerston; = Cowdray Park; = Pimms; = Windsor Park, 3
7 = Casarejo; = Jersey Lillies; = Woolmer's Park; = Falcons; = Southfield, 2

TOP 10 COUNTIES WITH THE MOST WINS IN THE ALL-IRELAND HURLING CHAMPIONSHIPS

(County/wins)

1 Cork, 28 **2** Kilkenny, 25
3 Tipperary, 24 **4** Limerick, 7
5 = Dublin; = Wexford, 6
7 = Galway; = Offaly, 4 **9** Clare, 3
10 Waterford, 2

EYE ON THE BALL

Table tennis is believed to have originated in England in the 1880s, with cigar box lids used as paddles and books as nets. Now a world sport, it is dominated by Chinese players like Song Ding, 1997 World Champion.

LAST WINNERS OF THE ROLLER HOCKEY WORLD CHAMPIONSHIP

YEAR	WINNER
1999	Argentina
1997	Italy
1995	Argentina
1993	Portugal
1991	Portugal
1989	Spain
1988	Spain
1986	Spain
1984	Argentina
1982	Portugal

Roller hockey, a five-a-side game formerly called rink hockey, has been played for more than 100 years. The first international tournament was held in Paris in 1910, the first European Championships in Britain in 1926, and the men's World Championship biennially since 1936 (odd-numbered years since 1989). Portugal is the overall winner, with 14 titles to its credit.

OLYMPIC ARCHERY COUNTRIES

	COUNTRY	GOLD	MEDALS SILVER	BRONZE	TOTAL
1	US	13	7	7	27
2	France	6	10	6	22
3	South Korea	10	6	3	19
4	Soviet Union	1	3	5	9
5	Great Britain	2	2	4	8
6	Finland	1	1	2	4
7 =China	0	3	0	3
7 =Italy	0	0	3	3
9 =Sweden	0	2	0	2
9 =Japan	0	1	1	2
9 =Poland	0	1	1	2

Archery was introduced as an Olympic sport at the second modern Olympics, held in Paris in 1900. The format has changed considerably over succeeding Games, with events such as shooting live birds being discontinued in favor of target shooting. Individual and team events for men and women are now included in the program.

UP AND OVER DOWN UNDER
Mathew Allan (Carlton) and Steven King (Geelong) battle for possession in an Australian football match.

LATEST COUNTRIES TO WIN THE WORLD CURLING CHAMPIONSHIPS

WOMEN'S CHAMPIONSHIPS	YEAR	MEN'S CHAMPIONSHIPS
Canada	2000	Canada
Sweden*	1999	Scotland
Sweden*	1998	Canada
Canada+	1997	Sweden
Canada	1996	Canada
Sweden*	1995	Canada
Canada#	1994	Canada
Canada#	1993	Canada
Sweden*	1992	Switzerland
Norway+	1991	Scotland

* The same team won four times

\# The same team won three times

\+ The same team won twice

Source: Sweep! *Curling's Magazine*

Curling is a quintessentially Canadian sport. By one estimate, more than 90 percent of the world's curlers are Canadian. Since the first world championship was held in 1959, Canada has dominated world-level competition, winning 26 out of 42 men's world championships and 11 out of 22 women's world championships.

OLYMPIC FIELD HOCKEY COUNTRIES

	COUNTRY	GOLD	MEDALS SILVER	BRONZE	TOTAL
1	India	8	1	2	11
2	Great Britain*	3	2	5	10
3	Netherlands	2	2	5	9
4	Pakistan	3	3	2	8
5	Australia	2	3	2	7
6	Germany#	1	2	2	5
7 =Spain	1	2	1	4
7 =West Germany	1	3	–	4
9 =South Korea	–	2	–	2
9 =US	–	–	2	2
9 =Soviet Union	–	–	2	2

* Including England, Ireland, Scotland, and Wales, which competed separately in the 1908 Olympics

\# Not including West Germany or East Germany 1968–88

OLYMPIC VOLLEYBALL COUNTRIES

	COUNTRY	GOLD	MEDALS SILVER	BRONZE	TOTAL
1	Soviet Union*	7	5	1	13
2	Japan	3	3	2	8
3	US	2	1	2	5
4 =Cuba	2	–	1	3
4 =Brazil	1	1	1	3
4 =China	1	1	1	3
4 =Poland	1	–	2	3
8 =Netherlands	1	1	–	2
8 =East Germany	–	2	–	2
8 =Bulgaria	–	1	1	2
8 =Czechoslovakia	–	1	1	2
8 =Italy	–	1	1	2

* Includes United Team of 1992; excludes Russia since this date

Did You Know? At the 1932 Los Angeles Olympics, India's field hockey team beat the US by a record 24–1 (with 12 of the goals scored by one player, Roop Singh) and Japan by 11–1.

Water Sports

WINNERS OF MEN'S WORLD WATER-SKIING TITLES

SKIER/COUNTRY	OVERALL	SLALOM	TRICKS	JUMP	TOTAL
1 Patrice Martin, France	6	0	4	0	10
2 Sammy Duvall, US	4	0	0	2	6
3 = Alfredo Mendoza, US	2	1	0	2	5
3 = Mike Suyderhoud, US	2	1	0	2	5
3 = Bob La Point, US	0	4	1	0	5
3 = Andy Mapple, UK	0	5	0	0	5
7 = George Athans, Canada	2	1	0	0	3
7 = Guy de Clercq, Belgium	1	0	0	2	3
7 = Wayne Grimditch, US	0	0	2	1	3
7 = Mike Hazelwood, UK	1	0	0	2	3
7 = Ricky McCormick, US	0	0	1	2	3
7 = Billy Spencer, US	1	1	1	0	3

TOP 10 ★

WINNERS OF WOMEN'S WORLD WATER-SKIING TITLES

SKIER/COUNTRY	OVERALL	SLALOM	TRICKS	JUMP	TOTAL
1 Liz Shetter, US	3	3	1	4	11
2 Willa McGuire, US	3	2	1	2	8
3 Cindy Todd, US	2	3	0	2	7
4 Deena Mapple, US	2	0	0	4	6
5 = Marina Doria, Switzerland	1	1	2	0	4
5 = Tawn Hahn, US	0	0	4	0	4
5 = Helena Kjellander, Sweden	0	4	0	0	4
5 = Natalya Ponomaryeva, USSR	1	0	3	0	4
9 = Maria Victoria Carrasco, Venezuela	0	0	3	0	3
9 = Yelena Milakova, Russia	2	0	0	1	3

TOP 10 POWERBOAT DRIVERS WITH MOST RACE WINS

(Owner/country/wins)

1 Bill Seebold, US, 912 **2** Jumbo McConnell, US, 217
3 Chip Hanauer, US, 203 **4** Steve Curtis, UK, 184 **5** Mikeal Frode, Sweden, 152 **6** Neil Holmes, UK, 147
7 Peter Bloomfield, UK, 126 **8** Renato Molinari, Italy, 113
9 Cees Van der Valden, Netherlands, 98 **10** Bill Muney, US, 96

Source: Raceboat International

TOP 10 COLLEGES IN THE INTERCOLLEGIATE ROWING ASSOCIATION REGATTA*

(College/first and last winning years/wins)

1 Cornell, 1896–1982, 24 **2** Navy, 1921–84, 13 **3** = Washington, 1923–97; = California, 1928–99, 11 **5** Pennsylvania, 1898–1989, 9 **6** = Wisconsin, 1951–90; = Brown, 1979–95, 7 **8** Syracuse, 1904–78, 6 **9** Columbia, 1895–1929, 4 **10** Princeton, 1985–98, 3
Men's varsity eight-oared shells event

TOP 10 ★

OLYMPIC YACHTING COUNTRIES

COUNTRY	MEDALS			
	GOLD	SILVER	BRONZE	TOTAL
1 US	16	19	16	51
2 Great Britain	14	12	9	35
3 Sweden	9	12	9	30
4 Norway	16	11	2	29
5 France	12	6	9	27
6 Denmark	10	8	4	22
7 Germany/West Germany	6	5	6	17
8 Netherlands	4	5	6	15
9 New Zealand	6	4	3	13
10 = Australia	3	2	7	12
10 = Soviet Union*	4	5	3	12
10 = Spain	9	2	1	12

* Includes United Team of 1992; excludes Russia since this date

TOP 10 ★

OLYMPIC ROWING COUNTRIES

COUNTRY	MEDALS			
	GOLD	SILVER	BRONZE	TOTAL
1 US	29	28	19	76
2 East Germany	33	7	8	48
3 Soviet Union*	12	20	11	43
4 Germany#	19	12	11	42
5 Great Britain	19	15	7	41
6 = Italy	12	11	9	32
6 = Canada	8	12	12	32
8 France	4	14	12	30
9 Romania	12	10	7	29
10 Switzerland	6	7	9	22

* Includes United Team of 1992; excludes Russia since this date
# Not including West Germany or East Germany 1968–88

Did You Know? John B. Kelly (1891–1960), father of actress Grace Kelly, later Princess Grace of Monaco, won three rowing gold medals at the 1920 and 1924 Olympics.

TOP 10 ⭐
OLYMPIC SWIMMING COUNTRIES

	COUNTRY	MEDALS			
		GOLD	SILVER	BRONZE	TOTAL
1	US	230	176	137	543
2	Australia	41	37	47	125
3	East Germany	40	34	25	99
4	Soviet Union*	24	32	38	94
5	Germany#	19	33	34	86
6 =	Great Britain	18	23	30	71
6 =	Hungary	29	23	19	71
8	Sweden	13	21	21	55
9	Japan	15	18	19	52
10	Canada	11	17	20	48

* Includes United Team of 1992; excludes Russia since this date
 # Not including West Germany or East Germany 1968–88

The medal table includes medals for the synchronized swimming, diving, and water polo events that form part of the Olympic swimming program. Swimming has been part of the Olympics since the first modern games in 1896, at which only members of the Greek navy were eligible for one event – the 100-m (328-ft) swimming race for sailors. Events were held in the open water until 1908, when specially built pools were introduced.

TOP 10 ⭐
OLYMPIC CANOEING COUNTRIES

	COUNTRY	MEDALS			
		GOLD	SILVER	BRONZE	TOTAL
1 =	Hungary	10	23	20	53
1 =	Soviet Union*	30	13	10	53
3	Germany#	18	15	12	45
4	Romania	9	10	12	31
5	East Germany	14	7	9	30
6	Sweden	14	10	4	28
7	France	2	6	14	22
8 =	Bulgaria	4	3	8	15
8 =	US	5	4	6	15
10	Canada	3	7	4	14

* Includes United Team of 1992; excludes Russia since this date
 # Not including West Germany or East Germany 1968–88

PADDLE POWER

Canoeing has been an Olympic sport since 1936. Six of Sweden's golds were won by one contestant, Gert Fredriksson, who also gained a silver and a bronze, in Games from 1948–60.

SWISS ROLL

The bobsled event has been part of the Winter Olympics since 1924. Switzerland has won more medals than any other country.

TOP 10 ★
MEN'S WORLD AND OLYMPIC FIGURE SKATING TITLES

	SKATER/COUNTRY	YEARS	TITLES
1	Ulrich Salchow, Sweden	1901–11	11
2	Karl Schäfer, Austria	1930–36	9
3	Richard Button, US	1948–52	7
4	Gillis Grafstrom, Sweden	1920–29	6
5=	Hayes Jenkins, US	1953–56	5
5=	Scott Hamilton, US	1981–84	5
7=	Willy Bockl, Austria	1925–28	4
7=	David Jenkins, US	1957–60	4
7=	Ondrej Nepela, Czechoslovakia	1971–73	4
7=	Kurt Browning, Canada	1989–93	4

TOP 10 OLYMPIC BOBSLEDDING COUNTRIES
(Country/medals)

1 Switzerland, 26 **2** US, 14 **3** East Germany, 13
4 = Germany*; = Italy, 11 **6** West Germany, 6 **7** UK, 4
8 = Austria; = Soviet Union,# 3 **10** = Canada; = Belgium, 2

* Not including West or East Germany 1968–88
 # Includes United Team of 1992; excludes Russia since then

TOP 10 ★
SKIERS WITH THE MOST ALPINE SKIING WORLD CUP TITLES (FEMALE)

	SKIER/COUNTRY	YEARS	TOTAL
1	Annemarie Moser-Pröll, Austria	1971–79	16
2	Vreni Schneider, Switzerland	1986–95	14
3	Katia Seizinger, Germany	1992–98	11
4	Erika Hess, Switzerland	1981–84	8
5	Michela Figini, Switzerland	1985–89	7
6	Lise-Marie Morerod, Switzerland	1975–78	6
7=	Maria Walliser, Switzerland	1986–87	5
7=	Hanni Wenzel, Liechtenstein	1974–80	5
9=	Renate Goetschl, Germany	1997–2000	4
9=	Nancy Greene, Canada	1967–68	4
9=	Petra Kronberger, Austria	1990–92	4
9=	Tamara McKinney, USA	1981–84	4
9=	Carole Merle, France	1989–92	4

The Alpine Skiing World Cup was launched as an annual event in 1967, with the addition of the super-giant slalom in 1986. Points are awarded for performances over a series of selected races during the winter months at meetings worldwide. In addition to her 16 titles, Annemarie Moser-Pröll won a record 62 individual events in the period 1970–79, and went on to win gold for the Downhill event in the 1980 Olympic Games.

TOP 10 ★
SKIERS WITH THE MOST ALPINE SKIING WORLD CUP TITLES (MALE)

	SKIER/COUNTRY	YEARS	TOTAL
1	Ingemar Stenmark, Sweden	1976–84	18
2	Pirmin Zurbriggen, Switzerland	1984–90	15
3	Marc Girardelli, Luxembourg	1984–94	11
4=	Gustavo Thoeni, Italy	1971–74	9
4=	Alberto Tomba, Italy	1988–95	9
6	Hermann Maier, Austria	1998–2000	8
7=	Jean-Claude Killy, France	1967–68	6
7=	Phil Mahre, US	1981–83	6
9=	Luc Alphand, France	1997	5
9=	Franz Klammer, Austria	1975–83	5

Did You Know? At the Third Winter Olympics, in Lake Placid, New York, in 1932, an early thaw meant that snow had to be taken to the venue from Canada by a fleet of trucks.

TOP 10 ★
WOMEN'S WORLD AND OLYMPIC FIGURE SKATING TITLES

	SKATER/COUNTRY/YEARS	TITLES
1	Sonja Henie, Norway, 1927–36	13
2=	Carol Heiss, US, 1956–60	6
2=	Herma Planck Szabo, Austria, 1922–26	6
2=	Katarina Witt, E. Germany, 1984–88	6
5=	Lily Kronberger, Hungary, 1908–11	4
5=	Sjoukje Dijkstra, Holland, 1962–64	4
5=	Peggy Fleming, US, 1966–68	4
8=	Meray Horvath, Hungary, 1912–14	3
8=	Tenley Albright, US, 1953–56	3
8=	Michelle Kwan, US, 1996–2000	3
8=	Annett Poetzsch, E. Gemany, 1978–80	3
8=	Beatrix Schuba, Austria, 1971–72	3
8=	Barbara Ann Scott, Canada, 1947–48	3
8=	Kristi Yamaguchi, US, 1991–92	3
8=	Madge Syers, UK, 1906–08	3

TOP 10 ★
OLYMPIC FIGURE SKATING COUNTRIES

	COUNTRY	GOLD	SILVER	BRONZE	TOTAL
1	US	12	13	14	39
2	Soviet Union*	13	10	6	29
3	Austria	7	9	4	20
4	Canada	2	7	9	18
5	Great Britain	5	3	7	15
6	France	2	2	7	11
7=	Sweden	5	3	2	10
7=	East Germany	3	3	4	10
9	Germany#	4	4	1	9
10=	Norway	3	2	1	6
10=	Hungary	0	2	4	6

* Includes United Team of 1992; excludes Russia since then

\# Not including West Germany or East Germany 1968–88

Figure skating was part of the Summer Olympics in 1908 and 1920, becoming part of the Winter program in 1924.

TOP 10 ★
WINTER OLYMPIC MEDAL-WINNING COUNTRIES, 1908–98

	COUNTRY	GOLD	SILVER	BRONZE	TOTAL
1	Norway	83	87	69	239
2	Soviet Union*	87	63	67	217
3	US	59	59	41	159
4	Austria	39	53	53	145
5	Finland	38	49	48	135
6	Germany#	66	38	32	116
7	East Germany	39	36	35	110
8	Sweden	39	28	35	102
9	Switzerland	29	31	32	92
10	Canada	25	25	28	79

* Includes United Team of 1992; excludes Russia since then

\# Not including West or East Germany 1968–88

Only skating and ice hockey were featured in the 1908 and 1920 Summer Olympics. The first Winter Olympics was held at Chamonix, France, in 1924.

TOP 10 ★
FASTEST WINNING TIMES OF THE IDITAROD DOG SLED RACE

	WINNER	YEAR	DAY	HR	MIN	SEC
1	Doug Swingley	2000	9	0	58	6
2	Doug Swingley	1995	9	2	42	19
3	Jeff King	1996	9	5	43	19
4	Jeff King	1998	9	5	52	26
5	Martin Buser	1997	9	8	30	45
6	Doug Swingley	1999	9	14	31	7
7	Martin Buser	1994	10	13	2	39
8	Jeff King	1993	10	15	38	15
9	Martin Buser	1992	10	19	17	15
10	Susan Butcher	1990	11	1	53	28

Source: Iditarod Trail Committee

TOP DOUG

Doug Swingley from Simms, Montana, is one of the few non-Alaskans to win the grueling 1,864-km (1,158-mile) Anchorage-to-Nome Iditarod dog sled race.

Background image: **IDITAROD DOG SLED RACE, 1999**

Sports Roundup

TOP 10 — PARTICIPATION SPORTS, GAMES, AND PHYSICAL ACTIVITIES IN CANADA

	ACTIVITY	PARTICIPANTS IN 1998 (000s)
1	Golf	1,802
2	Hockey (ice)	1,499
3	Baseball	1,339
4	Swimming	1,120
5	Basketball	787
6	Volleyball	744
7	Soccer	739
8	Tennis	658
9	Skiing (downhill, alpine)	657
10	Cycling	608

Source: *Statistics Canada*

TOP 10 — MOST COMMON SPORTS INJURIES

	COMMON NAME	MEDICAL TERM
1	Bruise	A soft tissue contusion
2	Sprained ankle	Sprain of the lateral ligament
3	Sprained knee	Sprain of the medial collateral ligament
4	Low back strain	Lumbar joint dysfunction
5	Hamstring tear	Muscle tear of the hamstrings
6	Jumper's knee	Patella tendinitis
7	Achilles tendinitis	Tendinitis of the Achilles tendon
8	Shin splints	Medial periostitis of the tibia
9	Tennis elbow	Lateral epicondylitis
10	Shoulder strain	Rotator cuff tendinitis

WINGS WINNER
Soviet-born Detroit Red Wings star Sergei Federov is one of the highest scoring and highest earning of all sports personalities.

TOP 10 — SPORTING EVENTS WITH THE LARGEST TV AUDIENCES IN THE US

	EVENT	DATE	RATING
1	Super Bowl XVI	Jan 24, 1982	49.1
2	Super Bowl XVII	Jan 30, 1983	48.6
3	XVII Winter Olympics	Feb 23, 1994	48.5
4	Super Bowl XX	Jan 26, 1986	48.3
5	Super Bowl XII	Jan 15, 1978	47.2
6	Super Bowl XIII	Jan 21, 1979	47.1
7=	Super Bowl XVIII	Jan 22, 1984	46.4
7=	Super Bowl XIX	Jan 20, 1985	46.4
9	Super Bowl XIV	Jan 20, 1980	46.3
10	Super Bowl XXX	Jan 28, 1996	46.0

Source: *Nielsen Media Research*

Those listed here, along with 10 further Super Bowls, back to VI in 1972, are among the Top 50 networked programs of all time in the US. In this extended list, the XVII Lillehammer, Norway, Winter Olympics makes two showings, on Feb 23 and Feb 25 1994 (the latter achieving a rating of 44.2). Despite the national enthusiasm (fueled by media interest in figure skater Nancy Kerrigan, who had been physically attacked before the Games), the US finished a disappointing 5th in the overall medals table.

TOP 10 — HIGHEST-EARNING SPORTSMEN

	SPORTSMAN*	SPORT	1999 INCOME (US$)
1	Michael Shumacher, Germany	Motor racing	49,000,000
2	Tiger Woods	Golf	47,000,000
3	Oscar De La Hoya	Boxing	43,500,000
4	Michael Jordan	Basketball	40,000,000
5	Evander Holyfield	Boxing	35,500,000
6	Mike Tyson	Boxing	33,000,000
7	Shaquille O'Neal	Basketball	31,000,000
8	Lennox Lewis, UK	Boxing	29,000,000
9	Dale Earnhardt	Stock car racing	26,500,000
10	Grant Hill	Basketball	23,000,000

* From the US unless otherwise stated   Source: Forbes *magazine*

TOP 10 UNIVERSITY SPORTS IN CANADA

(Sport/participants)*

1 Track and field, 1,593   2 Soccer, 1,314
3 Swimming, 1,188   4 Hockey, 1,164   5 Basketball, 988
6 Football, 960   7 Volleyball, 744   8 Rugby, 625
9 Cross country, 441   10 Wrestling, 282

Source: *Canadian Interuniversity Athletic Union (CIAU)*

Did You Know? The Tour de France bicycle race is believed to be watched by more spectators than any other sport, with some 10 million people lining the route during the three-week event.

THE 10 ★
LATEST TRIATHLON WORLD CHAMPIONS

MAN/COUNTRY	TIME	YEAR	TIME	WOMAN/COUNTRY
Dimitry Gaag, Kazakhstan	1:45:25	**1999**	1:55:28	Loretta Harrop, Australia
Simon Lessing, UK	1:55:31	**1998**	2:07:25	Joanne King, Australia
Chris McCormack, Australia	1:48:29	**1997**	1:59:22	Emma Carney, Australia
Simon Lessing, UK	1:39:50	**1996**	1:50:52	Jackie Gallagher, Australia
Simon Lessing, UK	1:48:29	**1995**	2:04:58	Karen Smyers, US
Spencer Smith, UK	1:51:04	**1994**	2:03:19	Emma Carney, Australia
Spencer Smith, UK	1:51:20	**1993**	2:07:41	Michellie Jones, Australia
Simon Lessing, UK	1:49:04	**1992**	2:02:08	Michellie Jones, Australia
Miles Stewart, Australia	1:48:20	**1991**	2:02:04	Joanne Ritchie, Canada
Greg Welch, Australia	1:51:37	**1990**	2:03:33	Karen Smyers, US

The Triathlon World Championship has been contested since 1989 and consists of a 1.5-km (1-mile) swim, a 40-km (25-mile) bike ride, and a 10-km (6¼-mile) run.

TOP 10 ★
ALL-AROUND CHAMPION COWBOYS

	COWBOY	YEARS	WINS
1	Ty Murray	1989–98	7
2=	Tom Ferguson	1974–79	6
2=	Larry Mahan	1966–73	6
4	Jim Shoulders	1949–59	5
5=	Lewis Feild	1985–87	3
5=	Dean Oliver	1963–65	3
7=	Joe Beaver	1995–96	2
7=	Everett Bowman	1935–37	2
7=	Louis Brooks	1943–44	2
7=	Clay Carr	1930–33	2
7=	Bill Linderman	1950–53	2
7=	Phil Lyne	1971–72	2
7=	Gerald Roberts	1942–48	2
7=	Casey Tibbs	1951–55	2
7=	Harry Tompkins	1952–60	2

The All-Around World Champion Cowboy title is presented by the Professional Rodeo Cowboys Association (PRCA) each year. The winner is the rodeo athlete who wins the most prize money in a single year in two or more events, with minimum earnings of US$2,000 per event. During the 1990s, several winners earned more than US$250,000 a year.

TOP 10 ★
FASTEST WINNING TIMES FOR THE HAWAII IRONMAN

	WINNER/COUNTRY*	YEAR	TIME HR:MIN:SEC
1	Luc Van Lierde, Belgium	1996	8:04:08
2	Mark Allen	1993	8:07:45
3	Mark Allen	1992	8:09:08
4	Mark Allen	1989	8:09:16
5	Luc Van Lierde	1999	8:17:17
6	Mark Allen	1991	8:18:32
7	Greg Welch, Australia	1994	8:20:27
8	Mark Allen	1995	8:20:34
9	Peter Reid, Canada	1998	8:24:20
10	Mark Allen	1990	8:28:17

* From the US unless otherwise stated

In perhaps one of the most grueling sporting contests, competitors engage in a 3.86-km (2½-mile) swim, a 180-km (112-mile) cycle race, and a 42.2-km (26¼-mile) run.

DANGER BELOW

The risk of injury or becoming trapped underground has resulted in spelunking being ranked among the world's most hazardous sports.

TOP 10 ★
MOST DANGEROUS AMATEUR SPORTS

	SPORT	RISK FACTOR*
1	Powerboat racing	15
2	Ocean yacht racing	10
3	Cave diving	7
4	Spelunking	6
5=	Drag racing	5
5=	Karting	5
7	Microlyte	4
8=	Hang gliding	3
8=	Motor racing	3
8=	Mountaineering	3

* Risk factor refers to the premium that insurance companies place on insuring someone for that activity – the higher the risk factor, the higher the premium

Source: *General Accident*

Index

Acknowledgments

US research: Dafydd Rees

UK research assistants: Harriet Hart, Lucy Hemming

Thanks to the individuals, organizations, and publications listed below who kindly supplied information in the preparation of this book.

Caroline Ash, Mark Atterton, John Bardsley, Richard Braddish, Lesley Coldham, Pete Compton, Stanley Coren, Luke Crampton, Sidney S. Culbert, François Curiel, Bonnie Fantasia, Christopher Forbes, Professor Ken Fox, Darryl Francis, Simon Gilbert, Russell E. Gough, Monica Grady, Stan Greenberg, Duncan Hislop, Andreas Hoerstemeier, Tony Hutson, Alan Jeffreys, Robert Lamb, Dr. Jaquie Lavin, Dr. Benjamin Lucas, John Malam, Ian Morrison, Vincent Nasso, Christiaan Rees, Linda Rees, Adrian Room, Bill Rudman, Joanne Schioppi, Robert Senior, Lisa E. Smith, Mitchell Symons, Tony Waltham, Professor Edward O. Wilson

Academy of Motion Picture Arts and Sciences, *Advertising Age,* American Athletic Association, American Film Institute, American Forestry Association, American Kennel Club, American Library Association, American Pet Classics, American Theater Wing, *Amusement Business, Art Newspaper,* Art Sales Index, Associated Press, Association of Tennis Professionals (ATP), Audit Bureau of Circulations, Beverage Marketing Corporation, *Billboard,* BPI, *BP Statistical Review of World Energy,* Breeders Cup, British Cave Research Association, British Columbia Vital Statistics Agency, British Library, Bureau of Federal Prisons, Bureau of Justice Statistics, Canadian Football League (CFL), Cannes Film Festival, Carbon Dioxide Information Analysis Center, Cat Fancier's Association, Center for Disease Control, Central Intelligence Agency, Central Statistics Office/An Príomh-Oifig Staidrimh, Ireland, Champagne Bureau, Championship Auto Racing Teams (CART), Channel Swimming Association, Christian Research, Christie's, *Classical Music,* Coca-Cola, Columbia University/ Pulitzer Prizes, Computer Industry Almanac, Inc., Country Music Association, *Crime in the United States, Criminal Statistics England & Wales,* Dateline International, Death Penalty Information Center, De Beers, Duncan's American Radio, *Economist, Editor & Publisher Year Book,* Electoral Reform Society, Energy Information Administration, Environmental Protection Agency, Environment Canada, Euromonitor, *FBI Uniform Crime Reports,* Federation of Canadian Municipalities, Feste Catalogue Index Database/Alan Somerset, *Financial Post, Financial Times, Flight International,* Food and Agriculture Organization of the United Nations, Food Marketing Institute, *Forbes, Fortune,* Gemstone Publishing, Inc., Generation AB, Gold Fields Mineral Services Ltd., H. J. Heinz, Helpard Publishing, Hollywood Foreign Press Association (Golden Globe Awards), Home Office, UK, Indianapolis Motor Speedway, Iditarod Trail Committee, Interbrand, International Associatiion of Ports and Harbors, International Atomic Energy Agency, International Civil Aviation Organization, International Cocoa Organization, International Coffee Organization, International Commission on Large Dams, International Dairy Foods Association, International Game Fish Association, International Union for the Conservation of Nature, Inter-Parliamentary Union, Interpol, Jockey Club, Jumbo Video, Kellogg's, Korbel Champagne Cellars, League of American Theaters and Producers, Lloyds Register of Shipping/ MIPG/PPMS, Major League Baseball, Mansell Color Company Inc., Mars, Inc., Meat and Livestock Commission, Metropolitan Opera House, New York, Modern Language Association of America, Desmond Morton, McGill Intitute for the Study of Canada, MRIB, M Street, MTV, NASA, National Academy of Recording Arts and Sciences (NARAS), National Academy of Television Arts and Sciences (Emmy Awards), National Association of Stock Car Auto Racing, Inc (NASCAR), National Basketball Association (NBA), National Center for Health Statistics, National Climatic Data Center, National Collegiate Athletic Association (NCAA), National Dairy Council, National Football League (NFL), National Hockey League (NHL), National Hockey League Players Association, National Hurricane Center, National Safety Council, National Sporting Goods Association, National Steeplechase Association, National Thoroughbred Racing Association, National Trotting Association, Natural Resources Canada, New South Wales Registry of Births, Deaths and Marriages, Niagara Falls Museum, ACNielsen MMS, Nielsen Media Research, Nobel Foundation, *NonProfit Times,* NOP, Northern Ireland Statistics and Research Agency, NPD TRSTS, Toy Tracking Service, Nua Ltd., Office for National Statistics, UK, Peabody Awards, PC Data Online, Pet Industry Joint Advisory Council, Phillips Group, Phobics Society, Popular Music Database, Produktschap voor Gedistilleerde Dranken, Professional Rodeo Cowboys Association (PRCA), Project Feeder Watch/Cornell Lab of Ornithology, Public Broadcasting System (PBS), *Publishers Weekly, Raceboat International, Railway Gazette International,* Recording Industry Association of America (RIAA), Rock 'n' Roll Hall of Fame, Royal Aeronautical Society, Royal Canadian Mint, *Screen Digest,* Shakespeare Birthplace Trust, Siemens AG, *Slimming World,* Songwriters Hall of Fame, Sotheby's, *Spaceflight, Sporting News, Sports Illustrated, Statistical Abstract of the United States,* Statistics Canada, Statistics Norway, STATS Inc., *Steeplechase Times,* Stockholm International Peace Research Institute, *Take One, Time,* Tourism Industries, International Trade Administration, Ty Inc., UNESCO, United Nations, Universal Postal Union, US Board on Geographic Names, US Bureau of Engraving and Printing, US Bureau of the Census, US Consumer Product Safety Commission, US Department of Agriculture/ Economic Research Service, US Department of Justice, US Department of the Interior, US Fish and Wildlife Service, US Geological Survey, *Variety,* VideoScan, Inc., *Video Store,* Ward's Automotive, Whitbread Literary Awards, Sgt. Larry Wilson, RCMP, Women's National Basketball Association (WNBA), World Association of Newspapers, World Bank, World Health Organization, World Meteorological Organization, World Resources Institute, World Science Fiction Society, World Tourism Organization, Zenith International

Index
Patrica Coward

DK Picture Librarians
Denise O'Brien, Melanie Simmonds

Packager's acknowledgments:
Cooling Brown would like to thank the following: Pauline Clarke for design assistance; Peter Cooling for technical support; Carolyn MacKenzie for proofreading; Chris and Eleanor Bolus for the loan of the Beanie Babies.

Advertising Archives: 205tl, 218tl
Allsport: 243br, 244tr, 248tr, 259bl, 264br; Al Bello 253br; Hamish Blair 273tr; Sean Botterill 276tl, 249r; Clive Brunskill 271br; Simon Bruty 252l; David Cannon 246–247, 264–265; Michael Cooper 260tr; Tim Defrisco 244bl; Stephen Dunn 251r; Stu Forster 270b; John Gichigi 272; Otto Greule 247tl; Elsa Hasch 278tr; Tom Herbert 266–267; Mike Hewitt 245tr; Harry How 265br; Doug Pensinger 246bl, 260–261; Gary M Prior 259tr; Pascal Rondeau 274–275; Ezra Shaw 276–277
Apple Computers: 209br
Austin Brown/Aviation Picture Library: 236bl, 236–237, 237tr
British Museum: 97bc
Camera Press: 69tr, 76–77, 103; Richard Open 114bl; R Stonehouse 194; Brian Snyder 77br
Capital Pictures: Phil Loftus 143tl
China Photo Library: 92b
Christie's Images Ltd: 102bl, 112tr, 113br; Edward S. Curtis 117tr; *Kiss II, 1962* by Roy Lichtenstein © DACS 115br
Bruce Coleman Ltd: John Cancalosi 42bl; Geoff Dore 43b; Jeff Foott 40l; Earl Kowall 50bl; Fritz Prenzel 48b
Colorsport: John Varley 258tl.
Corbis UK Ltd: 75tr; Paul Almasy 114tr; Yann Arthus–Bertrand 92–93, 238–239; Bettmann 9tl, 29bl, 63, 67tr, 130tl, 146bl, 162br, 226; Jonathan Blair 14–15b; Ralph A Clevenger 40–41; Sheldan Collins 99, 198–199; Dean Conger 26br; Jonathan Smith/Cordaiy Photo Library 23tr; Philip James Corwin 72–73; Jay Dickman 213; Henry Diltz 126tl; Wayne Lawler/Ecoscene 22–23; Trisha Rafferty/Eye Ubiquitous 204; Jack Fields 58t, 79br; Kevin Fleming 50–51; Natalie Fobes 212bl; Stephen Frink 41br; Marc Garanger 230bl; Mitchell Gerber 128l; Mark Gibson 230t; Dallas and John Heaton 242tl, 242–243; Robert Holmes 100tl; Jeremy Horner 59r, 208tl; Hulton Deutsch Collection 125t, 127tl; Kelly–Mooney Photography 185tl; Earl Kowall 93br; Daniel Laine 84t; Jean–Pierre Lescourret 228bl; James Marshall 21tr; C Moore 89; Kevin R Morris 234–235t; David A Northcott 38tr; Richard T Nowitz 24t, 71br; Neal Preston 129tr, 133bl; Bob Rowan/Progressive Image 199tr, 210–211; Neil Rabinowitz 51tr; Steve Raymer 82r; Jim Richardson 28bl; Kevin Schafer 42–43; Lee Snider 9br; Paul A Souders 90–91t, 210tl; Keren Su 8–9; Chase Swift 37r; Liba Taylor 201br; Peter Turnley 74–75; David Turnley 202; Underwood and Underwood 124b; UPI 77tl; Nik Wheeler 27tr; Staffan Widstrand

83br; Michael S Yamashita 157br, 229tl
DC Comics: 119tr
Ferrari UK: 227
Galaxy Picture Library: Gordan Garradd 12tr
Ronald Grant Archive: *Purple Rain* 149; *The Spy Who Loved Me* © 1977 EON Productions 148br; *Back to the Future* ©1985 Universal UIP 165tl; *Misery* ©1990 Columbia 181bl; *Terminator II* ©1991 Columbia Tristar 159br; *Wayne's World* ©1992 Paramount (UIP) 182tr; *Batman Returns* ©1992 Warner Bros 176br; *Independence Day* ©1996 20th Century Fox 162–163t; *The Rock* ©1996 Buena Vista 174tr; *Escape from LA* ©1996 Paramount; photo Robert Zuckerman 183; *Jackie Brown* ©1997 Buena Vista 180t; *Tomorrow Never Dies* ©1997 EON Productions; photo Keith Hamshere 174bl; *The Prince of Egypt* ©1998 Dreamworks 147t; *You Got Mail* ©1998 Warner Bros 176tl; 20th Century Fox 186t; MGM 187br
Mike Griggs Photography: 67br
H J Heinz: 216; **Chris Howes:** 279br
Johnson Space Centre: 18t
Kobal Collection: *Cabaret* ©1972 ABC/Allied Artists 169tl; *Jaws* ©1975 Universal (UIP) 163br; *Arthur* ©1981 Orion 168tl; *On Golden Pond* ©1981 Universal 170bl; *Gandhi* ©1984 Indo-British/International Film Investors 184l; *Ghostbusters* ©1989 Columbia 164bl; *Reservoir Dogs* ©1992 Live Entertainment 179; *Jurassic Park* ©1993 Amblin/Universal (UIP) 158; *Much Ado About Nothing* ©1993 Sam Goldwyn/ Renaissance Films/BBC 156tr; *Forest Gump* ©1994 Paramount (UIP) 165br; *Braveheart* ©1995 Icon/Ladd Co/Paramount 167br; *The Full Monty* ©1995 20th Century Fox 159tl; *Seven* ©1995 New Line Cinema/Entertainment Film 175tr; *Waterworld* ©1995 Universal, photo Ben Glass 160b; *Copycat* ©1995 WB Monarchy Enterprises 181tr; *Shine* ©1996 Momentum Films 172tr; *Fargo* ©1996 Polygram Filmed Entertainment/ Gramercy Pictures; photo James Bridges 178tr; *The English Patient* ©1996 Tigermoth/Miramax 166tr; *Jackie Brown* ©1997 Buena Vista 178bl; *My Best Friend's Wedding* ©1997 Columbia Tristar 177; *As Good As It Gets* ©1997 Tristar/Gracie Films 170tr; ©1999 Paramount Pictures and Touchstone Pictures Company; photo Ron Batzdorff 182bl; *The Matrix* ©1999 Warner Bros; photo Jasin Boland 161l; *The Truman Show* © 1997 Paramount Pictures Corp., photograph Melinda Sue Gordon 173; 193tr; *There's Something About Mary* © 1998 20th Century Fox, photograph Glenn Watson 195tr
Lebrecht Collection: Peter Mares 153tl
London Features International: 139r, 192bl; Jen Lowery 132; *The Sound of Music* © 1965

Argyle Enterprises, Inc./Twentieth Century Fox 148tl; David Fisher 62bl
Moviestore Collection: *American Beauty* ©1999 Dreamworks 167tl; *Boys Don't Cry* ©1999 Fox Searchlight 171t
NASA: 15tr, 16–17, 25br; Finley Holiday Films 13t
Natural History Museum, London: 35b
Network Photographers Ltd: Greg Smith/SABA 70t; Homer Sykes 207tr
© Newspapers International Newspapers Limited, 1st January 2000: *The Sun*, London 107tr
Nickelodeon International Ltd: 190–191
Nordfoto: Liselotte Sabroe 222bl
Oxford Scientific Films: G I Bernard 47tl; Alastair MacEwan 34tl; Rob Nunnington 49t
Panos Pictures: Caroline Penn 100br
PetExcellence, Florida USA: 277br
Photodisc: 24–25, 79, 254–255, 256–257
Popperfoto: 238bl; Reuter 30bl, 64tr, 214–215, 231tr, 239tl
Redferns: 130br; Fin Costello 145br; Kieran Doherty 135b; Paul Hampartsoumian 134tr; Mick Hutson 133tr, 140–141l; Jm Enternational 142b; Michel Linssen 131r,145tl; Keith Morris 137; Michael Ochs Archive 123bl, 136br; Rb Collection 127br; David Redfern 123tr, 136tl; Ebet Roberts 134bl, 141tl, 144tl; Barbara Steinwehe 150bl; Gai Terrell 122bl; Des Willie 143r
Royal Caribbean Cruises Ltd: 234bl
Royal Geographical Society: Ranulph Fiennes 66tr
Science & Society Picture Library: Science Museum 188br
Science Photo Library: 54l; GJLP 55br; Laguna Design 29tr; Johnson Matthey 203br; Hank Morgan 54tr; NASA 19b; Novosti 17br; Dr Linda Stannard 31; Peter Thorne
Sotheby's Picture Library, London: 116, 118–119
Frank Spooner Pictures: De Kerle/Gamma 106bl; Peter Orme/Gamma 105r; Frederic Reglain/Gamma 104bl
Still Pictures: 68bl; Fritz Polking 39r
The Stock Market: Charles Gupton 221tr; M Smith 20–21; Ken Straiton 200
Tony Stone Images: Thierry Cazabon 110–111; Paul Chesley 78tl; Will and Deni McIntyre 20br; Nicholas Parfitt 26–27; Peter Pearson 90–91; Antonia Reeve 98tl; Ron Sherman 100–101
Sveriges Riksdag: 65bc; **Sygma:** Corbis 235br
Toyota (GB) PLC: 229br
Jerry Young: 46